THE WAY

THE WAY

An Ecological World-View

———

Edward Goldsmith

Revised and enlarged edition

THE UNIVERSITY OF GEORGIA PRESS

ATHENS

Published by the University of Georgia Press
Athens, Georgia 30602

Typographic design and photosetting
in 10.5 on 14pt Mergenthaler Sabon
by Five Seasons Press, Hereford, England.
The paper in this book meets the guidelines
for permanence and durability
of the Committee on Production Guidelines
for Book Longevity of the Council on Library Resources.

Printed in the United States of America
02 01 00 99 98 C 5 4 3 2 1
02 01 00 99 98 P 5 4 3 2 1

Library of Congress Cataloging in Publication Data

Goldsmith, Edward, 1928–
The way: an ecological world-view / by Edward Goldsmith.—
Rev. and enl. ed.
p. cm.
Includes bibliographical references and index.
ISBN 0-8203-1976-7 (alk. paper). —ISBN 0-8203-2030-7 (pbk. : alk. paper)
1. Human ecology—Philosophy. 2. Environmental protection.
3. Conservation of natural resources. 4. Gaia hypothesis.
I. Title.
GF21.G63 1998   97-20009
304.2—dc21

An earlier version of this book was published in the United Kingdom
by Themis Books, an imprint of Green Books,
and another by Shambhala in the United States.

Contents

CONTENTS

CONTENTS

CONTENTS

Introduction

Modern man is rapidly destroying the natural world on which he depends for his survival. Everywhere on our planet, the picture is the same. Forests are being cut down, wetlands drained, coral reefs grubbed up, agricultural lands eroded, salinized, desertified, or simply paved over. Pollution is now generalized—our groundwater, streams, rivers, estuaries, seas and oceans, the air we breathe, the food we eat, are all affected. Just about every living creature on Earth now contains in its body traces of agricultural and industrial chemicals—many of which are known or suspected carcinogens and mutagens.

As a result of our activities, it is probable that hundreds of species are being made extinct every day, with only a fraction of these being known to science. The Earth's magnetic field is being changed, with no one knows what possible consequences. The ozone layer that protects humans and other living things from ultraviolet radiation is being rapidly depleted; and our very climate is being so transformed and destabilized that within the next forty years we will probably experience climatic conditions in which no human has ever lived before.

By destroying the natural world in this way we are making our planet progressively less habitable, and if current trends persist, in no more than a few decades it may cease to be capable of supporting complex forms of life. This may sound far-fetched; unfortunately, it is only too realistic. My colleagues and I have documented the trends and the likely outcome ad nauseam in *The Ecologist* over the last twenty-three years.

Why, we might ask, are we doing this? The answer is that our society is committed to economic development or progress—a process that by its very nature must systematically increase the impact of our economic activities on an environment ever less capable of sustaining it, and ever more deeply degraded by it. An idea of the gross mismatch between the impact of human activities and the environment's capacity to sustain them is provided by the fact that we now co-opt for our own use and for our various economic activities, fully forty percent of the biosphere's terrestrial net primary production (NPP). What is more, if economic activities continue to expand at the present rate, within no more than a few decades we would be co-opting one hundred percent of NPP—which, of course, is not remotely conceivable.

All this is of little if any concern to our political leaders. They continue to go about their normal business as if the problem did not exist. Thus, though 170 scientists sitting on the Inter-Governmental Panel on Climate Change (IPCC), set up by the United Nations, have warned them that carbon dioxide emissions must be reduced by sixty to eighty percent immediately in order to stabilize climate, the British government has just undertaken the largest road-building program in the country's history and talks happily of doubling the number of cars on the roads by the end of the century. The last American administration openly admitted that, whatever the climatic consequences, it planned to go on increasing carbon dioxide emissions into the foreseeable future. Industrialists are, if anything, even less concerned. The oil industry has been very active in lobbying governments to prevent them from taking any measures that, in the interests of reducing CO_2 emissions, might lead to a reduction in oil consumption with a consequent dip in sales. In general, the main constraint on governmental action to tackle the serious environmental problems that face us are the lobbying campaigns of powerful industrial groups intent on defending their petty short-term interests, come what may.

More surprising, however, has been the almost total indifference with which the scientific world has viewed this critical problem. Its acknowledged role is to provide governments and society at large with knowledge that serves the public interest and maximizes the general welfare. But how can it achieve this task if it systematically ignores the fatal process that is rendering our planet ever less habitable and that if unchecked, must inevitably lead to the extinction of our species along with countless others? Our scientists bring to mind those Australian Aborigines, who, when they first sighted Captain Cook's impressive ship sailing up the Australian coast north of Botany Bay, went about their normal activities as if this strange monster were simply not there. Perhaps they hoped—consciously or unconsciously—that by ignoring it to the point of not recognizing its very existence they might induce this aberration to go away and leave them alone.

The parallel is more than superficial. In both cases a life-threatening challenge is systematically ignored because its occurrence is irreconcilable with the prevailing world-view that would be totally discredited were the challenge shown to be real. The American anthropologist A.F.C. Wallace shows convincingly that tribal peoples will go to any lengths to preserve their "cognitive structure or mazeway" (see chapters 18 and 66) as he refers to it. A scientist will go to equal lengths to do so—as Thomas Kuhn, Michael Polanyi, Gunther Stent and other enlightened philosophers of science have shown.

The world-view that today's scientists share with everybody else in our society, I refer to in this book as the world-view of modernism, that is faithfully reflected in the paradigm of economics and the paradigm of science. One of the two most fundamental tenets of the world-view of modernism and its derivative paradigms is that all benefits, and therefore our welfare and real wealth, are man-made (see chapter 34)—the product of science, technology and industry and of the economic development that these make possible. Thus health is seen as something that is dispensed in hospitals, or at least by the medical profession, with the aid of the latest technological devices and pharmaceutical preparations. Education is seen as a commodity that can be acquired in schools and universities. Law and order, rather than being natural features of human society, are seen instead as provided by our police force in conjunction with the law courts and the prison system. Even society is seen as man-made, brought into being by the "social contract." Not surprisingly, a country's wealth is measured by its per capita Gross National Product (GNP), that provides a rough measure of its ability to provide its citizens with all such man-made commodities, a principle faithfully reflected in modern economics. The inestimable benefits provided by the normal functioning of the ecosphere—such as a favorable and stable climate, fertile soil and fresh water, without which life on this planet would not be possible —are totally ignored and assigned no value of any kind. It follows that to be deprived of these non-benefits cannot constitute a "cost" and the natural systems that provide them can therefore be destroyed with economic impunity.

The second fundamental tenet of the world-view of modernism follows quite logically from the first: it is that to maximize all benefits, and hence our welfare and our wealth, we must maximize economic development or progress, that is above all the methodical substitution of the technosphere or surrogate world (the source of man-made benefits) for the ecosphere or real world (the source of natural benefits). To question the efficacy of this fatal process, or to suggest that it might not be entirely beneficial, is to blaspheme against the holy writ of what is in effect the religion of the modern world. No true believer will accept that the terrible social and environmental destruction we are witnessing today is the inevitable product of this sacred process. Instead, it will be imputed to deficiencies or difficulties in its implementation—government interference, corruption among local officials, or freak conditions that are unlikely to recur.

In this way, the world-view of modernism and its specialized paradigms prevents us from understanding our relationship with the world we live in and adapting to it so as to maximize our welfare and our real wealth. Instead, it serves primarily to rationalize economic development or "progress"—the very process that is leading to the destruction of the natural world with consequences that are only too evident to all (see chapter 65).

How, one might ask, is it possible for our "objective" scientists to behave in so unobjective a manner? The answer is that science is not objective—a fact that has been well established by Michael Polanyi, Thomas Kuhn and other philosophers of science (see chapter 13). One reason why scientists accept the paradigm of science and hence the world-view of modernism is that these rationalize the policies that have given rise to the modern world in which they, and indeed all of us, have been brought up. It is very difficult for people to avoid regarding the world they live in—the only one they have ever known —as the normal condition of human life on this planet. Just as an abandoned child who sleeps in the sewers of Rio de Janeiro and lives off petty crime and prostitution regards his or her lot as totally normal, so scientists regard it as normal that our rivers have been transformed into sewers, that our drinking water is contaminated with human excrement, pesticide residues, nitrates, radionuclides and heavy metals, that our agricultural land is eroding faster than soil can possibly form by natural processes, that our natural forests are being systematically replaced with ecologically vulnerable and soil-destroying monocultures of fast-growing exotics, that our cities are increasingly ugly, chaotic and polluted—and that our children spend most of their spare time watching violent and sadistic films on television. All this, and much else that is totally aberrant and destructive, most mainstream scientists will take to be normal.

This general human tendency to regard the only world we know as normal is reflected in just about all the disciplines that are taught in our schools and universities. Thus the modern discipline of economics is based on the assumption that the destructive economic system that is operative today is normal; the discipline of sociology on the assumption that our modern atomized and crime-ridden society is normal; our political science on the assumption that the elected dictatorships that govern modern nation states are normal; and our agricultural science on the assumption that large-scale, mechanized, chemical-based agriculture (that rapidly transforms arable land into desert) is normal. It simply does not occur to many academics that what they take to be normal is highly atypical of humanity's total experience on this planet —necessarily short-lived, and totally aberrant. They are like biologists who have only seen cancerous tissue and understandably mistake it for a healthy organism.

Another reason why our scientific community still accepts the paradigm of science is that, though it paints the most misleading picture of reality, it is nevertheless totally coherent and self-consistent. This must be so, for scientific theories are not adopted by mainstream science because they have been proved to be true by experimentation in controlled laboratory conditions, or even as a result of simulation on a mathematical model, but because, above all, they happen to fit in particularly well with the paradigm of science. Those that do not conform, what is more, are systematically tortured into that shape that enables them to do so.

In the last sixty years, the Behaviorists made psychology conform to the paradigm of science. The neo-Darwinists and, even more so, the sociobiologists did the same for biology. Modern sociology has also become mechanistic and reductionistic, and the development of the new ecology in the 1940s and 1950s has engendered a Newtonian ecology that rather than provide the theoretical foundations for the environmental movement of today (as most environmentalists firmly believe) serves instead further to rationalize and hence legitimize the very process of economic development or progress that is the principal, if not the only, cause of the environmental degradation that they seek so ardently to bring to an end (see chapters 4, 23 and 51). In this way all academic knowledge has been forced, Procrustean-like, into the paradigm of science, stretched or shrunk to fit an atomized and mechanistic vision of the world in which people are no more than machines and their needs purely material and technological— precisely those that the state and the industrial system are capable of satisfying. At the same time, any social and ecological problem that might arise is interpreted in such a way as to appear amenable to a technological solution, the only one that our modern industrial society can provide. It is all very neat and very logical but it is a pure figment of the scientist's imagination.

Another reason why our scientists are still wedded to the paradigm of science is that it is capable of perpetuating itself, however wide the gap may be between the world it depicts and the world as it really is. For if knowledge is only accepted to the extent that it fits the paradigm, any knowledge that does not fit, however true and important it might be, is by the same token ruthlessly rejected (see chapter 18). This disposes of all theories based on the assumption that the world is orderly and purposive rather than random; organized rather than atomized; co-operative rather than purely competitive; dynamic, creative and intelligent rather than passive and robot-like; self-regulating rather than managed by some external agent; tending to maintain its stability or homeostasis rather than geared to per- petual change in an undefined direction: in other words, all theories based on the assumption that the world is alive rather than dead and machine-like.

In terms of this false paradigm we can never correctly interpret the problems that threaten our survival, nor can we, on the basis of the world-view of modernism, justify the policies needed to bring to an end the destruction of the planet and to develop a sustainable and fulfilling way of life. In these conditions, an ecological world-view in the light of which all this becomes possible can only be a most urgent requirement.

I have tried in this book to state clearly the basic principles under- lying an ecological world-view. These principles are all closely inter- related, forming an all-embracing and self-consistent model of our relationship with the world in which we live. I have worked at the book, on and off, for several decades, but in recent years it has undergone a considerable change. It was always clear to me that the inspiration must come from the world-view of vernacular societies, in particular from the chthonic world-view of the earliest period when people everywhere really knew how to live in harmony with the natural world. I have often been criticized on this score. However, it has always seemed to me as presumptuous to postulate an ideal world-view as it is to postulate an ideal society for which there is no precedent in the human experience on this planet and whose biological, social and ecological viability has never been demonstrated. If Karl Marx made that mistake, so too do today's adepts of economic development or progress, who seek to create a man-made technological world without asking themselves whether we are capable of adapting to it (see chapter 43) or whether the ecosphere is capable of sustaining it for more than a few decades.

What has struck me more recently is that the main features of the world-view of early vernacular societies were everywhere basically the same. They emphasized two fundamental principles that necessarily underlie an ecological world-view. The first is that the living world or ecosphere is the basic source of all benefits and hence of all wealth (see chapter 34), but will only dispense these benefits to us if we preserve its critical order (see chapters 36 and 61). From this fundamental first principle follows the second, which is that the overriding goal of this behavior pattern of an ecological society must be to preserve the critical order of the natural world or of the cosmos that encompasses it.

A cursory study of the world-view of vernacular and, in particular, chthonic peoples, shows that many societies actually had a word for such a behavior pattern: the R'ta of the Hindus in Vedic times; the Asha of the Avestas; the Maat of the ancient Egyptians; the Dharma, another Hindu concept later taken up by the Buddhists; and the ancient Chinese Tao (see chapter 61). These terms can often refer to the critical order of the cosmos, but they are generally used to denote that path or Way that must be taken in order to preserve its critical order. If many other societies do not have a specific term for it, the concept of the Way is nevertheless built into their world-view (see chapters 62 and 63). Explicit or implicit adherence to the Way is critical. It is only by following it that a society can subordinate the petty, short-term, political and economic considerations that at present alone preoccupy us, to fundamental social, ecological and moral imperatives—the basic condition for survival on this beleaguered planet. Hence the title of this book.

The task of trying to formulate the underlying principles of a coherent and self-consistent world-view has been more difficult than I originally thought, because it has meant describing each one in terms of all the others, and hence in terms of the whole. Its structure is thus circular; there is thus no logical place to begin and the book can, in theory, only be understood by someone who has already read it. However, to assist the diligent reader, I have placed, after each principle that needs to be seen in a wider context, a bracketed chapter reference that can be consulted if necessary, while a glossary is available on page 467.

Like all syntheses of this sort, the book cannot be regarded as the work of a single person. I owe much to many people, both dead and alive. I started the work that led to its writing in the 1950s. For a long time, I worked in isolation. One of the first people I discussed it with was Ion Gresser of the Institut du Cancer at Villejuif near Paris. Another was Joel de Rosnay who in the early 1960s introduced me to the General Systems Theory of Ludwig von Bertalanffy, that has colored all my thinking ever since. I am very grateful too, to Armand Petitjean, Alain Hervé, Jacques Grinevald, and Richard Wilson, with whom I have had endless discussions on the various subjects dealt with in this book. I am also particularly indebted to that remarkable man, James Lovelock, who was my neighbor in Cornwall for many years, and whose Gaia thesis I regard as vital to the development of an ecological world-view.

I am indebted too, to Eugene Odum, one of the few remaining academic ecologists whose work has not been perverted to fit the paradigm of mechanistic science. His writings have been an important part of my education. The history of ecological thought I learned primarily from Donald Worster, from his seminal book *Nature's Economy*. I would like to mention my friend, Helena Norberg-Hodge, whose world-view just about coincides with my own. I am indebted, too, to Robert Mann, Grover Foley and Andrew McFarlane for the many evenings we have spent together discussing these issues in Auckland, New Zealand; to Rajni Kothari, Ashis Nandy, Vandana Shiva and their colleagues at the Centre for the Study of Developing Societies in Delhi; to Paul Blau and my other friends of Ecoropa, with whom I have had many enlightening discussions and to that scientific arch-heretic, Rupert Sheldrake. I am also indebted to Satish Kumar, who introduced a new dimension into my life in 1974 by arranging for me to spend four months with the Gandhi Peace Foundation in New Delhi. It was as a result of my stay there that I realized the incalculable relevance of the thought of Mahatma Gandhi to the development of an ecological world-view. It was also then that I met most of my Indian friends from whom I have learned so much. I must thank, too, Sunderlal Bahuguna and Mohammed Idris, who, along with Richard St Barbe Baker, "the Man of the Trees," are among the most inspiring people I have met.

I am particularly indebted to Krishna Chaitanya, possibly the greatest polymath of all time, who is not only one of India's leading art critics, but has written an eight-volume history of Mayalayam literature and a ten-volume history of world literature, and has still found time to write a remarkable five-volume synthesis of the physical and social sciences of which I have made shameless use. Krishna Chaitanya is also the author of many erudite studies of India's cultural heritage: it is from him that I learned of the Vedic principle of the R'ta (the Way), the behavior pattern adhered to by early Indian society to maintain the critical order of the cosmos. I must acknowledge too the encouragement I have received from my very close colleagues, Peter Bunyard and Nicholas Hildyard, with whom I have worked for many years. Nicholas, by taking over the task of running *The Ecologist* with its associated activities, that he does incomparably better than I ever did, has provided me with the leisure to write this book. I must also thank Arne Naess who, after reading a summary of this book in *The Ecologist*, urged me to complete it and get it published. I thank my very close friend John Aspinall for having so enriched my life during all the years I have been writing this work, my brother Jimmy for his great support and my wife, Katherine, for her support; also for putting up, over the years, with the anti-social way of life that is the lot of a writer committed to a long-term project of this sort.

I must also thank Brian Goodwin, Jacques Grinevald, Nicholas Hildyard, Donald Hughes, James Lovelock, Arne Naess, Jerry Ravetz, Wolfgang Sachs, Guiseppe Sermonti, Denys Trussell and Donald

Worster, who so kindly consented to read the original manuscript of this book, pointing out errors and making other valuable comments.

Finally, I must thank Tessa Strickland, my editor, for her enthusiasm. Without her, this book would never have been published—also Denys Trussell who has helped me finish it; Mike Kirkwood my very patient copy editor; Annie Ouvry, who has typed it over and over again; Hilary Datchens, Lynda Wright and Simone Hawkins, who over the years have typed a mountain of notes and various drafts.

Chinook Blessing Litany

WE CALL upon the Earth, our planet home, with its beautiful depths and soaring heights, its vitality and abundance of life, and together we ask that it

Teach us, and show us the Way.

WE CALL upon the mountains, the Cascades and the Olympics, the high green valleys and meadows filled with wild flowers, the snows that never melt, the summits of intense silence, and we ask that they

Teach us, and show us the Way.

WE CALL upon the waters that rim the Earth, horizon to horizon, that flow in our rivers and streams, that fall upon our gardens and fields and ask that they

Teach us, and show us the Way.

WE CALL upon the land which grows our food, the nurturing soil, the fertile fields, the abundant gardens and orchards, and ask that they

Teach us, and show us the Way.

WE CALL upon the forests, the great trees reaching strongly to the sky with Earth in their roots and the heavens in their branches, the fir and the pine and the cedar, and we ask them to

Teach us, and show us the Way.

WE CALL upon the creatures of the fields and the forests and the seas, our brothers and sisters the wolves and the deer, the eagle and dove, the great whales and the dolphin, the beautiful Orca and salmon who share our Northwest home, we ask them to

Teach us, and show us the Way.

WE CALL upon those who have lived on this Earth, our ancestors and our friends, who dreamed the best for future generations, and upon whose lives our lives are built, and with thanksgiving, we call upon them to

Teach us, and show us the Way.

And lastly, WE CALL upon all that we hold most sacred, the presence and power of the Great Spirit of love and truth which flows through all the Universe . . . to be with us to

Teach us, and show us the Way.

I

I

Ecology is a unified organization of knowledge

~

What we find among the Zuni of New Mexico is a veritable arrangement of the universe. All beings and facts in nature, the sun, moon and stars, the sky, Earth and sea, in all their phenomena and elements; and all inanimate objects as well as plants, animals and men, are classified, labelled and assigned to fixed places in a unique and integrated system in which all the parts are coordinated and subordinated one to another by "degrees of resemblance."
Emile Durkheim and *Marcel Mauss*

Each profession makes progress, but it is progress in its own groove. Now to be mentally in a groove is to live in contemplating a given set of abstractions. The groove prevents straying across country, and the abstraction abstracts from something to which no further attention is paid, but there is no groove of abstractions which is adequate for the comprehension of human life. Thus in the modern world, the celibacy of the medieval learned class has been replaced by a celibacy of the intellect which is divorced from the concrete contemplation of the complete facts.
A.N. Whitehead

Normal science is a strenuous and determined attempt to force nature into the conceptual boxes supplied by professional education.
Thomas Kuhn

3

ECOLOGY EMERGED as an academic discipline towards the end of the last century, largely in response to the realization that biological organisms and populations were not arranged randomly but, on the contrary, were organized to form "communities" or "associations" whose structure and function could not be understood by examining their parts in isolation. Victor Shelford,[1] one of the most distinguished of the early ecologists in the USA, defined ecology as the "science of communities." "A study," he wrote, "of the relations of a single species to the environment conceived without reference to communities and, in the end, unrelated to the natural phenomena of its habitat and community . . . is not properly included in the field of study."

In the 1930s, the Oxford ecologist Arthur Tansley[2] coined the term "ecosystem" which he defined as a community taken together with its abiotic environment. It is probable that were Clements or Shelford living today, they would see ecology as the "science of ecosystems." Eugene Odum,[3] possibly the most distinguished of modern ecologists (and one of the few remaining holists), defines ecology as "the science of the structure and function of nature," or "the structure and function of Gaia,"[4] as James Lovelock refers to the biosphere taken together with its atmospheric environment, or what I refer to as the ecosphere, a term coined by the ecologist Lamont Cole. For Odum, ecology is thereby a superscience or unified science, as it was for Barrington Moore, the first president of the American Ecological Society. For him, ecology was not just another scientific discipline, but a science "superimposed on the other sciences," a science of synthesis essential to our understanding of the structure and function of the ecosphere. He asked his colleagues in his address to the St Louis branch of the society in 1919,

> Will we be content to remain zoologists, botanists, and foresters, with little understanding of one another's problems, or will we endeavour

4

to become ecologists in the broad sense of the term? The part we play in science depends upon our reply. Gentlemen, the future is in our hands.[5]

His words would sound singularly out of place at a meeting of the American Ecological Society today, still more so at a meeting of its British counterpart.

J.H. Woodger, the great British theoretical biologist, also considered that

> there ought to be a most general science, not immersed in a particular subject matter, but dealing with the relationship between various special sciences, and trying to synthesize their most general results.[6]

Neither the ecosphere nor any of its constituent processes can be fully explained in terms of the separate impermeable disciplines into which modern knowledge has been divided. As Russell Ackoff, the founder of Operations Research, notes,

> Some of the questions that we ask of Nature—in contrast to the problems it presents to us—can be classified as physical, chemical, biological and so on, but not the phenomena themselves . . . Automobile accidents can be viewed at least as physical, biological, psychological, sociological, and economic phenomena. To study them in any one of these ways is to exclude variables that are relevant from other points of view.[7]

J.W. Craik makes the same point: "Getting used to the dark," he asks, "is it physics, chemistry or physiology?"[8] For him, it is at once quantum physics, photochemistry, chemistry, physiology and psychology. Even what appears to be a purely physical phenomenon, like tracing the movement of planets, cannot be understood in purely physical terms. As Ackoff writes,

> Experience of planetary motion is as much a biological, psychological, sociological and economic phenomenon as it is physical.[9]

The ecosphere, in fact, cannot be understood in terms of the arbitrary divisions into which knowledge has been divided. Even the best established barriers turn out to be of relative value only. Thus when Wolfgang Wohler synthesized urea, the barrier between the *organic* and the *inorganic* was suddenly shattered, as was that between the *animate* and the *inanimate* once the virus was found to manifest certain conditions associated with life on being confronted with a source of protein and at other periods to display the normal behavior pattern of a crystal. A.N.Whitehead even refused to accept that there was any fundamental barrier separating physics from biology. For him, physics was the study of small organisms, biology of big organisms. Ludwig von Bertalanffy, the father of General Systems Theory, showed that, at a certain level of generality, the behavior of all living entities or natural systems is very similar and must, in fact, be governed by the same laws. This basic principle underlies his General Systems Theory (see chapter 38).

The compartmentalization of knowledge into different disciplines makes possible the erection of artificial barriers between different life processes, permitting them to be viewed in isolation from all the others so that they can be made to appear subject to laws of their own which have nothing in common with those that govern other life processes.

In this way totally aberrant theories have been constructed and have, in some cases, remained to this day the official doctrine of science, theories whose absurdity would be apparent to all were we to accept the fundamental unity of life processes. An example is the mechanomorphic theory of life (see chapter 23).

René Descartes divided the things of this world into two categories —the *res extensa* and the *res cogitans*. The former, Descartes maintained, was the domain of science, the latter the domain of theology. The object of this totally artificial division was to carve out a sphere of influence for science so that it would be freed from the shackles of theological control, and at the same time, to reassure the Church that science was not threatening to take over its territory.

This may have been politically expedient but it was undoubtedly a sort of intellectual Yalta—and the frontiers it established were as arbitrary and as pernicious as those set up by that infamous treaty, for it is impossible to understand the *res extensa* without reference to the *res cogitans*, the soma without reference to the germ, the body without reference to the mind.

The compartmentalization of knowledge has also led to the erection of a barrier that separates economic activity, i.e. the distribution of resources within a society, from the society itself and from the rest of the Gaian hierarchy. As a result, in terms of that discipline, the economic process, as Nicholas Georgescu-Roegen points out, is depicted as a

> circular diagram, a pendulum movement between production and consumption within a completely closed system.[10]

It is thus seen as governed exclusively by its own laws rather than by those that govern all the other processes occurring within the natural world. As a result, the fact that there is

> a continuous mutual influence between the economic process and our physical environment carries no weight with the standard economists. And the same is true of Marxist economists who swear by the Marxist dogma that everything nature supplies man is a spontaneous gift. In Marx's famous diagram of production too, the economic process is presented as a completely circular and self-sustaining affair.

Once it is admitted that the economic process influences and is in turn influenced by biological, social and ecological factors, generally known as "externalities," then an effort is made to "internalize" them by quantifying them in the language of economics. This may be a reasonable procedure as Herman Daly and John Cobb concede, when the externalities involved are of a minor nature; but once it is the very capacity of the Earth to support life that has to be internalized, then "it is time to restructure basic concepts and start with a different set of abstractions that can embrace what was previously external."[11] This means, in effect, completely rewriting economics in the light of a unified theory of the ecosphere (see chapter 19).

Further barriers separate the disciplines in terms of which we study behavior, ontogeny and evolution with equally obscurantist consequences, for these life processes are part of the same ecospheric process, are governed by the same general laws, and cannot be understood separately from each other. Thus to say that a population has evolved is to say that neither its ontogeny nor its behavior is the same today as it was at some moment in the past. To understand evolution we therefore need to understand ontogeny and behavior—the processes that have actually undergone change—not separately as do the neo-Darwinists, but as part of the whole evolutionary process to whose constraints they are subjected.

Ontogenic development is clearly goal-directed since it leads to the development of a fertilized egg into an adult. It is also dynamic and highly coordinated, since all its different stages are closely interwoven into a single process. The developing system can also monitor its responses and correct diversions from the course it must take to achieve its goal and hence implement its strategy. That the day-to-day behavior of non-human animals also displays these same features few will deny yet it is denied by neo-Darwinists, indeed by all mainstream scientists, to the evolutionary process itself. The geneticist Theodosius Dobzhansky, for instance, while accepting that ontogeny is purposive, since organs grow to fulfill future functions, still dogmatically insists that this is not true of phylogeny.

Furthermore with the hardening of Darwinian theory, under the auspices of August Weissmann and William Bateson, any feedback between behavior and ontogeny on the one hand and evolution on the other is also fervently denied. This means that the instructions that determine the evolutionary process are seen as issued blindly —uninfluenced by their effects on the processes to which they give rise—a phenomenon that is unknown in the living world and cybernetically impossible in an adaptive life-process. However, once ontogeny, behavior and evolution are seen together as part of a single process, the operation of feedback processes of some sort becomes incontestable (see chapter 19).

The compartmentalization of knowledge also makes possible the totally artificial distinction between behavior occurring *within* the highly orderly and co-operative internal environment of an organism and that occurring *outside* it. It is only by insisting on that arbitrary dichotomy that the idea of natural selection, closely associated as it is with the "survival of the fittest" (Charles Darwin suggested the two might be different terms for the same thing) can possibly be postulated as the basic mechanism of evolution. Indeed, the notion put forward by the German biologist Wilhelm Roux that selection occurs at different levels of organization within the internal environment of an organism—for instance at the level of the cell and the tissue—did not gain full acceptance because natural selection and the struggle for survival were difficult to envisage within an internal environment where co-operation and homeostasis are so marked. In general, it is only by studying evolution in a restricted context that it has been possible to perpetuate the neo-Darwinian myth that the process is individualistic, competitive, random and hence non-directive—one that is not subject to Gaian control and hence that cannot be distinguished from the anti-evolutionary enterprise to which our industrial society is committed (see chapter 64).

If ecology is to become Barrington Moore's superscience, in terms of which we can understand the structure and function of the ecosphere, then it must be non-disciplinary or superdisciplinary and serve above all to provide the *generalities* of a coordinated set of new, ecologically-inspired, disciplines in terms of which the particularities of Gaian life processes can alone be understood.

2

Ecology seeks to establish the laws of nature

—

All things under Providence are regulated and measured by the Eternal Law, by those of the individual, who participates in this Law, by the Natural Law: not that these two are different laws, but only the universal and the particular aspects of one and the same Law.
St Thomas Aquinas

There is no law except the law that there is no law.
John Archibald Wheeler, Professor of Physics, Princeton University

The basic laws of nature have not been repealed.
Eugene Odum

Almost everywhere in the world, man has been disregarding the Divine Law and the Laws of Nature to his own undoing. In his pride, he has rampaged over the stage of the earth, forgetting that he is only one of the players put there to play his part in harmony and oneness with all living things.
Richard St Barbe Baker

To study the structure and function of the ecosphere and its constituent natural systems is to seek out their pattern. The general features of this pattern are relatively non-plastic, which is another way of saying that they are subject to constraints—in this case, that particular set of constraints required to ensure that their behavior will serve to maintain the stability of the ecosphere. It is these constraints that we must refer to as the laws of nature or Gaian laws. They are not absolute laws as were those that Laplace and La Mettrie saw as applying to the mechanistic world that they depicted. Gaian laws can be violated, but only at a cost—that of reducing stability, both directly at a specific level of organization and indirectly at other levels in the Gaian hierarchy including that of the biosphere itself.

Adherence to a specific set of laws is required to maintain the order and hence the stability of a natural system; if these laws are disregarded the degradation and eventual demise of the system will follow. As we move from one level of organization to the next, up the hierarchy of the biosphere, so do new sets of laws—usually referred to as "emergent laws"—become operative. These laws do not supersede those that are operative at lower levels, but complement them.

Thus if a man is to remain healthy, his behavior must be subject to a set of physical, chemical, biological, psychological, social and ecological constraints. Among other things, he must breathe fresh air, drink clean water, feed himself properly and live in an environment that has not diverged too drastically from that to which he has been adapted by his evolution and upbringing (see chapter 46). He is of course free to violate these laws, but he will pay the penalty, for his health must suffer as a result. As a member of a larger natural system, the family, he must behave in a husbandly way towards his wife and in a fatherly way towards his children, or his family will simply disintegrate. The family in turn is part of a community, and the community is part of a wider society contained within one of the ecosystems that constitute our ecosphere. If the latter is to maintain its stability, all the individual living things that compose it must obey a veritable hierarchy of laws, that together constitute the laws of nature. It is the failure of modern man to observe the constraints necessary for maintaining the integrity and stability of the various social and ecological systems of which he is part that is giving rise to their disintegration and destabilization, of which the increased incidence of discontinuities such as wars, massacres, droughts, floods, famines, epidemics and climatic changes are but the symptoms (see chapter 65).

Unfortunately, the very principle of Gaian law is incompatible with the reductionist thesis that is essential to modern science, according to which natural systems are no more than the sum of their constituent parts and thus have no identity, no integrity and no stability. It is incompatible too with the notion of randomness, also critical to modern science, in terms of which life processes are no more than accidental, chance happenings. It is incompatible with the notion of causality. Thus Robert Boyle objected to the notion of laws because for him, as for all other reductionist scientists, events cannot be "caused" by laws, only by antecedent events. When an arrow is shot from a bow he insisted "none will say that it moves by a law, but by an external impulse."[1] It is also incompatible with the empiricist thesis that only observable events are real, all theoretical explanations of life processes being largely ignored.

Since laws cannot be totally denied, scientists have demoted them to the status of "statistical regularities." This means that there is no reason why any laws should apply to the world we live in other than that they have, on the whole, been observed to do so. This statistical view of the world provides a means of reconciling the embarrassing evidence for an orderly world and hence one governed by laws with the paradigm of science (see chapter 35).

However, even this concession to reality is regarded as unacceptable by Ilya Prigogine,[2] the Belgian Chemist and Nobel Laureate who has become an intellectual cult figure in France, Belgium and elsewhere. Prigogine considers that the only universal laws are those of classical thermodynamics (see appendix 1). However, they only apply to those things that are near "thermodynamic equilibrium" and are thereby in a "state of homogeneity"—to a world in which all energy is in its final degraded or homogeneous state, and all matter, by inference, in a state of disorder or randomness—the primeval soup, in other words. Since living things do not fall within this category, the laws of classical thermodynamics cannot apply to them, and since there are no other laws, it must follow that the behavior of living things is not subjected to any laws at all.

This sounds very much like the worst sort of medieval casuistry, yet Prigogine[3] assures us that it is the only view that a scientist can possibly adopt—for it is the only one that is reconcilable with statistical theory. When the Newtonian paradigm was in fashion, he admits, there were indeed laws. However, it was by specifically rejecting the notion that nature is governed by laws that it became possible to free science from the "Newtonian Myth" (see appendix 1).

The French philosopher and social theorist Edgar Morin[4] seems also to have accepted the Prigogine mythology in its entirety. It is only in "popular epistemology," he tells us, that one finds reference today to the laws of nature. In other words, only the stupid and the uneducated still believe that nature is governed by laws. Modern science has abolished them all and has thereby liberated man so that he is free to create his own laws and to determine the course of his own evolution, and hence of his own destiny. This is exactly the message required to rationalize our modern individualistic and competitive society—the global free-for-all that is leading to the rapid destruction of our planet to satisfy short-term economic and political interests.

In terms of the world-view of ecology, the opposite is true. The main feature of the ecosphere is its incredible order (see chapter 35). This order is critical, and it can only be maintained if all life processes within the ecosphere are subjected to laws or constraints—which are at once self-imposed (see chapter 41), as well as further imposed by the larger systems of which they are part and that make up the Gaian hierarchy (see chapter 45). These constraints, what is more, are not of a random nature—they are precisely those that must lead living things to contribute to the maintenance of the ecosphere's critical order (see chapter 61) and that thereby cause them to behave homeotelically towards it (see chapter 41). Significantly, chthonic man has always recognized a hierarchical set of laws governing at once his own behavior, that of his society, of the natural world and of the all-encompassing cosmos itself, laws which it is his moral duty to observe as rigorously as possible (see chapter 61).

3

Ecology studies natural systems in their Gaian context

If perception is ordinarily highly dependent on context, then stripping away context may be a strategy of doubtful value.

Karl Popper

Whereas the laboratory method's power lies precisely in its isolation of the phenomenon to be studied, ecological science is, in principle, anti-isolationist. It is the science of totalities. As such it is anti-scientific, as science at present is usually conceived and practiced.

Lynn White

SCIENTIFIC METHOD INVOLVES studying the behavior of living things in "controlled laboratory conditions"—which means isolating them from the larger systems of which they are part. The information thus gained would be less questionable if these larger systems were no more than random arrangements, but they are not. Living things are the differentiated parts of the hierarchy of natural systems that make up the ecosphere, and the ecosphere has a critical structure which enables it to maintain its homeostasis in the face of environmental challenges (see chapter 36) and to provide each of its subsystems with an optimum environment (see chapter 43).

This principle has obvious implications. A natural system behaves very differently within its natural environment from the way it behaves once subjected to an artificial environment which bears little relationship to that in which it evolved, and hence one removed from the natural systems of which it is a differentiated part. This is true at all levels of organization within the Gaian hierarchy.

Thus, at a molecular level, a hemoglobin molecule in solution has a different affinity for oxygen than when it is inside a red blood cell. A cell that has been removed from an egg at an early stage in its development, as the famous German embryologist Hans Driesch showed, can develop into a whole organism, instead of developing into a differentiated part of an organism. As Michael Polanyi has pointed out so eloquently, the behavior of a cell depends on its position in a total pattern which means that "cell interaction . . . is of crucial importance," an embarrassing fact that cannot be explained in terms of reductionist science. This is true not just of isolated cells, but also of tissues—that is why grafting and budding and in general modern tissue culture are practicable.

Paul Weiss, though himself a laboratory biologist, notes that

Biochemists tend to study organic chemical interactions (e.g. enzyme reactions) in physically orderless or deliberately disordered states (test tube solutions or tissue pulp). This is a technical necessity and a lot can be learned through these methods. But they fall far short of reproducing the way things happen in the living system. They can show, at best, what might happen, but not what actually does happen in the organized state; for in an organism, chemical reactions occur, in the first place, not ubiquitously and indiscriminately, as in a mixture, but rather in critical patterns of localization and segregation, and, secondly, without the pampering and nursing care of a learned experimenter.[1]

The same is true of the behavior of organisms. As Eugene Odum notes, many insects are destructive pests in an agricultural habitat but not in their natural habitat where parasites, competitors, predators or chemical inhibitors keep them under control.

The more the environment of living things differs from that in which they evolved, the more their behavior is likely to be maladjusted, unadaptive or heterotelic. Thus, until recently, it was generally assumed that baboons were individualistic, competitive and aggressive creatures—a notion based on a study conducted by Lord Zuckerman,[2] at one time chief scientist to the British government, of baboons in the London Zoo. When they were actually studied in the wild however they were found, on the contrary, to be orderly, co-operative and peaceful. It then became clear that Zuckerman's baboons were asocialized and delinquent, their behavior resembling that of the equally asocialized and delinquent inhabitants of urban slums (see chapter 42).

In the same way, the responses to the sight of a piece of cheese of a laboratory animal confined in a box or cage are likely to provide very little valid information as to the normal behavior of the members of its species towards the food on which they normally feed, because such animals have not been adapted by their evolution or upbringing to living in boxes or cages, nor to dealing with isolated pieces of cheese. They have not in fact been biologically, socially and cognitively adjusted to dealing with such an artificial situation (see chapters 46, 47, 48). In addition, living things do not react blindly to stimuli. They seek to make sense of them, and as the Gestalt psychologist Keith Oatley notes, "that sense will include the whole context in which the material is presented."[3] But how can they make sense of something when its context has been systematically removed—when a "context-free situation" has been created to satisfy the exigencies of scientific method?

Experiments carried out in the impoverished environment of a laboratory, as Krishna Chaitanya notes, are biased "against cognition and intelligence."[4] They have been set up in such a way as to lend credence to the myth that living things simply react blindly and robot-like to specific stimuli. This is even more the case if the animals have actually been *brought up* in the aberrant conditions of a laboratory where their cognitive faculties have been stunted.

Living things, studied in isolation from the natural systems within which they developed phylogenetically and ontogenetically, are little more than freaks, their behavior providing little valid information on normal homeotelic behavior within the ecosphere. The study of the behavior of living things is of value to the extent that it be allowed to occur in conditions resembling as much as possible those in which they evolved and grew up.

4

Ecology is holistic

Our final aim is to bring human behavior within the framework of the
physical sciences.
Lord Adrian

If the organism is a hierarchical system with an organization above the
chemical level, then it is clear that it requires investigation *at all levels*,
and the investigation of one level (e.g. the chemical) cannot replace that
of higher levels.
J.H. Woodger

All particulars become meaningless if we lose sight of the pattern which
they jointly constitute.
Michael Polanyi

To say . . . that a man is made up of certain chemical elements is a satisfactory description only for those who intend to use him as fertilizer.
Edmund W. Sinnott

We have to start with the concept of the whole organism as the fundamental entity in biology and then understand how this generates parts that
conform to its intrinsic order—resulting in a harmoniously integrated,
though complex, organism.
Brian Goodwin

THE EARLY ACADEMIC ECOLOGISTS were so impressed by the way living things are organized to form a community, and hence the extent to which they are interrelated, that they compared the community to a biological organism. C.C.Adams, in the first American book on animal ecology published in 1913, insisted that

> the interactions among the members of an association are to be compared to the similar relations existing between the different cells, organs, or activities of a single individual . . . The physiological needs and states of an association have as real an existence in individual animals as similar needs in the cell or cells that compose the animal's body.[1]

This view of the ecological community became so well established that Daniel Simberloff refers to it as "ecology's first paradigm."[2] F.S.Bodenheimer wrote in 1953 that the concept of the community as an organism is stressed in nearly every textbook of ecology and, " . . . backed by established authority, is generally regarded if not as a fact, then at least as a scientific hypothesis not less firmly founded than the theory of transformation." (Or evolution.) It is this concept above all, he wrote, "that distinguishes ecology from biology proper."[3]

However, the holism of early ecologists was irreconcilable with the paradigm of science in terms of which the world is seen as random, atomized and mechanistic. Unfortunately, it is the latter view of the world that is alone capable of generating the science-based manufactured goods required to satisfy commercial ends (pesticides, antibiotics and genetically engineered micro-organisms, for instance). The holistic approach, on the other hand, does not yield the sort of practical information required for this purpose. As the biochemist N.W.Pirie notes,

> Those who are obsessed by the interactions of everything with everything else . . . are of necessity diffuse. Practical conclusions are not drawn from the holistic contemplation of totality.[4]

For that reason alone, ecology had to be transformed, but there are other reasons too. Ecology had to become respectable if it was to be taught in universities, and this meant making it conform to the paradigm of reductionistic science. This process started in the 1940s.

The Cambridge zoologist and ethologist W.H.Thorpe defines reductionism as the attribution of reality exclusively to the smallest constituents of the world and the tendency to interpret higher levels of organization in terms of lower levels. The justification for this is the dogma that only discrete particle-like entities are real; larger more diffuse natural systems being no more than abstractions that can only be studied in terms of their particle-like constituents.

Because it is physics that deals with the smallest constituents of the world (those at the lowest level of organization) it is considered the only real science—"aristoscience" as the Australian philosopher of science, John Passmore, calls it.[5] The New Zealander Lord Rutherford —one of the fathers of Nuclear Physics—went so far as to say that "Science is either physics or stamp-collecting."[6]

The gratuitous assumption that all knowledge about the world we live in can be reduced to the language of physics is still largely unquestioned in scientific circles—and scientific progress consists largely in the achievement of this task. The Nobel Laureate Francis Crick, co-discoverer of the genetic code, states the reductionist credo very explicitly. "Eventually," he writes, "one may hope to have the whole of biology 'explained' in terms of the level below it, and so on right down to the atomic level . . ."[7] It is becoming quite clear, however, that the enterprise Crick proposes will never be realized, nor can it be. Nevertheless, the basic philosophy of reductionism has survived unscathed, and it has led to the most obscurantist trends in the disciplines dealing with life processes at the higher levels of organization.

As Alexandre Koyré, perhaps the foremost Newtonian scholar, notes:

> The unholy alliance of Newton and Locke produced an atomic psychology, which explained (or explained away) mind as a mosaic of "sensations" and "ideas" linked together by laws of association (attraction;) we have had, too, atomic sociology, that reduced society to a cluster of human atoms, complete and self-contained each in itself and only mutually attracting and repelling each other.[8]

Koyré disowns these products of "physics envy" in the name of Newton himself, assuring us that he is "by no means responsible for these, and other monstra, engendered by the overextension—or aping —of his method."

The reductionist and mechanistic ecology that came into being in the 1940s is another such monster. One of its main architects was the Oxford ecologist, Arthur Tansley. He denied the basic holistic principle that the whole is more than the sum of its parts and hence that it is not amenable to study by the reductionist method of science. "These 'wholes'," he wrote, "are in analysis nothing but the synthesized actions of the components in associations." A mature science, in his view,

> must isolate the basic units of nature [and must] split up the story into its individual parts. It must approach nature as a composite of strictly physical entities organized into a mechanical system. The scientists who knows all the properties of all the parts studied separately can accurately predict their combined results.[9]

The reductionist approach to ecology, however, is usually traced to the earlier writings of the botanist Herbert Gleason, whose famous article "The Individualistic Concept of the Plant Association"[10] was first published in 1926 and presented and discussed at the International Botanical Congress that year. Gleason's main argument was that only the individual is "real." Larger associations—such as ecological communities or human communities—he saw as abstract entities that only exist in the eyes of the beholder. "An association has no real identity of its own," he wrote, from which it must follow that "its behavior is only understandable in terms of that of its components." It merely represents "the coincidence of certain plant individuals and not an organic entity itself." For only the latter are measurable, and only they can be studied with precision in controlled laboratory conditions. It is these assumptions that still underlie "analytical" or "reductionist" science.

Initially, Gleason's thesis was very badly received. In the words of Robert McIntosh, the best known historian of ecological thought, Gleason was "anathema to ecologists."[11] Gleason himself admitted that, for ten years after the publication of his article, he was "an ecological outlaw,"[12] for his thesis simply did not fit in with the ecological paradigm of the times. However, as the latter was transformed so as to make it conform with the paradigm of science and hence with the world-view of modernism, so Gleason's ideas became increasingly acceptable until they eventually became an integral part of accepted biological wisdom (see chapter 66). Today McIntosh refers to them as "a viable and expanding tenet of current ecological thought,"[13] while P.A.Colinvaux, in a well known textbook of ecology, goes so far as to describe the holistic view of the community as a "heresy."[14] Other modern ecologists go further and actually claim that their work has provided incontestable proof of the validity of Gleason's philosophy. J.T.Curtis for instance, tells us that "the entire evidence of the plant ecology study in Wisconsin (in which he was involved) can be taken as conclusive proof of Gleason's individualistic hypothesis of community organization . . ."[15] The American ecologist P.H.Whittaker regards his "gradient analysis" as providing similar evidence.[16]

How, one might ask, can they possibly make such claims? The answer is that science provides a means of collating data but not of interpreting them, and inevitably data are interpreted in terms of a scientist's particular paradigm. Thus if Curtis and Whittaker believe that the biosphere is "atomized" and "random" they will probably interpret the results of their experiments in such a way as to rationalize their reductionist faith.

The truth is that small systems *are not more real but merely simpler than bigger systems*. It is for that reason alone that they can be studied by physicists in terms of the crude methodology of science.

Natural systems however, especially those at the higher levels of organization such as societies and ecosystems (and, of course, the ecosphere itself) are incomparably more complex than the relatively simple entities that physicists study. As Wolfgang Kohler notes,

> If organisms were more similar to the systems which physics investigates, a great many methods of the physicist could be introduced in our science without much change. But in actual fact, the similarity is not very great. One of the advantages which makes the physicist's work so much easier is the simplicity of his systems . . . An ameba is a more complicated system than all the systems of the inanimate world.[17]

Living systems display all sorts of qualities that inanimate things do not display, or do so in an embryonic or latent way—qualities that become very much more developed as we move up from simple forms of life to more complex ones such as humans. The important point is that these qualities are not apparent from a study of the system's constituent parts but only once we see the system as a whole. Thus, the coordination of the behavior of the parts by the whole (see chapter 45) is only apparent once one has identified the whole. That living systems co-operate not just with each other but with the whole (i.e. that they are homeotelic to it), is also only evident if one looks at them within the context of the whole.

As the great Indian polymath Krishna Chaitanya notes, "seen from below, a mechanism may look self-sufficient; but from above, it can be seen as being utilized for a purpose that transcends the apparent self-sufficiency of its operations."[18] Von Bertalanffy also notes that the essential difference between events ordered "so as to maintain the system" and "those running wild to destroy it" is also clearly obscured by considering biology and indeed sociology in physical terms.[19] "What does 'health' or 'norm' mean in contrast to 'disease' and 'pathology'?" he asks. "Nothing, so far as the laws of physics and chemistry are concerned . . . But without these and similar notions, there would be no science of medicine and indeed biology." Nor, one may add, would it be possible to establish the essential distinction between heterotelic and homeotelic processes (see chapters 41 and 42) or between evolution and anti-evolution (see chapter 64).

Nor can reductionist science help us understand the problems caused by the disintegration of a larger system such as an ecosystem or Gaia herself, whose principal features it continues to deny, and whose very existence except in a metaphorical sense it continues to question. Passmore feels that it is precisely because of this insistence in trying to understand the world in terms of physics that scientists have been so unsuccessful in understanding the real problems that face us today.

> If we are still ignorant about most of the phenomena we encounter in our daily life—whether it be human nutrition or the life history of animals—this ignorance can in part be set down to the aristo-scientific emphasis on a very different kind of knowledge.[20]

Eugene Odum, though he admits the successes of the reductionist approach, considers that cell-level science will contribute very little to the well-being or survival of human civilization if we understand the higher levels of organization so inadequately that we can find no solutions to population overgrowth, social disorder, pollution and other forms of societal and environmental cancer.[21]

It is probably by seeking to understand the simple in terms of the complex rather than the complex in terms of the simple, that one can best understand the true nature of our relationship with the world of living things. Whitehead intimated this when he suggested that the concept of organism should be extended downward to include the particle. Thorpe was more explicit: "We have to work back into the physical sciences," he wrote, "equipped with the concept of organism derived from the biological sciences."[22] Better still, he might have said, from the self-regulating ecosystem, or from Gaia herself. This would reveal structures and functions that, though clearly visible at the higher levels of organization, are but embryonic at the lower levels. It would reveal too that these structures and functions, rather than being autonomous, are, in effect, the differentiated parts of larger natural systems and life processes, indeed of the spatio-temporal Gaian hierarchy as a whole, to whose control they are subjected and to whose stability they necessarily contribute. (See chapters 41 and 45.)

5

Ecology is teleological

—

The attitude of biologists to teleology is like that of the pious towards a
source of temptation which they are unsure of their ability to resist.
P.B.Medawar

Teleology is like the kind of woman people do not want to be seen with
in the street, yet are prepared to tender their love to in secret.
Von Brucke (the elder)

Still, all the while like warp and woof, mechanism and teleology are
interwoven together, and we must not cleave to the one nor despise the
other: for their union is rooted in the very nature of totality.
D'Arcy Thompson

Teleological explanations in academe are a sin against the holy spirit of
scientific rationality; they deny the objectivity of nature.
James Lovelock

The Gaia hypothesis . . . is an alternative to that pessimistic view which
sees nature as a primitive force to be subdued and conquered, and that
equally depressing picture of our planet as a demented spaceship, forever
traveling, driverless and purposeless, around an inner circle of the Sun.
James Lovelock

THE TELEOLOGICAL EXPLANATION of a life process centers on its goal—Aristotle's "final cause"—rather than on its antecedent cause, which alone is accepted by the scientific community. Teleology, the neurophysiologist and Nobel laureate Ragnar Granit tells us, is required to answer the question of *why* things happen, that we must know if we are to understand *how* things happen.[1]

This must be true of any entity or process. Thus Robert Fuller and Peter Putnam tell us that

> a skilled electronics engineer is often unable to derive the function of a rather simple electronic circuit, despite a complete knowledge of the network and the properties of its elementary units. On the other hand, if one has a guiding idea as to the overall function of the circuit, then it is possible to examine the component parts and see just what role they play in this function.[2]

Granit also notes how this is true in determining how the eye adapts to light and darkness.

> When rods and cones were discovered in the vertebrate retina, had it not become evident that rods dominated in retinas of the night animals and cones in those of daylight animals, this discovery would have remained an observation of but limited consequence. Instead, understanding of its meaning (why) made it a cornerstone in a large body of biological research dealing with the adaptation of the eye to light and darkness, rod vision and cone vision, and the rod-free central fovea of the human retina.[3]

In the same way, it is by establishing what is the goal of any organism or natural system that one is in a position to ask how it sets out to achieve it. This is often referred to as the cybernetic method.

It is by using this method that James Lovelock developed his famous Gaia thesis.

To examine the Earth cybernetically, he writes, is to ask the question "What is the function of each gas in the air or of each component of the sea?" Outside the context of Gaia, such a question would be taken as circular and illogical, but from within it is no more illogical than asking: what is the function of the hemoglobin or of the insulin in the blood? We have postulated a cybernetic system; therefore, it is reasonable to question the function of the component parts.[4]

Lovelock starts off by pointing to the extraordinary constancy of the chemical composition of the ecosphere—the oxygen and carbon dioxide content of the atmosphere, for instance, and the salt content of the sea. He then searches for mechanisms that could assure this constancy. Ralph Gerard notes how the physiologist proceeds in precisely the same way.

The physiologist's whole life is concerned with problems of organic purpose, though he rarely likes to say it, particularly in public. We see purposeful behavior all through the body; it is the only way it makes sense to us. And then we look for the mechanisms to account for it.[5]

In terms of the paradigm of science, this teleological method of building up knowledge is totally illegitimate. To accuse a scientist of using a teleological argument is to accuse him of being unscientific, indeed, of being a veritable charlatan. Very few scientists would be willing to take that risk. Even Lovelock did not originally admit that his argument is teleological. The Daisy World model, that he developed with Andrew Watson, is primarily designed to show that cybernetic processes need not be teleological. However, it is but a rudimentary and indeed hypothetical cybernetic process and it would prove very much more difficult to build a realistic model to demonstrate that the dynamic, sequential and creative cybernetic strategies of complex forms of life in the real world are non-teleological.

Mainstream scientists will go to the most extraordinary lengths to make it appear that the statements they make are non-teleological. One ruse is to deny the purposiveness of life processes altogether and to argue that nature only *appears* purposeful. Julian Huxley tells us that "at first sight the biological sector seems full of purpose. Organisms are built *as if* in purposeful pursuit of a conscious aim. But the truth lies in those two words "*as if.*" As the genius Charles Darwin showed, the purpose is "*only an apparent one.*"[6] He adds that

No conscious seizing of opportunities is here meant (by the use of the word purpose) nor even an unconscious sensing of an outcome. The word is only a convenient label for these tendencies in evolution; that what can happen usually does happen; changes occur as they may and not as would be hypothetically best; and the course of evolution follows opportunity rather than plan.

The opposite is true. The "seizing of opportunities" is itself a teleological concept. An adaptive individual does not seize any opportunity to bring about a random change, but the one that suits its purposes, the one that it judges to be "hypothetically best" for itself and for the hierarchy of natural systems of which it is part.

More devious expedients are resorted to in order to make it appear that scientists can avoid arguing teleologically. Thus David Merrell notes how throughout the modern biological literature we find

> a great array of teleological jargon bearing witness, as it were, to the homeorhetic tendency of living systems. Biologists are always talking of one thing occurring, "for the purpose of something" or, "in order that something might happen" or, "serving the function of something" and so on.[7]

However, philosophers still go to great lengths to show that these statements can be translated into a non-teleological form. This often leads them "into a morass of circumlocutions." Thus, biologists, as Peter Calow notes, have been prepared to say "a turtle came ashore *and* laid its eggs," but not that "it came ashore *to* lay its eggs."[8]

Calow also shows how it is possible to translate teleological propositions into non-teleological language.[9] Thus the teleological statement "the function of the vertebrate heart is to pump blood" can be translated into non-teleological language simply by saying that "the heart is a necessary condition for the circulation of blood in vertebrates."

Another device resorted to by mainstream scientists is to provide a purely mechanistic explanation of purpose. The inspiration came from the machine with feedback. These machines are programmed in such a way that they seek to achieve a goal. They avoid teleology in the sense that they are not seen as tending towards a final cause, hence their behavior is not seen as requiring some sort of supernatural explanation. The principle involved is also reconcilable with causality, reductionism, statistical method and, of course, mechanomorphism.

As Henri Atlan puts it, "this new type of goal directedness is acceptable in that it is not derived from theological idealism, but from neo-mechanism," and hence from a *scientifically acceptable* rather than a *scientifically unacceptable* metaphysics.[10] It came to be known as "teleonomy," a term first used by the biologist Colin Pittendrigh and later taken up by many leading biologists.

The acceptance of teleonomy enables us to ask the question "why" rather than "how" but only within a limited sphere, that of the functioning of a machine. It may indeed tell us what is the immediate goal of a natural process, but it tells us nothing of the ultimate goal to which its achievement contributes. It even implies that there is no such ultimate goal. More recently, the development of molecular biology culminating in the decoding of the genetic code by Francis Crick and his colleague James Watson has further increased the credibility of the notion of teleonomy. Living things, molecular biologists maintain, *give the impression* of seeking to achieve a goal or final cause, but this is only because they have been genetically programed to move in this direction. Instead of taking the form of a computer program, the Deus ex machina is now a genetic program.

However, no life process can be understood in terms of the information with which it has been programed, for it is under the control of the larger systems of which it is part, that provide it with the environment with which it is constantly interacting, and from which it derives much of the information required for its development. Thus a developing embryo acquires information during the entire embryological process, first from the cytoplasm, then from the womb and later, when the child is born, from its family, and as it grows up, from the community and ecosystem of which it is part.

It is one of the main attractions of Darwinism for scientists that it appears to be non-teleological, but that is an illusion. Competition, for example, implies competition for something. Since competition, for Darwinists, is intimately linked with the notion of the "survival of the fittest," it means competition to survive. But why should living things want to survive? We assume that they do, but this is a gratuitous assumption. Stones do not want to survive particularly. At least they make no visible effort to do so. Lamp bulbs, nylon stockings and many other consumer products are designed specifically not to survive, since it is "economic" to build into them "planned obsolescence."

Another key Darwinian concept, natural selection, is equally teleological, a point made by Grassé.[11] "There cannot be selection without purpose (intention)," he writes, and, "by explaining the evolution of the fittest in terms of selection, they (the neo-Darwinists) are endowing all living things with an inherent goal."

In reality, the concept of selection is of use to neo-Darwinists because it provides a means of delegating *surreptitiously and, it is hoped, imperceptibly*, to a vague and undefined environment the teleological functions *that organisms alone are capable of fulfilling adaptively*. In this way, of course, the latter's own behavior can be made out to be random. It is a desperately feeble subterfuge especially as the environment, if one considers it, must itself be made up of other organisms the purposiveness of whose behavior is, of course, never questioned.

Ecology has to be teleological, for purposiveness is possibly the most essential feature of the behavior of living things (see chapter 27). It is only in terms of a teleological ecology that we can understand the role of living things within the Gaian hierarchy, in particular their fundamentally homeotelic or whole-maintaining character (see chapter 41) which above all makes possible the order, integrity and stability of the living world.

6

Ecology explains events in terms of their role within the spatio-temporal Gaian hierarchy

———

The microbe is nothing, the environmental conditions (le terrain) everything.
Louis Pasteur

At the present day, the whole subject of causation is in a chaotic state. Men of science, on the one hand, who use the notion, appear to be too busy amassing facts to trouble themselves much about what they mean by it, and philosophers, on the other hand, seem, for the most part, from the time of Hume onward, to entertain beliefs on this subject which are very difficult to harmonize with the use of the notion in biological science.
J.H. Woodger

The meaning of any natural thing or event cannot be fully grasped or explained scientifically until we discover its relations to the components of the orderly flow of process we call our cosmos.
C. Judson Herrick

MAINSTREAM SCIENCE sees an event in the real world as the product of a "cause." A cause is another discrete event that has been observed empirically by the process of induction to precede it in time, on the basis of which it is assumed that it will always have the same effect.

This principle of explanation fits in perfectly with the paradigm of science. It is reductionist, the cause being a discrete event; mechanistic, since the cause is a switch that triggers off a specific effect; predictable, since switches are not creative or intelligent; compatible with the notion of randomness since the causal process occurs in isolation from all other processes; and non-teleological, since the cause must necessarily precede the effect.

However, it provides a very misleading picture of events in the real world, for a life process—contrary to the impression conveyed by neo-Darwinism—does not occur in a void but as an integral part of a much wider process: the evolution of the ecosphere itself. As such, it is subject to homearchic control (see chapter 45) by the ecosphere, seen as a spatio-temporal system. Such control of the part by the whole can be termed holistic causation, or as it has been referred to "emergent" or "downward" causation.

A life process also evolves for a purpose, that of fulfilling a specific function within the hierarchy of the ecosphere so as to contribute to the maintenance of its critical order and hence its stability. For this reason it can only be explained in terms of its role or purpose within the spatio-temporal Gaian hierarchy. It is this explanation that must be taken to be its cause—that is if the term "cause" is to be of any use in the understanding of life processes.

What is more, the same cause will not always trigger off the same effect, for if a living thing cannot achieve its goal in the normal way, it will seek to do so in a different way; for life processes display "equifinality." For this reason alone the scientific principle of causality

34

must be rejected, for how can one explain a life process in terms of a single causal event if it can achieve its goal *even when the event does not occur* (see chapter 25).

If a normal homeotelic process cannot be explained in terms of isolated discrete causes, nor can a heterotelic process (see chapter 42) that disrupts the functioning of natural systems and prevents them from achieving the goal they were designed to achieve. The reason is that such a heterotelic event can trigger off a veritable chain reaction of ever more heterotelic events. That event which is taken to constitute a cause may thus be but one of a very long series of events, each one of which can be regarded as constituting a cause. Consider the following passage from the writings of George Perkins Marsh, a nineteenth century American diplomat, and one of the most important precursors of today's ecology movement.

> The aquatic larvae of some insects constitute, at certain seasons, a large part of the food of fresh water fish, while other larvae, in their turn, prey upon the spawn and even the young of their persecutors. The larvae of the mosquito and the gnat are the favorite food of the trout in the wooded regions where those insects abound. Earlier in the year, the trout feeds on the larvae of the Mayfly, which is itself very destructive to the spawn of the salmon, and hence by a sort of house-that-Jack-built, the destruction of the mosquito that feeds the trout, that preys on the Mayfly, that destroys the eggs, that hatch the salmon, that pampers the epicure, may occasion a scarcity of this latter fish in waters where he would otherwise be abundant. Thus all nature is linked together by invisible bonds, and every organic creature however low, however feeble, however dependent, is necessary to the well-being of some other among the myriad forms of life with which the Creator has peopled the Earth.[1]

What then is the cause of the epicure's frustration? Why has he been deprived of his smoked salmon? The obvious answer is that the mayfly has eaten the salmon's eggs. But is that a sufficient cause? Obviously not, since mayflies would not have been a problem if there had been enough trout around to eat them. The absence of the appropriate number of trout is thus another cause of this sad event. But it is not a sufficient cause either, since if there had been enough mosquito larvae around for the trout to eat they would not have left the area. Hence the absence of mosquitoes can also be regarded as a cause, though still not a sufficient cause, for if people had not killed the mosquitoes there would still have been plenty of larvae. Clearly we must consider the problem in greater depth. To begin with, it would appear that the people in the area once used to put up with the mosquitoes, why then do they not do so now? Perhaps people had recently moved into the area who were particularly sensitive to mosquito bites. Perhaps too, they had been persuaded by a chemical company to get rid of the mosquitoes, which they would otherwise have tolerated, by spraying them with an insecticide that the corporation happened to manufacture. But why should people be stupid enough to poison their environment with carcinogenic pesticides? Why too should chemical companies be allowed to manufacture them? To answer these questions would mean describing the dynamics of our industrial society and how it actually came into being.

Of course in such a society it is politically and commercially convenient to take the most immediate cause as determinant and ignore all others. This appears to justify the most superficial treatment possible, accommodating rather than changing the aberrant social and economic structures on which we have become dependent for the satisfaction of our short-term interests. If the cause of crop damage is seen to be a specific pest, this justifies waging chemical warfare against it (which suits the pesticide manufacturers). If the cause of an infectious disease is taken to be a specific microbe, this justifies the use of antibiotics to eliminate it (which suits the pharmaceutical industry). The adoption of these solutions, moreover, stimulates other commercial activities, such as transport, banking and retailing, all of which provide jobs, contribute to the tax revenue of the State and, temporarily at least, improve our material welfare.

Unfortunately, technological expedients only solve technological problems. They cannot reverse the disruption of natural systems. Alleviating the symptoms, they render the problems more tolerable and thus serve to perpetuate them. René Dubos, the Franco-American microbiologist, and father of what might be referred to as the Ecology of Health, pointed out over 40 years ago that microbes are not the cause of infectious disease.[2] Man will always be inhabited by vast populations of microbes; indeed, according to the American microbiologist Lynn Margulis, known for her work on microbial ecology and the Gaia thesis, we harbor in our bodies as many microbial cells (prokaryotes) as animal cells (eukaryotes), most of them playing an essential role in our metabolism.[3] Dubos traces the source of diseases to a breakdown in the critical balance between man and his microbial populations, brought about by a range of possible factors such as old age, malnutrition, exposure to low-level radiation or to chemical pollutants, or to a virus that disrupts the immune system.

Louis Pasteur, who was the first to incriminate the microorganism, eventually saw the error of his ways. W. R. Day, an authority on plant diseases, also saw very clearly that blaming the parasite leads to the neglect of fundamental causes.[4] An infectious disease may be caused by a subtle combination of factors which reduces the resistance of an organism, making it vulnerable to an attack which, under normal conditions, it would repel with ease. The recent deaths of dolphins in the North Sea, for example, point to its contamination by low levels of all sorts of heavy metals, chemicals and radionuclides, that combine to reduce the effectiveness of the immune system of sea mammals against the viruses that have been officially implicated. The truth is that the highly-polluted North Sea has simply ceased to provide a viable habitat for dolphins and many other complex forms of life.

The same is probably true of the degradation of forests in Europe and on the East Coast of North America where trees have died in increasing numbers. The designated killer is "acid rain" containing high levels of sulfuric acid created when sulfur dioxide emissions from factories combine with the moisture in the atmosphere. But trees are ill and dying in areas where there is little or no sulfur dioxide pollution. It is more likely that a subtle combination of pollutants of all sorts— in the air, in the rainfall and in the soil itself—is responsible, leaving us to face the depressing fact that our industrial society is giving rise to conditions which are ever less capable of sustaining complex forms of life like large trees. Such conditions are the opposite to those that obtain in a climax ecosystem where everything conspires to reduce the incidence of such problems to a minimum.

It is impossible to understand the daunting problems that confront us today in terms of the narrow scientific concept of causality. They should be examined instead within their total ecospheric context. In this way, it would become clear that these problems cannot be solved by technological means—but only by correcting the social and ecological maladjustments of which they are but the symptoms. It would also be clearer that this must mean bringing about the most fundamental changes to our society, our economy and their relationship with an increasingly degraded ecosphere so that the restoration and preservation of its critical order, on which our survival necessarily depends, becomes our overriding goal (see chapter 61).

7

Fundamental knowledge is inherited

~

No proposition can be said to be in the mind which it never yet knew,
which it was never yet conscious of . . .
John Locke

Deductivism in mathematical literature, and inductivism in scientific
papers are simply the postures we choose to be seen in when the curtain
goes up and the public sees us.
P. B. Medawar

It is fundamental to modern science that all knowledge is obtained by empirical observation. This implies, among other things, that a child is born with a virgin mind—the "tabula rasa" of the empiricist philosophers—on which, during its upbringing, empirical knowledge is systematically registered. This thesis is consistent with the view that a living thing is a temporal isolate, but it is incompatible with our knowledge of the continuity and stability of natural systems.

The ethologist Robert Fantz noted how new born chicks, from the moment they were born, pecked one hundred times more often at spherical than at pyramidal objects.[1] The Nobel Laureate Niko Tinbergen found that newly hatched herring gull chicks preferred pecking at objects which resembled the bill of the parents from which they were fed. Marked preferences for certain specific objects were also established among baby chimps. Fantz also showed that children displayed a greater interest in flat objects that were painted to look like human faces than at flat objects on which the features of a human face were painted in a scrambled pattern, while they largely ignored similar objects on which no human features were painted.

Fantz regards his experiments as demonstrating that living things are born with an "innate knowledge of the environment"—a knowledge that "provides a foundation for the vast accumulation of knowledge built up through experience."[2] This must be so, for each generation of living things inherits genetic information that reflects the experience of its ancestors going back into the mists of time. Only in this way can a species (and the Gaian hierarchy of which it is part) display continuity or stability. Morphogenesis—including the morphogenesis of the individual's brain, and hence of its capacity to build up knowledge—must also display continuity or stability. But what is true of morphogenesis is also true of behavior, for these processes are but different stages in the same Gaian process. It follows that the behavior of successive generations also displays continuity—which in any case we know empirically to be true—and this requires that an individual inherit a rudimentary model of its relationship with its environment (see chapter 10), reflecting the long-term behavioral experience of its cultural group, its race or variety, and its species.

We know that the evolutionary development of all life processes proceeds from the general to the particular, and this is also true of the development of the hierarchical organization of knowledge on the basis of which behavior is mediated. The generalities of this knowledge, what is more, being non-plastic, must color the rest of the information that is built up through experience. It is thus the most general and hence the most fundamental knowledge that must be inherited, while that which is built up through experience is derived from it during the interplay between the individual's behavior and its field—the ordered environment within which behavior occurs (see chapter 44).

8

Fundamental knowledge is ineffable and we mainly have access to it by intuition and via our sense of aesthetics

~

What we cannot speak of, we must be silent about.
Ludwig Wittgenstein

The Tao that can be told is not the eternal Tao.
Lao Tzu

The intuitive powers of the investigator are always dominant and decisive.
Michael Polanyi

When you have satisfied yourself that the theorem is true you start proving it.
G. Polya

The servant of Tao, realizing the perfect beauty of the universe, attains understanding.
Lao Tzu

For empiricist philosophers, and hence for our mainstream scientists, knowledge must be entertained consciously and must be expressible in language, for only such knowledge is observable. However, there is every reason to suppose that knowledge that is entertained subconsciously, and cannot thereby be articulated, plays an essential part in determining our behavior pattern.

Michael Polanyi refers to such knowledge as "ineffable" and notes how "all professionals possess a mass of professional knowledge of this sort . . . they know many more things than they can tell, knowing them only in practice, as instrumental particulars, and not explicitly as objects." All the knowledge that they cannot tell, he takes to be "ineffable" and its use to guide our behavior, "an ineffable process of thought."[1]

Arthur Koestler notes that our emotions are "notoriously inarticulate." "We can describe intellectual processes in the most intricate detail, but have only the crudest vocabulary even for the vital sensations of bodily pain—as both physician and patient know to their sorrow."[2] Neurophysiologically, the seat of our instincts, of our emotions and of our values too, lies in our primitive brains, the first to develop during the course of our cerebral evolution. It is the knowledge organized in these brains of which we are unconscious and cannot articulate. The seat of our readily articulated conscious knowledge, on the other hand, seems to be in the neo-cortex, the newest of our brains. Significantly, attempts to mediate at the "high" conscious level functions designed to be mediated at a "lower" one lead to maladjustments and failures. The psychologist Victor Frankl notes how many psychological problems and failure on the part of patients to fulfill basic behavioral functions are attributable to this cause.

> In clinical practice, often we are confronted with patients who are, so to speak, over-conscious of what they are doing, and this interferes with

44

performance, be it the performance of the sexual act (sexual neurosis) or the performance of any artistic work (vocational neurosis).[3]

In Frankl's terms this is the phenomenon of *hyper-reflection* to be countered by *de-reflection*, which means turning a patient's attention away from himself and his own activity.

Polanyi describes the same phenomenon in slightly different terms.

> If a pianist shifts his attention from the piece he is playing to the observation of what he is doing with his fingers while playing it, he gets confused and may have to stop. This happens generally if we switch our focal attention to *particulars* of which we had previously been aware only in their subsidiary role.[4]

This is usually referred to as self-consciousness. In the example of "stage fright," it consists in "the anxious riveting" of the would-be actor's attention on the next word—or note or gesture—to be remembered. This accent on the details "destroys one's sense of the context which alone can smoothly evoke the proper sequence of words, notes or gestures." The cure is to allow one's mind to "operate with a clear view to the comprehensive activity in which we are primarily interested."

This suggests that different types of behavior—if they are to be adaptive—*must be mediated at the appropriate cerebral level.* An essential part of the skills displayed by Polanyi's professionals, pianist and actor, and by Frankl's lover and artist is closely bound up with their instincts, emotions and values and must be mediated at the level of the primitive brains. This is even more obviously true of our basic physiological functions, such as the digestion of our food and the circulation of our blood. If they were to depend for their proper functioning on the conscious knowledge organized into our neo-cortex, we would probably not survive for a single day.

It is probably also true of our most fundamental knowledge of our relationships with the world around us. Thus, the basic features of the behavior of vernacular man towards his society and his environment are mediated on the basis of his traditional world-view, which is largely organized in the primitive brains. But once the conscious and rational mind, whose seat is the neo-cortex, seeks to take them over, disaster follows, for it was simply not designed for that purpose. This fundamental but ineffable knowledge must also be passed on from generation to generation largely intact. It is only the particularities of such knowledge that can be modified with impunity by articulate consciousness. The process whereby we acquire ineffable knowledge is usually referred to as "intuition." It is itself mysterious and ineffable.

A fundamental principle of the vernacular world-view is the unity or "one-ness" of the living world. For the Bantu, as Father Placide Tempels writes, this is the supreme wisdom that cannot be acquired in schools or universities. For Alexander von Humboldt, "the harmonious unity of nature" lies "beyond the realms of positive knowledge" and "is accessible only to the vivid and deep emotions."[5] The Haiku scholar R.H.Blyth also feels that only our intuition can enable us to understand the whole, while the intellect can understand something as a part but not as a whole. For deep ecologists this one-ness of the natural world is "the central intuition of deep ecology"—but they do not stress its ineffable and intuitive character.

Our sense of aesthetics is closely related to our intuition. It is also an important means of apprehending and of understanding our relationship to the world around us, as it is of attaching us emotionally to that which is important to us and to the cosmic hierarchy of which we are part.

It is above all the natural world, in which our aesthetic sense—like all our other faculties—evolved, that we find beautiful, as we do the human artefacts that mimic it. A Gothic cathedral, for instance, is beautiful; for its vault is that of the forest, its pillars the forest trees.

On the other hand, we abhor what is foreign to nature: unnatural colors, the straight lines of modern buildings, the uniformity of a conifer plantation that contrasts only too sharply with the mosaic of different greens of a natural forest.

Things that are beautiful also tend to be socially and ecologically desirable. Thus the traditional farm, carved out of the woods, with its diminutive fields, its patchwork of different crops, enclosed by hedgerows, looks good and is good. As William Cobbett used to say, "Farm right and you can be sure the land will look right." On the other hand the modern intensive farm, with its huge asbestos sheds and its endless stretches of monoculture enclosed by barbed wire fences, looks wrong and is wrong—very wrong.

We see beauty too in the natural pattern and order of nature. For Weiss the beauty of natural forms is not a "random configuration, scattered haphazardly through the universe" but rather the outcome of lawful and orderly processes in nature.[6]

Not surprisingly, then, we see beauty in the wholeness of living things and of the natural world. As American poet Robinson Jeffers notes,

> A severed hand
> Is an ugly thing, and man dissevered from the Earth
>   and stars and his history
>   . . . for contemplation or in fact . . .
> Often appears atrociously ugly. Integrity is wholeness,
>   the greatest beauty is
> Organic wholeness, the wholeness of life and things,
>   the divine beauty of the universe.
>   Love that, not man
> Apart from that, or else you will share man's
>   pitiful confusions,
>   or drown in despair when his days darken.[7]

9

Ecological knowledge is built up by organizing knowledge in the mind

—

Overt intelligent performances are not clues to the working of the mind,
they are those workings.
Gilbert Ryle

How can one explain scientific discovery and artistic originality without
reference to mind and imagination?
Arthur Koestler

The proper understanding of matter requires the imagination to invent
entities not apparent in everyday phenomena. It is the enduring miracle
of creative thought that the mind is equal to this task.
Gerald Feinberg

Complex concepts are not built up out of simple ones, simple concepts
are abstracted from complex ones.
Russell Ackoff

IF THE CONCEPTS of "ineffable knowledge" and "intuition" are foreign to the paradigm of science, so until the development of the new "cognitive" or "mentalist" school in the Behavioral Sciences in the 1970s was that of the mind itself, for its workings are not observable in the sense in which material objects are observable. Thus to David Hume only impressions (sensations) and ideas were real, the mind being regarded as no more than the sum total of our impressions and ideas. Gilbert Ryle insisted that there could be no mind as distinct from its workings and that any statement about the mind was meaningless.[1] This, in broad terms, has been the position of empiricist philosophers ever since.

When John B. Watson and the American Behaviorist school sought to eliminate from their field of study all the metaphysical speculation of their predecessors and turn their subject into a "hard science" they denied the existence of the mind in the same way as did Hume and Ryle. Any introspective concept that could not be observed and quantified was taken to be non-scientific and had to be eliminated. Consciousness for instance, which empiricists since Descartes had always taken to be the seat of knowledge, Watson regarded as "neither a definable or usable concept" and as "merely another word for the concept of the soul . . . of more ancient times."[2] As he pointed out, "no one has ever touched a soul or seen one in a test tube." This too was E.C. Tolman's position. "All that can ever be observed in human beings," he insists, "is behavior";[3] and he intimates that this is all one can talk about scientifically. Also, since all behavior is seen as random, there is no need for the mind as an instrument of coordination.

According to Watson, when a dressmaker designs a new gown, he does not have any picture in his mind of what the gown is going to look like when it is finished; this would be teleological behavior, which is quite unacceptable to science. Besides, how can one quantify a picture and explain it in the scientifically respectable terms of physics and mechanics? All the dressmaker does is

> call his model in. She picks up a new piece of silk, and throws it around her; he pulls it in here, he pulls it out there . . . He manipulates the material until it takes on the semblance of a dress.[4]

A painter, too, plies his trade in this way. "Nor can the poet boast of any other method." Indeed, we get new verbal creations such as a poem or a brilliant essay, he insists, "by manipulating words, shifting them about until a new pattern is hit upon." The same attitude is displayed by the members of the Behaviorist school of sociology. Thus, George A. Lundberg considers the search for human motives to be unscientific on the grounds that it is "an animistic pursuit."[5] It is under the influence of such ideas that sociology has degenerated into the study of the observable atoms of social behavior.

Evolution is seen by neo-Darwinists and Sociobiologists in just the same way. As Watson writes

> The organic raw material is manipulated in a random manner—a tail is added here, a pair of wings there, and eventually, the appropriate pattern is hit upon and preserved because it happens to be the fittest.[6]

The only scientifically acceptable method of acquiring "synthetic" knowledge is referred to as induction which involves the acquisition of data by cumulative individual observations and correlations. The more often a correlation can be made, the more are we justified in believing that the events will continue to occur together and, indeed, that they constitute a "cause and effect" relationship.

This method of acquiring knowledge fits in perfectly with the paradigm of science. It is a reductionist concept, since each observation can be regarded as an "atom" of cognition, just as each "bit" is an atom of information, each "reflex" an atom of behavior, each sense-datum an atom of perception, and each "meme" (to use Richard Dawkins's term), an atom of culture. Each of these reductionist concepts can be quantified, since observations can be counted. It also fits in with the view of behavior as random rather than orderly or teleological, and also passive and robot-like rather than dynamic and creative. But it has very serious failings. Hume was the first to point to the limitations of induction. There was no logical reason, he argued, for supposing "that those instances of which we had no experience, resemble those of which we have had experience,"[7] which means that "even after the observation of the frequent or constant conjunction of objects we have no reason to draw any inference concerning any object beyond those of which we have had experience."[8]

However, in spite of this failing, Hume considered that induction still provides the only valid way of building up knowledge. Indeed, he is usually regarded as its original proponent.

Other epistemologists, including both Immanuel Kant and later Karl Popper, have taken the logical objection to induction more seriously. However, this issue does not seem to be the critical one, for no method of acquiring "synthetic" knowledge can provide us with logically indubitable knowledge. What we require is a means of acquiring knowledge that has the greatest likelihood of being true—different degrees of likelihood being required for different purposes. The critical question is whether induction is the means of satisfying even this more modest criterion, and it can be shown that it is not. One reason is that one can push Hume's argument against the validity of induction a stage further. Because of the nature of life processes themselves (which logicians do not appear to be concerned with), the fact that events have been observed to occur together does not mean that they will continue to do so indefinitely. As Polanyi notes,

> Our expectation of life does not increase with the number of days we have survived. On the contrary, the experience of living through the next twenty-four hours is much less likely to recur after it has happened 30,000 consecutive times than after only 1000 times. Attempts to train a horse to do without food will fall down precisely after the longest series of successes; and the certainty of amusing an audience by one's favorite joke does not increase indefinitely with the number of its successful repetitions.[9]

The truth is that the building up of knowledge requires more than the accumulation of individual observations. These must be interpreted in the light of a model of our relationship with our environment. Thought is required—a non-quantifiable, non-reductionist, non-mechanistic activity, whose very existence is not consistent with the paradigm of science. Without it, "without theoretical interpretation," in Popper's formulation, "observation remains blind—uninformative."[10]

Cause and effect relationships established on the basis of indiscriminate empirical observations must indeed provide very questionable conclusions. After the racial riots in Britain in 1981, a public enquiry was set up under the chairmanship of Lord Scarman to determine its causes and propose measures to prevent their recurrence. The Brixton residents group "Concern" argued that simply to engage more policemen would not solve the problem. To confirm this thesis, they published a study establishing that between 1977 and 1980, the period during which crime really began to escalate in Brixton, "the number of policemen exceeded the established level for the area by 113 percent." From this they drew the conclusion that "more police increased the crime rate."[11] They may, of course, have been right, but it is more realistic to see the growing crime rate in Brixton and elsewhere as but a symptom of social and cultural deprivation against which the police, however numerous, can do very little.

It is only among the most simple forms of life for whom mental activity (i.e. thinking) is still relatively rudimentary that knowledge is acquired by something approaching the inductive method. To train an Earthworm to find its way through a maze must require considerable patience. The correlation between taking the wrong path and receiving an electric shock is made only after repeated lessons. On the other hand, as we move to more complex forms of life so is there a corresponding increase in cybernismic complexity (see chapter 52) and hence in the ability to think and to interpret experiences, and the number of empirical observations required before learning occurs is proportionately reduced. In fact one could formulate a law to the effect that the role of induction is inversely proportionate to the complexity of the mental model an animal builds of its relationship with its environment. Indeed, the more one knows about something, the smaller the number of observations needed to understand it and predict how it is likely to change. Otherwise why should an authority on the subject be better at doing this than one who knew nothing about it at all?

As we shall see (in chapter 28), perception or observation involves detecting rather than merely receiving signals—a living thing detecting only those signals that appear to be relevant to the achievement of its behavioral goal. Such signals are said to attract its "attention." Polanyi notes that the role of attention is ignored by psychologists and other inductive scientists.[12] Popper tells of an experiment that he carried out with his students, in which he simply asked them to *observe*. The students looked a little flummoxed. He then said

> I hope you are all co-operating and observing. However, I fear that at least some of you, instead of observing, will feel a strong urge to ask what do you want me to "observe"?[13]

If this were so, he told them, then his experiment had been successful for its object was to show that "in order to observe, we must have in mind a definite question which we might be able to decide by observation."

Interestingly enough, Darwin, in his autobiographical sketch, insisted that he "worked on Baconian principles, and, without any theory, collected facts on a wholesale scale."[14] But later in the same book he admitted that he could not resist forming a hypothesis on every subject. In a letter to the naturalist Henry Fawcett, he observed "how odd it is that anyone should not see that all observation must be for or against some view," [15] and later in a letter to H. W. Bates he agreed that for him "a good observer really means a good theorist." Medawar considers that these comments reflected "his true opinions as opposed to the opinions which he felt became him."[16]

Polanyi also denies that a scientist's discoveries are the product of the inductive method. He considers that de Broglie's wave theory, the Copernican system and the theory of Relativity "were all found by pure speculation guided by criteria of internal rationality."[17]

Thorpe sees scientific progress as being largely achieved by

> great leaps of imaginative insight; leaps which, at the time they were made, may have had very little experimental or observational basis . . . In some respects . . . many of the most important theories in the history of science are arrived at as much by the modes of thought of the artist and of the pure mathematician as by those popularly considered to be characteristic of scientists.[18]

They were achieved by a mysterious process, he might have put it, that could well be referred to as intuition.

10

The mind contains a hierarchical organization of instructions and an associated model or dynamic map

For living processes to occur a ready made model of the final product i.e. of the goal, is required, or at any rate a template with the same degree of specificity to guide a proper order of assemblage.
Paul Weiss

For a natural system to be capable of undertaking a co-ordinated sequence of actions or a strategy for maintaining itself along its path or chreods, and achieve the requisite end-state (a baby in the case of an embryological process or a climax ecosystem in the case of an ecological one), its cybernism must be endowed with the requisite set of instructions. But that is not enough. It must also provide a model of the relationships between the system and its goal or end-state, or the path or chreods to be followed, and of all the probable sources of disturbance that must be counteracted if the goal is to be achieved.

For Norman Horowitz, the gene provides such a model.

> It seems evident that the synthesis of an enzyme—a giant protein mol-ecule consisting of hundreds of amino acid units arranged end to end in a specific and unique order—requires a *model* or *set of instructions* of some kind. These instructions must be characteristic of the species; they must be automatically transmitted from generation to generation, and they must be constant yet capable of evolutionary change. The only known entity that could perform such a function is the gene. There are many reasons for believing that it transmits information by acting as a *model* or *template*.[1]

The relationship between the genome, which is more realistically seen as providing such a model, and set of instructions, and the proteins that it synthesizes must be functionally the same as that existing between *any* cybernism and the life process that it helps to mediate. In each case, information organized in a cybernismic medium is translated into behavior, in other words, instructions are translated into action. The model must thus be highly purposive—not objective or, in Oatley's words, "neutral in the sense in which an encyclopedia typically is."[2] On the contrary, the model is best seen as formulated in the language of the system's pattern of instructions. For instance, it is because a traditional society's fundamental instructions are of a moral nature that its cultural model is formulated in the language of morality.

Instructions and potential instructions are organized in accordance with the stage in the process at which they will be required; in accordance too, with the probability of their being required, and hence of the occurrence of conditions to which the behavior they mediate is adaptive. The model thereby provides a picture of those aspects of the system's relationship with its field or environment relevant to the implementation of the instructions required to enable it to achieve its goal in the face of the predictable obstacles. This is the very essence of cybernetic or self-regulating behavior.

In a military campaign, the commander issues his orders, organized hierarchically, as all orders must be. The most general order will be to defeat the enemy; the less general orders specify how, in the changing conditions of the battlefield, this goal is best to be achieved. The instructions will be constantly revised in the light of the data gathered by intelligence officers on the deployment of friendly and enemy troops. Of course, they will not just be piled up somewhere, for adaptive behavior cannot be mediated on the basis of data, or even a databank. For behavioral purposes, the data must be organized to constitute a model, only then can they be taken to constitute information.

Specialized staff officers do this, methodically moving little symbols representing friendly and enemy formations across a map that usually covers one wall of the room, tent or caravan, that serves as the general's headquarters. It is only by consulting this "dynamic map" that the general knows what instructions, at any given point in the campaign, will make victory more probable. Any other approach would simply be "muddling through," very much as our politicians do today. But theirs is not the way of nature. The behavior of the ecosphere and its component sub-systems we know to be coordinated and committed to a long term strategy of survival. We can thus postulate that all behavior, including the evolutionary process itself, must be controlled with the aid of a dynamic model analogous to that used by the general.

It is a comparatively recent idea that humans and other animals possess in their minds a dynamic model of their relationship with their environment. H. Head, the neurologist, was possibly the first to suggest that information was organized in the brain to form representations or "schemata." This idea was taken up by Karl Lashley, who found it useful as a means of understanding the behavior he observed in his own animal experiments. In 1932, F.C.Bartlett published his classic *Remembering*.[3] He showed that remembering could only be understood if it be realized that "the past operates as an organized mass rather than as a group of elements each of which retains its specific character," and that "remembering is not the re-excitation of innumerable fixed, lifeless traces, it is *an imaginative reconstruction*."

Thus, if a group of people are told a story and are, at a later date, asked to repeat it, each will do so very differently, for each will reconstruct it in the light of his personal mental model or world-view. What remains of the original story is a person's general attitude to it, which reflects all the attitudes and prejudices, if we like to call them that, that underlie its own particular world-view. His principal preoccupation thereby is not to recall the events with the greatest possible precision, but to reconstruct the story in accordance with his world-view.

At about this time, C. Judson Herrick also noted that in order to explain the subtleties of behavior, one must postulate the existence of stable arrangements of information in the brain which he referred to as "neurograms."[4] The first really explicit statement of the thesis, however, was Kenneth Craik's.[5] He contended that the brain, in order to fulfill its function, *must provide a model of the physical world*. Only an organism equipped "with a small scale model of externality and of its own possible actions within its head" can try out various alternatives, determine which is the most adaptive, and react to future situations before they occur—thus making use of the knowledge of past events to deal with the present and future and to adapt successfully to its environment.

Polanyi also found it necessary to explain learning in this way.

> A rat which has learned to run a maze, will show a high degree of ingenuity in choosing the shortest alternative path when one of the paths has been closed to it. This behavior of the rat is such as would be accounted for by it *having acquired a mental map of the maze*, which it can use for its guidance when faced with different situations within the maze.[6]

In this way, a rat does not have to rely on induction and hence on random trial and error to find its way out of the maze, any more than does a man.

The rat, in fact, can best be regarded as being endowed with a mind. This mind must be seen to be the seat of its instincts, emotions, values and sociability, which provide it with the appropriate guidelines of an adaptive homeotelic behavior pattern. It also provides the rat with a closely associated cybernismic model of its relationship with its environment. Each move the rat makes, what is more, will be that which seems most likely to prove successful in the light of its mental model that is constantly brought up to date with the experience of each successive move. What is true of the rat must be true of all self-regulating natural systems, whether they be organisms, vernacular societies, ecosystems or the ecosphere itself.

11

Ecology is qualitative

~

That which cannot be measured and reduced to numbers is not real.
Galileo Galilei

What is exact about mathematics except its own exactitude?
Johann Wolfgang von Goethe

The further away economics strays from reality, the better it can be sold
as "scientifically precise."
Jude Wanniski

It is perfectly meaningless to measure something with higher and higher
degrees of precision, if the thing you measure is more or less
meaningless.
Ralph Gerard

as long as we have lips and voices
which are to kiss and sing with
who cares if some one-eyed son of a bitch
invents an instrument to measure Spring with?
e.e. cummings

THE BASIC KNOWLEDGE of vernacular man was contained in his myths and was formulated in the language of abstract concepts, such as "fate," "justice," and "law," and in the language of gods and spirits —concepts that had a clear meaning to him in terms of his world-view. It was a language of the people, a human language. Plato also sought to understand the world in terms of abstract ideas or "universals," while abstract concepts such as "origins," "essences," "qualities" and "goals" continued to be in vogue during the medieval period.

Quantification came with the search for objective and precise knowledge. Galileo Galilei laid down that only that which was quantifiable was real, which meant that the non-quantifiable was outside the field of science. The new philosophy of nature developed by Descartes and Galileo anticipated the Newtonian idea that nature could be understood in terms of physical atoms moving through space and time. To isolate the characteristics of matter in motion, that could be measured and related by mathematical laws, was to understand the workings of nature. As Descartes himself said, "Give me extension and motion and I will construct the universe."

Quantifiable concepts such as space, time, weight, velocity, acceleration, inertia, force and momentum were the subject matter of Galileo's new science, replacing the more subjective knowledge that could not so easily be quantified. The seventeenth century saw the development of further quantifiable abstractions such as "the force of gravity," "space-pervading ether," "mass" and also "power" and "energy." The two great eighteenth century works on mechanics, Lagrange's *Traité de Mécanique Analytique* and Laplace's *Mécanique Celeste*, purported to prove that nature is governed by precise and all embracing mathematical laws—they served to enshrine the quantitative method.

Since then science has not looked back. As Morris Kline writes, "The history of modern science is the history of the gradual elimination of gods and demons and the reduction of vague notions about light, sound force, chemical processes and other concepts to number and quantitative relationships."[1] This process has been a great success in the field of physics, where the concepts used have been relatively simple and hence easy to quantify, especially when employed in isolation from the more complex systems studied by biologists and sociologists. As C.P.A. Pantin notes, physics has been able to become exact and mature "just because so much of the whole of natural phenomena is excluded from this study,"[2] and the more complex the natural system studied *the more must be excluded*. But surely, as Weiss argues, "There is no reason to downgrade nature to meet the physicist's inadequacy,[3] which, of course, is precisely what science has done and continues to do.

If scientific method is unsuitable for the study of complex systems so are the concepts that science uses. Few have even been defined. As the theoretical biologist J.H. Woodger notes,

> Nothing in biology is more striking than the contrast between the brilliant skill, ingenuity and care bestowed upon observation and experiment, and the almost complete neglect or caution in regard to the definition and use of the concepts in terms of which its results are expressed.[4]

This is also a problem in psychiatry. The Nobel Prize-winning novelist Isaac Bashevis Singer notes how accurately the textbooks have "defined" the idiot, the cretin, the imbecile, the epileptic, the hysteric, the hypochondriac and the neurasthenic,

> but as he observes, instead of admitting that little was known about what went on in the human brain, either healthy or sick, the professors stacked up Latin words. What do the impressive Latin words actually refer to? A vague set of symptoms at best. As the cynic puts it, "the psychotic builds a castle in the air; the neurotic lives in it; and the psychiatrist collects the rent."[5]

Similarly, the most basic terms used by ecologists have never been properly defined. Thus G.H. Orians distinguishes between nine types of *stability* and David Merrell notes twenty-one different ways in which scientists use the term *competition*.[6] In the philosophy of science, the terms used are equally vague. Margaret Masterman once accused Thomas Kuhn of using the term *paradigm* in twenty-two different ways.[7] The term *diversity* is used at once to denote the number of species in an ecosystem and at the same time, their "equitability" or their relative sizes. These are basically two different concepts that could only be represented by a single quantity if they were known to be precise functions of each other, so that a change in the value of one would automatically lead to a predictable change in the value of the other. This is not so: in fact, the relationship between the two concepts has yet to be determined with any sort of accuracy. Other terms used in ecology are also very difficult to quantify. Biomass is an example. Ramon Margalef points out that a tree "includes much dead tissue" to which the term biomass cannot strictly apply.[8]

The preoccupation with quantification has led scientists to develop concepts and indeed whole theories partly at least because they could be quantified regardless of whether or not anything in the real world corresponded to them. Many of the concepts of neo-Darwinism fall into this category, natural selection being a case in point. It should realistically be seen as acting on the phenotype—the living animal. As Waddington notes, if a horse is to survive in the natural world, it must run fast enough to escape from predators and "it is irrelevant whether it can run fast because it has been trained by a good horse-trainer, or because it has a nice lot of genes."[9] However, natural selection acting on the phenotype is extremely difficult to quantify, for which reason selection has been seen very misleadingly by neo-Darwinists as acting on the genotype—a process very much easier to model.

"Complexity" (see chapter 52) is also defined in terms that makes it easily quantifiable. A complex system is simply seen as one made up of many interrelated parts *without reference to the way they are organized*, for organization is very difficult to quantify. Such complexity, however, corresponds to nothing in the real world.

If modern ecologists are so preoccupied with energy flux it is also largely because this concept is particularly easy to quantify. Putman and Wratten, who see ecology as "a quantitative exact science, with certain underlying principles and laws, as fundamental as the laws of pure physics" assure us that it is via energy that an ecological science can be developed. They also insist that it is by studying organisms in terms of their energy flux that it is possible to see them "in context" and "to define their actual function."[10]

Modern ecologists have been at pains to define ecosystems in such a way as to rationalize this thesis. Thus O'Neill states explicitly that the ecosystem is fundamentally an energy processing system. Putman and Wratten also see a biological system—individual, population or community—as a system for the transfer, storage and dissipation of energy, a thesis with which McIntosh seems to concur.

But this is but a gratuitous dogma. Why should energy be the currency of nature? Why not resources, or information, or organization? Why should we not seek to understand nature in terms of a model that makes use of all these and many other relevant variables?

Quantifiable or not, the idea that the basic role of living things is to process energy cannot really be very much more simplistic and naive. It is of course reconcilable with the paradigm of science, that sees living things as no more than machines, but it bears no possible relationship with reality.

Polanyi has shown how mental knowledge undergoes simplification as it is translated into language, for all that which cannot be articulated must be left out. As it is further translated into mathematics still more information is left out—all that which cannot be quantified—which is often that which is most relevant to the understanding of any given issue.

Scientists are unlikely to entertain the possibility that a proposition about the behavior of complex systems couched in the language of mathematics can provide *less* rather than *more* accurate information. Robert Mann of Auckland University, however, accepts that it can. He distinguishes between precision and accuracy. By formulating a proposition quantitatively, he argues, one undoubtedly makes it more precise but only at the cost of reducing its ability to represent the real world.[11] Precision, in fact, is only achieved at the cost of accuracy.

12

Only qualitative vernacular models can provide the informational basis for adaptive behavior

~

Anything can be proved with a model if the right assumptions
are specified.
Cheryl Payer

It is only in quantitative ecosystem ecology that the rich details of natural
history become reduced to "brute" transfers of conservative substances,
because the real details have so far proved too diverse, complex and
generally difficult to represent and quantify. Every ecologist who has
ever made an energy or material flow model of an ecosystem, is painfully
aware of its deficiencies in terms of relevant information omitted . . . A
model reduces the intricate beauty and awesome complexity of a piece of
living nature to what is by comparison a flat, pallid image of the reality . . .
An ecosystem model, no matter how sophisticated or difficult to produce,
is but a shadow of its prototype.
B. C. Patten and Eugene Odum

Knowledge is seen by mainstream science as organized into man-made structures, such as logic or mathematics, from which propositions can then be deduced. The philosopher of science W.M. Elsasser considers, in fact, that if science were sufficiently advanced, all scientific propositions could be deduced in this way. However, it is increasingly considered by mainstream scientists that to understand the structure and function of a complex system such as a society or an ecosystem requires modeling it mathematically. This involves first determining what are the relevant variables to take into account (systems analysis) and then determining just how they are interrelated (modeling). A change occurring in the real world can then be simulated by modifying the value of the appropriate variables and interrelationships—the effect that this will have on all the other variables and interrelationships providing an indication of how the change is likely to affect the real world. Simulation can be seen as a very much more sophisticated form of deduction. It is particularly attractive because living things seem to proceed in a very similar way when they seek to understand events in the real world. Unfortunately, however, this methodology is fraught with problems.

To begin with, there is no established methodology for choosing the variables and interrelationships. They are chosen first of all because they are modelable—which means above all that they can be quantified and unfortunately many of the most relevant variables and interrelationships of a mental model of a complex system are non-quantifiable.

What is more, there is no valid methodology for choosing which of those quantifiable and hence modelable variables and interrelationships should be taken into account. This is left to the initiative of the modelers, and inevitably the choice will faithfully reflect the world-view with which they have been imbued. In view of the very high cost of building mathematical models of complex systems, which can often run into hundreds of thousands if not millions of dollars, the chances are that it is the world-view of modernism—that which is most fanatically entertained by governments, multinational corporations and international agencies—that the choice of the variables and interrelationships will reflect.

The same problem occurs in the choice of the basic assumptions underlying a mathematical model, which the modelers are expected to state explicitly. Such assumptions are not those that must underlie the model if it is to represent the real world with the greatest accuracy, but those that are required for purely technical model-building reasons. Thus, among the assumptions underlying a model built by the ecologist A.J. Nicholson to mimic the stable relationship between predators and their prey are firstly that the predator and the prey have synchronized generations, which means that they are of the same length and start at the same time. Needless to say, this simply does not occur in the real world.[1]

Further assumptions in Nicholson's model are equally unrealistic. The generations are assumed to be discrete, with no overlap between them. The predator searches randomly, contrary to the known behavior of predators which is dynamic, intelligent and consistent with a specific interpretation of the situation in which they find themselves. The predator never becomes satiated, and goes on eating members of the prey species indefinitely, which again we know not to be the case. Finally, the robot-like predator has a "constant searching efficiency" which means that it is unaffected by the food it eats, the mood it is in, or the time it has spent seeking out his prey, which is also very unrealistic.

In short to build a mathematical model at all, its architect must simplify his creation until it bears very little relationship to the real world it is supposed to be modeling. This does not seem to concern our modelers unduly, their principal preoccupation being to assure that their model is a self-contained and logically consistent construct. At this they are very skillful.

Consider the mathematical model provided by Putman and Wratten of the process of ecological succession towards a climax (see chapter 50).[2] For them succession, rather than being a goal-directed ecological strategy that ends once its goal (the climax or most stable state) is achieved—a scientifically unacceptable thesis that makes nonsense of progress—is simply an example of a statistical process known as a "regular Markov chain," in which "characteristic probabilities depend only on a current state and not any previous state," and which, as it develops, eventually settles into a pattern "in which various states occur more or less with characteristic frequency that are independent of initial states."

It is argued that this final "stationary distribution" of states is the analogue of the climax community and that climaxes must occur by the statistical certainty that the Markov process always settles into a stable pattern. What is more, if a community is temporarily disturbed, something like the original community returns. This too is a function of Markovian processes. Finally, Markovian development, like succession, is characterized by rapid changes followed by undetectably slow changes. This means that stability, in the naive sense of "absence of change," increases "tautologically" as succession proceeds. What is important is that "none of these characteristics," Putman and Wratten insist, are "necessarily of biological origin."[3] In other words, it is not in terms of the behavior of biological systems, let alone of natural systems in general, that we must seek to explain succession, but in terms of a mathematical formula fed into a computer. Researchers, we are told, have shown the "close fit" between Markovian processes and succession. The most "sophisticated" of such researchers, we are told, is F.S. Horn who insists that the general properties of succession are direct statistical consequences of a species-by-species replacement process, and have no uniquely biological basis.

The whole argument is an example of a fallacy we can best refer to as "mathematical realism." Children often think that because a word exists there must be something in the real world to correspond to it, a notion known as "nominal realism." Jean Piaget cites, among many examples, a child who says that "pigs are rightly named because they are so dirty," and "the sun is rightly named because it is so hot."[4]

Oxford linguistic philosophers are similarly guilty of what might be called "linguistic realism" when they assume that there must be some intrinsic and universal wisdom in the structure of the English language which casts light on the workings of the ecosphere when in reality what is offered is a very crude representation suitable only for normal conversational purposes.

Putman and Wratten, like Horn and other modern ecologists, are in fact committing the same error. They suppose that because someone has developed a mathematical model that simulates in a rudimentary manner some aspects of the real world, then it must be capable of simulating accurately all aspects of the real world. It is, of course, astonishing that a mathematical model of a Markov chain can imitate, however crudely, any aspect at all of such real-world processes as succession to a climax. That one must thereby be able to derive from it other ecologically acceptable information about succession is absurd, just as absurd as to suppose that because a puppet can be made to resemble a policeman, an examination of the cotton wool with which it is stuffed will enable you to understand the policeman's digestive system or the circulation of his blood. What they are proposing is in fact little more than a modern form of divination—but because the diviners are scientists, performing their rituals on scientifically consecrated premises, they enjoy credibility among the naive and the gullible (see chapter 51 and appendices 2 and 3).

Simulation on a mathematical model is no substitute for the interpretation of real-world situations in the light of a qualitative model provided by a vernacular world-view of a person's relationship with his or her environment. It can, of course, be argued that such a model is not "scientific" in that it does not conform to "objective" reality. However, the role of knowledge is not to depict reality in the manner of an encyclopedia, but to help mediate adaptive homeotelic behavior.

Roy Rappaport sees vernacular knowledge as organized to constitute "cognized models," which he sees as providing vernacular populations with a distinctive means of maintaining themselves in their environment.[5] Rather than being objective or encyclopedic, such models are thus *purposive to the achievement of this goal*. Nor, as Rappaport writes, should they be simply judged in accordance with

> the extent to which they are identical with what the analyst takes to be reality, but the extent to which they direct behavior in ways that are *appropriate to the biological well-being of the actors and of the ecosystems in which they participate*. The criterion of adequacy for the cognized model is not its *accuracy* but its *adaptive effectiveness*.

The Colombian anthropologist Gerardo Reichel-Dolmatoff sees the mythology of a vernacular society as providing its members with a model of their relationship with the society and to its natural environment in the light of which they seek to interpret environmental changes and monitor their behavior pattern so as to assure that such changes are reduced to a minimum and their society's stability is maintained.[6] The vernacular model is naturally formulated in the language of the society's mythology, and the interrelationships that are seen to exist between the gods and spirits who control society and the natural world are carefully established and explained in mythological terms (see chapter 22). Thus among the Canelos Quichua Indians of Ecuador, as N.E. Whitten tells us,

> playing flutes, singing songs and telling myths punctuates discussion of Amasanga (who controls the weather, the thunder and lightning), Nungui (who controls the soil-base for the roots of garden-life and pottery clay), and Sanghui (who controls water). These activities are, among other things, mechanisms for associational or analogic linking of cosmological and ecosystem knowledge to social rules and breaches, and social dynamic to cosmological premises.[7]

Problems such as a shortage of game, soil erosion, a lack of clay for making pots, and bad weather, can all be interpreted in terms of the model and attributed to some maladjustment in the relationships between the various gods that control these resources, which in turn can be related to some failure on the part of society to fulfill its obligations towards them. The model is holistic rather than reductionist: the spirits are not the atomized components of the ecosphere but on the contrary reflect its truly hierarchical nature. In addition, the model, rather than being divided up into watertight disciplines between which interrelationships are almost impossible to establish is, on the contrary, totally non-disciplinary, which is necessary if it is to permit the mediation of an integrated behavior pattern as opposed to that mere patchwork of expedients that is the policy of a modern nation state.

The vernacular model, what is more, is usually formulated in a language which each member of the society can understand and which can guide the behavior of the society as a whole. This is in stark contrast with a mathematical model, formulated in an esoteric tongue, which only a handful of specialists can really understand and act upon.

What is more, the interrelationships on which it is based are constantly brought home to people in songs and other ritual activities, so that everyone is properly imbued with the world-view it reflects. Also, because it is couched in the moral and emotional language of the society's mythology, people are emotionally motivated both to entertain it and to adopt that behavior pattern that is consistent with it, and indeed feel morally bound to do so.

For all these reasons a cognized or vernacular model satisfies the basic cybernetic requirements of a social system in a way that the scientific mathematical model cannot. The vernacular model, in fact, is alone capable of providing the informational basis for homeotelic and hence homeostatic behavior at the social level.

13

Ecology is subjective

—

Te matauranga o te Pakeha
The knowledge of the white man
He mea whakato hei tinanatanga
is propagated
Mo wai ra?
For whose benefit?
Mo Hatana?
For Satan's?
Kia tupato i nga whakawai
Be wary of its temptations
Kia Kaha ra, kia kaha ra
Be strong and firm.
Te matauranga o te Pakeha
The knowledge of the white man
Patipati, a ka mura whenau
Engulfs you, then confiscates land.
Kia kaha ra, e hoa ma
Be strong, friends.

Ka mutu ano
Land is all we have
Te tanga manawa
To rest a beating heart
Oranga, a oranga
And for our livelihood
Te matanranga o te Pakeha
The knowledge of the white man
Ka tuari i te penihana oranga
Gives out social security benefits.
Hei aha ra?
Why?
Hei patu tikanga
To kill customs
Patu mahara
To kill memory
Mauri e
To kill our sacred powers.

Tuini Ngawai of the Maori tribe of Ngati Porou

75

Scientific knowledge purports to be objective; that is seen to be its main virtue, distinguishing it from the sort of knowledge entertained by ordinary people. Objective knowledge is knowledge that is free of the personal beliefs, values and metaphysical ideas of its entertainer; hence it is knowledge that is neutral with regard to the achievement of any specific goal.

Actually, scientific knowledge is epistemologically no different from other forms of human knowledge. We like to think that the latter (whether scientific or not) is something very special, but it is simply a particular kind of information, and there is every reason to suppose that it is organized and made use of in the same way as other forms of information. It is thus significant that objective information plays no part in the strategy of the biosphere. The information used by natural systems at all levels of organization is not objective but subjective.

Thus the information contained in a fertilized egg is not objective; it consists of that which is required to permit the development of the embryo into a child. The information contained in the cultural "cognized" model of a vernacular society is not objective. As Roy Rappaport makes clear, its role is to ensure the adaptation of a particular society to the specific environment in which it lives; it is thus only in terms of its ability to achieve this goal that it can be judged.[1]

Though scientists will deny it, this is also how scientific models are really judged. Francis Bacon, "the father of modern science," was the first to insist that science be ruthlessly separated from values ("the idols of the understanding")—but he did nothing of the sort. His scientific knowledge, far from being "value free," set out explicitly and purposefully to give man power over nature. "Truth and utility are perfectly identical," he wrote in *Novum Organum*, and "that which is most useful in practice is most correct in theory."[2]

76

Instead of putting aside the old values of good and evil to create a value-free factual knowledge, Bacon simply replaced them with the values of "useful" and "useless." It was a critical time in the history of human affairs. The New World had just been discovered and the financial opportunities provided by plunder and the slave trade seemed limitless. It is not surprising, as Benjamin Farrington notes, that the Christian values of mercy and love should, in such circumstances, have been so easily forgotten, nor that the cynical values of Baconian science should have been so readily accepted.[3] After all, they were precisely those that best served to rationalize our efforts to exploit these new opportunities. "In Baconian ideology," Donald Worster writes, "the good shepherd of the Christian tradition had become a scientist and technocrat. Science offered the means for building a better sheepfold and creating greener pastures."[4]

All the models developed by human societies, including the world-view of modernism and the closely associated paradigm of science, are necessarily "cognized" and hence subjective. One reason is that man, like all other living things, is a *participant* in the life of the biosphere, whereas in the Western philosophical tradition he is regarded as a *spectator* and hence as an entertainer of "objective" knowledge. This has now been accepted, in theory at least, in modern physics. Werner Heisenberg showed that it is impossible to eliminate the influence of the observer and this led him to formulate his "principle of uncertainty." Unfortunately, this principle has yet to affect the way most physicists look at the world, let alone the practitioners of such disciplines as chemistry, biology, anthropology, sociology and ecology.

For vernacular man, on the other hand, there was what Ashis Nandy calls "a continuity between the observer and the observed."[5] For Toshihiko Izutsu,

> The highest degree of knowledge is always achieved when the knower, the human subject, becomes completely unified and identified with the object so much so that there remains no differentiation between the two. For differentiation or distinction means distance, and distance in cognitive relationships means ignorance.[6]

That knowledge, whether scientific or not, must be subjective also follows from the fact that the faculties with which our evolution

77

has equipped us for perceiving our relationship with our specific environment are purely subjective; for contrary to the assumptions of our empiricist philosophers, they are simply not designed to provide us with an objective representation of the world. This principle is worth looking at in some detail.

Observation or perception, which is supposed to be the source of all our knowledge, begins with the detection of data. This process is *active* rather than *passive*—data being detected, rather as a mine is detected by a mine detector, not just *received*—and it is *highly selective*. Instead of accumulating available data in a random fashion, as empiricists assume we do, we isolate those which appear relevant to our behavior pattern (a minute percentage of the total) from those which do not. As Herrick notes:

> The skin is sensitive to mechanical vibrations up to 1,552 per second, but beyond that point feels only a steady push. The ear is aware of sound traveling by wavelengths of thirteen mm up to 12,280 mm, but does not hear sounds below or above these limits. The skin is aware of heat-waves only from .0008 mm to .0004 mm, but misses electric waves, ultra-violet waves, X-rays, gamma rays and cosmic rays, running from wavelengths of .0004 mm to .000,000,000,008 mm.[7]

We have no biological means of apprehending sense data outside these ranges, presumably because during the course of our evolution they have not proved of any relevance to the achievement of our behavioral goal.

This genetically determined selection is complemented by a culturally determined one. At any given moment, we detect only a minute proportion of the data we are biologically equipped to detect—those that our upbringing and experience within a particular culture have taught us to regard as relevant to our behavior, and hence on the basis of our mental model (see chapter 10) whose generalities reflect the experience of the species and whose particularities are largely those of the individual within his cultural group. It is in the light of this model that the relevance of different data to his behavior pattern is determined.

What is more, what we detect with our sensing apparatus is not what we *see*. We do not detect the actual constituents of our environment, such as dogs, trees and rocks, but only patterns of light and shade. These are then interpreted by us in the light of our mental model. A perception is thus a *hypothesis* based on a particular paradigm. Only in this way can we explain how we can differentiate between movements in our environment and shifts of the image on the retina due to the movement of our own eyes, how we are capable of perceiving "phantom colors" such as white and purple, which constitute gaps in the spectrum in terms of our detecting faculties, or how we can distinguish between extreme cold and extreme heat, both of which transmit identical messages to the brain. Only in this way can we understand why babies see everything the right way up, for if they were to depend on their detecting faculties, they would see everything upside down.

Only in this way, too, can we understand our extraordinary ability to handle fragmentary data. When we read a page of print we may not even notice printing mistakes such as missing letters or even missing words. We subconsciously fill in the gaps. This is possible, Oatley points out, "because we have a prior knowledge of what we are looking at." More precisely, we interpret the signals we detect in terms of the mental model we have built up of the subject matter.

Many experiments, including those carried out by Solomon Asch at Harvard, reveal that people can be induced by suggestion and the force of public opinion to *see* things very differently from the way they previously saw them.[8] Thomas Kuhn wrote that this is precisely what occurs in the scientific world after a "paradigm shift."[9] Thus Antoine Laurent Lavoisier, who discovered oxygen, "*saw* oxygen" where Joseph Priestley had *seen* dephlogisticated air and where others had *seen* nothing at all. In learning to see oxygen, however, Lavoisier also had to change his view of many other more familiar substances. He had, for example, to see a compound ore where Priestley and his contemporaries had seen elementary Earth, and there were other such changes besides. At the very least, as a result of discovering oxygen Lavoisier *saw* nature differently. One might even say that he "worked in a different world."

If observation is a purely subjective process, then so are the other means whereby we acquire knowledge, such as intuition and thought itself. Thus we judge the validity of a proposition or hypothesis by determining to what extent it fits in with our subjective model of our relationship with our environment.

The truth is that man is simply not designed by his evolution to entertain objective knowledge. As Karl Popper put it, "Knowledge in the objective sense is knowledge *without a knower*." Empiricist philosophers have totally failed to realize this. For this reason, Popper discards the epistemology of John Locke, George Berkeley, David Hume and even Bertrand Russell, for they all assume the possibility of objective knowledge in the conventional sense of the term.[10] He thereby dismisses the entire school of empiricist philosophy which they created, and which provides the basic epistemological foundations of modern science.

Polanyi[11] goes further than Popper. If knowledge is objective, he considers, then "we must accept the virgin mind, bearing the imprint of no authority, as the model of intellectual integrity." Only a new-born child possesses such a virgin mind and is thereby able to pass judgments on all questions "without any preconceived opinions." But such judgments would necessarily be of a rudimentary nature, as a child would not yet be intelligent enough to understand fully the issues it was called upon to judge. To do so, it would have to grow up, but for its mind to remain virgin and hence objective, the child "would have to be kept unshaped until then by any kind of education. It must be taught no language, for speech can be acquired only a-critically, and the practice of speech in one particular language carries with it the acceptance of the particular theory of the universe postulated by that language." An entirely untutored maturing of the mind, would however, result in a *state of imbecility*. For these reasons, Polanyi considers that objective knowledge is an illusion and that we should accept that knowledge, whether scientific or not, is necessarily subjective.

Popper on the other hand, still thinks that objective knowledge is possible—even though it may be, strictly speaking, "knowledge without a knower." Such scientific knowledge he sees as made up of logical constructs of different sorts: "conjectural theories," "arguments" and, presumably, mathematical models. It is precisely the role of science to build up such constructs. Popper postulates "three worlds." The first world is the real world, the second that of subjective knowledge of the real world, and the third that of objective knowledge of the real world which he sees as the product of humans, just as "honey is a product of bees or spiders' webs of spiders."[12]

It is true that such constructs have a measure of autonomy in that changes occurring in the real world can be translated into or "simulated" by changes in the structure of the construct in accordance with clear rules. If the construct is a particular language, for instance, simulation is achieved in accordance with the grammatical rules of the language in question. If it is symbolic logic, it is done in accordance with the rules of symbolic logic; if a mathematical model, in accordance with the rules of mathematics. Changes occurring within these constructs, it can be argued, are insulated from human subjectivity by virtue of the fact that they occur in accordance with the laws that govern them.

That is undoubtedly the case once the constructs have been brought into being, but we must not forget that the constructs are *man-made in the first place* and for that reason reflect human cultural patterns which are clearly highly subjective. Indeed, Benjamin Lee Whorf maintained that each language faithfully reflects the metaphysical system of the society that developed it,[13] a thesis much discussed and generally confirmed by semanticists and anthropologists over the last decades. That a mathematical model reflects the metaphysical system of the society that developed it, is perhaps even more evident. It is generally accepted that a mathematical model is no better than its basic assumptions. If these are wrong, then the answers obtained by simulating real-life changes on the model will also be wrong. As the critics of model building put it: "garbage in, garbage out."

The subjectivity of all the various disciplines into which we have divided modern knowledge is equally clear. Their function is above all to help rationalize, and hence legitimize, different aspects of the enterprise of economic development or progress to which our society is so resolutely committed. Thus Adam Smith's *Wealth of Nations* postulated that by behaving in the most egoistic way possible we maximize not only our own material interests but also those of society at large—a cheerful philosophy which rationalized the individualism and egoism that marked the breakdown of society during the industrial revolution. Darwinism was rightly described by Oswald Spengler as "the application of economics to biology,"[14] Darwin's "natural selection" being but a biological version of Smith's "invisible hand" and serving, above all, to legitimize the Promethean enterprise to which our modern society is committed by making it appear to be a natural process.

Scientific knowledge, as is pointed out throughout this book, serves to rationalize the paradigm of science and hence the world-view of modernism on the basis of which economic development or progress alone makes sense. There is no reason to suppose that ecological knowledge—in its different variants—is any more objective, less value-laden or less purposive. It is, or should be, designed purposefully to rationalize the world-view of ecology and the associated ecological society geared as it must be to maintaining the critical order of the cosmos.

14

Man is cognitively adjusted to the environment in which he is evolved

～

It is by Earth that we see Earth.
Empedocles

How exquisitely the individual Mind
(And the progressive powers perhaps no less
Of the whole species) to the external World
Is fitted:—and how exquisitely, too—
Theme this but little heard of among men—
The external World is fitted to the Mind;
And the creation (by no lower name
Can it be called) which they with blended might
Accomplish:—this is our high argument
William Wordsworth

What a curious idea it is, this fear that has haunted us since the age of Bacon, that knower and known cannot be trusted alone in one another's company but must be chaperoned by a sober and censorious methodology . . . lest they should have illegitimate intercourse and produce bastards of fantasy.
Theodore Roszak

THE PERFECTION of man's cognitive endowment for the purpose of assuring his adaptation to his biological and social environment is an essential principle of the ecological world-view. This principle was always clear to vernacular man and has been expressed in a wide variety of ways. Philosophers since the days of Parmenides have insisted that the mind can understand reality only because they both have the same structure or logos. It was also the first article of faith of Goethe's philosophy of nature that there is "a perfect correspondence between the inner nature of man and the structure of external reality, between the soul and the world."[1] Henry David Thoreau referred to it as "nature looking into nature."[2] Paul Tillich refers to what he regards as the rational structure of the mind as "subjective reason" and to the rational structure of reality as "objective reason."[3]

This principle is incompatible with the scientific assumption that subjective knowledge is necessarily imperfect and that only objective scientific knowledge displays sufficient accuracy to provide the basis of rational and hence adaptive behavior. Darwin would have agreed with this on interesting grounds.[4] Intuitively, he felt that the natural world could not really have been brought into being by random changes. However, he did not feel that he could trust "the convictions of man's mind" for it "has been developed from the mind of lower animals," and he asks, "would anyone trust in the convictions of a monkey's mind if there are any convictions in such a mind?" This is also the view of the neo-Darwinists and sociobiologists. Thus R.L. Trivers, a noted sociobiologist, regards as "very naive" the view that "natural selection favors nervous systems which produce ever more accurate images of the world." On the contrary, he tells us, it is very much more probable that "our genes are deceiving us and filling us full of the glow of having achieved absolute truth."[5] Edward O. Wilson sees things in much the same way. His attack on "intuitionism" is based on the notion that we cannot depend on our judgments precisely because they are the product of evolution and thereby totally undependable.

It is also true that, in terms of the neo-Darwinian theory of evolution, an individual need not be capable of correctly apprehending his environment in order to survive, for behavior is not taken to be part of the evolutionary process (see appendix 4). What is more, living things are not seen as correctly apprehending or understanding their relationship with their environment (see chapter 31), but as reacting to it blindly like Pavlov's dogs. Behavior, like evolution, is thus regarded as a passive process stage-managed by an anonymous environment.

It is encouraging, however, that a number of our more thoughtful scientists have, by implication at least, rejected such assumptions, realizing that the living brain, after millions of years of being shaped by the environment, is suited to it with an accuracy that is both remarkable and profound. Waddington points to a "congruity between our apparatus for acquiring knowledge and the nature of the things known" and suggests that the human mind "has been shaped precisely to fit the character of those things with which it has to make contact."[6] Konrad Lorenz goes still further. He notes that the way we experience the outside world, and indeed, the "a priori" forms of intuition, are "organic functions based on physical and even mechanical structures of our senses and of the nervous system" and these "have been adapted by millions of years of evolution."[7] Jean Piaget goes so far as to say that our cognitive functions are an extension of organic regulations and must be seen as differentiated organs for regulating our relationship with the external world, which must therefore clearly serve the ends of human life.[8]

15

Ecology is emotional

A physiologist is not an ordinary man: he is a scientist, possessed and absorbed by the scientific idea that he pursues. He does not hear the cries of animals, he does not see their flowing blood, he sees nothing but an organism that conceals from him the problem he is seeking to solve.
Claude Bernard

Reason is the slave of the passions and should be.
David Hume

Reason flows from the blending of rational thought and feeling. If the two functions are torn apart, thinking deteriorates into schizoid intellectual activity and feeling deteriorates into neurotic life-damaging passions.
Erich Fromm

People need more than to understand their obligation to one another and to earth; they also need the feeling of such obligation.
Wendell Berry

Nineteenth-century naturalists were unashamedly emotional in their descriptions of nature. This is particularly true of von Humboldt, who described the tropical forests of Brazil with emotion and with awe. Darwin, who particularly admired Humboldt, wrote of the Brazilian forests in the same vein, in a letter to John Henslow:

> Here I first saw a tropical forest in all its sublime grandeur . . . Nothing but the reality can give any idea how wonderful, how magnificent it is . . . I formerly admired Humboldt, I now almost adore him; he alone gives any notion of the feelings . . . on first entering the tropics.[1]

This is very different from the detached, impersonal, "objective" approach of today's scientists, for whom, as Worster notes, a tropical forest is but

> a resource to be mapped and dissected, and whose constituents are classified and cataloged increasingly for the benefits of some organization that is only interested in their utilitarian potential.[2]

Modern science has banned the emotions. This is the inevitable consequence of decreeing that scientific knowledge must be objective—a vain decree since man, by his very nature, is incapable of entertaining objective knowledge, just as he is incapable of effectively suppressing his emotions. Polanyi[3] speaks of "the overwhelming elation felt by scientists" at the moment of making a scientific discovery, "an elation of a kind which only a scientist can feel and which science alone can evoke in him." He cites as an example Kepler's elation at discovering his Third Law: "Nothing holds me," he wrote, "I will indulge my sacred fury."

The same degree of passion is displayed by scientists in their diatribes against those who attack their beliefs, and threaten their "cognitive structure" (see chapter 18). Against these critics veritable witch-hunts have been mounted comparable to those the medieval church launched against the proponents of new heresies. Take the witch-hunt against Rachel Carson, who dared suggest that synthetic organic pesticides, whose development in the 1940s was seen as one of the great scientific achievements of that period, actually did more harm than good and should be phased out. Rachel Carson's message was undoubtedly a very subversive one. "The 'control of nature' is a phrase conceived in arrogance," she wrote,

> born of the Neanderthal age of biology and philosophy, when it was supposed that nature exists for the convenience of man. The concepts and practices of applied entomology for the most part date from that Stone Age of science. It is our alarming misfortune that so primitive a science has armed itself with the most modern and terrible weapons, and that in turning them against the insects it has also turned them against the Earth.[4]

This was clearly more than mainstream scientists could take: the reaction was quick and venomous. Dr. William B. Bean wrote in *Archives of Internal Medicine* that *Silent Spring*, from the scientific point of view, is "so much hogwash."[5] The reaction to *The Limits to Growth* (1972) (the first report to the Club of Rome, written by Donella and Dennis Meadows and others)[6] was equally emotional. It was lambasted by the editors of both *Nature* and *Science*, the two principal scientific journals in the English-speaking world, and by Lord Zuckerman, then chief scientist to the British Government, who referred to it as "arbitrary speculation" and "unscientific nonsense."[7]

The reaction of the scientific world to Immanuel Velikowsky's heretical book *Ages of Chaos* (1952) was even more hysterical, as is well documented by Harold Brown.[8] Among other things, there was a concerted effort to force the publisher to take the book out of print. Scientists wrote numerous infuriated letters to the publishers, and actually boycotted their salesmen and text books. The attack was so powerful that the publishers simply had to give in, even though it was one of their most profitable books. This does not seem to be the way that truly objective scientists would react to the publication of a dissenting book. It was the reaction of highly emotional, indeed almost hysterical people who felt that the dissenter threatened to undermine scientific doctrines to which they were professionally and psychologically committed.

The truth is that man (whether a scientist or not) is simply not designed to behave in a non-emotional way, which is one of the reasons why he is incapable of entertaining objective knowledge and behaving "rationally." Those imbued with the paradigm of science see this insuppressible human emotionality as a terrible human failing. Some go so far as to attribute it to a defect in our neuro-psychological evolution which has prevented our neo-cortex—the seat of our intelligence—from dominating our primitive reptilian brain—the seat of our emotions.

Koestler considers that this terrible evolutionary blunder can only be remedied by systematically subjecting man to some form of chemotherapy.[9] But the suppression of man's emotions would mean the eclipse of his closely associated values, his religiosity, his spirituality, his ability to sing and dance, laugh and weep, love and hate, *everything in fact, that makes him human*—all in the interests of making him more rational and machine-like, and hence better adapted to the aberrant and necessarily short-lived surrogate world that science has helped bring into being.

Up to a certain point, man can "isolate" himself, to use Sigmund Freud's expression, from his emotions—splitting "cognition from affect."[10] Freud saw this as an "ego defense" or, in Nandy's words, "a psychological mechanism to help the human mind cope with unacceptable or ego-alien inner impulses, and external threats."[11] It involves distancing himself emotionally from a situation or an act that to a normal emotional human would otherwise be intolerable, "distancing," as Bruno Bettelheim notes,[12] being in the words of Nandy a "psychological device, which both the victim and his oppressor have to use." It is precisely by reducing a victim to an object that one can face treating him in an inhuman way, which is why Aimé Césaire equates colonialism with "thingification."[13]

Scientists involved in designing instruments of mass destruction such as nuclear bombs must also be capable of distancing themselves emotionally. Robert Jungk describes his encounter with a mathematician he met on his last visit to Los Alamos.

> His face was wreathed in a smile of almost angelic beauty. He looked as if his gaze was fixed upon the world of harmonies. But in fact, he told me later, he was thinking about a mathematical problem

whose solution was essential to the construction of a new type of H-bomb.[14]

Jungk adds that this scientist never bothered to watch the trial explosion of any of the bombs he had helped produce. To him, "research for nuclear weapons was just pure mathematics untrammelled by blood, poison or destruction."

But is Jungk's mathematician as unemotional as he seems? Undoubtedly not. Scientific education does not suppress the emotions; it merely displaces the object of the emotions. Instead of teaching people to feel emotional about their family, their community, their traditional culture, their religion and the beauty of their natural environment, they are taught instead to feel emotional about the scientific enterprise and the surrogate world it brings into being. Nor is the emotional attachment of the scientist to his work irrelevant to its achievement. Polanyi notes that "scientific passions are no mere psychological by-product"; instead they have a logical function that contributes an indispensable element to science: "passions charge objects with emotions, making them repulsive or attractive; positive passions affirm something as precious."[15] It follows that "the excitement of the scientists making the discovery is an intellectual passion, telling that something is intellectually precious, and more particularly, that it is precious to science." In the same way, it can be argued that the witch-hunts mounted by the scientific community against those who threaten the credibility of the scientific enterprise are also "precious to science."

The ecology we need is not the ecology that involves viewing the ecosphere on which we depend for our survival at a distance and with scientific detachment. We will not save our planet by means of a conscious, rational and unemotional decision, a sort of ecological contract based on a cost-benefit analysis. A moral and emotional commitment is required. Indeed, one of the key tasks of ecology must be to redirect our emotions so that they may fulfill the role they were designed for: to commit us to what should be the overriding human enterprise of maintaining the critical order of the ecosphere.

16

Ecology is a faith

———

Unless ye believe ye shall not understand.
St Augustine

Science is a new religion, and disinfectant is its holy water.
G. Bernard Shaw

Science has remained predominantly an anti-rationalistic movement,
based upon a naive faith.
A. N. Whitehead

We must recognize belief once more as the source of all knowledge.
Michael Polanyi

VERNACULAR MAN BELIEVED unquestioningly in the sacred principles underlying the cultural pattern with which he was imbued. Since they had been first formulated by his ancestors, who lived at the beginning of time, they had to be true. Who was he to doubt the ancestral wisdom which these principles so clearly embodied?

For St Augustine, knowledge was a gift of grace for which we must strive under the guide of antecedent belief. He dominated Christian thought for nearly a thousand years—until the end of the seventeenth century. Then came the development of "objective science" which was and still is seen as free of all contamination from subjective and "irrational" human emotions, values and beliefs.

John Locke, in particular, distinguished between faith and knowledge, persuasion and certainty. It was particularly important to root out faith or belief, for it was associated with religion and superstition. As Polanyi writes, "all belief was reduced to the status of subjectivity, to that of an imperfection by which knowledge fell short of universality." Without belief, however, there can be no knowledge. "For all truth," as Polanyi notes, "is but the external pole of belief, and to destroy all belief would be to deny all truth."[1]

This is the overall theme of his seminal book *Personal Knowledge*. Into every act of knowing, he writes, "there enters a tacit and passionate contribution of the person knowing what is being known," and this rather than being imperfect is "a necessary component of all knowledge."[2] For him the idea that reason and intelligence alone are the source of our understanding is sheer illusion.

> Tacit assent and intellectual passions, the sharing of an idiom and of a cultural heritage, affiliation to the like-minded community; such are the impulses which shape our vision of the nature of things on which we rely for our mastery of things. No intelligence, however critical or original, can operate outside such a fiduciary framework.[3]

That this must be so follows from the fact that the human neo-cortex, which is possibly the seat of our intellectual activities, has not been designed by its evolution to function by itself as an autonomous instrument of control any more than has the gene. The lower parts of the brain which may be regarded as the seat of our values and emotions have an equally and indeed possibly greater role to play in determining adaptive human behavior.

Our leading philosophers of science and our more thoughtful scientists fully realize that science too is a faith in that scientists accept uncritically the basic assumptions that underlie it. Karl Popper considers that "scientific discovery is impossible without faith in ideas which are of a purely speculative kind," and which is "completely unwarranted from the point of view of science."[4] Whitehead considers that "faith in the order of nature which has made possible the growth of science is a particular example of a deeper faith," which "cannot be justified by any inductive generalization."[5] Waddington agrees that a scientist's work is influenced by his metaphysical beliefs—a point also made by von Bertalanffy, Paul Feyerabend and others. To say this is no more than to say that the nature of a scientist's work reflects the paradigm in terms of which he seeks to understand it and indeed the wider paradigm of science which has shaped his whole professional life.

Science, in many respects, is just another religion. Kuhn actually describes the scientific community as a sort of priesthood. John Passmore compares "aristo-scientists" with medieval theologians.[6] In many ways they are the priests of our industrial society. It is they who provide the information on the basis of which the industrial process is mediated and without which it could not occur. It is they who have formulated the world-view that provides its rationale, and like other priesthoods, they have couched their holy texts in an esoteric language of their own which no outsider can understand. What is more they have defined truth in such a way that they alone have access to it, for it must be established by a set of scientific rituals which only they can perform, for only they possess the necessary scientific skills, only they are equipped with the requisite scientific technology, and only they have access to the holy places where, in order to be effective, these rituals must be performed.

It is not surprising that their writings are imbued with an aura of sanctity previously reserved for the holy texts of the established religions. Indeed, if a proposition is classified as "scientific," then it must be true, indeed incontestable; if on the other hand it is branded as "unscientific" then it must be the work of a charlatan. This has provided the scientific-priesthood with the power to prevent any undesired deviation from scientific orthodoxy, just as the Catholic establishment of the Middle Ages could excommunicate any heretic whose teachings were a challenge to its authority. Science thereby has not banished faith. It has substituted faith in modern science for faith in conventional religion.

Ecology, with which we must replace it, is also a faith. It is a faith in the wisdom of those forces that created the natural world and the cosmos of which it is part; it is a faith in the latter's ability to provide us with extraordinary benefits—those required to satisfy our most fundamental needs. It is a faith in our capacity to develop cultural patterns that can enable us to maintain its integrity and stability.

17

Ecology reflects the values of the biosphere

———

Nature is the first ethical teacher of man.
Peter Kropotkin

For primitive man, the universe as a whole is a moral or social order,
governed not by what we call natural law, but rather by what we might
call moral or ritual law.
A.R.Radcliffe Brown

A thing is right when it tends to preserve the integrity, stability and beauty
of the biotic community. It is wrong when it tends otherwise.
Aldo Leopold

For vernacular man, the laws of nature were essentially moral laws. In Ancient Greece, the natural world was seen to be governed by abstract cosmic forces, in particular, *Moira* (fate) and *Dike* (justice, law and morality). These concepts are not really distinguishable. As F.M.Cornford notes, "The ordinance of fate is not a mere blind and senseless barrier of impossibility: *it is a moral decree*—a boundary of right and wrong."[1]

Hesiod states clearly, that for him, the course of nature is governed by a moral law. "When men do justice" he said, "and do not go aside from the straight path of right, their city flourishes and they are free from war and famine. For them the Earth brings forth food in plenty, and on the hill, the oak tree bears acorns at the top and bees in the middle; their sheep have heavy fleeces, their wives bear children that are like their parents."[2]

On the other hand, if man does not do justice, if he diverts from "the straight path of right," and hence violates the moral laws of the cosmos, then taking the form of Nemesis, the cosmos will strike back. Thus when Oedipus committed incest, even if his crime was an unconscious one, both he and the whole land of Thebes were made to pay the penalty for violating the cosmic laws.

That the order of nature was a moral order, Cornford considers was for the ancient Greeks an "obvious, unchallengable truth," and, indeed, "the most important truth about the world,"[3] and this could probably be said of all vernacular people even today. What is more, their idea of what constitutes morality is likely to be exactly the same as it was for the ancient Greeks.

The moral philosophers of today, on the other hand, do not see morality as in any way connected with our behavior towards society, nature, or the cosmos. Instead morality is seen as a unique and isolated phenomenon. Thus Anthony Flew writes of G.E.Moore, probably the most influential moral philosopher of this century, that his "argument proceeds as if it were in suspense outside space and time, and, incidentally, in complete isolation from the progress of the natural and human sciences."[4] He could have said much the same for the arguments of most of the other moral philosophers of recent times (see Appendix 3).

The importance of ethics is today also seriously played down. Thus T.L.S. Sprigge tells us that "our moral life is not the most important aspect of our life" and that "we should conform to morality but seek our satisfaction elsewhere."[5] The so-called "emotivist" school of moral philosophy goes even further, regarding moral statements as "non-factual": neither true nor false, but merely reflecting someone's non-rational emotions. This is clearly the view that best fits the paradigm of science.

The ethical attitudes of leading modern biologists and sociologists cast considerable light on the metaphysical assumptions and the world-view underlying their scientific beliefs. The social Darwinists such as Herbert Spencer in the UK and William Graham Sumner in the USA, saw nature as random, chaotic, atomized, competitive and aggressive. They felt that it was natural, desirable and indeed moral, that man should behave in the same way. Another school of thought on morality is represented by T.H. Huxley, Gaylord Simpson and Jacques Monod as well as Edward O. Wilson, Richard Dawkins and the other sociobiologists. They agree that nature is "red in tooth and claw" but they consider that it is man's duty, on the contrary, to declare war against nature. As Huxley puts it "the ethical progress of society depends not on imitating the cosmic process, still less in running away from it, but in *combating it.*"[6]

The third school can be represented by Waddington and Julian Huxley. They too saw nature as "red in tooth and claw." However, they rejected T.H. Huxley's view that man's behavior is equally unpleasant, and also that we should wage war against nature. They felt that nature was evolving and as it did so, would become more co-operative. It was thus by observing the laws of evolution that man could be moral.

In spite of their obvious differences, the scientists of all three schools have much in common—above all, their view of morality faithfully reflects the fundamental principles underlying the paradigm of science.

Thus, they all agree that morality begins with modern man and that one cannot talk of primitive man, or of other forms of life, as being "moral." This was the view of both T.H. Huxley and Julian Huxley after him. Waddington felt that it is only when we pass on from the sub-human world to deal with the evolution of man that ethics must, in its own right, enter the picture. In a similar vein, Simpson tells us that "there is no ethics but human ethics and a search that ignores the necessity that ethics be human, relative to man, is bound to fail."[7]

Morality is also associated by such scientists with the acquisition of knowledge and hence with the development of science. Monod and Simpson actually preached an "ethic of knowledge." The former saw this as being the only possible ethic for modern man and regards him as differing from "animistic" or primitive man, who, by contrast believed also in teleology, which is irreconcilable with objective or "authentic" knowledge.[8] Julian Huxley considers that knowledge is good, its acquisition being essential for assuring the march of progress; it must follow that "social morality" includes "the duty of providing an immense extension of research, and its integrated planning to provide the basis for desirable change."[9] Scientific knowledge is also regarded as alone making democracy possible. Joseph Needham goes so far as to say that "Democracy might . . . be termed that practice of which science is the theory," while "the subjective and the irrational are anti-democratic; they are the instruments of tyranny."[10]

Ethics is also seen as depending on consciousness, purpose, knowledge and all the other supposedly unique endowments of modern man, for it is only by means of them that there can be reason and choice, and thus morality. Monod tells us that the ethic of knowledge differs from all other previous ethics in that it has been adopted by an act of *objective* choice.[11] Simpson insists that choice is morally good.[12] "Blind faith" on the other hand "is morally wrong." It must follow that as knowledge builds up, our rational choices will change or rather "evolve." This means that our ethics must be flexible rather than absolute or universal. Change, Simpson insists, is "the essence" of evolution and for that reason alone, "there can be no absolute standard of ethics." Waddington also considers that an evolutionary ethic "cannot be expected to be absolute but must be subject to evolution itself"; in particular it must "be the result of responsible and rational choice in the full light of such knowledge of man and of life as we have."[13] This was also essentially the view of Julian Huxley.

The ethic of modernism is also an *individualistic* ethic. Simpson argues that even if we wished to derive an ethic from nature, it would still be individualistic, for evolution tends towards individualization as opposed to higher integration, as ecologists once maintained. Man must be aware of "the goodness of the maintenance of this individualization" and promote "the integrity and dignity of the individual." For sociobiologists, only an individualistic ethic is even conceivable, for man's overriding goal is the proliferation of his genes. The notion that in the natural world, this goal may be subordinated to the needs of the community, the species, or the natural world *itself*, is considered "unscientific," and those who suggest it, as does V.C. Wynne-Edwards, are mercilessly derided. The occasional occurrence of such "altruistic behavior" is acknowledged but is explained away as but serving to provide, in specific circumstances, the best means of satisfying the individual's overriding goal of maximum gene-proliferation.

There is a terrifying logic to this argument. For "conscious" and "rational" modern man, supposedly bereft of a subconscious, of emotions, of faith, who is allowed no attachments save of a rational and contractual nature and who is deprived of any identity in an anonymous megasociety committed to perpetual growth, there *can* be no alternative to the individualistic ethic.

It is logically justified in another way. The ethic of modernism is the product of the conscious choice of the individual who is seen to be external to the Gaian hierarchy and free of the laws that govern its behavior. Based on "objective" and hence "scientific" knowledge, this ethic can be sanctioned or authenticated by no authority *but that of the individual himself*, endowed as he supposedly is with unique intellectual and moral gifts, and armed with the unique potentialities of scientific knowledge. Not surprisingly, Simpson tells us that "man can cherish values if he wishes to," but they are *his own, self-imposed values*.[14] No absolute ethics can be found "outside of man's own nature." Monod is of the same mind. "The ethic of knowledge," he writes, "would not be imposed on man. It is he on the contrary who would impose it on himself."[15] For the evolutionists (among them Julian Huxley and Waddington) modern man also authenticates his own moral choices—although they are further authenticated by being *natural* and because they reflect the fundamental direction of the evolutionary process.

Above all, the ethic of modernism is *the ethic of progress*. As Julian Huxley writes, "Social organization should be planned not to prevent change, nor merely to permit it, *but to encourage it*."[16] This is also logical, for if all benefits are derived from the technosphere and are thereby the product of economic development or progress which brings that organization into being (see chapter 34), then ethical behavior must clearly be that which most favors that fatal process and best serves to preserve the order of the technosphere which it must improve and expand.

Fortunately, others—mainly non-scientists—have in recent times, returned to a more realistic view of morality. The Romantic poets, for instance, reacted against the ethic of modernism as did the early ecologists. For Aldo Leopold, "that land is a community is the basic concept of ecology, but that land is to be loved and respected is an extension of ethics." "We abuse land," he wrote, "because we regard it as a commodity belonging to us," but "when we see land as a community to which we belong we may begin to use it with love and respect."[17] This is Leopold's famous "land ethic"—it remains today the basic principle of ecological ethics.

In the 1940s, Gerard and the other members of the Chicago school of ecology saw nature as providing moral inspiration. The nature they saw was essentially co-operative, rather than "red in tooth and claw." "If nature is found to be a world of interdependence," Gerard wrote, "then man is obliged to consider that characteristic a moral dictum."[18] The evolutionary trend towards closer integration was, he argued, "like a straight path through a dense wood, requiring of the pathfinder that he remain on the track and follow it through." The only problem is that Gerard's path seems to lead to an overintegrated ecosphere—one that does not respect its critical order. He does not realize—and the same can be said for all those who believe integration or co-operation to be a good thing in itself—that the degree of integration that characterizes a biological organism is incomparably higher than that which characterizes a family, which in turn is greater than that required at the level of a community, still more so than at the level of society at large, and still more so than at that of an ecosystem or indeed of the ecosphere itself.

It follows that the only path or "Way" that is truly moral must be that which leads to the maintenance of the degree of integration required at the level of the different natural systems that make up the Gaian hierarchy. Only if this condition is respected can they fulfill their essential homeotelic functions towards it, and only in this way can its critical order be maintained.

18

A proposition can only be verified
in terms of the paradigm or model
of which it is part

⌒

A new scientific truth does not triumph by convincing its opponents and making them see the light, but rather because its opponents eventually die, and a new generation grows up that is familiar with it.
Max Planck

Scientific knowledge in any era is what the scientist actively takes as such, and the scientific knowledge of one era may be rejected as error in the next.
Harold Brown

The test of proof or disproof is in fact irrelevant for the acceptance or rejection of fundamental beliefs, and to claim that you strictly refrain from believing anything that should be disproved is merely to cloak your own will to hide your beliefs behind a false pretense of self-critical severity.
Michael Polanyi

IF MAINSTREAM SCIENTISTS assure us that a thesis, however likely it may seem, has not been verified empirically, it will be branded as unscientific and unworthy of being taken seriously. The consecrated formula is that there is "no scientific evidence" that it is true, the evidence being exclusively provided by empirical verification in "controlled laboratory conditions" and hence in isolation from the world of living things. If complementary evidence is admitted—epidemiological evidence in the field of health, for instance—this too must be empirical. Empirical verification can also be complemented by theoretical arguments, but these are considered of secondary importance.

Logical positivism is the epistemological doctrine that justifies this position. Its main tenet is that the criterion for the acceptability of a proposition—distinguishing a scientific from a metaphysical proposition, or sense from nonsense—is empirical verification. Verification is based on induction and is invalid on that count alone. The reason is that neither an observation, nor an experiment, nor even a series of observations and experiments can establish a thesis or general principle. At best these procedures can only show that the observation or experiment is *compatible* with that thesis. But of course, most propositions can be shown to be compatible with a large number of different theses, many of which are likely to be irreconcilable with each other. The philosopher of science Jerry Ravetz shows that one could "verify" in this way "the hypothesis that the moon is made of mouldy cheese. One need only deduce that it would then have spots, and then establish that the predicted spots do exist."[1]

The philosopher Harold Brown regards the fact that "universal propositions cannot be conclusively verified by any finite set of observation statements" to be the "central difficulty" of logical positivism.[2] To be consistent, logical positivists would have to regard universal propositions as but meaningless metaphysics, but this they clearly cannot do without losing all credibility. They have got round the problem by insisting that they are not propositions at all but merely "rules which allow us to draw inferences from observation statements to other observation statements." This is playing with words in the worst tradition of medieval casuistry.

On the other hand, more sensible logical positivists have given up the strict verificationist position. While they require that a meaningful proposition must at least be testable by observation and experiment, they accept that the results need not be conclusive. Rudolf Carnap, one of the fathers of logical positivism, proposed replacing the principle of verification with that of "gradually increasing confirmation."[3] This marked the establishment of a new school of epistemology called "logical empiricism."

Another problem with empirical verification is that it is based on observation. As we have seen, to observe something means forming a hypothesis about it in the light of one's world-view, while the act of observation which serves to verify the hypothesis is itself the product of this paradigm or world-view, and hence no more objective than the proposition it serves to verify.

Thus Popper noticed as far back as 1919 how currently accepted theories such as Marx's theory of history, Freud's psychoanalysis and Adler's individual psychology seemed to explain almost everything within the fields to which they were applied; so much so that those who studied them underwent what could be described as an "intellectual conversion or revelation." "Once your eyes were thus opened," Popper writes, "you saw confirming instances everywhere: the world was full of *verifications* of the theory. Whatever happened always confirmed it."[4] Koestler, who in his youth in Hungary was a member of the Communist Party, later admitted that this is precisely what used to happen to him. "My party education," he wrote, "had equipped my mind with such elaborate shock-absorbing buffers and elastic defenses that everything seen and heard became automatically transformed to fit a preconceived pattern."[5]

Popper regards such behavior as "uncritical." Scientists do not behave that way. Science is distinguished from metaphysics by its application of the "critical approach," which means that scientific theories must be formulated in such a way that they can be refuted by empirical means. Newton's theory, for example, predicted deviations from Kepler's laws (due to the interactions of the planets) which had not been observed at the time. It exposed itself thereby to attempted empirical refutations whose failure invalidated the success of the theory. Einstein's theory was tested in a similar way. "Only if a theory successfully withstands the pressure of these attempted refutations," Popper asserts, "can we claim that it is confirmed or corroborated by experience."[6] Scientists, in formulating a theory, are thereby "taking a risk," which astrologers, Marxist historians, psychoanalysts and individual psychologists do not take. In other words, "the criterion of the scientific status of a theory is its falsifiability or refutability, or testability."

This thesis has in turn been much criticized on a number of obvious counts. To begin with, falsifiability still depends on observation, and is thereby still subject to all the limitations applying to the empirical method. As Medawar notes,

> We could be mistaken in thinking that our observations falsified a hypothesis; the observations may themselves have been faulty, or may have been made against a background of misconception; or our experiments may have been ill-designed. The act of falsification is not immune to human error.[7]

Popper himself admits this. Falsifiability, what is more, is also based on induction, and as we have seen, one cannot argue from observations or experiments to theories, nor can one disprove theories in this way.

Waddington considers that the falsifiability principle applies only to very simple events such as those studied by physicists. The reason is that all sorts of devices can be resorted to in order to maintain the validity of a hypothesis concerning the behavior of complex natural systems. Imre Lakatos sought to replace the principle of "naive falsification" by "sophisticated falsification," which involved confronting the scientific theory with an alternative one. "There is no falsification," he wrote, "but the emergence of a better theory," though this is still not enough; what is required is a "series of theories . . . usually connected by a remarkable continuity which welds them into a 'research program'."[8] This, Lakatos admits, is roughly what Kuhn refers to as normal science.[9] However a program takes a long time to develop, and it must not be killed off prematurely by pointing to a single inconsistency. For this reason, "one must treat budding programs leniently," for it is unfair to falsify theories until they are fully developed. Falsifiable theories must therefore be tolerated at least in their early stages.

For Kuhn, this is not sufficient. He rejects Popper's view that science is still concerned, as was Greek science, with fundamental issues. This is simply not true of modern science in which the accent shifts from the discussion of fundamentals to that of what he calls "problem solving." Those involved in this latter activity share the same paradigm whose validity is taken for granted and hence does not require testing. Kuhn actually goes so far as to say that "it is precisely the abandonment of critical discourse that marks the transition to a science," after which "the critical discourse recurs only at moments of crisis when scientists must choose between competing theories," and it is only then that they behave like Greek scientists or philosophers.[10]

Of course in normal conditions, testing still occurs, but it is not the fundamental issues (current theory), that are tested but only the details or technicalities of the theory, the experimenter's skill at "problem solving," while the paradigm itself is never tested *and could be guaranteed to emerge unscathed even if it were.* As John Watkins notes

> If the outcome of such a "test" is negative, it does not fit the theory but backfires on the experimenter. His prestige may be lowered by the failure of his attempt to solve a puzzle; but the prestige of the paradigm within whose framework he makes the attempt is so high that it will scarcely be affected by such little local difficulties.[11]

Not surprisingly, Kuhn considers that it is only very superficial propositions that are falsified, except when the paradigm of which it is part, is in crisis, and is due to be replaced with a new paradigm.

The trouble is that when there is a confrontation between two paradigms, the victor is not necessarily that which would be chosen on the basis of any sort of empirical verification or falsification. For there is no rational discourse between the proponents of different paradigms. They speak different languages, see things in a fundamentally different way, and therefore cannot really communicate. Moreover, as Polanyi observes, scientific controversies never lie altogether within science,[12] which is perhaps an understatement. Indeed such controversies are likely to be highly emotive indeed quasi-religious affairs. In general, one can say that people, whether they be primitive tribesmen, businessmen, bureaucrats or professional scientists, will do everything they can to preserve their paradigm in the face of knowledge that appears to undermine it. This is referred to by the anthropologist A.F.C. Wallace as "the principle of the preservation of cognitive structure."

Polanyi describes three strategies currently in use for preserving a cognitive structure when confronted with experiences which would appear to invalidate it. The first is to defend the principle that seems to be invalidated with reference to another principle; this is possible because of the circularity of world-views or paradigms. Edward Evans-Pritchard notes how this is done by the Azande tribe of Uganda when faced with such experiences.[13] For them "the contradiction between experience and one's mystical notion is explained by references to other mystical notions." Polanyi points out that belief in the usefulness of mathematics as a means of understanding the world is based on the same self-reinforcing circularity, since

> every assertion of a deductive system can be demonstrated by, or else shown to be, implied as axioms of the others. Therefore, if we doubt each assertion in its turn, each is found confirmed by circularity and the refutation of each consecutive doubt results in strengthening the belief in the system as a whole.[14]

Another technique mentioned by Polanyi for maintaining the stability of beliefs in the face of conflicting evidence is to "expand the circle in which an interpretive system operates."[15] In this way, an "elaboration of the system" can be readily supplied to cover "almost any conceivable eventuality." This device he calls "the building up of ancillary hypotheses." Scientific theories which "possess this self-expanding capacity," he writes, are "epicyclical"—an allusion to the epicycles which were used in the Ptolemaic and Copernican theories to represent the uniform and circular movement of planets. According to Polanyi, all major interpretive frameworks have an epicyclical structure "which supplies a reserve of subsidiary explanations for difficult situations."[16] Polanyi cites Evans-Pritchard's description of the epicyclical character of Azande beliefs.[17] The Azande believe in the powers of the poison oracle. The oracle answers questions through the effects on a fowl of a poisonous substance called *benge*. The oracle poison is extracted from a creeper gathered in a traditional manner, which is supposed to become effective only after it has been addressed in the words of an appropriate ritual. Suppose that the oracle, in answer to the same question, says "yes" and immediately afterwards, "no." For us, this would discredit the oracle, but Azande culture provides ready-made explanations for such contradictions. Evans-Pritchard lists no fewer than eight ready-made explanations which can account for the oracle's failure.[18] They may insist that the wrong type of poison had been used, or a breach of taboo committed, or that the spiritual owners of the forest where the poisonous creeper grows had been insulted and avenged themselves by making the poison ineffectual.

Scientists, Polanyi points out, behave in just the same way. They are no more likely than an Azande medicine man to accept evidence that could invalidate any aspect of their beliefs. This could not be better illustrated than by Lakatos's story of the imaginary pre-Einsteinian physicist.

On the basis of Newtonian mechanics, of Newton's law of gravitation (N) and of the accepted initial conditions (I), the physicist calculates the trajectory of a newly discovered small planet, (p). Unfortunately, however, the planet does not follow the expected trajectory. How does the physicist react to this? Does he accept that Newtonian mechanics are wrong? That the law of gravity (N) does not apply? Undoubtedly not. He suggests that there must be a hitherto unknown planet, (p'), which perturbs the path of p. He calculates the mass, orbit, etc., of this hypothetical planet and then asks an experimental astronomer to test his hypothesis. The planet p' is so small that even the biggest available telescopes cannot possibly observe it: the experimental astronomer applies for a research grant to build yet a bigger one. In three years' time, the new telescope is ready. Were the unknown planet p' to be discovered, it would be hailed as a new victory of Newtonian science. But it is not. Does our scientist abandon Newton's theory and his idea of the perturbing planet? No. He suggests that a cloud of cosmic dust hides the planet from us. He calculates the location and properties of this cloud and asks for a research grant to send up a satellite to test his calculations. Were the satellite's instruments (possibly new ones, based on a little-tested theory) to record the existence of the conjectural cloud, the result would be hailed as an outstanding victory for Newtonian science but the cloud is not found. Does our scientist abandon Newton's theory, together with the idea of the perturbing planet and the idea of a cloud which hides it? No. He suggests that there is some magnetic field in that region of the universe which disturbed the instruments of the satellite. A new satellite is sent up. Were the magnetic field to be found, Newtonians would celebrate a sensational victory. But it is not. Is this regarded as a refutation of Newtonian science? No. Either yet another ingenious auxiliary hypothesis is proposed or . . . the whole story is buried in the dusty volumes of periodicals and the story never mentioned again.[19]

The third technique proposed by Polanyi to maintain the stability of a hypothesis in the face of evidence that refutes it, is to "deny to any rival conception the ground in which it might take root."[20]

Polanyi refers to this third technique or "defense mechanism" as the principle of "suppressed nucleation." He regards it as complementary to the operations of circularity and self-expansion.

While these protect an existing system of beliefs against doubts arising from any adverse piece of evidence, suppressed nucleation prevents the *germination of any alternative concepts* on the basis of any such evidence.

Again, this is not only done by members of vernacular societies but by mainstream scientists, who will purposefully ignore and if necessary suppress any information, however well-documented, that appears incompatible with the paradigm of science.

In this way, scientists today are both ignoring and suppressing today the ecological knowledge that makes nonsense of their methodology, of many of the practices of the Promethean enterprise to which they are committed, and of the paradigm of science itself.

For Polanyi, to preserve the stability of one's world-view, paradigm or cognitive structure is entirely human. To suppose that it can be avoided by developing a more objective science is no more than a pious hope, based on no knowledge of any kind. It is also an error to suppose that this is a human *failing*. It is not. It is, in fact, *highly adaptive, indeed essential in order to maintain the continuity or stability of a human social system*. Indeed, all organizations of information in the natural world are and must be capable of maintaining their stability in the face of environmental challenges.

The problem of course, as Polanyi does not fail to point out, is that the devices used for stabilizing a true view of the universe, may equally stabilize an erroneous one. That, of course, is in the nature of things. The faculties that make possible homeotelic life processes (see chapter 41) can be misdirected to promote heterotelic ones instead (see chapter 42). But the possibility of such errors is systematically reduced as we move from a "disclimax" or neo-pioneer society (see end of chapter 64) in which people's ideas will be largely random and individualistic, to a climax society in which people will be imbued with a world-view consistent with that behavior that best assures the preservation of the critical order of the cosmos.

19

The ecosphere is one

—

The most fundamental of my intellectual beliefs is that the idea that the world is a unity is rubbish. I think the universe is all spots and jumps, without unity and without continuity, without coherence or orderliness or any of the other properties that governesses love.
Bertrand Russell

For primitive man, the supreme wisdom consists in recognizing the unity and order of the living world, a term we must take as including the world of the spirits.
Placide Tempels

The entire range of living matter on Earth, from whales to viruses, and from oaks to algae, could be regarded as constituting a single living entity capable of manipulating the Earth's atmosphere to suit its overall needs and endowed with faculties and powers far beyond those of its constituent parts.
James Lovelock

TRADITIONAL MAN knew that the world is one, that it is alive, hierarchically organized and that all the myriad living things that inhabit it are closely interrelated, and co-operate in maintaining its integrity and stability. Among the ancient Greeks, as Hughes writes, "the Pythagoreans held that the world is spherical, animate, ensouled and intelligent."[1] Plato saw it as "a living creature, one and indivisible, containing within itself all living creatures that are by nature akin to itself."[2] What is more, this living creature is "endowed with soul and reason." The Stoics, Hughes tells us, also saw the cosmos as a sentient being, that is rational, harmonious, and of which all living things are part.[3] It is also self-sufficient since it nourishes and is nourished from itself.

This view of the world was largely that of Linnaeus and his follow-ers in the seventeenth century, and that of the Natural Theologians of the eighteenth century, such as John Ray, William Paley and Thomas Morgan.[4] The latter wrote of the "perfect unity, order, wisdom and design" of the natural world, "by which every individual is necessarily related to and made a dependent part of the whole." For him, the living world could only be the work of a "universal designing mind" which "contrived, adjusted and disposed the whole into such order, uniformity, concordant beauty and harmony and which continues to support govern and direct the whole." Aldo Leopold also saw the Earth as one: "We must realize the indivisibility of the Earth," he wrote, "—its soil, mountains, rivers, forests, climate, plants and animals, and respect it collectively, not as a useful servant but as a living being."

More recently, advances in cytology and molecular biology have led scientists, whose interest had previously been monopolized by the extraordinary diversity of living things, to realize that underlying it all is a basic unity that is very difficult to explain in terms of the paradigm of science in terms of which knowledge is so strictly compartmentalized. Thus the geneticist Theodosius Dobzhansky notes that underlying the great diversity of living things there are profound similarities.[5] The genetic information in all living things can be read in the language of DNA and RNA, and the protein building blocks of all living things are made of the same twenty amino-acids. Both François Jacob and Jacques Monod also note how similar are all living things at the microscopic level. And if the materials are the same throughout the living world, so is the pattern of construction. Thus the French biologist Armand de Ricqles is struck by the fact that all vertebrates, fish, amphibians, reptiles, birds and mammals are built according to the same organizational plan in spite of important anatomical differences. "What," he asks, "does this unity of design imply? This is a big question which comparative anatomy began to ask in the eighteenth century and has not ceased to ask."[6]

It implies of course, that as evolution proceeds, so do superficial changes occur to adapt different forms of life to specialized environments and yet the basic features of life remain the same—an evolutionary achievement that it is very difficult to reconcile with currently accepted evolutionary theory. It implies too that the overriding goal of living things is to preserve the critical order and hence the stability of the Gaian hierarchy of which they are part. It also suggests that Gaia is a single self-regulating natural system and at once a life-process and the unit of evolution (see chapters 20 and 21).

The Scottish geologist and natural philosopher James Hutton, writing in 1788, was possibly the first scientist in the modern world to recognize the unity of nature. The idea was put forward once again by the Austrian scientist Edouard Suess in 1875. He saw the Earth as "a Living World that is a system of living animals and plants" and coined the term "biosphere" to apply to this entity together with its geological substrata.[7] The modern idea of the biosphere, however, is usually attributed to the Russian scientist Vladimir Vernadsky. He saw it as a "living organism" and quite rightly claimed that this had the widest possible implications for all the other disciplines in terms of which modern man seeks to understand the natural world and its functioning.

The notion that the world of living things, together with its geological substrate and atmospheric environment, also constitute an entity (that I refer to in this book as "the ecosphere" or Gaia) can probably be traced to Jean-Baptiste Lamarck. He saw the development of living organisms as an integral part of a wider subject (the physics of the Earth) that included the study of the atmosphere (meteorology) and of the Earth's crust (hydrogeology).[8] None of these disciplines could be understood without reference to the others, pointing to the need for a truly holistic science of the natural world. Suess also saw the biosphere in this way and described plants reaching deep into the soil to feed and, at the same time rising into the atmosphere above to breathe—thus accentuating the close interaction between the lithosphere and the atmosphere.[9] Vernadsky's biosphere included "the whole atmospheric troposphere, the oceans and thin layer in the continental regions expanding down about three kilometers or more."[10] His position contrasted with that of Frederic Clements and Victor Shelford. Though they were among the fathers of holistic ecology, they nevertheless insisted that the community and its environment should not be regarded as forming part of the same ecological entity.

Critical to the development of the modern theory of the biosphere was the realization that the atmosphere was the creation of living things rather than the product of purely physical and chemical forces. This was first suggested by Alfred Redfield and later, in 1841, by the French scientists Jean Baptiste Dumas and Jean Baptiste Boussingault. In the early 1970s the idea was taken up by James Lovelock who described the process involved in great detail. "The atmosphere of dead planets, like Mars and Venus," he notes, "is in chemical equilibrium." On the other hand,

> the chemical composition of the atmosphere (of our planet) bears no relation to the expectations of steady-state chemical equilibrium. The presence of methane, nitrous oxide, and even nitrogen in our present oxidizing atmosphere represents a violation of the rules of chemistry to be measured in tens of orders of magnitude.[11]

What is still more extraordinary is that many of the gases that compose the atmosphere are unstable in each other's presence. Yet chemically they should not coexist, which suggests that they have to be continuously emitted on a very large scale if they are to persist in the atmosphere. As Lovelock puts it,

> we have an abundance of oxygen, twenty-one percent of the atmosphere, and a trace of methane, at 1.5 per million. We know from

chemistry that methane and oxygen will react when illuminated by sunlight, and we also know the rate of this reaction. From this, we can confidently conclude that the coexistence of the two reactive gases, methane and oxygen, at a steady level requires a flux of methane of 1000 megatons a year. This is the amount needed to replace the losses by oxidation. Furthermore, there must also be a flux of oxygen of 4000 megatons a year, for this much is used up on oxidizing the methane. There are no reactions known to chemistry that could make these vast quantities of methane and oxygen starting from the available raw materials, water and carbon, and using solar energy.[12]

For Lovelock there is only one answer:

There must be some process at the Earth's surface which can assemble the sequence of unstable and reactive intermediaries in the programmed manner to achieve this end. Most probably this process is life.[13]

As Lynn Margulis and Dorion Sagan also point out,[14] if our planet were a dead one, like Venus or Mars, the atmosphere would be composed of more than 95 percent carbon dioxide, yet it contains no more than 0.3 percent—that which is required to support life. Why? The explanation is photosynthesis—that essential activity of plant and algal life that is at the same time responsible for maintaining the requisite level of oxygen in the atmosphere. Thus living things, in taking up carbon dioxide and emitting oxygen, are creating precisely that combination of the two gases in the atmosphere that is required for maintaining life on our planet. They are also creating conditions most favorable to life when generating methane and other atmospheric gases or taking up or otherwise neutralizing gases in the atmosphere that are surplus to the requirements of life. For Lovelock this suggests "that the atmosphere is not merely a biological product, but more probably a biological construction; not living but like a cat's fur, a bird's feathers, or the paper of a wasp's nest, an extension of a living system designed to maintain a chosen environment."[15]

It is essential to Lovelock's thesis that living things could not create precisely the atmospheric environment they require nor maintain its homeostasis in the face of environmental change if they were not organized to constitute a single entity—the biosphere (a term he applies exclusively to the organization of living things on our planet exclusive of its abiotic constituents). This global living entity, in conjunction with its geological substrate and the atmospheric environment it has created, constitutes a bigger natural system that Lovelock refers to as Gaia, after the Greek goddess of the Earth, and that I also refer to in this book as the ecosphere. The relationship of the ecosphere to the biosphere is thus similar to that of the ecosystem to the ecological association or community. Lovelock defines Gaia as

> a complex entity involving the Earth's biosphere, atmosphere, oceans and soil; the total constituting a feedback or cybernetic system which seeks an optimal physical and chemical environment for life on this planet.[16]

In particular, he stresses that Gaia is thereby capable of maintaining its stability or homeostasis in the face of change, which can alone explain how global climate has remained remarkably stable over the last few hundred million years, even though the heat from the sun during this period has increased by about thirty percent.

No credible rebuttal of Lovelock's thesis has been published by the mainstream scientific community, nor is one likely to be. Many of its far-reaching implications are considered in this book.

20

Gaia is a spatio-temporal entity

~

Every existing object, whether at rest or in motion, is a strand of history
with some duration.
C.D. Broad

An object separated from its history is clearly not the kind of thing that
could possibly exist.
C.D. Broad

We are beginning to grasp that societies, like the individuals which
compose them, and like life in general, have a time dimension. They
are processes, and their direction in time is as important a part of their
nature as their organization at any particular time.
Julian Huxley

What are called structures are slow processes of long duration, functions
are quick processes of short duration.
Ludwig von Bertalanffy

GAIA, AND INDEED ALL NATURAL SYSTEMS, exist in time as well as in space. There can be no atemporal system any more than there can be a non-spatial process. As J. H. Woodger puts it:

> A frog without a life history is as impossible as a life history without a frog. A frog in pickle is a cross-section of its history as a living organism, and anatomy is biology with the time dimension omitted. Anatomy studies the organism in "timeless space."[1]

The languages of some vernacular societies, including a number of Indian tribes of the American Northwest, accentuate the temporal aspect of the world around them, as Benjamin Lee Whorf showed so convincingly.[2] Others, including those of European societies, tend to accentuate, on the contrary, their spatial aspect. The members of many North American Indian tribes, as Mircea Eliade tells us, saw the cosmos as "a living being that is born, grows and dies on the last day of the year, to be reborn with the new year." Thus instead of saying "a year has passed," the Yokuts say "the world has passed."[3] If the sacred houses of the Algonquins and the Sioux are designed to provide a representation of the cosmos, they provide at the same time a representation of the year. What is more, if the cosmos were seen as dying at the end of each year, then it was man's duty to assure that it was annually reborn. Indeed, many of the ceremonies of vernacular people were re-enactments of the original act of creation ("cosmogenesis") designed to assure the continuity of the cosmos. Vernacular man thus understood that the behavior of successive generations of men and other living things is critical to the maintenance of cosmic continuity and hence to prevent a reversion to the original chaos.

Mainstream science, on the contrary, sees no connection between the behavior of living things, their development (morphogenesis), their physiology and the fate of the ecosphere—whose very existence as a self-regulating natural system most mainstream scientists still deny.

They do not even see any connection between the behavior of man and other living things and the evolutionary process that is seen as occurring independently of adaptive changes undergone by them (see appendix 4). All these processes are seen as distinct, largely unrelated and governed by a different set of laws.

Fortunately, a few more enlightened scientists see things differently. Thus Woodger sees all adaptive changes as "different eras in the same process." In his classical studies of infant behavior, the psychologist Arnold Gesell notes that the early instinctive reactions of a child are no more than a continuation of the embryological activities that brought it into being. "The action systems of embryo, foetus, infant and child," he writes, "undergo pattern changes which are so sequential that we may be certain that the patterning process is governed by mechanisms of form regulation—the same mechanisms that are being established by the science of embryology . . . The growth of tissues, or organs, and of behavior is obedient to identical laws of development morphology . . ."[4] Henri Bergson also points to the continuity between embryogenesis and behavior. "How," he asks, "can one draw the line between the constructive processes of the bird's embryonic development and the constructive process by which it builds its nest?"[5] Charles Lumsden and Edward O. Wilson point to the same continuity, asserting that there is no fundamental break in the process between tissue formation and behavior.

If morphogenesis and behavior are part of the same process, physiology and behavior must be similarly linked. Edmund Sinnott notes that breathing, for instance, is a physiological process but also "a part of the way an animal behaves" and that "these two processes are part of a single strategy."[6] It follows that morphogenesis and physiology are also part of the same process. Indeed, "in any living system," Sinnott writes, "changes involved in growth are essentially the same as those concerned with the maintenance of vital activities and the repair of tissues."[7]

It is thus realistic to regard these processes, taken together, as constituting the wider process normally referred to as ontogeny. In turn, it is realistic to regard ontogenies as constituting key units of the evolutionary process itself. That this must be so should be clear from the following consideration: when we say that evolutionary change has occurred, we mean that ontogenetic processes at a particular moment in time are no longer the same as they were in the past, which means that they have been subjected to morphogenetic, physiological and behavioral changes. This being so, it seems very unrealistic to study these changes outside their evolutionary context, just as it is absurd to study evolutionary change, as does mainstream science, separately from the changes undergone by the constituent life processes in terms of which it manifests itself.

21

Gaia, seen as a total spatio-temporal process, is the unit of evolution

———

The family (in China) from its first ancestors to its latest generations was a unit.
Ralph Linton

To Freud the unconscious is chiefly a receptacle for things repressed. He looks at it from the corner of the nursery. To me it is a vast historical storehouse.
Carl Jung

It is doubtful whether life can be significantly lived without conscious relation to some tradition. Those who do live without it live as a kind of moral proletariat, without roots and without loyalties.
Dorothy Emmett

In terms of the neo-Darwinian thesis the individual organism is seen as the basic unit of evolution. But what is so special about the individual organism? Is there a fundamental difference between its adaptive strategies and those of other natural systems that it can be viewed as totally distinct from them? The answer is, unquestionably, no.

Life processes at all levels of organization including the evolutionary process itself are designed according to the same plan, being purposeful, dynamic, creative and intelligent. What is more, their adaptive strategies are all geared to maintaining the stability or homeostasis of the entire Gaian hierarchy—a *sine qua non* for the maintenance of their own homeostasis (see chapter 41). In addition, the larger systems control and coordinate the behavior of their constituent parts, Gaia herself co-ordinating the behavior of all the constituent members of the hierarchy and further assuring in this way that their behavior remains that which will assure its overall homeostasis, a process I refer to as homearchy (see chapter 44). For these reasons, the individual cannot conceivably be regarded as the unit of evolution. *It can only be Gaia herself, and we can best refer to evolution as the Gaian process.*

A process, however, is an abstraction unless it has a spatial aspect, just as any entity is an abstraction if seen atemporally. The temporal or spatial abstractions in terms of which we are accustomed to think about Gaia are in fact but different aspects of the same reality, the spatio-temporal system that is Gaia. It follows that there must be a *perfect correspondence* between the temporal Gaian abstraction and the spatial Gaian abstraction, just as there must be a perfect correspondence between our digestive process and our digestive system seen as a physical entity. The neo-Darwinian thesis involves, on the other hand, radically isolating the structure of the ecosphere, viewed spatially, from that of the ecosphere seen as a process—the former being seen in all its complexity and sophistication, the latter being reduced to the crude interplay between two machines—a generator of randomness and a sorting machine. This alone makes nonsense of the Darwinian thesis.

In terms of the world-view of ecology the main features of Gaia, seen as a spatial abstraction, *must also be its main features when seen as a temporal abstraction, and also its main features when seen as a spatio-temporal system.* Let us look at a few of its particularly significant features. The first is that Gaia, seen as a spatial abstraction, is hierarchical, being made up of larger systems that are divided into smaller and still smaller systems. The same must also be true of Gaia seen as a temporal abstraction or as a spatio-temporal process, which is a hierarchy made up of long-lived life processes that are divided up into ever shorter-lived life processes.

Thus there are tens of thousands of generations of cells within the lifespan of a single individual organism. Individuals also have very much shorter lifespans than do the families of which they are the temporal as well as the spatial constituents. Beyond families stretch communities; beyond communities, societies and ethnic groups; beyond these, the human species, which in turn is unlikely to survive for longer than a fraction of the history of the ecosphere itself.

Another essential feature of the ecosphere, seen as a spatial abstraction, is that it displays order. As we shall see (chapter 27), order in a spatial abstraction corresponds to purpose in a temporal abstraction. In a hierarchical spatio-temporal system this means that the parts must behave homeotelically to the Gaian hierarchy as a whole in order to maintain its stability and thus their own stability (see chapter 41). James Lovelock sees the development of Gaia and the maintenance of its stability over hundreds of millions of years as the result of the coordinated action of living things, in particular bacteria.

Thus the evolution of species, as opposed to the overall Gaian evolutionary process, can only manifest itself in terms of changes occurring to a succession of ontogenies. These ontogenies cannot be understood as separate, individual processes. They are the differentiated parts of phylogeny, which in turn is closely integrated with the myriad other phylogenies that make up the Gaian process. What then is the role of ontogenies and their constituent sub-processes—morphology, physiology and behavior? The answer can only be *to provide the evolutionary process as a whole with the localized and short-term information required to ensure that it remain adaptive to the changing circumstances in which it occurs.* In modern language, they provide the feedback without which no cybernetic process is possible. This was implicit at least to the evolutionary theory of Lamarck, but it is hotly denied by mainstream science which sees evolutionary change as exclusively the result of changes affecting the genes of individual living things. As neither morphogenesis nor the development of a child into an adult nor its physiological or behavioral experience is considered to affect the genetic material in any way, these processes are seen as totally isolated from the evolutionary process (see Appendix 4).

Another relevant feature of the Gaian hierarchy, seen as a spatial or perhaps more realistically as a contemporaneous entity, is that the smaller constituent entities are controlled and coordinated by the larger ones—Gaia herself controlling in this way the whole hierarchy that it constitutes. It can be shown that this must also be true of the Gaian process or evolution, and this means that the past and the future must control the present (see chapter 55).

In evolution, as in all natural processes, the whole precedes the part: in other words, the more general the features of a natural system, the earlier they must have been established. Thus the decision that a particular organism was to be a bird rather than a reptile or mammal was taken many millions of years ago. Those required to determine what family, genus, species or variety it would belong to, were taken correspondingly later and in that order. The more trivial or specific the characteristics that distinguish an individual from the other members of its variety or species, the later its period of development (see chapter 55).

The German philosopher and naturalist Ernest Haeckel very significantly showed that the embryos of different vertebrates such as chickens, tortoises and humans were, at particular stages in their respective developments, so similar that they could not be told apart. However, as they developed, so did they grow correspondingly different. This led him to formulate his "biogenetic law" according to which ontogeny recapitulates phylogeny, which, though it has been reconsidered and reformulated by Sir Gavin de Beer, remains, in its essence, fundamentally true.[1]

The similarity in the form of these different embryos at the specific stages of their respective developments *reflects their common early history*. This early history is largely indelible. The reason is that the information that is transmitted from one generation to the next *reflects the total experience of the species, not just its short-term experience*. This is essential since the short-term experience could be non-representative, indeed aberrant. Life processes based on it would then be heterotelic, serving to satisfy the short-term needs of individuals of a particular generation without, at the same time, serving those of the hierarchy of spatio-temporal systems of which they are part; the Gaian process losing its continuity or stability as a result. If life processes are to be based on information that reflects the total experience of a species, then this information must be non-plastic, which we know to be the case. It is only the shortest and most recent experience that is plastic and hence modifiable, and that can thereby change for the sake of preventing bigger and more destructive changes affecting the system's generalities.

The information transmitted from one generation to the next must reflect the total experience of the species for another associated reason. It is that evolution is cumulative and incremental. During the evolutionary process, new information does not replace the old—it merely supplements it. Significantly, the nervous system has evolved by a process of successive accretions, the second and later the third nervous systems being added without displacing the older ones. Paul MacLean and Arthur Koestler lament the fact that the neo-cortex does not completely dominate the older brains—which would be necessary if human beings were, as both of them feel they should be, truly "rational." As MacLean writes, "the reptilian brain is filled with ancestral lore and ancestral memories and is faithful in doing what its ancestors say, but it is not a very good brain for facing up to new situations."[2] Neither of them realizes that rationality by itself (if there is such a thing) could only lead to chaos and that it is a prerequisite for the continuity of our species and hence for its survival that our "rationality" be *controlled precisely by the "ancestral lore and ancestral memories" that they see as but an undesirable relic of an animal past.*

Social behavior must also be based on information that reflects the society's total experience. How this is achieved is well known. Vernacular and, particularly, chthonic societies, lacking formal political institutions, are effectively governed by a council of elders. These are the living custodians of the society's cultural wisdom which, in effect, reflects its total experience. For this reason, a chthonic society has often been referred to as a gerontocracy, or *government by the old*. However, the ultimate custodians of the traditional wisdom are the ancestral spirits who formulated it. For this reason, such a society is best seen as a necrocracy, or *government by the dead*. Ancestor worship (or rather "communion with the ancestors" as Kenyatta refers to it) is an essential feature of the religion of such societies, as it is the influence of the values of which the ancestors are the custodians that is determinant.

Lafcadio Hearn notes how this is true of traditional Japanese society. "In all matters," he notes, "the dead, rather than the living, have been the rulers of the nation and the shapers of its destiny"[3] —as indeed they have ruled and shaped the destinies of all chthonic societies. No voices from the grave have spoken with greater authority than the mythical ancestors—the "Dawn Beings" as Radcliffe-Brown[4] refers to them, who lived in that sacred period known by certain Australian tribes as the "World Dawn," Mircea Eliade's *in illo tempore*.[5]

In that sacred period they enacted the traditional law that was to govern for all time their society, the natural world and the cosmos itself. The traditional law was sacred on all these counts, and the non-plasticity of the traditional information that reflected the total experience of the society and that was passed down from one generation to the next was thus assured. Adaptation to new environmental changes, in such conditions, involved only the imperceptible changes that the shaman and the Council of Elders could reconcile with the society's mythology and the traditional law that it served to rationalize. Such a society can thus be seen as governed by the total spatio-temporal hierarchical entity of which it is part going back to the "Dawn Period" when it first arose. In this way, the principles governing the transmission of cultural information *are precisely those governing the transmission of genetic information which ensures the stability of natural systems at a biological level of organization*.

But it is not just the past, but also the future that controls the present; for the shorter processes serve the purpose of the larger processes *that encompass and outlive them*. Indeed, within the Gaian process, individual life processes are designed in such a way as to maintain the critical order of the Gaian process indefinitely—that is until such time as massive geophysical change gives rise to conditions that lie outside its "tolerance range."

Nothing is undertaken by the Gaian process in the interests of satisfying short-term requirements that can possibly interfere with its continuity or stability, and hence with its perpetuation. In the case of economic development, or progress, the opposite is true (see chapter 64). It is exclusively concerned with immediate political and economic benefits and its promoters show absolutely no interest in the consequences of such behavior for future generations; for the latter are not players in today's political and economic games: they neither vote, nor save, nor invest, nor produce, nor consume. Why then should they be consulted?

It must follow that if evolution is the Gaian process it cannot be understood by examining the behavior of that contemporaneous cross-section of the ecosphere of which we are part and that is normally taken to be evolving. For such a cross-section does not evolve in order to maintain its stability, but rather the stability of that vast spatio-temporal process-entity that stretches back to the beginning of life on Earth and whose experience is reflected in the information on the basis of which it evolves. It is the latter, in fact, that is evolving, not the former, which by itself is not capable of evolution.

From the cybernetic point of view, the total Gaian experience going back into the mists of time *exists* as does the present and as does its future experience, for together they constitute the Gaian process—the unit of evolution. A tribal society is said to be made up of the dead, the living and the yet to be born. That is precisely how Gaia must be seen.

22

Stability rather than change
is the basic feature of the living world

~

Wherever we seek to find constancy we discover change.
Daniel B. Botkin (Professor of Biology and Environmental Studies at the
University of California)

Nature, left undisturbed, so fashions her territory as to give it almost
unchanging permanence of form, outline and proportion, except when
shattered by geologic convulsion; and in these comparatively rare cases of
derangement, she sets herself at once to repair the superficial damage, and
to restore, as nearly as practicable, the former aspect of her dominion . . .
A condition of equilibrium has been reached which, without the action
of man, would remain, with little fluctuation, for countless ages.
George Perkins Marsh

What is it that holds so many groups of animals to an astonishingly
constant form over millions of years? This seems to be the problem now
—the problem of constancy, rather than of change.
W.H. Thorpe

THE ATTENTION of those imbued with the paradigm of science and hence with the world-view of modernism is monopolized by change. For them, the world is in perpetual flux, constantly changing in a direction seen to be desirable and progressive. This is true of species that are seen to be "evolving" and societies and their economies that are seen to be "developing." Reality is quite different. It is *continuity or stability* that has been the most striking feature of the world of living things.

Darwin himself was highly impressed by the constancy of the natural world and once even suggested that it may be more important than "the struggle for survival" with which he was so concerned. In a letter to the geologist Charles Lyell, he wrote, "If I had to commence *de novo*, I would have used 'natural preservation'."[1] A similar view has also been expressed by Gaylord Simpson, one of the founders of the Synthetic Theory of Evolution, who admits that

> heredity is, on the whole, a conservative factor tending to keep succeeding generations within a common pattern. The acorn produces an oak similar to the tree that produced the acorn, except in unessential details, and the egg produces a chicken essentially like the hen that laid it.[2]

But he cannot avoid accentuating that "offspring are nevertheless never exactly like their parents" and that "since evolution is a process of change, these differences are of special concern to us . . . ."

Theodosius Dobzhansky was also struck by the conservatism of nature:

> that the bones of Cretaceous opossums are similar to some modern ones, . . . modern horseshoe crabs (limulus) do not differ greatly from those having lived some two hundred million years ago; the brachiopod Lingula changed little if at all for four hundred and fifty million years.[3]

Both Waddington and Monod were also impressed by the constancy of living things, as was Thorpe who fully realized that the constancy of certain biological forms is more difficult to explain "than it is to account for their evolution." He notes for instance that

> The Wagtail (Motacilla) there in the garden was here before the Himalayas were lifted up! This constancy is so extraordinary, that it seems to demand a special mechanism to account not for the evolution but for the fixity of some groups.[4]

Weiss also realized this. There is so great a preoccupation with change, he noted, that we have totally neglected the less glamorous but more *fundamental constancy* of the living world. "In our educational system," he writes, "we are acting very much like newspaper editors, who highlight the spectacular and neglect the far more constant phenomena."[5] Thus we accentuate evolution, but we do not impress on our children that the most fundamental features of all living things are exactly the same and "have remained the same from the simplest living system that we know, all the way up to man." They should all be told that

> all the biochemical mechanisms of macromolecular synthesis, energy utilization, respiration, storage, proliferation, cell division, membrane structure and function, contractility, excitability, fibre-formation, pigmentation, and so forth, have all *remained unaltered in essence through the ages.*[6]

This has been noted by the Harvard palaeontologist Stephen J. Gould and also by his colleagues, Steven Stanley and Niles Eldredge, who, between them, developed the theory of Punctuated Equilibrium in terms of which long periods of stability are punctuated by short periods of dramatic and rapid evolutionary change. Like the similar notion put forward in the 1940s by Richard Goldschmidt it is difficult to reconcile with the Darwinian view that evolution occurs as the result of a gradual succession of small changes. Punctuated equilibrium is much easier to reconcile with the fossil record, as has always been known, and fits in much better with our knowledge of life processes.

What then explains this stability? As Dobhzansky asks, "What caused the living fossils to stop evolving?" A possible answer, he suggests, is that evolution simply stopped when a sufficient degree of adaptiveness was achieved.[7] However he admits that it is not obvious that opossums or horseshoe crabs are in any way better adapted than mice, cats or lobsters. His own tentative answer is that "the living fossils occupy ecological niches that have become perhaps more confining, otherwise not much altered for a long time." In what way though are they more confining? Why should this confinement not imply a better degree of adaptation? Dobhzansky provides no answers to these questions.

For Monod, the answer is to be found in the "extreme coherence of a teleonomic system, which, during evolution, at once played the role of guide and of break and has preserved, amplified and integrated, but an infinitesimal fraction of the astronomic number of possibilities offered to it."[8] However, a teleonomic system is one that is programed to achieve a specific goal—but what is the goal? Monod does not say. He implies that it is to "preserve, amplify, and integrate" the favored minority of living things—the fittest in the Darwinian language; but why should this be so? For Monod, as for the rest of the scientific establishment, the explanation lies in the mysterious workings of "the roulette of nature"; so randomness is introduced once again, to play the role of the *"deus ex machina."*

Waddington more realistically attributes the stability of the living world to the constancy of the genetic material throughout the evolutionary period and to the shuffling and recombination of genes that may be present within the population. These are both critical considerations. None of the scientists mentioned, however, entertains the possibility that it is the overriding goal of all living things to maintain their own stability within the context of the critical order of the Gaian hierarchy, and that the dynamics of this process is such as to assure that this goal—in normal conditions—be achieved.

If gradual evolutionary change were the norm, as neo-Darwinists assume, then we would expect that the incidence of random mutations would be high and that it would increase as systems become more highly developed. But the opposite seems to be the case. Random mutations are extremely rare, and this is no coincidence, as natural systems develop the most elaborate methods to avoid their occurrence and reduce their incidence to a minimum. Monod realizes this. "Because of the conservative nature as well as of the perfection of the mechanism of replication," he writes, "individual mutations are very rare events." What is more, once mutations do occur, special mechanisms, that are perfected during the course of evolution, exist for assuring their elimination.[9] As Bryn Bridges points out, cells that have mutated as a result of exposure to radiation and to other mutagenic agents are, in normal conditions, eliminated by the body's immune system.[10] If it were not for this, the incidence of cancer would be even higher than it is today.

This must lead us to ask an embarrassing question. If genetic mutations play such an important part in evolutionary change, as neo-Darwinists tell us, yet a natural system does everything to prevent their occurrence and indeed seeks desperately to neutralize their effects when they do occur, how can it be considered to be geared to the achievement of such change? Richard Dawkins is fully aware of the contradiction in the neo-Darwinian thesis. "How," he asks, "can we reconcile the idea that copying errors are an essential prerequisite for evolution to occur with the statement that natural selection favours highly copying fidelity?"[11] The answer, he suggests, is that although evolution may seem, in some vague sense, a "good thing," especially since we are the product of it, *nothing actually "wants" to evolve*. Evolution is something that happens, in spite of all the efforts of the replicators (and nowadays of the genes) to prevent it happening, a point also made by Jacques Monod in his Herbert Spencer Lecture.

Quite clearly, natural systems are not geared towards change but towards the *avoidance of change*. Change occurs, not because it is desirable *per se*, but because in certain conditions, it is judged to be necessary, *as a means of preventing predictably larger and more disruptive changes*. This must be true of social evolution as well as biological evolution. The main feature of vernacular societies, within which man has spent well over ninety percent of his experience on this planet, has also been their stability. This is particularly true of hunter-gatherer societies. During the old stone age, for instance, flint-chipping techniques did not change for some 200,000 years, nor did the lifestyle of Australian Aborigines for at least 30,000 years. "The Australian ethos," writes the anthropologist, W.E.H. Stanner,

> appears to be continuity, constancy, balance, symmetry, regularity.
> There are no great conflicts for power, no great contest for place and

office. There is no idea of a formal chief in fact . . . They do not fight over land. There are no wars or invasions to seize territory. They do not enslave each other. They place a very special value on things remaining unchangingly themselves, on keeping life to a routine which is known and trusted. Absence of change which means certainty of expectation, seems to them a good thing in itself. The value given to continuity is so high that they are not simply a people "without history." They are a people who have been able, in some sense, to "defeat" history, to become a-historical in mood, outlook and life.[12]

It is probable that the same could be said of all hunter-gatherer societies and tribal societies in general when living in the environment to which they have been adapted by their social evolution.

All this is unlikely to impress anyone. We have all been brainwashed into regarding change as desirable in itself. Hunter-gatherers, most of us feel, must have had a very boring life—for they underwent no change—they had no history. But is it so desirable to have a history? It is very doubtful. Our history books contain little more than the history of wars, invasions, massacres, revolutions, assassinations and intrigues. History makes very depressing reading and does little more than illustrate the extreme squalor of human behavior once vernacular communities and their cultural patterns have broken down. Indeed, if "no news is good news" then one can equally well say that "no history is good history." The fact that hunter-gatherers did not have one reflects above all the orderliness and harmony of their lives, which were not punctuated by the increasingly intolerable discontinuities that today are rendering our lives ever less supportable.

In ecology, one of the problems with the term "stability" is that it is used differently by different ecologists. Eugene Odum distinguishes between two different types of stability. The first is "resistance stability" which he defines as "the ability of an ecosystem to resist perturbations and maintain its structure and function intact." The second is "resilience stability" which he takes to be "a system's ability to recover when a system is disrupted by a perturbation."[13] An example of the former is provided by the California Redwood which is resistant to fire by virtue of its thick bark and other features, but which, if it happens to burn, will recover but very slowly or perhaps never at all. An example of the latter is provided by the Californian chaparral vegetation which is very easily burned but which recovers quickly.

G.H. Orians, who distinguishes between no fewer than seven different types of stability, makes a similar distinction between "inertia" or "the ability of a system to resist external perturbations" and "amplitude" which he defines as "the area over which a system is stable"[14] (the extent to which it can be displaced from a previous state and yet return to it), a concept similar to Odum's "resistance stability."

The Canadian ecologist C.S. Holling refuses to accept that either Odum's "resistance stability" or Orians' "inertia" is a viable strategy for survival, one that leads to "persistence."[15] For him, a stable system is one which returns to "an equilibrium state" after a temporary disturbance and "with the least fluctuations." He includes in this category living things that have not been subjected to change for a long time. These are very vulnerable to environmental change, and thereby cannot be regarded as "persistent." He then contrasts stable systems with resilient systems which are characterized by large fluctuations and which alone are "persistent." He does not seem to notice the irony of classifying as "non-persistent" such organisms as the horseshoe crab which has not changed for some five hundred million years while reserving the term persistent to "resilient" species like the fruit-fly that is constantly developing new forms. This is quite clear to Waddington. The distinction that Holling makes between stability and resilience he sees as based on "a confusion between two different types of stability."[16]

But Holling is a disciple of Ilya Prigogine and thus committed to the most extreme form of the paradigm of science and the world-view of modernism. For him, stability means stagnation, a bad word. In the world in which we live, in any case, it is not an option. Increasingly, he writes, "we must learn to live with disturbances and live with variability and live with uncertainties."[17] Discontinuities, such as floods, droughts, epidemics, wars, pollution disasters, the erosion of the ozone layer and global warming are, presumably, desirable because out of such "fluctuations" emerge progress and order.

I think we can reject Holling's views on stability. Eugene Odum's distinction between "resistance" and "resilience stability" on the other hand seems very sensible. Of course, we can refine the concept as Orians sought to do. In particular, we can regard a resilient system as more or less stable in accordance with the size of the discontinuities that affect it and from which it must then recover. What is important is that if a system evolves, so it becomes capable of reducing such discontinuities to a minimum (see chapters 39 and 40). As this occurs, it comes to enjoy a more co-operative relationship with the other systems that make up the larger system of which it is part. And as this larger system becomes more highly integrated, so resilience stability evolves into resistance stability.

23

Gaia is alive

—

. . . every part of the universe is body, and that which is not body is no part of the universe; and because the universe is all, that which is no part of it is nothing, and consequently nowhere.

Thomas Hobbes

Man is a self-balancing, 28-jointed adapter-based biped, an electrochemical reduction plant, integral with the segregated storages of special energy extracts in storage batteries, for subsequent actuation of thousands of hydraulic and pneumatic pumps, with motors attached; sixty-two thousand miles of capillaries, millions of warning-signals, railroad and conveyor systems; crushers and cranes . . . and a universally distributed telephone system needing no service for 70 years if well managed; the whole, extraordinary complex mechanism guided with exquisite precision from a turret in which are located telescopic and microscopic self-registering and recording range finders, a spectroscope, et cetera.

Buckminster Fuller

A machine is made to realize some conscious human purpose. Its parts work together to secure that purpose, not to secure its own persistence.

J.H. Woodger

I was born a thousand years ago, born in the culture of bows and arrows . . . born in an age when people loved the things of nature and spoke to it as though it had a soul.

Chief Dan George

For vernacular man throughout the ages, nature was alive and his religious life was above all his relationship with the spirits that inhabited all natural things. Theodore Roszak talks of the Pagan view of nature as "alive and infused with purpose" and "aglow with seductively sensuous qualities."[1] Morris Berman tells us that nature was seen until the scientific revolution, as "enchanted," "alive" and as "the place of belonging." Man was not "an alienated observer" of the cosmos but "a direct participant in its drama." His destiny was "bound up with its destiny" and this gave meaning to his life.[2]

It is no coincidence that vernacular man was an animist for, as the anthropologist Weston La Barre writes, animism "is deeply linked with the biological nature of the human species."[3] Indeed, it is part of that intuitive heritage that enables man to be cognitively adjusted to the world in which he lives. However, with the development of the world-view of modernism, and in particular of the paradigm of science, the world became "disenchanted," secularized and mechanomorphized.

The mechanistic view of the world, like all the different aspects of the paradigm of science, can be traced back to the sixteenth and seventeenth centuries but it was more explicitly formulated in the eighteenth century by Julien La Mettrie in his *L'Homme Machine*, Joseph Louis Lagrange in his *Mécanique Analytique*, and Pierre Simon Laplace in his *Mécanique Celeste*. The mechanomorphic thesis has gone through at least three distinct phases. In the first, with Galileo, Newton and Descartes, life processes were explained in terms of pure mechanics. Scientists sought purely mechanical explanations of digestion, embryogenesis, nerve reactions and even the workings of the mind.

During the next phase, living things were compared to heat engines and life processes to physical burning processes. This notion can be traced to Priestley, who thought that living things like mice and candles emitted a substance that he called "phlogiston." Since, when there is no phlogiston left, the candle stops burning and the mice die, living and burning are one.

Lavoisier replaced phlogiston with oxygen. The process was then reformulated in the language of thermodynamics. It was shown that, during metabolism, energy is conserved (first law of thermodynamics) and heat is dissipated (second law). It was then noticed that life is more than just the burning up of food to release energy; it also involves synthesis, the switching of potential energy from one state of matter to another. These considerations led to the third phase, called by Peter Calow "the chemical plant analogy."[4] Like a chemical plant, an organism makes use of raw materials and adds to them a "biological reaction flask" to produce new compounds. This process can also be expressed in the language of thermodynamics: life processes being seen as overcoming the influence of the second law because the biosphere within which they occur is an open system, at least from the point of view of energy (see appendix 1).

The mechanomorphic thesis suffers from a very serious flaw. Descartes is regarded as the first to have explicitly formulated it— but officially at least, Descartes remained a deist. It was God who created man the machine, as He created all other living machines that make up the biosphere. The position of mechanistic science however is quite different. God has been abolished, and so man and other living things *have neither a manufacturer nor an operator*.

Mechanistic scientists, as J.H. Woodger notes,

> want to have a machine without a mechanic. Their problem is to show how it is possible to have a machine that comes into existence, runs, repairs and regulates itself, and finally divides into two machines, *without a mechanic.*[5]

They have, in fact, completely forgotten that *"machines presuppose organisms,"* and hence all those features of organisms whose very existence the mechanomorphic thesis sets out to deny. Professing to eliminate them, our scientists have merely externalized them on the sly, hoping that no one would notice. In reality, as Woodger notes, "the choice is not between mechanism and mystery, but between one mystery and another."[6]

It will be argued that this dogma is no longer entertained by physicists today. Quantum mechanics has revealed that behavior at the sub-atomic level cannot be understood in terms of Newtonian physics. Quantum physicists, we are told, now view the world in terms of waves and fields. But outside the discipline of quantum mechanics, mainstream science remains very definitely Newtonian. If the sub-atomic constituent is no longer seen as a machine, *molecules, organisms and ecosystems still are, and so indeed are human societies.*

Why then, we may ask, do mainstream scientists still maintain this untenable thesis? The main reason seems to be that machines are simple and predictable. Their behavior is explicable in terms of cause and effect and is also eminently quantifiable. They can be studied in isolation from other machines and hence in controlled laboratory conditions. Indeed, scientists should be honest enough to admit, as Woodger does, that living things are taken to be machines largely *because they have to be, if they "are to be studied by means of scientific method."*[7] This is of course to admit that scientific method can only enable us to understand the behavior of living things once their *most important features, precisely those that distinguish them from mere machines, have been eliminated.*

But there is another reason why the mechanomorphic view of life has been adopted by mainstream scientists. If they faced up to the real nature of man as a complex form of life, they would also have to face the fact that his real needs—biological, social, ecological, spiritual and cognitive—*are ever less adequately satisfied* by progress or economic development. If man is a machine, on the other hand, one can maintain that his only needs are material and technological—precisely those that economic development is capable of satisfying. As Polanyi writes, "the Laplacean universal mechanics induces the teaching that material welfare and the establishment of an unlimited power for imposing the conditions of material welfare are the supreme good."[8] Worster makes the complementary point that "by reducing plants and animals to insensate matter, mere conglomerates of atomic particles devoid of internal purpose or intelligence," mechanistic science has removed "the remaining barriers to unrestrained economic exploitation."[9]

The mechanomorphic view of the world, moreover, is not only alienating but grossly flawed. In his heart, man has always known this, and has constantly reacted against this soul-destroying vision, as did Henry More in the early seventeenth century. He was much influenced by the animism of Plato and Plotinus, and revived the idea of the "soul of the world" or "spirit of nature" or *anima mundi*. He described this as a "substance incorporeal but without sense and animadversion, pervading the whole matter of the universe, and exercising a plastical power therein . . . raising such phenomena in the world . . . as cannot be resolved into mere mechanical powers." He also posited a vital organizing power in plants and animals. It is because of this power, he maintained, that they are more than "mere motion of matter."[10]

The notion of the *anima mundi* was taken up by the Romantic poets and writers of the eighteenth and nineteenth centuries in their reaction against mechanistic science and the associated technological ethic. Goethe saw nature "at work and alive, manifesting herself in her wholeness in every single part of her being."[11] The Romantics developed a highly ecological world-view. Wordsworth, for instance, talked of "an intertwined togetherness" and "a community of existence."[12] A living thing for the Romantics could not be disassembled and then reconstructed like a clock. The world was alive, not dead as the scientists were telling us.

Even scientists began to react against the mechanistic picture of the world. Driesch found that he could not explain, in terms of mechanistic science, the ability of the sea-urchin embryo that he studied in his laboratory to develop into a more or less normal phenotype, even after parts of it had been removed. To do so required that he posit a vitalistic principle which he referred to as "entelechy," Aristotle's *entelekhia* (from the Greek *en* meaning internal, and *telos* meaning goal). He saw life processes as controlled by a hierarchy of entelechies that were all derived from and controlled by the organism's overall entelechy.[13]

In his *Creative Evolution*, Bergson also insisted that the evolutionary process could not be explained in mechanistic terms but had to be seen as a "current of life" flowing from one generation to the next and triggered off by a vital impetus or *élan vital*. "This impetus," he writes, which he saw as "sustained right along the lines of evolution, among which it gets divided," is a "fundamental cause of variations, at least of those that are regularly passed on, that accumulate and create new species."[14] The problem with both Driesch's entelechy and Bergson's *élan vital*, however, is that they are very vague notions, so much so that to postulate their existence does not tell us a great deal. Bergson realized this, but argued that at least his *élan vital* could serve as a "sort of label affixed to our ignorance, so as to remind us of this occasionally, while mechanism invites us to ignore that ignorance."[15]

Vitalism, however, is not an alternative to the mechanomorphic thesis. It is just something that is added on to make it more realistic. What is really required is a *totally non-mechanistic theory of life* and such a theory must by its very nature be holistic. Living things are alive *because they are part of a whole*: the Gaian hierarchy. The main features of living things, those that make them alive—their dynamism, creativity, intelligence, purposiveness—are not apparent if one studies them in isolation from the hierarchy of natural systems of which they are part. Living things are alive in a very important sense of the term *because they are part of this hierarchy*. As Joseph Needham puts it, "life is the whole in which the parts, instead of going their separate ways, work together." If they did not, life would be chaotic, random, uncoordinated. "The whole," Needham continues, "requires its components (of all levels) in order to be 'alive,' while the parts require the whole in order to make their particular contribution to it by virtue of which it is 'alive,'" expressing in this way what I refer to as the principle of hierarchical mutualism. He goes so far as to say that "a molecule, an atom or an electron, if it belongs to the spatial hierarchy of a living organism, will be just as much 'alive' as a cell, while on the contrary, an entity that does not belong to such a spatial hierarchy will be 'dead.'"[16]

One can see for oneself that if one kills a living thing, it loses its wholeness. The parts, in so far as they can survive, regress to a state of chaos and randomness and their behavior can then be understood in terms of the reductionist and mechanomorphic paradigm of science. For instance, purposiveness, in the living world, can be identified with the *tendency of living things to maintain the whole*. Once the whole disintegrates however, the parts cease to be purposive and their behavior can then be explained in terms of the crude mechanistic theory of causality.

Though Needham was only concerned with life up to the level of the biological organism, one can apply his criterion of life with some reservations to higher levels of organization such as that of the society, the ecosystem and Gaia herself. At these levels, living things are not so closely integrated, which means that their separation from the whole does not immediately entail their demise. However social isolates are alienated beings, incapable of normal homeotelic behavior; they can no longer fulfill the task for which they were designed—the maintenance of the critical order of the living world within which their life alone has meaning. Under these conditions their meaningless lives are either devoted to instant gratification, attempting, via drugs, alcohol and the like, to cut themselves off from a meaningless world with which they cannot cope, or to recreate, by various contrived means, some illusory semblance of the social environment of which they have been deprived. They are freaks—not truly alive—in the full sense of the term. James Lovelock has been criticized for stating that "Gaia is alive." "This notion 'alive'," he writes, "bothers a lot of my scientific colleagues," and he asks them to think of it "as no more than the capacity of the Earth to regulate itself and keep cool, when things are changing adversely."[17]

In his latest book, *Gaia: The Practical Science of Planetary Medicine*, Lovelock tells us that he sees as alive "everything that metabolizes and self-regulates . . . so that life is something shared in common by cats and trees, as well as by beehives, forests, coral reefs and Gaia."[18] In other words, to be alive is to display homeostasis (see chapter 24).

However for a natural system to assure its homeostasis it must above all seek to maintain the integrity of the Gaian hierarchy of which it is part (see chapter 53), *for homeotely is a sine qua non of homeostasis*. Since for Lovelock, *Gaia is the whole*, to assure her homeostasis means maintaining her own wholeness in the face of change. When Lovelock says that Gaia is alive, he must therefore also imply that she is whole.

24

Natural systems are homeostatic

—

All the vital mechanisms, varied as they are, have only one object, that of preserving constant the conditions of life in the internal environment.
Claude Bernard

Homeostasis is the totality of steady states maintained in an organism through the coordination of its complex physiological processes.
Walter Cannon

Health is a continuing property, potentially measurable by the individual's ability to rally from insults, whether chemical, physical, infectious, psychological or social.
J. Ralph Audy

Biological organisms are self-regulating cybernetic systems capable by their own efforts of maintaining their stability (both resistance and resilience) in the face of internal or external challenges—a quality referred to as homeostasis. A natural system controlled by an external agent, however, cannot be stable. Because the external agent is not part of the Gaian hierarchy, it is not subjected to homearchic control, and so does not behave homeotelically towards the whole of which it is part. Instead, it will steer a system towards a random, heterotelic goal—one that satisfies its own specific interests regardless of the effects on biological, social and ecological systems.

Hippocrates considered that diseases were cured by the natural actions of the body. As the physiologist Walter Cannon notes, this implies the existence of agencies that are ready to operate correctively when the normal state of the organism is upset. The nineteenth-century French physiologist Claude Bernard was also impressed by the way in which living cells maintain the constancy of what he was the first to call their "internal environment"(*milieu interieur*).[1] For him, "this constancy of the internal environment is a condition for life to be free and independent"—a principle still fundamental to physiology. The same principle was noted in 1885 by the German physiologist Edward Pfluger, and also by his Belgian colleague, Leon Fredericq. "Each disturbing influence," the latter wrote,

> induces by itself the calling forth of compensatory activity to neutralize or repair the disturbance. The higher in the scale of living beings, the more numerous, the more perfect and the more complicated do these regulatory agencies become. They tend to free the organism completely from the unfavorable influences and changes occurring in the environment.[2]

For Bernard, to achieve this must be the fundamental goal of all living things.

The term "homeostasis" was first coined by Cannon in his seminal book *The Wisdom of the Body*. It is worth considering the concept in some detail. Cannon was struck by the fact that organisms "composed of material which is characterized by the utmost inconstancy and unsteadiness, have somehow learned the method of maintaining constancy and keeping steady in the presence of conditions which might reasonably be expected to prove profoundly disturbing." For instance mammals can maintain the constancy of their body temperature in spite of external changes.

> For a short time, men may be exposed to dry heat at 115 to 128 degrees centigrade (239 to 261 degrees Fahrenheit) without an increase of their body temperature above normal. On the other hand, arctic mammals when exposed to cold as low as thirty-five degrees centigrade below freezing (thirty-one degrees below zero Fahrenheit) do not manifest any noteworthy fall of body temperature.[3]

Resistance to changes induced by external circumstances (what ecologists would call the resistance stability of living things), Cannon notes, is not the only evidence of adaptive stabilizing arrangements. Natural systems are also capable of resisting disturbances from within. For instance

> The heat produced in maximal muscular effort, continued for twenty minutes, would be so great that, if it were not promptly dissipated, it would cause some of the albuminous substances of the body to become stiff, like a hard-boiled egg. Again, continuous and extreme muscular exertion is accompanied by the production of so much lactic acid (the acid of sour milk) in the working muscles that within a short period it would neutralize all the alkali contained in the blood, if other agencies did not appear and prevent that disaster.[4]

The constancy that living things achieve some might be tempted to term equilibrium. That word, however, has come to have a fairly exact meaning as applied to relatively simple physico-chemical states in which physico-chemical forces are balanced. Homeostasis is a far more complex condition. It is not "something set and immobile, a stagnation," but "a dynamic situation." What is more "the coordinated physiological processes" required to maintain it "are complex and peculiar to living things—involving as they may the brains and nerves, the heart, the lungs, kidneys and spleen, all working co-operatively."[5]

Homeostasis is also diachronic. All the co-operating factors can be brought into action successively as well as at the same time. Cannon notes, as did Fredericq, that as an organism evolves, the homeostatic mechanisms that assure the constancy of its internal environment also become correspondingly more elaborate.[6] Thus "lower animals which have not yet achieved the degree of control of stabilization seen in the more highly evolved forms, are limited in their activities and handicapped in the struggle for existence." A frog, for instance, is not capable of preventing water from evaporating from its body, nor can it regulate its own body temperature. This means that if it leaves the pond in which it normally lives, it soon dries up, and when it gets cold, it must seek refuge in the mud at the bottom of its pond and hibernate until spring.

Reptiles have developed more effective homeostatic mechanisms against rapid loss of water, which means that they no longer have to remain close to ponds or streams and can even survive in very dry conditions. But, like amphibians, they have no homeostatic mechanisms to insulate their internal environment against changes of temperature. This is because they are still "cold-blooded," which means that during the winter, they too must give up an active existence. As Cannon writes, "only among the higher vertebrates, the birds and mammals, has there been acquired that freedom from the limitations imposed by cold that permits activity even though the rigours of winter may be severe."

Interestingly enough, Cannon considers the probability that such mechanisms may not only be operative in biological organisms but also in other natural systems which could also explain their constancy. A comparative study, he suggests, might show that every complex organization must be capable of "more or less effective self-righting adjustments in order to prevent a check on its functions, or rapid disintegration of its parts, when it is subjected to stress."[7]

Significantly, B.C.Patten and Eugene Odum also see homeostatic mechanisms or "checks and balances (or forces and counter-forces) that dampen oscillations" as operating "all along the line," and hence not only at the level of the individual where for instance, they "keep body temperature fairly constant despite fluctuations in the environment" but also at the level of the population, the community and the ecosystem.[8]

Roy Rappaport was probably one of the first anthropologists to show that tribal societies are also capable of such behavior. In his seminal book *Pigs for the Ancestors*, he interpreted the ritual cycle of a small social group in New Guinea in cybernetic terms, showing it to be above all a means of controlling its impact on its natural environment so as to assure its sustainability or stability.[9] Gerardo Reichel-Dolmatoff, quite independently of Rappaport, interpreted the cultural pattern of the Tukano Indians of Colombia in much the same way.[10] Thomas Harding also sees tribal societies as capable of homeostatic behavior and thereby of maintaining their stability. "When acted upon by external forces," he writes, "a culture will, if necessary, undergo specific changes only to the extent of, and with the effect of preserving unchanged its fundamental structure and character."[11]

That ecosystems are geared to the maintenance of their homeostasis is denied by mainstream ecologists today as it is difficult if not impossible to reconcile with the paradigm of science. However, if ecosystems are not cybernetic (and hence self-regulating), as Patten and Odum ask,[12] *then by what other means could the perceived harmony of the biosphere have evolved?* Most modern ecologists would give the neo-Darwinian answer: by natural selection from random mutations and hence by a crude and rudimentary mechanism largely determined by external factors such as competition and selection. Thus Putman and Wratten insist that self-regulatory behavior at the level of an ecosystem is largely due to intra-specific competition for a resource. They nevertheless admit that such competition seems to achieve an equilibrium "well before the limiting resource starts to act as a finite shortage." This suggests that natural systems are capable of foresight and planning (see chapter 30), but Putman and Wratten deny this. Such a notion is irreconcilable with the paradigm of science.

Patten and Odum do not believe that competition alone can explain the order displayed by ecosystems. "Either the ecosystem is orderly," they write, "or its lack of chaos just happened to develop from unregulated Darwinian struggles between competing populations all alone and uninfluenced except by each other on the mutual stage of life. The latter seems to us implausible to us."[13]

Eugene Odum notes how ecosystems are endowed with the necessary mechanisms for self-regulation and hence homeostasis.

> Besides energy flows and material cycles, ecosystems are rich in information networks comprising physical and chemical communication flows that connect all parts and steer or regulate the system as a whole. Accordingly, ecosystems can be considered cybernetic in nature, but control functions are internal and diffuse rather than external and specified as in human-engineered cybernetic devices.[14]

These information networks Howard Odum refers to as "the invisible wires of nature" or alternatively as "the hormones of ecosystems."[15]

A number of experiments have been carried out to determine whether ecosystems display resilience stability and if so, whether this can be attributed to their own efforts, and hence whether they are cybernetic or self-regulating systems capable of maintaining their homeostasis. The best known of such experiments are those conducted by Simberloff and Wilson. They removed all the fauna from several small mangrove islets and then closely watched the way these were recolonized by terrestrial arthropods. They established that though the islets were eventually populated by very different species from the original ones, the total number of species was very much the same as before.[16]

Three years later, H. Heatwole and R. Levins examined the same data. Their interest was to classify the different species to be found there in terms of trophic organization, noting the number of species in each of the trophic categories (herbivores, scavengers, detritus feeders, predators etc.). The results were highly significant. They showed that the trophic structure of the communities on the different islets displayed a remarkable stability even though the species composing each of the trophic levels had undergone a considerable change.[17] This experiment clearly illustrates the principle of homeostasis, though this is denied by Putman and Wratten. They insist that what Heatwole and Levins witnessed, was not "the recovery of a disturbed system" but *the creation of a completely new one*, which means that there is no evidence for any cybernetic process at work.[18]

Putman and Wratten's error is that they assume that a goal-directed life process (that they refer to as "deterministic") must, like a machine, display *"microdeterminacy."* But as Weiss has taken so much trouble to show, it only displays *"macrodeterminacy."* In other words, to be stable a natural system need only preserve its basic pattern or basic features, not every detail of its structure as in the case of a homeostatic machine. Indeed, the details must necessarily change in answer to changing environmental conditions, as it is only in this way that bigger and more devastating changes can be avoided. What is important is that the basic trophic structure of the ecosystem studied by Heatwole and Levins was restored. The fact that the actual species that took over the different trophic functions were no longer the same is irrelevant. Indeed, that the same functions can be taken over in this way by different species demonstrates just how adaptive are the mechanisms assuring the homeostasis or stability of ecosystems. It provides a perfect illustration of Weiss's "principle of the conservation of overall pattern" which is really but another way of stating the principle of ecological homeostasis.

James Lovelock, in his seminal book *Gaia: a New Look at Life on Earth*, shows that Gaia herself displays homeostasis. Sagan and Margulis are also struck by the extraordinary stability of the Earth's relationship with its environment, the atmosphere.[19] It must have been maintained very much as it is now, at least "since the time that air-breathing animals have been living in forests"—or for about 300 million years. Fossil records show that the climate has changed very little since life first appeared on Earth about 3500 million years ago. Yet the output of heat from the sun, the surface properties of the Earth, and the composition of the atmosphere have almost certainly varied greatly over the same period.

For the incredible stability of world climate to have been the result of pure chance, is for Lovelock "as unlikely as to survive unscathed a drive blindfolded through rush-hour traffic."[20] Again the only explanation is that life must have developed the capacity for self-regulation, so maintaining its own stability. Lovelock refers to Cannon's work on the homeostasis of biological organisms and considers that there must be a similar homeostatic process regulating the temperature of the planet, a conclusion that has the widest possible implications for our view of the natural world and man's interrelationship with it.

The principle of homeostasis is somewhat of an embarrassment to science. It is difficult to reconcile with the dogma that living things are in a permanent state of flux, as it is with the notion that living things learn by the crude process of trial and error, or that their adaptive responses are selected by an undefined environment, or alternatively are simply *ad hoc* responses triggered by specific environmental stimuli. Nonetheless, that biological organisms are geared to maintaining their homeostasis is now difficult to deny, but that vernacular communities, or ecosystems, do as well is accepted by but a small minority of social scientists and ecologists and that the ecosphere itself also does so, by a still smaller minority.

What is missing however from the whole discussion of homeostasis is the realization that natural systems are integral parts of the Gaian hierarchy, and that a system cannot maintain its homeostasis *unless the hierarchy of natural systems of which it is part is also capable of doing so*. In other words, a system can only be stable if the larger systems of which it is part are also stable. There is no stable economy, for instance, within an unstable society, no stable society within an unstable ecosystem, and no stable anything when the ecosphere itself is being destabilized, as is happening today. Hence for a natural system to maintain its homeostasis, its behavior must be homeotelic (see chapter 53) to the Gaian hierarchy, which means subordinating all other considerations to that of maintaining the critical order or stability of the ecosphere.

25

Natural systems are homeorhetic

~

Homeorhesis makes homeostasis possible by assuring the structural development of the organs.
Jean Piaget

We use the word homeorhesis when what is stabilized is not a constant value but is a particular course of change in time.
C.H. Waddington

IN SPITE OF THE BASIC TENDENCY in nature towards relative constancy, living things are changing dynamically all the time. Thus a fertilized egg develops into a foetus, a child into an adult, a pioneer ecosystem into a climax ecosystem and unicellular organisms (sometimes) into multicellular organisms. How does one reconcile this tendency towards change with the thesis of overall stability?

From the evolutionary point of view these processes of change do not violate the principle of stability so long as one sees them holistically. Individual generations or ontogenies can be regarded as feelers enabling the long-term evolutionary process—the Gaian process—to monitor its interactions with and thereby permit its adaptation to its spatio-temporal environment.

Seen cybernetically, ontogenetic development occurs along a closely integrated constellation of set-paths which Waddington refers to as "chreods" (from the Greek root *chre* it is necessary, and *odos* a route or path). The total constellation of chreods along which a system develops constitutes what Waddington refers to as the "epigenetic landscape"—the developmental path the system is constrained to follow by virtue of the instructions with which it is endowed and the homearchic constraints imposed upon it by the larger systems of which it is part. A developing system thereby displays "a certain lack of flexibility"; its development has

> a strong tendency to proceed to some definite end-point. For instance, the adult tissues such as muscle, nerve, lung, kidney etc., are quite distinct from one another and it is rather difficult to persuade developing cells to differentiate into something intermediate between these main types. Again, the animal as a whole will very often succeed in "regulating," that is to say, in reaching its normal adult state in spite of injuries or abnormal circumstances it may have met during the course of its development.[1]

This ability has been noticed by many students of development, among them Driesch who noted the remarkable "equipotentiality" of the sea-urchin embryo (see chapter 23). He and others also pointed to the ability of a fertilized egg to develop into a normal embryo even after undergoing severe amputations. This goal-seeking behavior of a developing embryo remains inexplicable in terms of mechanistic science.

The tendency of a developing system to maintain itself on its pre-set path along its constellation of chreods and to correct any disturbances that might divert it, Waddington refers to as "homeorhesis" (from the Greek *homeo*—same and *rhesis*—flow). Homeorhesis is the principle of homeostasis applied to a predetermined path or trajectory rather than to a fixed point in space-time. Orians refers to it as "trajectory stability," that he defines as "the property of a system to move towards some final end point or zone despite differences in starting points." This, he tells us, is the sort of stability which plants tend to achieve during plant succession, "where a single 'climax' state may be reached from a variety of starting points."[2] (Equifinality)

It is reasonably clear that a climax is not a point fixed in space and time. Life processes are dynamic, creative, intelligent and anticipatory. This means that, in changing environmental conditions, a living thing can develop in a new direction so as to achieve a new end-state: one which, on the basis of its model of its relationship with its environment, would appear to constitute a new climax and hence a position of still greater stability, one in which discontinuities would be still further reduced.

Of course, this process is subject to homearchic control by the Gaian hierarchy. It is Gaian homeostasis which homeorhetic systems seek to achieve—since this is a prerequisite of their own stability. During the course of this book, I shall seek to show that all life processes, including evolution—the Gaian Process—are homeorhetic regardless of the level of organization at which they occur (see chapter 62).

26

The Gaian process is not random

Man is the product of causes which had no prevision of the end they were achieving; that his origin, his growth, his hopes and fears, his loves and beliefs, are but the outcome of accidental collocations of atoms . . . all these things, if not quite beyond dispute, are yet so nearly certain that no philosophy which rejects them can hope to stand. Only within the scaffolding of these truths, only on the firm foundation of unyielding despair, can the soul's habitation henceforth be safely built.
Bertrand Russell

It is on the notion of randomness that geneticists have based their case against a benevolent or malevolent deity, and against there being any overall purpose or design in nature.
Sir Peter Medawar

That living things have been brought into being by purely random forces is a gratuitous statement, which we regard as wrong and as irreconcilable with the facts.
P.P. Grassé

THE NOTION THAT THE ECOSPHERE and everything in it are the product of pure chance is critical to the paradigm of science. Jacques Monod refers to the mechanism of determining the evolution of life and of culture as "a gigantic lottery" or as "nature's roulette." "Chance alone" he sees,

> as the source of every innovation, of all creation in the biosphere. Pure chance, absolutely free but blind, is at the very root of the stupendous edifice of evolution. This central concept of modern biology is no longer one among other conceivable hypotheses. It is *the sole conceivable hypothesis*, the only one that squares with observed and tested fact. And nothing warrants the supposition—or the hope—that on this score our position is likely ever to be revised.[1]

Many neo-Darwinists however (including Dobjzansky and Julian Huxley) have adopted a less extreme position. They admit that mutations may well be caused by factors that we ignore. However they insist that

> they are random *in relation to evolution*. Their effects are not related to the needs of the organism, or to the condition in which it is placed. They occur *without reference to their biological uses*.[2]

This means that though something makes a mother feed her child, that something is unconnected with the child's need to be fed by its mother.

In the real world, however, life processes are not random, even in this less extreme sense of the term. Art styles, for instance, closely reflect the character of the cultures in which they developed. The clothes people wear are indicative of the image of themselves they wish to communicate to others. The way people walk, eat, light cigarettes, blow their noses, do up their shoelaces—all convey some information as to the personality of the individuals concerned.

Behavior is indeed so ordered, so little random, that it is questionable whether people are capable of behaving in a random way. This appears to be confirmed by various experiments such as those described by the psychologists Anne Broadhurst and W.R. Ramsey who experimented with a panel of seventy-two people by asking them to repeat in time to a metronome a series of numbers, one to nine, in as random a manner as possible. They found that "even when subjects try to be random, there is a high degree of stereotype."[3] It has been suggested that it is even possible to identify a particular individual by his "random number matrix" and also that a pathological configuration of a matrix may reveal a mental illness and a set of random numbers has actually been used to enable a practitioner to differentiate between brain-damaged patients and normal subjects.

The British cybernetician Stafford Beer also rejects the view that randomness is a natural feature of behavior in the natural world.

> There are random number tables on my book-shelf; there are computer tapes for producing pseudo-random numbers next door; there is a large electronic machine for generating noise upstairs; down the road there is a roomful of equipment designed to hurl thousands of little metal balls about in a random way; and I use ten-sided dice as paper-weights. The upkeep of this armoury is considerable; think of all the time we spend trying to ensure that these artefacts produce results which are "genuinely random"—whatever that may mean. This tremendous practical problem of guaranteeing disorderliness ought to be enough to satisfy any systems man that *nothing is more unnatural than chaos*.[4]

How then do scientists know that a process is random? How do they know it is not part of an orderly pattern that they simply have not been able to identify? Lamarck is often quoted as stating that the word randomness only expresses our ignorance of causes. The French physicist Henri Poincaré said much the same thing, as did the French theoretical biologist Albert Jacquard, and also Waddington, in particular with regard to the randomness of genetic mutations.

Recent studies have tended to confirm this view. Biologist John Cairns and his colleagues at Harvard University recently conducted studies which suggest that mutations are not random but are on the contrary highly directive. At first, Cairns's studies were dismissed by the scientific establishment; however, Barry Hall of Rochester

University has now come up with similar results. He has found that certain mutations in bacteria occur more often when they are useful to the bacteria than when they are not. Cairns refers to such mutations as directed mutations while Hall refers to them instead as "Cairnsian mutations," in honor of their original discoverer.

There is every reason to doubt too the concept of "genetic drift" which has been postulated to explain evolutionary changes that do not appear to have been "selected." This concept is far less in use today than it was twenty years ago and is increasingly seen as a convenient device for masking our ignorance of the role of such changes. Indeed, more and more processes which originally appeared to be random are found upon closer examination to be highly functional and indeed *purposive*.

However, one does not need experimental "evidence" for rejecting the idea that evolution is based on random mutations. We know that single gene mutations can only determine extremely superficial changes. Significant changes can only be brought about by changes occurring to a whole constellation of associated genes (polygeny). This means that "for a functional unit to make an adaptive change," as Rupert Riedl notes, "requires not just one happy accident, but *an accumulation* of happy accidents."[5] Does this seem likely? Waddington did not believe it in spite of his insistence on remaining within the neo-Darwinian fold. He admitted that to suggest that evolution was based on selection from random mutations was "like suggesting that if we went on throwing bricks together into heaps, we should eventually be able to choose for ourselves the most desirable house."[6] Murray Eden rejects the thesis on the grounds of its sheer mathematical improbability. It is as unlikely as it is that "a child arranging at random a printer's supply of letters would compose the first 20 lines of Virgil's *Aeneid*."

How then can the absurd notion of the randomness of life processes have been raised to the elated status of "the central concept of modern biology"? I shall suggest some possible answers. To begin with, randomness was postulated as an argument against teleology, which was seen as ushering in all sorts of unacceptable supernatural principles such as God or various forms of vitalism. Secondly, it is essential in order to rationalize the reductionist nature of modern science. If the biosphere displays order, worse still, if the whole evolutionary process is seen as a single coordinated strategy, involving all life processes at all levels of organization, then the reductionist approach would make no sense. Thirdly, the postulate of randomness is also required to justify statistical method which, in turn, rationalizes other key features of the paradigm of science—the principle of causation for instance, and reductionism itself.

Finally, randomness is seen as essential because it is impossible to justify the Promethean enterprise to which our industrial society is committed and which involves systematically transforming the biosphere so that it may best satisfy short-term commercial interests if it is seen as organized to achieve a grand overall project of its own. By seeing the ecosphere as random, on the other hand, it is possible to make out that what order there is in the world has been created by science, technology and industry, rather than by God or the evolutionary process. "The cardinal tendency of progress," as J.D. Bernal writes, "is the replacement of an indifferent chance environment by a *deliberately created one*."[7]

The insistence by mainstream scientists on maintaining the principle of the randomness of life processes in the teeth of all the evidence, both empirical and theoretical, shows what a negligible role is played by "scientific method," or by human rationality in any shape or form in the formulation and acceptance, by the scientific community, of even the most fundamental principles of modern science. This particular principle, like many others, is accepted for one reason only: it is essential to help make sense of the paradigm of science which, by the same token, it helps so effectively to rationalize and hence legitimize.

27

Gaian life processes are purposive

~

The problem of evolution is now essentially solved and the mechanism of adaptation is known. It turns out to be basically materialistic, with no sign of purpose as a working variable in life history, and with any possible Purpose pushed back to the incomprehensible position of First Cause . . . Man is the result of a purposeless and materialistic process that did not have him in mind. He was not planned.
George Gaylord Simpson

Purpose is not imported into nature, and need not be puzzled over as a strange or divine something else that gets inside and makes life go . . . it is simply implicit in the fact of biological organization.
Herbert Mueller

THE EVIDENCE FOR the purposiveness of life processes at every level of organization within the hierarchy of the ecosphere is so great that its denial seems inconceivable. Who could deny that the evolution of gills and fins by fish is purposive to enabling them to breathe and move about in their aquatic environment, or that the development of mammary glands by the females of all species of mammals is purposive to feeding their babies or that the human milk provided in this way is designed to satisfy the nutritional needs of their young in the first one or two years of their lives?

To Charles Sherrington it seemed obvious that the embryological process, whereby "a pin's head ball of cells in the course of so many weeks becomes a child," is purposive.[1] Joseph Barcroft points to

> the levers laid down in gristle, becoming bone when wanted for the heavier pull of muscle which will clothe them. Lungs, solid glands, yet arranged to hollow out at a few minutes notice when the necessary air shall enter. Limb-buds, futile at their appearing and yet deliberately appearing, in order to become limbs in readiness for existence where they will be all-important.[2]

Barcroft is particularly impressed by the development of embryonic organs, useless at the time to their possessor, but which will be indispensible later on during the course of its development. "Organs of skin, ear, eye, nose, tongue," he writes, "superfluous all of them in the watery dark where formed, yet each unhaltingly preparing to enter a daylit, airy, object-full manifold world which they will be wanted to report on."[3]

Purposiveness is also evident in physiology. As Gavin de Beer notes:

> The structure of an animal shows a number of exquisitely delicate adjustments; the splinters inside a bone are situated exactly where they are required to withstand the pressure to which the bone is subjected; the fibres of a tendon lie accurately along the line of strain between a

muscle and the bone to which it is attached; centers of nerve cells in the brain are situated close to the ends of the nerve fibres, from which they habitually receive impulses.[4]

The same principle is equally evident in animal behavior. For Bierens de Haan,

> that the weaving of the web by the spider is purposeful for the catching of insects, and the collecting and storing of caterpillars by the wasp purposeful for the nourishing of its future larva are facts that are so self-evident that it is not necessary further to elucidate them.[5]

If life processes achieve their purpose it is because they are under control, but they could not be controlled in the first place unless they had a purpose to achieve. Control serves to assure that life processes achieve their pre-set purpose. This is clear if we consider that a basic ingredient of control is "negative feedback" *which is totally useless to a non-purposive system.*

An essential constituent of control is perception, and perception is essentially purposive. As Keith Oatley notes "the way we see is in terms of our human purpose in the environment."[6] What we see "depends on our particular purpose at the time, what we are trying to do, what aspect of the thing we are seeing that is relevant to what we are trying to achieve." What is more, it is not just in terms of a short-term purpose that we see things but ultimately in terms of our long-term strategic purpose, that itself must be seen in the overall context of the purpose of our society, our ecosystem and the entire ecosphere.

Thoughtful scientists recognize this as a serious problem. Monod for instance, as Gunther Stent notes, insists that "the cornerstone of scientific method is to postulate that nature is 'objective,' which means systematically denying the purposive character of life, however, such purposiveness is nevertheless *prima facie* apparent."[7] Monod admits that "this self-same contradiction is in fact the central problem of biology."[8] But it is only for modern scientists that it is a problem, for their ability to understand the functioning of the ecosphere is seriously hindered by their adherence to the paradigm of science. In the light of the world-view of ecology, on the other hand, purposiveness is a necessary feature of life processes at all levels of organization, and in particular that of the ecosphere whose critical order they seek purposefully to assure.

28

Life processes are dynamic

—

The distinctive aspect of primitive thought is the accent that it places on the dynamic aspect of living things, while in Western scientific thought, on the other hand, the accent is put on the static aspect of things.

Placide Tempels

Even under constant external conditions, and in the absence of external stimuli, the organism is not a passive, but a basically active system.

Ludwig von Bertalanffy

Almost from the moment a creature is hatched or born it lashes out at the environment, be it liquid or solid, with cilia, flagellae, or muscles; it swims, crawls, glides, pulsates; it kicks, yelps, breathes, feeds on the environment. It does not merely adapt to the environment but adapts the environment to its needs—it eats and drinks its environment, fights and mates with it, burrows and builds in it.

Arthur Koestler

THAT LIFE PROCESSES are dynamic was self-evident to vernacular man. For Father Placide Tempels, author of a seminal book on Bantu philosophy, it is traditional man's accent on the dynamic aspect of living things that characterizes his view of the world. This view contrasts only too starkly with the modern scientific view of living things as essentially static and passive, a view that is consistent with the paradigm of science but not with our knowledge of the real world (see chapter 54).

All the different processes involved in adaptive behavior are necessarily dynamic. Perception is dynamic. Signals are not merely received, they are detected; the organism seeks out those signals that are seen to be relevant to its behavior pattern in the light of its mental model of its relationship with its environment. Mental activities do not merely occur to interpret external stimuli, they also occur quite spontaneously. Even in the absence of any external stimuli, the brain remains constantly active. We think, in fact, even when sitting in an armchair in a dark room.

Erich von Holst has shown that primitive locomotor activities function without the aid of external stimuli. Movements continue to occur even after "the connection of motoric to sensory nerves have been severed."[1] Konrad Lorenz has pointed to the existence of what he calls "innate releasing mechanisms" (IRM) which play a dominant role in our behavior and can function without the presence of external stimuli.[2] This fits in very well with Granit's description of nerve cells that are specified at birth, that are not affected by outside stimuli and that are subject to the presence of genetically determined instructions whether or not they are operative and whether or not they are triggered off by an environmental stimulus.[3]

It must be clear from our own experience that we are not only led to do things by the mere presence of an external stimulus. When I am hungry I shall look for food; it is not just the sight of food that triggers off my food-seeking behavior. It may undoubtedly stimulate my appetite, but appetite there must be. A good indication that this must be so is furnished by the possibility of redirecting different behavioral trends such as aggression into relatively harmless activities such as sport, rather than into destructive ones such as war (see chapter 40).

When the normal outlet for a behavioral tendency or urge is unavailable, living things can even imagine it or create it. Thus the Comanche Indians of Nevada, once they were confined to a reservation and deprived of their hereditary enemies, compensated for this by increasing the number and the threatening nature of the evil spirits with which they saw themselves surrounded, thereby creating or imagining the stimuli needed to trigger off their aggressive tendencies.[4] In the field of sex, this could not be more evident. If the normal stimulus that triggers off sexual behavior is not available, others are sought out, and the degree of improvisation seems considerable. In other words, we modify, or even invent, by our own efforts, the stimuli that alone are supposed to trigger off behavioral responses. This dynamism what is more, does not only occur at the behavioral level, but is a feature of all life processes.

Alister Hardy, like Jean Piaget, has pointed to the close relationship between the dynamism of behavior and that of evolution. "It is adaptations which are due to the animal's behavior, to its restless exploration of its surroundings, to its initiative, that distinguish the main diverging lines of evolution . . . giving the lines of runners, climbers, burrowers, swimmers and conquerors of the air."[5] Evolving systems are not puppets, controlled by the whims of a distant environmental puppeteer as Darwin and his successors have implied. On the contrary, it is the dynamism of living things that makes evolution possible.

29

Life processes are creative

—

I am astonished at the amount of creative force, if such an expression
may be used, displayed on these small barren and rocky islands [The
Galapagos].
Charles Darwin

Creativity is ultimate. It is not a philosophical postulate but an observed
fact that creative activity or formative process is an intrinsic property of
anything in the natural cosmos that is known to man.
A.N. Whitehead

CLEARLY, HUMANS HAVE a vast capacity for improvisation and have developed diverse and highly imaginative cultural patterns for dealing with the challenges of life in different environmental conditions. The creative capacity of non-human animals is also well documented. Living things have developed the most diverse strategies for adapting to different and often highly challenging environments. Thus a warm-blooded animal can learn to survive the rigors of the winter by developing a thick fur coat, by going into hibernation, by migrating to a warmer area, or by lighting a camp fire. Desert plants can learn to avoid dessication by developing leaves covered with oily substances or that become spine-like, or that are simply shed during the dry season or by changing their life cycle so that it is compressed into the wet season.

The creative development of new and often more complex forms of life is an essential feature of evolution. For instance, the development of the lichen provides a remarkable example of innovation arising from the partnership of two different organisms, a fungus and an alga. Lichens possess many morphological, chemical and physiological attributes that are absent from either partner when it grows independently.

Not only is nature creative and innovative in the extreme, but creative and innovative changes can occur very quickly as adaptations to environmental challenges. Consider how mosquitoes have adapted to DDT. According to David Merrell, resistance was first reported in 1946, and by 1965 it had been noted in one hundred and sixty-five pest species. More impressive than the speed at which this resistance had developed, were the very different strategies exploited by the mosquitoes for dealing with this new menace. Some mosquitoes learned not to alight on the walls that had been sprayed with DDT, others developed a thick cuticle that it could not penetrate. Others accumulated more body fat, thereby increasing their capacity to assimilate fat-soluble DDT. The nerves of others became less sensitive to DDT. Still others developed an enzyme that breaks down DDT into a harmless compound. The diversity of different mechanisms made use of by mosquitoes to adapt to DDT spraying programs, as Merrell notes, "bears testimony to the opportunism of evolution."[1]

Mainstream science seeks to explain this extraordinary innovativeness and creativity in terms of the neo-Darwinian thesis. The genetic resistance to DDT, Merrell insists, "already existed in the populations and was not induced by exposure to DDT."[2] But the DDT Molecule *did not exist in nature* before it was produced synthetically in the 1940s. How then could the mosquito's gene-pool have prior knowledge that this foreign substance would one day be synthesized by man and released into the environment? The answer, we are told, is by chance, by random pre-adaptation. This is the only scientifically respectable explanation of creativity—the only one reconcilable with such essential features of the paradigm of science as causality, mechanomorphism and statistical theory. Chance in the context of evolution means random mutations. It is only to them that evolutionary creativity can be imputed. "Natural selection," Merrell writes, "has a creative aspect . . . because it has a causal aspect . . . Looking back at a cause we can recognize it as creative; it has brought about something which could not have been predicted—something which cannot be referred back to antecedent events."[3]

It is like a "game of chance," he tells us; it is possible to conceive all the possible outcomes of the game—indeed, to calculate the relative probability of each one of them—but it is not possible to foresee exactly which one it will be. The scientific notion of causality is not thereby creative—in the true sense of the term, for a like cause must create a like effect and all Merrell is saying is that we cannot predict which particular causal relationship is going to occur as that will be decided by natural selection.

But natural selection, in spite of what our mainstream scientists tell us, cannot be a source of creative evolutionary change. One can understand that by selecting the most viable living things and allowing them to reproduce, their characteristics will be transmitted to the next generation which will become correspondingly more viable, but this is only possible *if living things already possess the capacity to transmit such characteristics to the next generation.* Billiard balls cannot, and it is difficult to see how they might be made to evolve by natural selection however much variability they might exhibit. As von Bertalanffy notes "selection presupposes self-maintenance, adaptability, reproduction, etc. of the living system. These cannot therefore, be the effect of selection. This is the oft-discussed circularity of the selectionist argument. Proto-organisms would arise, and organisms further evolve by chance mutations and subsequent selection. But, in order to do so, *they must already have had the essential attributes of life.*"[4]

For Woodger, the neo-Darwinian thesis is unacceptable on this count alone. "An explanation of this kind," he writes, "can only make out a case for itself by *begging the fundamental question at issue—* the essential characteristics of an organism have to be surreptitiously introduced in vague general language." They are so introduced largely by attributing to natural selection—the mechanical sorting machine— qualities, such as creativity, *which no machine can possibly display,* and that are, in effect, little more than the very "internal factors" whose role in determining the evolutionary process neo-Darwinists are at such pains to deny.[5]

That the extraordinary and highly complex ecosphere can be regarded as the product of such a crude process as selection from random mutations has to be seen in the context of other clumsy efforts by mainstream science to maintain the myth of mechanomorphism. Machines cannot create: their output (the effect) is a function of their input (the cause). It was to make sure that embryogenesis or development conformed to this principle that the theory of "preformation" was developed, according to which a fertilized egg contained a miniature replica of a child—the end product of the process. However, eventually it became clear that the information contained in the fertilized egg was nowhere near sufficient to give rise to the child, and preformation gave rise to epigenesis, a theory that is very difficult to explain in terms of the paradigm of science.

One of the most astonishing feats of creativity in the natural world is the working of the immune system, the most likely explanation for which is the process of genetic recombination. Immunologists tell us that a biological organism can produce 10^7 or so different antibodies —that is to say 10^7 different proteins designed to repel specific threats. All sorts of attempts have been made by mainstream scientists to explain this in the language of the neo-Darwinian orthodoxy. They have failed. One possibility with regard to our mosquito populations, for instance, is that though they were not endowed before the development of DDT with the genes that would confer resistance against that poison, they were, nevertheless, endowed with cells containing bits and pieces of the genes: a kit of components, as Philip Leder puts it, and those components are shuffled in the cells of the immune system which can lead to a different result in each of millions of lines of cells. Individual mutations amplify the diversity and, as a result, in the mature descendants of each line, a unique gene is assembled whose information is expressed in the form of a unique antibody.

If this is so, then it must be extremely unlikely that the mutations referred to are in any way random. The immune system, like the genome, is self-regulating and capable of maintaining its homeostasis in the face of external or internal challenges. That mutations are often not random but highly directive or purposive has now been established by Cairns and others. That such mutations should be brought about by the homearchic action of the genome or of any other cybernism such as that associated with the functioning of our immune system seems more than likely. Whether recombinations together with such induced mutations provide a sufficient explanation for the massive evolutionary leaps that have given rise to metazoans, vertebrates and mammals is uncertain. Grassé considers that this requires the development of new gene loci that previously had no particular functions.[6]

All in all, the creativity of the living world is only a problem if we insist in trying to reconcile it with the paradigm of science. It is totally reconcilable, on the other hand, with—and is indeed an essential feature of—the world-view of ecology.

30

Life processes are anticipatory

~

The essential nature of mind is to govern present action by anticipation of the future in the light of past experiences, to make, in fact, effects precede and determine their causes.
William McDougall

Every perceptual act anticipates its own confirmation by subsequent acts.
A. N. Whitehead

Man has lost the capacity to foresee and to forestall. He will end by destroying the Earth.
Albert Schweitzer

FOR NATURAL SYSTEMS to achieve their goal of maintaining their own stability and that of the Gaian hierarchy, they must be able to predict the changes to which they may have to adapt as well as the environmental effects of such adaptations. There is every reason to suppose that they are well capable of doing so—providing such changes occur within their tolerance range (see chapter 42).

Thus the Didiera of Madagascar, the Baobab tree of Africa and certain cacti seem able to store just the right amount of water required to help tide them over dry periods. It does not stretch the meaning of the word too far to say that they must be *predicting* the weather changes involved. Green turtles travel three thousand miles from the coast of South America to Ascension Island in the middle of the Atlantic Ocean where they lay their eggs. When embarking on such a journey, they can only be seen as *predicting* that their reproductive period is approaching and that, by laying their eggs on Ascension Island, rather than anywhere else, they will give their young the best chance of survival.

Many insects such as monarch butterflies, ladybird beetles, hover-flies, noctuid moths and other species migrate when winter approaches to warmer climes. They do not do so, however, because the cold has become insupportable for, as C.G.Johnson notes, they begin to migrate *long before cold weather sets in*.

> Neither food shortage nor "intolerable overcrowding" are evident to the human observer at the time of departure . . . The migration, therefore, usually comes in advance of any obvious change for the worse in living conditions.[1]

Such examples are not exceptional (see chapter 49). As H.Kalmus writes:

> Anticipatory actions occur widely in the organic world. A predator catching a moving prey, a tennis player hitting a ball, a spider

constructing a web, even a flower displaying its visual and olfactory attractions, all can be said to anticipate future events in their environments.[2]

Prediction is an essential component of perception, the first step in self-regulation. What people see is not a static image, but a hypothesis as to its history, why it is there, how it is likely to change and what the consequences will be. Perception, in fact, *involves prediction*.

Modern science cannot admit that living things predict. They are supposed to be passive and stage-managed by an external agent. In any case, they cannot predict the future, for, we are told, knowledge is only acquired by observation and one cannot observe what has not actually occurred. This explains to what lengths mainstream scientists will go to deny that prediction plays a necessary role in adaptive behavior. Thus the behavior of dogs in Pavlov's famous experiments has been interpreted in such a way *as to avoid having to admit that the dogs are making predictions*. When a dog is trained to salivate at the sound of a bell announcing food, it is seen as responding in a blind and unintelligent manner to the ring of a bell *as if the bell were food*. A "conditioned stimulus" is seen in this way as simply replacing the "unconditioned stimulus."

It is becoming increasingly difficult to maintain this myth. Indeed, C.L.Hull, a behaviorist and experimental psychologist inspired by Ivan Pavlov, sought towards the end of his life to modify his theories so as to reconcile them with the fact that living things display interest, planning, foresight, fore-knowledge, expectancy, purpose and so on —qualities whose very existence he and his predecessors would have previously denied.[3]

Prediction is not only possible on the basis of the information contained in the brain, but also on that organized in the genome. L.Z. Young has pointed out that the genes have to perform "a *task analogous* to prediction." The genes of the polar bear, for instance, are predicting that this great beast will live in the Arctic snow and that the snow-white coat will help to camouflage it from its prospective prey. If suddenly there were a radical warming of the Arctic area these predictions might then prove to be wrong, and, partly as a result, polar bears might not survive.

Thorpe is also struck by the ability of the genes to predict the sequence of chemical processes in metabolism. He quotes M. Dixon and E. C. Webb who ask

> how the gene-forming enzyme 2.4.2.14 "knows" that phosphoribosyl pyrophosphate will be converted by the consecutive action of ten or more different enzymes into a purine nucleotide, or how the gene for the first enzyme of histidine biosynthesis, which acts on the same compound, "knows" that its product will be converted into histidine by a different series of enzymes. Even with this information, how do these genes "know" what amino-acid sequences in their enzymes will act as specific centers combining with purine nucleotides or histidine respectively?[4]

For Dixon and Webb, this ability to predict is only possible if we postulate a mechanism "whereby information derived from the metabolic processes themselves is transmitted back to the genes and therefore incorporated in the form of polynucleotide sequences."[5] However, the existence of such a feedback mechanism violates Francis Crick's central dogma and is irreconcilable with the neo-Darwinian thesis.

Waddington accepts that evolution must be based on prediction. He tries to reconcile this with the neo-Darwinian thesis by attributing to the environment—that neo-Darwinists have never bothered to define —the capacity to select species for their ability to deal with future as well as present problems, producing "a system which is stable enough to deal with difficulties that may arise many generations in the future."[6] However, if it is to selection that we must attribute the capacity to achieve this long-term stability, then this crude mechanical process must be endowed with the ability to predict the future, for how else can it create precisely those genes and gene combinations required to permit an organism to adapt to conditions that have not yet occurred?

Without the capacity to predict, natural selection would not, among other things, be able to bring into being an organ that is still in its embryonic stage and is not yet really functional, for how else could embryonic and non-functional organs have an adaptive function in the short-term that would justify their selection by the environment? Clearly they could not. For Grassé, this provides yet another reason for rejecting the notion that natural selection plays a determinant role in evolution. If it did, then we would have to attribute to natural selection "the gift of divination, or of prophecy."[7]

For a living thing to predict the future is only possible on the basis of a model of its relationship with the Gaian hierarchy of which it is part. The accuracy of its predictions will not only depend on the accuracy with which its mental model represents this relationship, but also on the stability of the Gaian hierarchy, and hence upon the extent to which the living thing has adapted to it, biologically, socially and cognitively.

Chthonic man had no difficulty in predicting the future, for he inhabited a climax ecosystem and knew how to earn his living in it without disrupting its critical functioning in any way. In such conditions, he would predict with reasonable certainty that the future would be very much like the present, that in turn, would closely resemble the past.

Today, we are bringing about the most dramatic possible changes to the living world in which we live and our scientists have no hope of predicting their consequences, for the methodology that enables them to understand the functioning of the constituents of the ecosphere for the purpose of making such changes does not enable them to understand the effects of these changes on the Gaian hierarchy as a whole. Our scientists are capable of producing synthetic organic chemicals, but quite incapable of determining how exposure to them will affect the health of living things. They have developed methods of extracting fossil fuels from the bowels of the Earth, using them to generate power that drives countless devices to achieve all sorts of different and often impressive goals. However they are quite incapable of predicting, with any sort of accuracy, what the effect will be on biological organisms, societies, ecosystems and now on global climate.

If we are to be capable once again to predict the future with any sort of accuracy, it will not be by developing new technologies for this purpose, however ingenious and however sophisticated, but by dramatically reducing the impact of our activities on the ecosphere, thereby creating the conditions in which its critical order and hence its predictability can be restored.

31

Living things seek to understand their relationship with their environment

~

In animal and human behavior, trials are not chosen randomly.
Keith Oatley

Learning takes place not simply as the emission of a new response when
an error occurs. Rather it involves *understanding* the particular structure
of the mistake and deciding what to do next.
Keith Oatley

A LIVING THING apprehends its environment by detecting data that appear relevant to its behavior pattern and interpreting them in the light of its mental model of its relationship with it, within as wide a context as is necessary for the purposes of determining the appropriate adaptive response. This means that it seeks to establish their meaning or to *understand* them.

This thesis is, of course, irreconcilable with current wisdom on the subject. Behavioral psychologists fall into a number of schools, but for a long time, the dominant one was that of Behaviorism. It is associated with the work of Edward Thorndyke and E. R. Guthrie, also with John Broadus Watson and particularly and more recently with B. F. Skinner. Though many behavioral psychologists, such as the members of the Gestalt school, and more recently of the "Cognitive" or "Mentalist" school that we associate with the name of R. W. Sperry, did not accept Behaviorism, it remains true that it still underlies much of the thinking in this field. One reason is that it is the view that best fits in with the paradigm of science that rationalizes the methodology that experimental psychologists and ethologists must use if they are to be taken seriously by the scientific community. This highly reductionist theory of behavior is roughly as follows.

Living things apprehend their environment by acquiring sensations or "sense data"—the atoms of perception—which provide them with measurable atoms of information or "bits" (see appendix 2). It is accepted that living things have a memory but the memory too is atomized—the atoms of memory being referred to as "engrams" or memory traces. The atom of behavior is the reflex, a mechanism whereby an environmental event referred to as a "stimulus" triggers off a blind and automatic response. As far back as 1906, Sherrington wrote that the "simple reflex is probably a purely abstract conception . . . if not a probable fiction."[1] Herrick describes it as a pure abstraction, a "mere manifestation of what is clearly a very coordinated pattern of behavior."[2] However such criticisms have not deterred others from presenting the process even more mechanistically in terms of inputs and outputs, the stimulus being the input and the response the output, like a machine that switches on when the button is pressed.

Learning has to be explained of course, and mainstream scientists have done so very ingeniously, making it appear random, atomistic and mechanistic as is required by the paradigm of science. The learning process is not seen by them as occurring in any necessary order; living things are seen as simply responding to their environment in a purely random way. A rat trying to find its way out of a maze, for instance, will try out in random order a whole series of trial and error moves corresponding to the Darwinist's random variations and the random genetic mutations of the neo-Darwinists. If one such move is crowned with success, it is said to be "reinforced," the Darwinian and neo-Darwinian equivalent of being "selected." In laboratory experiments, rats are given rewards for making what the experimenter judges to be the right moves, and are often also given penalties, such as being administered electric shocks for the wrong ones—rewards and penalties being seen in the Benthamite tradition as the only motivations of living things.

Behaviorists attribute remarkable powers to reinforcement, just as neo-Darwinists do to selection. Thus Skinner informs his readers that "a man talks to himself . . . because of the *reinforcements* he receives";[3] that thinking is in fact "behavior which automatically affects the behavior and is *reinforcing* because it does so";[4] that "just as the musician plays and composes what he is *reinforced* by hearing, or as the artist paints what *reinforces* him visually, so the speaker engaged in verbal fantasy says what he is *reinforced* by hearing, or writes what he is *reinforced* by reading,"[5] while the creative artist is "controlled entirely by the contingencies of *reinforcement*."[6]

It is astonishing that serious people can really believe that the incredibly subtle and sophisticated behavior of living things can be explained in terms of so crude and rudimentary a mechanism. If we really believed it, as Michael Polanyi points out, we would also have to accept that "if a dog were consistently offered food whenever it was shown the radiogram of diseased lungs and no food when shown the radiogram of healthy lungs, it should learn to diagnose pulmonary diseases."[7]

Pure trial and error learning, however, except perhaps in the most rudimentary possible forms of life, is mere fantasy. This has been realized even within the ranks of experimental psychologists. Thus Karl Lashley has insisted strongly that normal animals do not behave in a random fashion. Oatley agrees: "In animal or human behavior," he maintains, "trials are not chosen randomly."[8] On the contrary, as Herrick notes, "the learning process is ordinarily directive and it is an organized activity, never a mere random fumbling."[9] I. Krechevsky considers that "we must change our description of the learning process so as to recognize the existence of organized and systematic responses at all stages of the process."[10] Indeed, the rat, "when placed in an unsolvable situation, does not respond in a helter skelter chance fashion, but makes all sorts of integrated, and informed attempts at solution. These systematic responses are, partly at least, initiated by the animal and are not altogether merely a resultant of the immediately presented external situation." This means that such animals are not just reacting blindly to various stimuli, but are seeking to interpret them correctly and thus *understand their meaning*; that, of course, involves establishing the role of the thing or event that attracts their attention within the context of the larger spatio-temporal system of which it is part.

When the Tahitians first saw a horse, introduced to the island by de Bougainville's French sailors, they immediately classified it in terms of the mammal they knew most resembled it . . . the pig. It was obviously closer to the horse than the other two mammals of which they had any experience: the dog and the Polynesian rat. Very sensibly, they referred to the horse as a "man-carrying pig." This was not a robot-like response; it was a sophisticated attempt to understand this strange beast in the light of their experience of similar beasts. There is no reason to suppose that rats do not do likewise.

Some of Lashley's experiments cast considerable light on this question. He showed that rats with large cortical lesions could learn to solve a problem in about the same time as normal rats but their behavior was simplified. They did so less elegantly. They stumbled on the solutions rather than find them in a more systematic or logical way. In other words, they did not really *understand* the nature of the problems they had to solve.

This reminds one of the behavior of children brought up in isolation, whose model of the world remains stunted and rudimentary. Peter of Hanover, the celebrated eighteenth century isolate brought to London as a curiosity, ended up working as a farm laborer. He would perform his tasks well, but could never really *understand* their meaning. When asked to load a wheelbarrow with manure, he would do so very efficiently but, not understanding the point of what he was doing, would proceed to empty it and fill it up again repeatedly until made to stop.

To understand something is to determine its function within a larger spatio-temporal system. This means that widening the context in which we study it will increase our knowledge of its function. This is how a detective tries to understand a crime. Each clue is related to an increasingly wider set of events, gradually acquiring ever greater meaning. Other clues are treated in the same way, until eventually, the crime is reconstructed, and the detective can be said to *have understood* exactly what has occurred. There is no other way of proceeding. The clue in isolation from its context cannot be interpreted, for it has no meaning and constitutes data, not information.

Living things, except for the very simplest ones, do not behave like robots. They are intelligent beings and whether mainstream science likes it or not, they seek desperately to understand their relationship with the world about them.

32

Living systems are intelligent

Of all the fictions with which mankind has allowed itself to be fooled,
none is vainer than the belief that the "instinct" of animals is absolutely
different from the "reason" of men, and that the lower races are a dumb
and soulless automaton, separated from the human by a deep and
impassable gulf.
Henry S. Salt

Existing scientific data indicate a greater degree of intellectual
communality among primates and probably a greater communality
among all other animals, than has been commonly recognized.
H. F. Harlow

THE NOTION THAT man's mental processes are categorically distinct from those of other animals is a gratuitous assumption based on no valid knowledge of any kind. In particular it is gratuitous to insist, as mainstream science does today, that only humans are *intelligent*— especially since the term has never even been satisfactorily defined. Admittedly, we have intelligence tests, but as Herrick notes "we do not know just what it is they measure."[1] Some authors, among them Ashis Nandy, suggest that intelligence is little more than "that which is tested by intelligence tests."[2]

A. Binet and T.H. Simon, the pioneers of intelligence testing, consider that "to judge well, to comprehend well, to reason well, these are the essential activities of intelligence."[3] For A.W. Heim, "intelligent activity consists in grasping the essentials in a given situation and responding appropriately to them."[4] Harlow defines intelligence as "all round intellectual ability, to learn, understand, improvise and create"[5]—qualities that all living things—in varying degrees—tend to display. With regard to learning, for instance, Harlow considers that

> there is no scientific evidence of a break . . . between primate and non-primate forms. Emergence from the oceans to the land produced no sudden expansion of learning ability. Indeed, there is no evidence that any sharp break ever appeared in the evolutionary development.[6]

Major Hingston would have agreed with Harlow.[7] For seventeen years he observed the behavior of lowly insects in the tropical forests of India and he concluded that they solved their problems much the same way as we do. "The notion that insects are nothing but animated machines," he wrote, and "that they lead purely reflex lives, these assertions I believe to be quite unfounded." Regardless of what particular mental qualities we judge as important, Hingston showed that insects seem to display them. They are quite capable of "reasoning" for instance. Hingston noted how dung-rolling beetles, when their ball was pinned to a long stake, examined the ball, discovered the stake and freed the ball by cutting it in two and putting the separate bits together. They are also quite capable of adapting means to ends. Thus, the wasp, *mellinus arvensis*, Hingston found, can capture flies on pads of dung. It normally does so by sneaking about, but on one occasion when the flies were particularly active, one of these wasps was seen to lie on the dung, simulating death and simply waited for the victims to walk into its grasp. "Is this not a plan perfectly adapted to meet a given end?" Hingston asks.[8]

Insects are quite able to improvise strategies for dealing with environmental challenges. Hingston describes how Swynnerton's ants dealt with a poisoned spine caterpillar. They ingeniously blocked the poisonous openings with crumbs of Earth and then amputated the spine. They are also capable of displaying judgment. Hingston describes the wasp that dragged its large victim to the opening of its nest. Before trying to get its victim in, the wasp went backwards and forwards between its victim and the hole, until, having "decided" that the victim would not fit, set about methodically to enlarge the hole.

They are also able to foresee the effects of their acts. Hingston describes a mason wasp, that, in building its nest, did not just build one cell after another in a random way, but started off by laying the foundation plan for all the cells of the finished nest. They are well able too to remember past experiences. A particular ant, Hingston assures us, can remember the place where it has found food after a prolonged period of time. A hive-bee can do the same thing. Wasps, he assures us, can not only remember one spot but can "keep in their minds a geographical picture of the territory which they work."

From all this evidence, Hingston claims that

> we are not justified in making barriers between insects and human mentality. I mean we have no right to regard their minds as being totally different in kind. In their main essential characteristics, *the minds of these humble creatures operate in the same way as the mind of man*, and this harmonizes well with those laws of continuity, which, as our knowledge of this world grows, become more and more firmly established.[9]

Mainstream science is unimpressed by these arguments. Non-human living things are indeed capable of very remarkable achievements, but these, it is insisted, are the products of *instinct* not of intelligence.

Yet man's behavior is as governed by his instincts as is that of other animals. Our intelligence does not lead us to substitute new goals for those set by our instincts. It merely enables us to satisfy them *with greater discrimination and in a greater diversity of different conditions* than can non-human animals. In normal conditions—those that fall within our tolerance range—there is no conflict between our instincts and our intelligence. Our instincts do not lure us, as MacLean and Koestler suggest, into "primitive types of behavior against the better judgment of our intelligence."

If the term intelligence is to be used in a functional manner, there is no reason why it should be limited to the behavior of organisms; on the contrary, it should be applied to all life processes. Lucien Cuenot, the Belgian theoretical biologist, goes so far as to attribute to the cell "a sort of intelligence and indeed, an eminent power equivalent to the purposiveness that is apparent in human behavior."[10] Piaget feels that Cuenot has gone too far, and accuses him of "psychomorphism";[11] but if the function is the same at both levels of organization, why not use the same term? Not to use it is to mislead people into supposing that the processes are different, helping to perpetuate the myth of the uniqueness of man on which the paradigm of science depends.

Sherrington was filled with awe at what we could refer to as the intelligence of the ontogenetic process:

> The body is made up of cells, thousands of millions of them, in our own instance about 1000 million. The one cell [out of which it grows] the original fertilized cell, grows into two and those two each into two and so forth. When that has gone on in the aggregate some forty-five times, there are 26 million million magic bricks, all of a family. That is about the number (of cells) in a human child at birth. They have arranged themselves into a complex, which is a human child. Each has assumed its required form and size in the right place.[12]

How do we explain this? "It is as if an immanent principle inspired each cell with the knowledge for the carrying out of a design."

Perhaps the most quoted miracle of nature is the eye. Even the eye of a relatively modest form of life such as an insect is of a degree of sophistication that defies the imagination. The Spanish neurologist Santiago Ramon y Cajal, describes it thus:

> From the insect's faceted eye, proceeds an inextricable criss-cross of excessively slender nerve-fibres. These then plunge into a cell-labyrinth which doubtless serves to integrate what forms from the retinal layers. Next follow a countless host of amacrine cells and with them again numberless centrifugal fibres. All these elements are moreover so small the highest powers of the modern microscope hardly avail for following them. The intricacy of the connections defies description. Before it, the mind halts, abased.[13]

The complexity and precision of the eye was an embarrassment to Darwin. As he wrote in *The Origin of Species*,

> to suppose that the eye with all its inimitable contrivances for adjusting the focus to different distances, for admitting different amounts of light, and for the correction of spherical and chromatic aberration, could have been formed by natural selection, seems, I freely confess, *absurd in the highest degree.*[14]

However, he pointed out, "when it was first said that the sun stood still and the world turned round it, the common sense of mankind declared the doctrine false; but the old saying of *Vox Populi, vox Dei* as every philosopher knows, *cannot be trusted in science.*" Reason, for him, was a better guide, and it told him that the eye, however sophisticated, could still only be the product of natural selection.

It is ironic that to explain what are the paltry, not to mention socially and ecologically destructive achievements of scientific and technological man, such as the invention of the internal combustion engine and the atom-bomb, we invoke his consciousness, his creativity and his intelligence, yet we categorically deny these qualities to all other living things, let alone to the miraculous processes of evolution and morphogenesis that brought them and him into being.

33

Consciousness is not a prerogative of man

—

Only human beings guide their behavior by a knowledge of what
happened before they were born and a preconception of what may
happen after they are dead; thus only human beings find their way by a
light that illuminates more than the patch of ground they stand on.
Sir Peter Medawar

The evidence for some degree of consciousness certainly in the higher
animals and perhaps far down the animal scale is overwhelming.
W.H.Thorpe

Even if it be admitted that all natural systems are intelligent, thus allowing the term to be used in a meaningful way, it will still be maintained by many that man remains unique as he alone displays consciousness. We are told (see chapter 17) that without consciousness there can be no reason and hence no real choice, no purposiveness and no morality. Also, because man is conscious, his evolution (as opposed to that of all other creatures) is seen as freed from all the biological, social and ecological laws that govern the rest of the natural world, which means that man can in effect determine his own evolution. Eric Jantsch puts this idea into religious language: "it is because man possesses consciousness." He tells us that "mankind is not redeemed by God, but redeems itself."[1]

Evolution, he tells us, is usually seen as the history of the organization of matter and energy. However, it can also be viewed as "the organization of information into complexity of knowledge."[2] This "may be understood as the evolution of consciousness," the highest state of evolution, corresponding to Teilhard de Chardin's noosphere.[3] "Once this state is achieved," he writes, "the whole universe can be identified with consciousness and it is this consciousness that determines the course of further evolution."[4] In this way, by identifying the universe with human consciousness, Jantsch has reconciled—to his satisfaction at least—the idea that conscious man can determine his own evolution with his principal thesis that the universe is a self-organizing entity. The Promethean enterprise to which modern man is religiously committed is thereby effectively justified.

Along with Herrick, I think we can best regard consciousness as a state of awareness, associated with enhanced mental activity, which may be required when it is necessary to identify and interpret very carefully an important environmental challenge to which an immediate and often innovative response is required—the unconscious mind only being capable of dealing with routine matters.[5]

Thorpe is perfectly willing to accept that man is not the only living thing to possess this faculty. He sees the same degree of consciousness in the higher animals (chimpanzees, like other "higher" animals, denoting specific states of mind by different facial expressions) and the possibility of its presence far down the animal scale. Conscious awareness, he feels sure, provides some adaptive advantage over the purely unconscious apprehension of the environment.[6] Julian Huxley talks of the "mind intensifying" organization of animals' brains. He sees this as providing a fuller awareness of both outer and inner situations and as enabling living things to deal with chaotic and complex situations.[7]

For some authors, all natural systems are endowed with consciousness, or "bio-conscience." Teilhard de Chardin goes so far as to attribute a primary consciousness to the atom. This may be going too far. It is probably more realistic to see consciousness as a feature of organisms—embryonic among the simpler organisms, and more highly developed with the evolution of the brain and in particular the neo-cortex. It is also important not to overrate the importance of consciousness as a factor in determining our behavior pattern. As motivation research has revealed, humans themselves are not conscious of their basic underlying motivations; the reasons they give to explain their actions being largely those that best serve to rationalize them. It is indeed one of the principal failings of modern epistemology that it is only concerned with *conscious knowledge*, completely ignoring the unconscious or ineffable knowledge that plays an incomparably greater role in shaping our world-view and in determining our behavior pattern and hence our influence on the Gaian hierarchy.

34

Gaia is the source of all benefits

—

Land that is left wholly to nature . . . is called, as indeed it is, waste.
John Locke

You can gauge a country's wealth, its real wealth, by its tree cover.
Richard St Barbe Baker

Wilderness is the bank on which all checks are drawn.
John Aspinall

All that great bare belt of country which now stretches south of the Ganges—that vast waste where drought seems to be perennial and famine is as much at home as is Civa in a graveyard—was once an almost impenetrable wood. Luxuriant growth filled it; self-irrigated, it kept the fruit of the summer's rains till winter, while the light winter rains were treasured there in turn till the June monsoon came again. Even as late as the Epic Period, it was a hero's derring-do to wander through that forest-world south of the Nerbudda, which at that time was a great inexhaustible river, its springs conserved by the forest. Now the forest is gone, the hills are bare, the valley is unprotected, and the Nerbudda dries up like a brook, while starved cattle lie down to die on the parched clay that should be a river's bed.
E. Washburn-Hopkins

It is fundamental to the world-view of modernism that all benefits are man-made—the products of scientific, technological and industrial progress, and made available via the market system. Thus health is seen as something that is dispensed in hospitals, or at least by the medical profession, with the aid of the latest technological devices and pharmaceutical preparations. Education is seen as a commodity that can only be acquired in schools and universities. Law and order, rather than being natural features of human society, are seen instead as provided by our police force in conjunction with the law courts and the prison system. Even society is seen as man-made, brought into being by the "social contract." Not surprisingly, a country's wealth is measured by its per capita Gross National Product (GNP), that provides a rough measure of its ability to provide its citizens with all such man-made commodities, a principle faithfully reflected in modern economics.

For economists trained in these ideas, natural benefits—those provided by the normal workings of ecospheric processes, assuring the stability of our climate, the fertility of our soil, the replenishment of our water supplies, and the integrity and cohesion of our families and communities—are not regarded as benefits at all; indeed, our economists attribute to them no value of any kind. It follows that *to be deprived of these non-benefits cannot constitute a "cost"* and the natural systems that provide them can thereby be destroyed with economic impunity.

Even economists who can see through this preposterous accounting system still deny that environmental destruction is a problem because they have been taught that the market system, in conjunction with science, technology and industry, can deal with any "resource shortage." For instance, the farmers of the San Joaquin valley, in the southern part of the great central valley of California, are faced with a serious water shortage that may put many of them out of business, but they do not seem unduly concerned and are making no effort to adapt highly wasteful water-intensive practices to the new conditions. It is taken for granted that, sooner or later, some massive water diversion scheme will, as in the past, bring them the water they require from some other part of America, or even Canada.

The same argument is used to persuade us that the degradation of our agricultural land is not a problem. For our economists, agricultural land is just another "resource." Gale Johnston, a university professor and well-known agricultural economist, insists that natural resources *play a relatively minor role in determining the wealth of nations.* Emery Castle of Resources for the Future, one of the USA's most influential research organizations, told a meeting on the availability of agricultural land in 1980 that "the loss of agricultural land is not a high-priority national concern."[1] The agricultural economist Philip Raup tells us that there can be no permanent shortage of agricultural land: to suppose the opposite is an error that stems from wrongly considering the availability of resources in physical rather than economic terms. Indeed, if some land is unsuitable for agriculture, this is only a reflection of current market conditions. If the land were really needed, then the necessary science, technology and capital would make it productive.

This aberrant attitude is further rationalized by mainstream scientists who set out systematically to denigrate natural processes. Thus Medawar talks of nature's "own artless improvisations."[2] Lester Ward attacks the inefficiency of nature: "Rivers, instead of flowing straight, and so delivering their water to the sea, with minimum expenditure of energy, lazily meander through plains and valleys." He complains of "the redundant fertility" of the organic world: the herring lays ten thousand eggs, of which only two will reach maturity, and a large chestnut tree produces up to a ton of pollen.[3] For Ward nature's shortcomings are an invitation to man to become nature's engineer and create a paradise on Earth of his own design, whose functioning he can plan and direct in all its detail.[4]

It is a basic principle of the world-view of ecology that real benefits, and hence real wealth, are on the contrary, derived from the normal functioning of the natural world and of the cosmos itself. Our greatest wealth must be the favorable and stable climate that we have enjoyed for hundreds of millions of years, our forests and savannahs and fertile agricultural lands, our rivers and streams, springs and ground waters, our wetlands and coral reefs, our seas and oceans, and the myriad forms of life that inhabit them.

It is usual today to depict our remote ancestors, who lived off this great wealth without pillaging it, as we are doing today, as poor and wretched. They are made out to have suffered from chronic malnutrition, living permanently on the edge of famine. Nothing is further from the truth. The incredible biological wealth of the vast area that is now the United States of America is attested by John Bakeless. In the great plains, where modern agriculture has eliminated most of the original vegetation, and where the top-soil is eroding so fast that much of the land will be reduced to low-grade rangeland within the next thirty years, there were

> prairies teeming with buffalo, in herds that would pass all day without end; lordly moose along the lake shores; deer everywhere. Wild grapes roofed much of the eastern forest; there were wild fruits of many kinds; plentiful fish in every lake or stream; oysters nine inches long—or longer—in great clusters, that some fortunate dwellers on Manhattan simply pulled out of the clear waters before their shelters; lobsters beyond twenty pounds easily caught; wild turkeys in flocks so large their gobbling in the morning might be deafening; passenger pigeons that literally did darken the sky. There were grouse, prairie chicken, ducks of every kind, wild geese so fearless that at times they tried to frighten off approaching hunters.[5]

It is straining one's credulity a little too far to pretend that the dwellers on Manhattan, as it was then, suffered from malnutrition and famine. On the contrary, they were almost certainly considerably better fed than the present inhabitants of that island. In Africa—a continent where famine has now become chronic, and where 27 million people were threatened with starvation in the year 1991 alone—food shortages appear to have been unusual. The anthropologist Richard Lee testifies that ¡Kung Bushmen had an extremely satisfactory diet and rarely suffered food privations.[6] James Woodburn assures us that the same is true of the Hadza, a tribe of hunter-gatherers in Tanzania.

Mungo Park in his *Travels in Africa*, tells us that the river Gambia abounds with fish and that nature "with a liberal hand" has bestowed on the inhabitants of that area "the blessings of fertility and abundance."[7] Two eighteenth-century French travelers, Poncet and Brevedent, note that in the Gezira area of the Sudan now occupied by eroded cotton fields, there were once "pleasant forests of flowering acacias full of little green parrots" and "fruitful and well cultivated plains" and that it was called God's Country (Belad-Allah) "by reason of the great plenty."[8] In Kenya, where now an exploding population must be fed from an increasingly degraded environment, food shortages were also uncommon. As B.D.Bowles notes,

> European explorers and Arab traders found little difficulty in obtaining food as they traveled through the area. European conquerors actually burned crops standing in the fields and still survived without the importation of food. They extracted a surplus by force and they would have been unable to do this if no surplus had been available.[9]

Bengal, which included modern Bangladesh and is now one of the most overpopulated and impoverished areas on our planet, was once known as "Golden Bengal." Francois Bernier in his *Travels in the Moghul Empire* was particularly impressed by its "richness." "Egypt," he writes, "has been represented in every age as the finest and most fruitful country . . . but the knowledge I have acquired of Bengal, during the two visits paid to that country inclines me to believe that the pre-eminence ascribed to Egypt is rather due to Bengal."[10] Nor is there any reason to suppose that the Australian Aborigines were short of food. Sir George Grey, who spent a good deal of time with Australian Aborigines in the early part of the nineteenth century, insists that he always found the greatest abundance in their huts.

Even if we are forced to admit that malnutrition and famine were not man's natural lot, we still insist that tribal man was poor because he was deprived of material goods and technological devices. This too is an illusion. For perhaps ninety-five percent of man's tenancy of this planet, he pursued a nomadic way of life as a hunter-gatherer, swidden agriculturalist or nomadic pastoralist. For the nomad, material goods that we associate with wealth are, above all, a burden he sees as "grievously oppressive," the more so the longer they have to be carried around.

When Laurens van der Post wanted to give a present to Bushman friends with whom he had sojourned, as a token of his gratitude for their hospitality, he simply did not know what to give them.

> We were humiliated by the realization of how little there was we could
> give to the Bushmen. Almost everything seemed likely to make his life
> more difficult for him, by adding to the litter and weight of their daily
> round. They themselves have practically no possessions: a loin strap,
> a skin blanket and a leather satchel. There is nothing that they could
> not assemble in one minute, wrap up in their baskets and carry on
> their shoulders for a journey of a thousand miles. They had no sense
> of possession.[11]

To label them as poor completely misses the point, for Bushmen, living in their natural environment, do not feel in any way deprived by their lack of material goods. Their priorities are simply quite different.

They were even different at the court of the Manchu emperors of China, before that country had been subjected to Western influence. Thus the Emperor Ch'ien Lung was not the least impressed by the gift of manufactured goods presented to him by the British emissaries of King George III who sought to establish diplomatic links with his country. He rejected the British request and sent a letter to King George that concluded with the following words:

> Swaying the wide world, I have but one aim in view, namely to
> maintain a perfect governance and to fulfill the duties of the State.
> Strange and costly objects do not interest me . . . As your Ambas-
> sador can see for himself, we possess all things. I set no value on
> objects strange or ingenious, and have no use for your country's
> manufactures.[12]

This attitude could not be more foreign to us. Our appetite for material goods and technological devices seems insatiable. Indeed, it is in terms of our access to them that our wealth, indeed our welfare, is normally gauged. It is undoubtedly true that today we need a lot of material goods and technological devices, but this is not because we have an intrinsic need for them but because, in the aberrant conditions in which we live, they are required for the purpose of satisfying our biological, social, spiritual and aesthetic needs—our real needs. The car, when it was first invented, was undoubtedly a luxury. Slowly, however, it became a necessity: as it came to be assumed that people possessed them, so they were expected to travel ever further to their place of work, to the schools where their children were educated, to shopping centers or for recreational purposes.

It is not religion that is the opiate of the people, as Karl Marx decreed, *but materialism*. The possession of material goods has only been man's chief preoccupation for a very short time, whereas religion permeated every aspect of the life of vernacular man. Material and technological goods can be regarded as little more than bribes to induce people to accept the systematic annihilation of their real wealth that inevitably accompanies economic development or progress.

It is unlikely that any man-made commodity, however sophisticated, can adequately replace the natural product that it mimics. The reason is that the latter is designed to satisfy the countless requirements of the smaller systems which compose it, as well as those of the larger systems of which it is part—whereas the man-made commodity is only designed to satisfy a few of these requirements. A good illustration is our attempt, as part of the developmental process, to substitute cow's milk for human milk. Needless to say, it is always easy to find experts, who, on the basis of a simplistic notion of human nutrition, assure us of its superiority. We are assured that cow's milk has a higher protein content, for instance. But as Ross Hume Hall notes, a calf needs more protein because, at birth, it grows more quickly than does a human baby. More important still, as S.H. Katz and M.V. Young point out, is the fact that cow's milk contains less polyunsaturated fat, but this fat is needed for building brain tissue and what is sufficient for this purpose in a growing calf is insufficient for the development of a human baby's much larger brain.[13] There are a host of other reasons why cow's milk is a poor substitute for human milk. It contains an almost equal ratio of calcium and phosphorus, unsatisfactory for a human baby which requires more calcium. The level of sodium in cow's milk is too high and may give rise to primary hypertension. The low level of copper in cow's milk has been related to the reduced transportation of iron and hence to the iron deficiency associated with anaemia, common among North American infants. On the other hand, human milk contains the proportion of long-chain fatty acids that most favors their absorption and conversion to energy in the human baby.

Furthermore, the gastro-intestinal tract of a baby fed on human milk is colonized by the bacterium *Lactobacillis bifidis*. The important role played by this bacillus appears to have been grossly underestimated. Its presence appears to be essential to the absorption of protein and other nutrients in the milk. Equally important is the role played by human milk in ensuring immunization to disease. Certain antibodies are transmitted by the placenta which is permeable to them, while other antibodies are excluded. This means that bottle-fed babies are born without immunity to the diseases against which the latter provide protection—including those of gastro-enteric origin that happen to be the leading cause of mortality among babies throughout the world. These antibodies, on the other hand, are present in human milk in sufficient concentrations to provide protection against many gastro-enteric diseases, though it appears that this immunization only occurs if the corresponding antigens are present in the child's immediate environment.

There is also growing reason to believe that the intimate relationship between mother and infant during breastfeeding has a significant effect on the child's digestive capacities. Katz and Young also consider that a real synergy is likely to exist among the nutritional, immunological, psychoendocrinological and maternal responses that foster infant development.[14]

It is both naive and irresponsible to suppose that so incredibly sophisticated a natural process as breastfeeding, that has evolved over millions of years, can be advantageously replaced by feeding an infant on milk that is designed by its evolution to satisfy the requirements of a baby ungulate, contained in a bottle that provides but a crude imitation of its mother's teat.

If human milk is one of nature's products that we cannot really do without, so are the natural forests that once covered significant proportions of our planet's land area, in particular the tropical rainforests. One can draw up an almost endless catalog of the irreplaceable services that rainforests provide. By means of their elaborate root systems, they literally hold the soil together, preventing erosion from even the steepest slopes. Even in rainforests that are subjected to three hundred inches of rain a year, the water that runs off into the rivers is crystal clear. Their elaborate root system also ensures that the Earth beneath it is sponge-like, which maximizes its capacity to retain the rains; by the same token, controlling run-off to the rivers, releasing only a fraction of what the Earth retains. Once the forests have been cut down, and the roots have rotted, the Earth hardens and ceases to be capable of retaining water. Most of the water runs off immediately into the rivers, whose beds have been raised by erosion from increasingly deforested slopes, giving rise to ever-worsening floods. The water table sinks; rivers become torrents that only flow during the rainy season; streams and springs dry up.

Forests also provide the perfect habitat for living things—it is said that between fifty and eighty percent of the tens of millions of different species of living things inhabit the tropical rainforests. Vernacular man, even after he has become a sedentary cultivator, still derives much of his food from neighboring forests. He also finds there the materials required for his houses or huts, his artefacts and tools, his medicinal herbs and his vegetable dyes—indeed, they provide the very material basis of his cultural pattern, that necessarily disintegrates once the forests go.

Forests also provide an important sink for carbon dioxide and, at the same time, generate the oxygen required for animals to breathe. The wholesale burning of forests that is occurring today is responsible for a significant proportion of the carbon dioxide released into the atmosphere to cause global warming. Where the destruction is irreversible, it reduces this sink and reduces too the availability of oxygen. Forests, via the transpiration from their leaves, give rise to much of the atmospheric moisture that will form into clouds and absorb much of the sun's heat, providing, in this way, a cooling system for the planet. In Amazonia, between fifty and seventy percent of the rain that falls on the three million square kilometers of Amazonian rainforest appears to be generated in this way. Thus over this vast area huge amounts of water are constantly falling and rising —yet another way in which these forests act as a cooling system for our planet. James Lovelock has sought to calculate the annual energy cost of achieving the same degree of cooling by mechanical means.

If the clouds made by the forests are taken to reduce the heat flux of sunlight received within their canopies by only one percent, then their cooling effect would require a refrigerator with a cooling power of six kilowatts per hectare. The energy needed, assuming complete efficiency and no capital outlay, would cost annually £1,300 per hectare.[15]

On the basis of this calculation, he regards "the refrigeration system that is the whole of Amazonia" as being worth about one hundred and fifty trillion dollars. This is probably a conservative estimate, and values only one of the large number of different services that the forest provides. Cattle ranching on the same low-grade land would yield a total income of less than one-thirteenth of this sum, and even then only for a few years after which this highly vulnerable land would have been largely transformed into dust.

Not surprisingly, even after one hundred and fifty years of economic development, the vast bulk of the services required to keep our planet functioning are still provided by the self-regulating process of the ecosphere. This was stated quite explicitly by Carroll Wilson in his seminal MIT report *Man's Impact on the Global Environment* (1967).

> Almost all potential plant pests are controlled naturally. Insects pollinate most vegetables, fruits, berries and flowers. Vegetation reduces floods, prevents soil erosion, air-conditions and beautifies the landscape. Fungi and minute organisms work jointly on plant debris and weathered rock to produce soil. Commercial fish are produced almost entirely in natural ecosystems. Natural ecosystems cycle matter through green plants, animals and decomposers to eliminate wastes. Organisms regulate nitrates, ammonia and methane in the environment. On a geological time scale, life regulates the amount of carbon dioxide, oxygen and nitrogen in the atmosphere.[16]

No more than a minute fraction of these essential self-regulating ecospheric functions, what is more, could be taken over—very inadequately at that—by the externally-regulated technospheric institutions and corporations of our modern world.

Why this must be so is clear if we compare the lot of the Indians of the north-west coast of America before the arrival of the white man with that of an astronaut. The region was once covered with luxuriant temperate rainforests, teeming with game and plentifully supplied with all sorts of wild fruits, berries, herbs and roots. At low tide, so abundant were the shellfish on the beaches that the Tlingit, a local Indian tribe, used to say that "when the tide goes out, the table is laid." Nor, it would seem, was there any need to build bridges across the rivers, for it was said that you could cross them on the backs of the salmon. All this ecological wealth was made available to the Indians, free, by the self-regulating processes of the ecosphere, in what—barring unforeseen catastrophes such as the arrival of the white man—was a totally sustainable manner.

The lot of the astronaut circling our planet in a small metal box, could not be more different. He is deprived of even the most rudimentary ecological wealth. No edible plants grow in his space capsule, there is no game to hunt, no fish to catch, no shellfish to gather from the shores. There are no rivers, no streams, no springs from which he can obtain water to drink. Even the oxygen he breathes has to be brought from afar. Indeed, the very conditions required for sustaining life in his capsule can only be maintained by the most sophisticated technological devices, and the cost of sustaining him in such degraded and artificial conditions is beyond calculation. The richest man in the world could not afford to enjoy his miserable lifestyle for more than a few days, while only the wealthiest nations at the height of their economic fortunes, could afford to provide it to a handful of their subjects and then but for a few days, weeks or at the most, months.

If the US government takes seriously the National Academy of Science's recent publication, *Policy Implications of Greenhouse Warming*, then we may all *be condemned to become astronauts on our own planet*.[17] Indeed, if we refuse to cut down global emissions of greenhouse gases by 60-80 percent which the United Nations' Intergovernmental Panel on Climate Change (IPCC) regards as necessary to stabilize world climate, the only method available to us for preventing a global climatic disaster may well be to resort to the geo-engineering "solutions" of the National Academy of Sciences. Among those suggested by this august body is the placing of "fifty thousand, one hundred square kilometer mirrors in the Earth's orbit, to reflect incoming sunlight." Another is "to use guns or balloons to maintain a dust cloud in the stratosphere to increase the sunlight reflection." Other strategies involve using aircraft "to maintain a cloud of dust in the low stratosphere to reflect sunlight," or decreasing the "efficiency of burning in engines of aircraft and flying in the low stratosphere, to maintain a thin cloud of soot to intercept sunlight."

But how do we know that these ludicrously crude geo-engineering strategies would work? Also, what happens if there is a general strike in the country that is responsible for producing them? or a civil war? or a Chernobyl-type accident to a nuclear installation, that leads to the compulsory evacuation of large numbers of people, or simply an economic collapse of the sort that occurred in 1929, and that is more than likely to recur in the next decade? Even if it does not, how do we know that the world economy would continue to be capable of sustaining the cost of applying these geo-engineering strategies? How do we know that the resources would always be available, or that our planet could sustain the social and ecological costs? or even that the climatic degradation caused by carbon-dioxide emissions from the burning of the fossil fuels required to power so gigantic a geo-engineering enterprise might not neutralize what beneficial climatic effects it might conceivably provide?

That our scientists should even suggest the remote possibility that all this absurd gimmickry could provide a substitute for the homeostatic mechanisms of the ecosphere that have so far regulated world climate, indicates to what extent they live in a world of their own—one that seems to be increasingly insulated against social, ecological and even economic realities.

35

The ecosphere displays
spatio-temporal order

~

Order is an expression of conformity to Law.
Rupert Riedl

Order is the condition for understanding the Universe. A world without
order would have no meaning. It would be neither recognizable nor
conceivable.
Rupert Riedl

. . . while for us the order of nature is one thing, and the social order is
another, to the Australian, they are parts of a single order.
A.R.Radcliffe-Brown

Heaven, Earth and man have the same Li (organic order).
Taoist saying

Li, then, is rather the order and pattern in Nature, not formulated Law.
But it is not pattern thought of as something dead, like a mosaic; it is
dynamic pattern as embodied in all living things, and in human relationships and in the highest human values.
Joseph Needham

ORDER IS A BASIC FEATURE of the Gaian hierarchy, as traditional man fully understood. His own body, his home, his temple, his society, the natural world and the cosmos itself—he saw as organized according to the same plan, governed by the same laws and hence as constituting a single organized whole. The word "cosmos" itself originally meant order. In many cosmologies, as Mircea Eliade notes, the cosmos came into being once God had succeeded in vanquishing a vast primordial monster or dragon that symbolized the original chaos.[1] Often, the monster's body served as the raw material out of which the cosmos was fashioned. Thus Marduk fashioned the cosmos out of the body of the marine monster Tiamat, and Yahveh built the cosmos out of the body of the primordial monster Rahab. However, so as to prevent the cosmos from reverting to the original chaos, that victory had to be re-enacted every year.

Evolution and its constituent life processes build up order. Individualistic systems become organized, differentiated, and hence specialized in the fulfillment of various functions. As this occurs, so competition yields to co-operation, so the incidence and severity of discontinuities are reduced, and so the systems become more stable. Indeed, order implies organization, differentiation, specialization, co-operation, and stability. *They are but different ways of looking at the same fundamental feature of the living world.* But order cannot increase indefinitely. There is an optimum degree of order at each level of organization in the Gaian hierarchy—as there must be for all its associated features. That degree of order required for best assuring the critical order of the ecosphere, can be referred to as homeotelic order (see chapter 41).

Order has also been defined as "the influence of the whole over the parts," though it is often forgotten that this influence takes the form of constraints that are imposed by the whole on the parts. Still less is it admitted that these constraints are best regarded as laws which the latter must observe if they are to fulfill their homeotelic functions within the larger system, and thereby maintain its integrity and stability. The reason is that this notion cannot be reconciled with the paradigm of science.

Another definition of order is limitation of choice. This makes perfect sense, since to submit systems to homearchic constraints or laws is necessarily to limit their choice by preventing them from undertaking activities that are inconsistent with the maintenance of the integrity and stability of the larger systems of which they are part, and by assuring, on the contrary, that they do precisely those things that most favor the achievement of that overriding goal. Thus, as largely autonomous systems are transformed into the differentiated or specialized parts of a larger system, so, by the same token, must the latter's influence over them correspondingly increase, so must they be subjected to correspondingly more rigid constraints or laws, and so must their freedom of choice be correspondingly reduced.

Thus when the slime mould takes the form of a largely autonomous protozoan living in a loose colony, the influence of the whole over the parts is correspondingly weak and the latter are only subjected to very loose laws or constraints, and thereby enjoy a wide range of choices. When, on the other hand, the loose colony is transformed into a multi-cellular organism, and its parts become more differentiated and specialized in the functions that maintain its integrity and stability, then the influence of the whole over the parts is increased, the constraints or laws to which the parts are subjected become more rigid and the range of choice more limited. The pattern of behavior which the constituents of such orderly systems are constrained to adopt is that which, in these optimum conditions, they themselves will "choose"—for it is *that which must best satisfy their own needs by providing them with their optimum environment or field* outside of which they have no meaning and their life becomes heterotelic and degraded. Hence the principle of hierarchical mutualism.

Natural systems display order whether we see them as spatial entities, as we usually do, or as processes. A disordered or random process can tend in any direction; its behavior is unpredictable. As order builds up, however, the process is subject to the influence of the whole of which it is part. Its range of choices is limited as it becomes a differentiated part of the larger ecospheric process committed to the achievement of a single overriding goal. Hence purposiveness is just another word for order applied to life processes.

As Pittendrigh notes, order, or organization without purpose,

> is an absurdity . . . there is no such thing as organization in any absolute sense pure and simple. Organization is always relative, and relative to an end. (Thus) the organization of an army is relative to the end of defeating an enemy; and doing so, moreover, in a particular environment or terrain, weapons and political system. A room may be organized with respect to relaxation. Certainly, neither a room nor an army can be organized with *respect to nothing*.[2]

Thus, if one states that living systems are organized, then one must be ready to face the question "With respect to what are they organized?" As von Bertalanffy notes, "The notion of 'organ,' of visual, auditory, or sexual organ, already involves the notion that this is a 'tool' for something."[3] Animals will eat and drink and breathe and reproduce because these processes are as much part of them as are the organs that assure these functions. Indeed, there are no such things as animals that do not eat and drink, breathe and reproduce, except as photographs, pictures, concepts and words, nor are there such processes as eating, drinking, breathing and reproducing taken apart from the organisms involved. This must follow from the fact that living things are spatio-temporal systems (see chapter 20), which means that the order they display is spatio-temporal order and this necessarily implies purposiveness (see chapter 27).

If the order of the living world, whether seen spatially or temporally, is not apparent to reductionist mainstream science, it is largely because *seeing the world as orderly means looking at it holistically*. Indeed, unless one sees a system within its correct field—as part of the hierarchy of larger systems in which it evolved, to which it is homeotelic and to whose influence it is subjected, one cannot see that it is orderly and hence purposive.

Weiss often points out how the parts of a cell are constantly changing, growing, dying, breaking up, recombining, in what appears to be a chaotic manner: but the chaos is illusory; the parts are under cellular control that is essential if the cell is to remain a viable unit of adaptive behavior. The cell maintains its order and identity in spite of the apparent disorder of its constituent parts. What is more, it outlives them, for it has greater persistence or stability than they do.[4]

Mainstream scientists would seek to explain this in terms of statistical method. The individual cells, they would maintain, behave in a disorderly manner, but a large number of cells would behave in an orderly manner. For this reason, one cannot make statements about individual cells, only about large numbers of cells and these statements are necessarily of a statistical nature. Such statistical statements, however, say nothing about the forces that give rise to this order, and hence do not explain why this order comes about. They do not relate order to differentiation, specialization, co-operation, or stability, nor even to the influence of the whole over the parts, nor to the operation of laws or constraints, nor to the reduction of choice, nor to the need for a system to behave in an orderly or purposive manner in order to maintain the integrity and stability of the whole. On the contrary, *the statistical approach is a tool for avoiding having to face the many fundamental implications of the orderliness of natural systems, all of which are irreconcilable with the paradigm of science which it thereby serves to perpetuate.*

It also makes it possible to avoid recognizing that in the ecosphere or real world, *a single order prevails*. In this way, Edgar Morin can tell us that "there is order in the universe but not one order."[5] This is just another way of stating that the ecosphere is atomized and random and that its constituents can thereby be seen as governed by very different sets of laws.

The statistical argument also enables mainstream scientists to avoid recognizing that the order displayed by the ecosphere is not only distinct from, but diametrically opposed to, that of the technosphere or surrogate world with which modern man is systematically replacing it. To confound ecospheric diversity and complexity with technospheric diversity and complexity is to obscure the essential fact that the expansion of the latter can only occur at the expense of the integrity and stability of the former.

In terms of an ecological world-view, the hierarchy of the ecosphere must be seen as displaying a single order and this order is sacred. At the same time the ecosphere must be seen as governed by a single set of equally sacred laws, whose generalities apply equally well to biological organisms, vernacular communities, societies and ecosystems and to

Gaia herself (see chapter 61). This was fully accepted by tribal man, as is pointed out by Jane Harrison, Radcliffe Brown and others. Modern man, if he is to have a future, must once more become aware of this fundamental principle.

36

Gaian order is critical

~

The atmospheric concentration of gases such as oxygen and ammonia is found to be kept at an optimum value from which even small departures could have disastrous consequences for life.

James Lovelock

The dominating interest [in Kono society] is to preserve and perpetuate social harmony, stability and welfare. Religious cults and magic practices have chiefly this purpose in view. Everyone who has lived with a "primitive" people and has tried to immerse his mind in theirs, knows the deep-rooted dread they foster towards any disturbance of the universal and social harmony and equilibrium and the intimate interdependence they assume as existing between these two. A violation of this harmony and equilibrium, whether this issues from the universal sphere— for example, by an unusual occurrence in nature—or from the social— by a dangerous transgression of tradition or by a disturbing event such as the birth of twins—calls forth a corporate and strenuous religious activity towards restoring the harmony and thereby saving the fertility of their fields, their health, the security of their families, the stability and welfare of their tribe from becoming endangered.

Hendrick Kraemer

VERNACULAR MAN knew that the order of the cosmos is critical so much so that his overriding preoccupation was to preserve it. The notion of critical order is reflected in such notions as harmony and balance, which were seen by all traditional peoples as being essential features of the living world and of the cosmos.

The essential principle, built into the cultural pattern of vernacular people, that everything within the living world has to be recycled (see chapter 56) was based on the need to maintain its harmony or balance; as was the principle of reciprocity, that governed economic relationships within the vernacular community. The principle of maintaining the balance between two complementary principles such as the Yin and the Yang among the Taoists was another means of maintaining the critical order of the living world, as was Greek medicine which, as W. H. S. Jones notes, sought above all to maintain what was referred to as the "balance of humors."[1] The great Swedish naturalist Linnaeus also saw the world as displaying balance and harmony, which to him reflected the "economy of nature," while for the Natural Theologians of the seventeenth and eighteenth centuries, the "balance of nature," as Frank Egerton points out, provided incontrovertible evidence of the wisdom of God.[2]

Unfortunately, economic progress cannot occur without disrupting the critical order of the natural world so, not surprisingly as the world-view of modernism and the associated paradigm of science slowly developed to rationalize and hence legitimize this anti-evolutionary enterprise (see chapter 64), the notion of balance or harmony was conveniently discredited by biologists, ecologists and sociologists alike.

When ecology developed as a reaction against the paradigm of science, not surprisingly it sought to revive the concept of the balance of nature. Thus S. A. Forbes saw "an ideal balance of nature as one promotive of the highest good of all the species."[3] W.C. Allee and the other principal members of the Chicago school of ecology in the 1940s also accepted the principle of the balance of nature, according to which "the community maintains a certain balance, establishes a biotic order, and has a certain unity paralleling the dynamic equilibrium and organization of other living systems."[4]

In the 1930s and 40s however, ecology was systematically transformed so as to make it conform with the paradigm of science, and ecologists sought to discredit the concept of the balance of nature in the same way as they questioned the established ecological principles that ecological succession leads to a climax (see chapter 51), that the whole is more than the sum of the parts (see chapter 4) and that complexity gives rise to stability (see chapter 52).

Alfred Russel Wallace, who developed the principle of evolution via natural selection at the same time as Darwin and independently of him, had argued that the occurrence of different types of ecological discontinuities made nonsense of the principle of the balance of nature —a principle that was clearly irreconcilable with his theory.

> Some species, he noted, exclude all others in particular tracts. Where is the balance? When the locust devastates the vast regions and causes the death of animals and man, what is the meaning of saying the balance is preserved? [Are the devastations of] the Sugar Ants in the West Indies and the locust which Mr. Lyell says have destroyed 800,000 acres an instance of the balance of species? To human apprehension there is no balance but a struggle in which one often exterminates another.[5]

The same argument was put forward again in the 1930s by the British ecologist Charles Elton who argued against the principle of the balance of nature on the grounds that species were constantly being made extinct. This argument, however, takes no account of the fact that, in a climax ecosystem, everything conspires to minimize the incidence and severity of such discontinuities. Their occurrence thus indicates that an ecosystem is still at a pioneering stage or has been reduced to a neo-pioneering stage—or "disclimax"—by an external agent, such as modern man.

This had been fully understood more than two hundred years ago by the famous French naturalist, Bernardin de Saint-Pierre. "If snails,

nay bugs, caterpillars and locusts ravage our plains," he wrote in his
Etudes de la Nature,

> it is because we destroy the birds of our groves which live upon them;
> or because on transporting the trees of foreign countries into our own,
> such as the great chestnut of India, the ebony and others, we have
> transported with them the eggs of those insects which they nourish,
> without importing likewise the birds of the same climate which destroy
> them. Every country has those peculiar to itself, for the preservation of
> its plants.[6]

It follows that the occurrence of plagues and other discontinuities,
rather than provide evidence that there is no such thing as the balance
of nature must, on the contrary, be seen as *part of the price we must
pay for disrupting this critical balance.* Of course, if we insist that
there is no such thing as the balance of nature, if the ecosphere has no
critical order, then it can be so modified with impunity and must be
seen as totally malleable. We can then pretend that plagues are *natural*
disasters; and rather than treat them by restoring the critical balance
of the affected ecosystems, we can justify waging chemical warfare
against their vectors—the remedy that best satisfies the requirements
of the agro-chemical industry and, it is assumed, of the economy
in general, though it merely serves to mask the symptoms of the
affliction.

Scientists have sought in all sorts of ways to deny that the order of
the natural world is critical. Lamarck believed that the human genetic
material—the genome—was so malleable that it could be moulded
into any form by environmental influences. That was his principal
error. For Descartes, living things in general—and for John Locke,
the human mind itself—are but pieces of wax: "flexible, malleable,
ours to shape as we please" as Passmore puts it.[7] Most modern historians and sociologists also see society in this way. H.A.L.Fisher, for
instance, tells us that man does not have a nature, only a history—
intimating that human behavior is infinitely malleable and that history
is just a record of random and disconnected events. Edward O.Wilson
also talks of the "extreme plasticity of social behavior," implying that
we can adapt to living in just about any social or environmental
conditions, including of course, those that economic development or
progress impose upon us.

If the living world is infinitely malleable, then it can have no needs. The Oxford anthropologist Edward Evans-Pritchard attacks the notion that a society has needs and hence that it has a critical structure. For him it is people, not societies, that exist and have needs. Modern economists also deny that people have needs. They only have "wants" which means that it can be left to sheer economic expediency to determine with which goods and services they should be provided.

All this is so much nonsense. Living systems or processes at all levels in the Gaian hierarchy *have a critical structure*—that which is consistent with the fulfillment of their homeotelic functions. Thus, clearly the structure of an organism, like that of any other natural system, is critical: its various body fluids, for instance, must have the "normal" chemical and biological composition, or what would be the point of pharmacological tests? The basic features of a human community are also critical. However much it may differ in its details, it must be composed of extended families, and intermediary social groupings which link people together to form a cohesive unit of social behavior capable of maintaining its homeostasis in the face of change.

Attempts to transform society so as to satisfy a particular ideology —for instance the systematic annihilation of these social forms so as to "liberate" man from the constraints they impose upon him—as occurred with the French Revolution—could only fail. The atomized mass-society that it produced could no longer run itself and was inevitably taken over by a ruthless dictatorship, giving rise to the "total State" committed to war and destruction that ravaged Europe for nearly two decades.

A cultural pattern must also display a critical order and cultural traits can only be understood in accordance with their functions within it. The suppression of vernacular customs and institutions because they appear undesirable, when judged by our particular standard of morality, can have fatal results on the culture involved, very much as the extraction of a key organ can result in the demise of an organism.

Let us take the case of the marital customs of the people of the Comores in the Indian Ocean. They practice polygamy and have a high frequency of divorce, so much so that it is perfectly normal for a woman to have been married five to ten times.[8] On the basis of the experience gained in our culture, we would tend to associate this high divorce rate with an equally high rate of emotional instability, drug-addiction and juvenile delinquency and crime. However, things do not work out that way. When I visited the Comores in 1971, I found that the incidence of all these problems was extremely low. Their society had thus adapted to marital instability, which ours has not. The reasons are twofold. Firstly, the society is both matrilineal and largely matrilocal; a child is partly the responsibility of the mother's clan, many of the functions of fatherhood being fulfilled by the mother's elder brother (inheritance being primarily through him rather than through the father). Secondly, by custom, the step-father (or baba-combo) also automatically assumes many of the responsibilities of fatherhood *vis-à-vis* the children that his wife has had with previous husbands. The step-father is in particular responsible for the payment of the very large expenses involved in the circumcision ceremony of his step-sons. In addition, the father's role is reduced by the fact that the children are brought up in the mother's home, while in any case, as the father probably has several other wives, he would probably have only been physically present in one particular house on one or two days a week.

For all these reasons, divorce does not have the same unsettling effect in the Comores as it does in our society. Now, supposing a busybody missionary or administrator suddenly decided to abolish matriliny and matrilocality—as vestiges of barbarity not to be found in modern advanced societies—the results would be disastrous: delinquency, crime and alienation and the other symptoms of social disorder would undoubtedly result, as they do with the breakup of the nuclear family in our society.

If societies have a critical order, so too must ecosystems. They must be made up of green plants that are capable, via photosynthesis, of mobilizing the energy of the sun, herbivores that can feed off the plants, predators that can feed off the herbivores applying quantitative and qualitative controls on their populations and decomposers that can break down biological material into its constituent parts to serve as the raw materials for the perpetuation of the whole cycle.

Though all terrestrial ecosystems are designed on this same basic plan, they will nevertheless differ in many respects. Very different species will, in different ecosystems, fulfill the basic ecological roles, and these will also display varying degrees of complexity and diversity, co-operation and competition (see chapters 39, 40, 52, 53).

The ecosphere itself, the overall ecosystem, must for the same reason display a critical order. That the Earth's atmosphere must do so at a chemical level is clearly noted by James Lovelock. Among other things, its carbon dioxide content is critical; if it were too low, the Earth would be too cold, and if too high, its temperature would exceed that which most forms of life could tolerate. Its oxygen content is also critical; if it were a little lower, then certain forms of life would not be able to breathe, while if it were too high, the Earth's atmosphere would become so inflammable that a single spark could set off uncontrollable fires.

It must follow that adaptive changes occurring to any natural system are those that serve to maintain its critical order and hence its stability within the context of the critical order or stability of the whole Gaian hierarchy.

In the vernacular world, the annihilation of a society's social and ecological forms would have been impossible, for this critical order was sacred (see chapters 62 and 63) and to violate it could only lead to the most terrible calamities. What vernacular man knew, our most highly regarded social philosophers such as Plato, Hobbes and Rousseau—whose ideas most influenced the course of the French Revolution—totally ignored, just as, tacitly at least, do contemporary sociologists who justify the further atomization of society and the further destruction of the natural world in order to accommodate further economic development, and worse still its globalization under the auspices of the World Trade Organization.

37

There is no fundamental barrier separating man from other living things

The fact that primitive man draws no strict line of cleavage between the animal, vegetable and mineral kingdoms, on the one hand, and human beings on the other, has been so often emphasised, that it can be regarded as an anthropological commonplace.
Raphael Patai

To man in the totemistic stage of thinking, Dike and Themis, natural order and social order, are not distinguished, not even distinguishable. Plants and animals are part of his group, factors in his social structure. It is not that he takes them under his protection; they are his equals, his fellow-tribesmen; naturally they obey the same law.
Jane Harrison

We have seen that the senses and intuitions, the various emotions and faculties, such as love, memory, attention and curiosity, imitation, reason of which man boasts, may be found in their incipient, or even sometimes in a well-developed condition, in the lower animals.
Charles Darwin

We and the beasts are kin. Man has nothing that the animals have not at least a vestige of; the animals have nothing that man in some degree does not share. Since, then, the animals are creatures with wants and feelings, differing in degree only from our own, they surely have their rights.
Ernest Thompson Seton

Humanity's greatest priority is to reintegrate with the natural world.
Jonathan Porritt

THERE IS NO fundamental difference between the structure and behavior of vernacular man and that of other living things. Both are governed by the same laws that govern the behavior of the natural systems which make up the Gaian hierarchy.

That the fellowship between man and other animals was strongly felt in Classical antiquity, during the middle ages and even as late as the nineteenth century in rural areas of Western Europe, is well documented by Edward Westermarck in his *Origin and Development of the Moral Ideas*. It played an essential part in the world-view of vernacular man, for without it there could be neither animism (see chapter 62), nor hylozoism (see chapter 63), nor could vernacular man see himself as an integral part of the Gaian hierarchy, let alone realize that this hierarchy is governed by the same fundamental laws. As Raphael Patai notes, it is "merely a recognition of the true state of things, the perception of the fundamental similarity underlying the apparent diversity of forms."[1]

It is particularly marked, of course, among "totemic" societies—those whose members were imbued with a chthonic world-view. For Sir James Frazer, this "sense of close relationship of man with the lower creatures," is the very essence of totemism.[2] He notes how a Bushman questioned by a missionary, could not see any difference between man and other animals—for instance "He did not know but a buffalo might shoot with bows and arrows as well as a man, if it had them."[3] The Giliaks of the Amoor attach no importance to the physical differences separating man from other animals:

> In substance every beast is a real man, just like a Giliak himself, only endowed with an intelligence and strength which often surpass those of mere ordinary human beings.[4]

The clans into which many tribal societies are divided are named after specific animals with whom they see themselves as very closely related. Indeed, they often actually identify themselves with their totemic animals. Cornford tells us that among Australian Aborigines, a member of a group that has the Kangaroo as its totem, literally believes that he is a kangaroo. "His belief that he is a kangaroo is so unquestioned that he has no need to pretend that he is one, all he has to do is to be a kangaroo by behaving as one."[5] Among the Ojibway, as Frazer notes, the members of the bear clan behave in a surly and pugnacious way and members of the crane clan affect "clear ringing voices like cranes."[6]

Needless to say, tribesmen will desist religiously from killing animals of the species with which they are associated in this way. Frazer tells us how a Mandingo porter offered to forego a whole month's pay in order to save a python, because the python was his totem and to kill it would threaten the survival of his whole family. Such an attitude is a serious impediment to economic development for if the tribesmen are to participate in this enterprise they cannot have such qualms about killing living creatures. It requires a very different attitude; rather than being our brothers and sisters, non-human animals must be seen as vastly inferior "beasts" or "brutes" to whom such qualities as purpose, creativity, intelligence, consciousness, even morality are denied. Instead, their behavior must be seen as blind and robot-like. In this way, we can feel justified in exploiting and killing them as much as we like in order to satisfy our sordid short-term economic interests.

Some mainstream scientists go further, insisting that "there is no evidence that animals actually suffer pain." This is another pretext for exploiting them—in particular for torturing them in their laboratories in order to obtain whatever "scientific evidence" will legitimize the use of new cosmetics, pesticides and pharmaceutical preparations.

Many of those who have sought to justify the colonial enterprise have insisted in a similar way that tribal man was "little more than an animal," hence little more than a machine. Darwin, for one, wrote in this vein of the Fuegians, the natives of Tierra del Fuego. The domination, indeed the annihilation of tribal cultures, was seen by him and the social Darwinists as part of the beneficial workings of natural selection. If tribal societies failed to survive, it was that they were not fit to do so. The fact that the colonial powers were capable of dominating and eventually of annihilating them was sufficient proof of the former's superiority. It was fully justified in the name of the "survival of the fittest" and was seen as a necessary condition for human Progress.

All this we must reject. In terms of the world-view of ecology, no fundamental barrier separates us from all the other living things with which we live on this planet—the particularities of their structure and behavior may be different, but the basic generalities are the same.

38

The ecosphere is a hierarchical organization of natural systems

～

The Chinese . . . visualized the universe as a hierarchy of parts and wholes
working in harmony—each according to its own Li or pattern—but all
fitting together in the great pattern.
Dolores La Chapelle

Hierarchical organization is the essential and distinguishing
characteristic of life.
Howard Pattee

Wholes and parts cannot exist by themselves either at a biological or
social level. What we find are intermediary structures on a series of levels
in ascending order of complexity, each of which has two faces looking in
opposite directions; the face turned towards the lower levels is that of an
autonomous whole, the one turned upward that of a dependent part.
Arthur Koestler

Insect societies, human and non-human animal societies, eco-systems, Gaia herself, have been compared to biological organisms. It would be more accurate, however, to regard them as instances of a more general category of entities. Gerard referred to them as "orgs" —not a particularly attractive term; von Bertalanffy, Ross Ashby, Paul Weiss and others called them "systems" or "natural systems," a term that is now in general use, while Koestler, and later Tom Starr and others, named them "holons."

Unfortunately the term "system," like most of the other basic terms used by scientists, is defined in many conflicting ways. A.D. Hall and R.E. Fagen originally defined it as "a set of objects together with the relationships between the objects and between their attributes."[1] It is more often defined as a set of entities in dynamic interrelationship with each other. However, both of these definitions could apply equally well to a disintegrated or "atomized" entity, such as a cancerous cell, or a modern industrial society or any of the groupings into which the latter is organized, such as state institutions or corporations, all of which are unnatural or heterotelic rather than natural or homeotelic to the ecosphere.

Koestler defines a "holon" as "any stable sub-whole in an organ-ismic, cognitive, or social hierarchy which displays rule-governed behavior and/or structural Gestalt constancy."[2] This definition is a little too loose. He should specify which rules govern the behavior of the holon, though of course, if a "sub-whole" displays structural con-stancy, then it can only be that it is subject to the rule of the whole.

Other authors have used the term "system" in a still more general way. Jantsch, for instance, includes "paradigms, the whole system of science, religions, the images we hold of ourselves and our roles in the evolution of the universe," together with cells, organisms, soci-eties and ecosystems in this category, which he mainly refers to, like Prigogine, as "dissipative structures."[3] This is simply a device to make it appear that all these things have more in common than they really do. Monod rightly criticizes the use of the term system as being too loose; "The trouble with embracing everything is that you can end up holding nothing," he writes,[4] though he would undoubtedly have used stronger language if he had seen Jantsch's definition.

With Ashby, von Bertalanffy developed an entirely new discipline called General Systems Theory whose object was to establish the laws governing the behavior of all "natural systems." He reserves the use of the term "system" to "complexes of elements in interaction to which systems laws can be applied." Weiss defines a system still more realistically as "a complex unit in space and in time, whose sub-units co-operate to preserve its integrity and its structure and its behavior and tend to restore them after a non-destructive disturbance."[5] In this way, he stresses the major features of the constituents of the biosphere; their complexity, their existence in space-time, their co-operative, self-regulatory, homeotelic nature, their dynamism, their purposiveness and their dedication to the maintenance of the larger systems of which they are part, a prerequisite for the preservation of their own integrity and stability. By defining a natural system in Weiss's way, one also distinguishes it from the components of the technosphere or surrogate world, that satisfy none of these conditions. The failure of many of those involved in General Systems Theory to grasp the significance of this distinction largely explains why this discipline has made remarkably little progress since the death of its founder.

It is clear that the laws governing the behavior of natural systems which von Bertalanffy tries to establish would have to be as general as the most general category of systems he describes. Thus the particularities of the behavior of humans can be seen as governed by a particular set of laws that apply only to humans. More general aspects of their behavior can be seen to be governed by more general laws that apply to mammals in general, still more general aspects by still more general laws that apply to all organisms in general, and so on. The most general aspects of their behavior must be seen as governed by laws that apply to all natural systems or holons, whether they be specified to be humans, mammals, organisms, non-human animal societies, vernacular human societies, ecosystems or indeed Gaia herself.

To determine what these most general laws are must provide the best means of developing a unified science, "not by the utopian reduction of all the sciences to physics and chemistry," as von Bertalanffy insists, "but by virtue of the structural uniformities, which exist between the different levels of the natural world."[6] Such a unified science would thereby constitute a truly holistic ecology in which there would be no place for the misleading dualisms that the paradigm of science has imposed on our understanding of the natural world, such as that which separates the natural sciences from the social sciences.

Von Bertalanffy lists two of the laws that he regards as essential and to which systems, in order to be classified as such, must presumably be subjected. The first is the Law of "biological maintenance" that states that "the organic system tends to preserve itself," another way of saying that it maintains its homeostasis. The Second Law is that a natural system is organized hierarchically. This he sees as applying both to organic systems and also to the inorganic world, "with its hierarchy of electron, atom, molecule, mycella and crystal."[7] This essential aspect of natural systems is also accentuated very forcefully by Weiss, Koestler and Eugene Odum.[8] The latter sees all natural systems as organized hierarchically from the biotic community, to the population, the organism, the organ and the cell. He sees them as forming a spectrum that theoretically can be extended infinitely in both directions. The upper end of the spectrum, covering populations and ecosystems, is the concern of ecology.

If every natural system is part of such a hierarchy, regardless of its level of organization, it must have two functions: on the one hand, *vis-à-vis* the larger systems of which it is part, and on the other *vis-à-vis* the smaller systems that comprise it. Weiss considers that the cell, the main object of his studies, must be seen "in a double light; partly as an active worker and partly as a passive subordinate to powers which lie entirely outside of its own competence and control, i.e. supra-cellular powers."[9] Koestler sees this as applying to all natural systems or "holons." He takes the double-faced Roman God Janus— whose two faces look in opposite directions—as the natural symbol of the holon, symbolizing its two roles within the hierarchy of nature.[10]

Scientific ecologists tend to ignore this key issue. For instance, there is no mention of hierarchy in Putman and Wratten's textbook, nor in the latest ecology textbook to appear in the United Kingdom, that by Michael Begon, John Harper and Colin Townsend.[11] The reason is probably that its many implications are largely unacceptable to those imbued with the paradigm of science. Hierarchy has, to my know-ledge, been the subject of only two major conferences, one organized by Lancelot Law Whyte[12] and the other by Howard Pattee.[13] Neither was particularly enlightening. M.D. Mesarovic and D. Macko, who attended the first symposium, noted how "the term 'hierarchy' was used to cover a variety of related yet distinct notions";[14] Marjorie Grene, another participant, also noted how loosely the term was used.[15]

Among ecologists, it is only Eugene Odum whose textbooks take the essentially hierarchical nature of the ecosphere into serious account. Yet unless they do so, they will never understand the structure and purpose of the living world and of its myriad forms of life.

39

Co-operation is the primary Gaian interrelationship

Mutual aid is as much a law of animal life as mutual struggle, but . . . as a factor of evolution, it most probably has a greater importance, in as much as it favors the development of such habits and characters as ensure the maintenance and further development of the species, together with the greatest amount of welfare and enjoyment of life for the individual, with the least waste of energy.

Peter Kropotkin

. . . in nature, the normal way in which trees flourish is by their association in a forest. Each tree may lose something of its individual perfection of growth, but they mutually assist each other in preserving the conditions for survival. The soil is preserved and shaded; and the microbes necessary for its fertility are neither scorched, nor frozen, nor washed away. A forest is the triumph of the organization of mutually dependent species.

A.N. Whitehead

Co-operation for mutual benefit, a survival strategy very common in natural systems, is one that humanity needs to emulate.

Eugene Odum

THE IDEA OF THE WORLD as a "vast co-operative enterprise" is a very ancient one. It was well understood by traditional man and, in our Western civilization, was embodied in the concept of the "Oeconomy of Nature," a term first used in 1658 by Sir Kenelm Digby, and taken up a century later by the Swedish naturalist Linnaeus when he sought to explain "the grand organization and governor of life on Earth, the rational ordering of all material resources in an interacting whole."[1] Thirty years later, Gilbert White noted how the cattle standing in the Selborne ponds provided, by their droppings, food for insects and thus indirectly for the fish. White marvelled at the ingenuity of the Creator. "Nature is a great economist," he wrote, "for she converts the recreation of one animal to the support of the other."[2] Darwin himself saw nature as "one grand scheme of co-operative integration." In his "General Observations" on the ecology of Rio de Janeiro, he writes

> I could not help noticing how exactly the animals and plants in each region are adapted to each other. Everyone must have noticed how lettuces and cabbages suffer from the attack of Caterpillars and Snails —but when transplanted here in a foreign clime the leaves remain as entire as if they contained poison. Nature when she formed these animals and these plants knew they must reside together.[3]

Dov Ospovat considers that it was only after reading Malthus that Darwin abandoned these ideas.[4]

The concept of co-operation also played an important part in the thinking of Johannes Warming, one of the earliest scientific ecologists. In particular he emphasized symbiosis, as in the case of the lichen, a quasi-organism made up of an alga and a fungus. Warming even regarded parasitism as a form of symbiosis since the parasite and its host eventually become very dependent on each other.[5] The academic discipline of ecology that developed towards the end of the nineteenth century regarded mutualism as a basic feature of ecological organization. Hundreds of articles appeared on this theme in early ecological texts.

The American naturalist Roscoe Pound, for example, described in a celebrated article all the various forms of mutualism that were known to occur in ecosystems, including pollination and the fixation of nitrogen by bacteria living on the root nodules of leguminous plants.[6] Mutualism within ecosystems was even compared to forms of co-operation within organisms—a comparison that no academic ecologist would dare make today. Thus, in the first American book on animal ecology, the ecologist C.C.Adams declared that

> the interactions among the members of an "association" are to be compared to the similar relations existing between the different cells, organs or activities of a single individual . . . The physiological needs and states of an association have as real an existence in individual animals as similar needs in the cells which compose the animal body.[7]

As late as the 1940s, Allee and the Chicago Ecology group continued to regard mutualism as the most basic feature of ecosystems. However, with the development of the world-view of modernism with its accent on individualism and competition, interest in mutualism rapidly declined, Eugene and Howard Odum being among the few ecologists who continued to produce work on the subject.

This was particularly so as ecologists strained to adapt their discipline to the paradigm of science, seeking respectability within the scientific community in which mutualism had little role to play. As a result, as J.H.Vandermeer and Douglas Boucher note, "although some of the most spectacular interspecific interactions in nature are obviously mutualistic, relatively little research, empirical or theoretical has been aimed at understanding this basic and perhaps prevalent form of interaction."[8]

A survey by S.Risch and D.Boucher of twelve ecology texts published between 1970 and 1975, clearly "substantiates the claim that practically the entire discussion of organismic interactions has centered on predation and competition. Of a total of 718 pages devoted to interspecific interactions in these texts, 321 pages concern predator-prey interactions, 362 pages concern interspecific competitive interactions and only thirty-five pages discuss any kind of mutualistic relationship. In addition to the disproportionate amount of space devoted to the different interactions, predation and competition are presented as important organizing principles, while examples of mutualism (such as cleaning symbiosis) are presented as interesting but eccentric exceptions to the general rule."[9]

Worse still, when co-operation or mutualism is admitted to exist at all, it is regarded by some of our most prestigious ecologists as thoroughly counter-productive. For instance, Princeton ecologist Robert May's view that mutualism has a destabilizing effect on ecosystems has gained general acceptance. Though this thesis is no doubt consistent with the mathematical model he built of co-operative relations, it bears little relationship with the real world in which mutualism is a basic condition of stability (see chapter 52).

Consider a human family. It is a mutualistic relationship between husband and wife, parents and children that holds it together. When mutualism is replaced by competition then the family falls apart; it ceases to remain a stable unit of behavior. If the co-operative members of a human community or of the populations that make up an ecosystem suddenly become competitive, so must these natural systems disintegrate. This is absolutely obvious. If a mathematical model proves the opposite, as May's does, *then it must necessarily be wrong*, which in any case it must be for at least two additional reasons. The first is that mathematical models of co-operation and competition can only take into account two co-operators or competitors at a time, whereas these relationships necessarily involve a large number of different co-operators and competitors—all those that make up the hierarchy of larger systems of which the systems are part and with which they must necessarily "co-operate" and "compete" if they are to ensure its overall stability. Secondly, the only sort of mutualism that can be modeled mathematically is "facultative" mutualism. "Obligate" mutualism, which alone is regarded by Odum as true mutualism, is, at present, very difficult to model. In any case, even if it could, it would probably still not be modeled, for obligate mutualism implies that organisms are "selected" for their capacity for mutualistic behavior, i.e. for their ability to fit into the differentiated system that is an ecosystem, and by implication, eliminated as "unfit" if they behave in an individualistic and competitive manner—a notion that is totally irreconcilable with the neo-Darwinian thesis and hence with the paradigm of science.

In the early 1970s, however, there was a sudden resurgence of interest in mutualism. It seemed to manifest itself independently in the work of ecologists at different universities, who were often unaware of each other's work. Well-known ecologists, who had previously downplayed the importance of mutualism, suddenly changed their minds about it. Thus Robert May stated in 1973 that the importance of mutualism "in populations in general is small." However, "in only a few years," to quote Boucher, "May's appreciation of mutualism changed considerably."[10] He suddenly announced that mutualism was now seen as "a conspicuous and ecologically important factor in most tropical communities." Indeed, in recent years, May has become one of the leaders in encouraging work on mutualism which he sees as "likely to be one of the growth industries of the 1980s."

Renewed interest in mutualism has focused attention (in the work of Boucher, S. James and K. H. Keeler[11] for example) on the role played by micro-organisms in the metabolism of complex organisms. Ecologists have also noted the increasing numbers of parasitic or predatory relationships that, on closer examination, turn out to be mutualistic. Thus S. J. McNaughton has pointed out that the normal view of the relationship between grazers and the grass they graze is false. Whereas "ecologists have tended to view plants as relatively passive" it now seems clear that plants are capable of reacting in a much more dynamic manner to grazing, and indeed are capable of "compensatory growth and assimilate reallocation." All in all, McNaughton found nine different ways in which the relationship between grazing animals and the grass on which they graze can be regarded as mutualistic.[12] D. F. Owen and R. G. Wiegert have carried this analysis a step further. They point to the obvious implication that grazers and the grasses they graze have co-evolved "to an extent that one would not be possible without the other."[13] They quote W. I. Mattson and N. D. Addy, who consider "that insects can act as regulators of primary production and nutrient cycling and this performs a vital function in ecosystems dynamics."[14]

Does this then mean, Boucher asks, that mutualism is "destined to be part of a new synthesis in which Newtonian ecology is replaced by a more organicist, integrated, value-laden view of the natural world?" He is not too optimistic on this score. The reason is that "our present theories of mutualism are still basically mechanistic, mathematical, fitness-maximizing and individualistic."[15] Unfortunately, this is only too true. D.H. Janzen, for instance, considers that "mutualisms are the most omnipresent of any organism-to-organism interaction." However, he still sees mutualism reductionistically in neo-Darwinian terms and insists that "natural systems larger than the individual cannot be mutualistic." The reason is that

> a mutualism is an interaction between individual organisms in which the realized or potential genetic fitness of each participant is raised by the actions of the other. The participants are called mutualists. Since a species has no trait that is analogous to the genetic fitness of an individual, mutualism cannot be defined with reference to species.[16]

Boucher considers it inevitable that ecologists should see mutualism in this way:

> While arguing that nature is an integrated whole and that everything is connected to everything else, we continued researching with theories that said that communities are no more than sets of individual organisms. The problem, in other words, is one of cognitive dissonance—the difficulty of working with two sets of ecological ideas, based on different fundamental assumptions and ultimately in conflict.[17]

Mutualism clearly cannot be understood in the light of the paradigm of science with which it cannot be reconciled. It is only when seen in the light of an ecological world-view that its essential role in maintaining the critical order of the cosmos becomes apparent.

40

Competition is a secondary Gaian interrelationship

~

All nature is at war.
Charles Darwin

From the point of view of the moralist the animal world is on about the same level as a gladiator's show. The creatures are fairly well treated, and set to fight—whereby the strongest, the swiftest and the cunningest live to fight another day. The spectator has no need to turn his thumbs down, as no quarter is given.
T. H. Huxley

The growth of a large business is merely a survival of the fittest . . . It is merely the working out of a law of nature and a law of God.
John D. Rockefeller Sr.

It is rare to see two animals, particularly animals of different species, tugging at the same piece of meat. And even when competition is observed, it often appears inconsequential. Perhaps a fiddler crab scurries into a hole on a beach only to come running out again, expelled by the current inhabitant. But the crab simply moves off to find another hole. Competition between species—interspecific competition—thus appears to be little more than a minor, temporary inconvenience.
Daniel Simberloff

THE INDUSTRIAL REVOLUTION transformed our vision of the natural world. Its proponents sought to show that even the most destructive aspects of industrialism were beneficial. The disintegration of society and the individualism, interpersonal competitiveness and aggression that are the inevitable concomitants of industrialization Adam Smith saw as a veritable boon providing, via the workings of "the invisible hand," the very basis of economic and hence social prosperity.

Herbert Spencer formulated the principle of "the struggle for survival," which he took to be the basic feature of human society, and which he regarded as a means of creating a more differentiated and hence a more efficient society. Thomas Malthus insisted that the struggle for food and resources was a mathematical necessity and that poverty, malnutrition and famine were quite normal, indeed desirable, since the victims of the struggle for survival would make way for the victors—the best adapted—who alone displayed the qualities required for creating an efficient and prosperous society.

Darwin, highly influenced as he was by Spencer and by Malthus, proceeded to show how the struggle for survival, that he loosely identified with competition, was the organizing principle in nature and provided the means for achieving evolutionary progress. For him, competition was everywhere. It was even the basic feature of inter-relationships *within* a biological organism where symbiosis most obviously takes its most highly developed form. He makes this clear in his treatment in *The Origin of Species* of the metaphor of the tree of life.

> The affinities of all the beings of the same class have sometimes been represented by a great tree. I believe this simile largely speaks the truth. The green and budding twigs may represent existing species: and those produced during former years may represent the long succession of extinct species. At each period of growth, all the growing twigs

have tried to branch out on all sides, and to overtop and kill the surrounding twigs and branches, in the same manner as species and groups of species have at all times overmastered other species in the great battle for life.[1]

If he saw competition to be the basic interrelationship *within* a biological organism in which symbiosis is most highly developed, one can imagine what little room there was, in his scheme of things, for symbiosis or mutualism *between* organisms, or within an ecological community, where the role of co-operation in its various forms may not be quite so obvious.

It was in 1895 that T.H. Huxley gave his famous Romanes Lecture, in which he stated most clearly what has come to be known as the gladiatorial view of the natural world.

In answer to it, Peter Kropotkin published in 1902 his famous *Mutual Aid*. For Kropotkin, co-operation and mutual aid were in evidence everywhere among non-human animals and among "savages," "barbarians" and "civilized men"; how then could our scientists possibly ignore them, let alone deny their very existence? "Sociability," he wrote,

> is as much a law of nature as mutual struggle. If we ask nature: "Who are the fittest: those who are continually at war with each other, or those who support one another?" We at once see that those animals which acquire habits of mutual aid are undoubtedly the fittest.[2]

Kropotkin's argument, however, fell on deaf ears, and until recently, other critics of the gladiatorial view of the natural world have fared no better. Everything had to be explained in terms of competition.

If Adam Smith showed that the competitive principle applied to economics, Spencer did the same for sociology, Malthus for demography, Darwin for evolutionary biology, and academic ecologists made sure that they were not left out. Boucher notes that "twentieth century ecology, while usually shying away from analogizing the natural and social worlds, has continued the tradition of seeing antagonistic interactions as the basis of community organization."[3]

R.E. Ricklefs, author of a famous textbook of ecology, confirms that "competition as a major organizing principle in ecology, is so widely accepted that it has achieved the status of a paradigm."[4]

Though competition, like natural selection, is a crude and rudimentary mechanism, ecologists have attributed to it the most sophisticated capacities. No feat is considered to be so daunting that competition cannot achieve it. Thus the Competitive Displacement Principle, otherwise known as Gause's principle, tells us that two species with the same lifestyle, and which in particular share the same diet, cannot occupy the same niche or co-exist on the same territory. In other words, *competition regulates diversity*. Again, since common species of plants referred to as dominants are declared the most effective competitors, while rare species, or non-dominants, are simply less effective competitors, it follows that *competition determines the relative size of populations*; while according to Putman and Wratten, competition for resources entirely *determines ecological organization, as well as ecological succession*. Indeed, mainstream ecologists attribute to competition those features of omnipresence, omnipotence and hence presumably omniscience that are normally attributed to God Himself.

It is the sociobiologists who have taken up the most extreme position. For them, it is individual self-interest that prevails in every sphere and it is in terms of this self-interest that any form of co-operation must be interpreted; no allusion to the larger system's need for such co-operation being regarded as scientific. This leads sociobiologists to see even the humblest of living things making precise cost-benefit calculations in the manner of modern economists in order to decide whether or not to co-operate with other members of their community, even with those of their immediate family. Even the most intimate mutualistic human relations such as those obtaining between a mother and her child are held to be explicable in such terms, displays of affection being seen as masking all sorts of sinister machinations on the part of the child *vis-à-vis* its unsuspecting mother, and presumably vice-versa. Thus Dawkins assures us that

> we can talk about a conflict between parents and young, a battle of the generations. The battle is a subtle one, and no holds are barred on either side. A child will lose no opportunity of cheating. It will pretend to be hungrier than it is, perhaps younger than it is, more in danger than it really is. It is too small and weak to bully its parents physically, but it uses every psychological weapon at its disposal: lying, cheating,

deceiving, exploiting, right up to the point where it starts to penalize its relatives more than its genetic relatedness to them should allow. Parents on the other hand, must be alert to the cheating and deceiving and must try not to be fooled by it.[5]

Cheating among the partners of apparently mutualistic interrelationships is now even regarded as a legitimate and respectable subject of research in those academic circles that take seriously the ideas of sociobiology.

The concept of competition as the ordering principle in nature, however, is not based upon any serious knowledge of any kind. To begin with there is no standard definition of competition, a term used in many different ways. Darwin, for instance, never established very precisely how he related the notion of competition to those of "the struggle for existence" or "the survival of the fittest." Opinions vary as to how he saw these relationships. Merrell considers that he regarded competition as one aspect of the struggle for existence. L.C. Birch, on the other hand, considers that he used the two terms in a different way. Merrell provides a veritable catalog of the different ways in which the term "competition" is defined. In his summing up he concludes that

> Some definitions apply only to animals, other to all organisms—plants as well as animals; some definitions refer only to interspecific competition, others to both intraspecific and interspecific competition; for competition to occur, resources must be in short supply in some definitions but not in others; sometimes the definition is so broad that it does not exclude predator-prey relations, but in others, the same trophic level is specified. Given these differences of opinion, it may be hazardous (not to mention presumptuous) to attempt to reach some workable definition of competition.[6]

Nor are the various applications of the competitive principle to ecology any better defined. The competitive exclusion principle, for instance, has been formulated by different ecologists in literally dozens of different ways. Merrell lists many of the formulations. Most of them make reference to limiting resources, but others do not mention resources at all. Furthermore, some definitions state that exclusion occurs if the ecological niches are "identical"; others only require them to be "similar." Worse still, the studies required to justify the thesis that competition is the ordering principle in nature have never really been undertaken. J.H. Connell notes that his review of the literature on the subject yielded only one study involving serious experimental work designed to determine if competition played a significant role in the interaction between species.[7] Peter Price goes so far as to say that

> competition theory lives in a dreamworld where everything can be explained, but the validity of these explanations has not been adequately established in the real world.[8]

In normal conditions, it would seem that competition is a minor feature of the interrelationship between living things, as the ecologist E.J. Kormondy and the entomologist E.S. Messenger maintain. The truth seems to be that animals seek to avoid competition, or rather avoid its more destructive manifestations. Thus living things will learn to occupy a different niche from potential competitors, even if it is one to which they may not be ideally suited and to which they may have to adapt by undergoing behavioral and structural modifications.

Robert Augros and George Stanciu also tell us how thousands of different species of living things are known to co-exist "without competing, because they eat different foods, or are active at different times, or otherwise occupy different niches." Some plant species for instance have learned to live on sandy soil, "others in rich humus, some prefer acid soil, others alkaline: still others require no soil, such as the lichens; some exploit the early growing season, others the late; some get by only because they are tiny, others only because they are huge."[9] Some animal species, to avoid competition, will simply move away to occupy a yet unexploited niche: this is why virtually every Galapagos island now has its own sub-species of finch, tortoise and lizard. In this way, rather than fight to the finish, competing groups spread out and become differentiated.

What is more, when real competition actually occurs it tends to be highly ritualized. Intraspecific conflict in the animal kingdom is indeed little more than a ritual and is conducted according to a set of rules designed, above all, to prevent the occurrence of death or mutilation. Thus rattlesnakes, capable of killing each other with a single bite, never actually bite each other. Their conflict, Charles Shaw reports, is a strange ritual resembling Indian wrestling.

> The successful snake pins the loser for a moment with the weight of his
> body and then lets him escape.[10]

The Oryx antelope, which is equipped with horns capable of putting
a lion to flight, does not use them in earnest in an intraspecific fight. As
Irenius Eibl-Eibesfeldt writes,

> A hornless bull observed by Walthe carried out the full ritual of combat
> as if he still had horns. He struck at his opponent's horns and missed by
> the precise distance at which his non-existent horns would have made
> contact. Equally remarkable, his opponent acted as though his horns
> were in place and responded to his imaginary blows.[11]

Much the same is true of vernacular human societies; for instance it
was the normal procedure in Australian aboriginal warfare for hostilities to cease at the death of one man. Among the Maori, leadership
was all important and hostilities came to an end once the leader of one
of the rival groups was put out of action. Andrew Vayda notes that an
attacking force of Maoris, even when "on the verge of victory," might
withdraw on the loss of its leader.[12]

Another form of ritualization is the substitution of a match or
tournament between two or more champions for a conflict between
two armies. The contest between David and Goliath is an obvious
example. This strategy was resorted to a great deal during the Middle
Ages in Europe. Sport also provides a means of ritualizing conflict
between two social groups. Baseball is apparently used for this purpose on the South Sea island of Truk, as the anthropologist George
Peter Murdock tells us, ever since tribal warfare was banned by the
then colonial powers. Football today increasingly takes the form of a
ritualized conflict between rival groups of "fans"—often representing
rival ethnic groups as in the case of the Celtic and Rangers football
clubs in Glasgow, and also between competing nation states.
Perhaps the most sophisticated and highly ritualized of such conflicts is the Palio of Siena, in which the "contrades"—medieval associations, each of which inhabits its own area of the city—compete
with each other by means of a horse race round the city's incredibly
beautiful central square, the Piazza del Campo. Significantly, there
is remarkably little crime in this city—people have learned to live
with each other and the Palio, into which their aggressive instincts

are channelled, plays a considerable role in enabling them to do so.

The thesis that competition is the ordering principle in nature is based on the fatal error committed by Malthus, Darwin, the social Darwinists, the sociobiologists and indeed, the bulk of mainstream biologists, ecologists and many sociologists, of regarding the atomized, individualistic and competitive societies of today as the norm; and seeing them, what is more, as reflecting the basic structure of the natural world. Such societies are, on the contrary, highly aberrant and necessarily short-lived, as is the economic system that they have developed.

This was clear to Frederick Engels when he came to London to study the great towns. He found there "the war of all against all," and had the wisdom to realize that it was not normal. "We know well enough," he wrote,

> that this isolation of the individual—the narrow minded egotism—is everywhere the fundamental principle of *modern* society. But nowhere is this selfish egotism so blatantly evident as in the frantic bustle of the great city. The disintegration of society into individuals, each guided by his private principles and each pursuing his own aims, has been pushed to its furthest limits in London. Here indeed, human society has been split into its component atoms.[13]

Today, London has been seriously outdone. It is in the slums of the larger industrial conurbations of North America that the war of all against all is most in evidence. Here crime, delinquency and violence of all sorts are the rule, and rather than being seen as normal, they can only be regarded as symptoms of social deprivation and hence of "evo-deviance" (see chapter 47) at the social level. If here the community has largely broken down, so has the family; even the nuclear family is no more. Most households are run by a single woman with children, whose fathers no longer have any interest in their upbringing. Such a society, or rather non-society, is maintained by a state welfare system that above all, serves to perpetuate the poverty and the misery it is supposed to combat; a state of affairs in which social relations are as far removed from the norm as they could possibly be.

We have seen that equally deviant relations among baboons in the London Zoo led Zuckerman to conclude that baboons were individualistic and aggressive creatures which most people believed for a long time afterwards.[14] Yet when ethologists had the opportunity to study them in the wild, they found them to be, on the contrary, both peaceful and socially integrated. It is important to note, too, that neither in the industrial slums, nor among the baboons of the London Zoo, is there the food shortage that Malthus and Darwin took to be the norm and that almost all ecologists regard as providing the motivation for competition. Aggression among asocialized and alienated individuals is but a symptom of their social isolation and alienation.

Obviously, competition has a role to play in the behavior of living things, in particular in a pioneer ecosystem, in which it serves to eliminate randomness and hence to increase the viability of natural systems, helping to maintain the ecosystem's critical order. Competition also serves in such conditions to space out living things which must, among other things, favor the development of increasing diversity which is adaptive to a greater range of environmental challenges, eliciting more numerous patterns of adaptive behavior and, eventually, structural forms. As living things evolve, however, as ecosystems develop from their pioneer states towards their climax states, so are such functions gradually internalized, or ritualized (see chapter 50), so does competition give way to co-operation and so is homeostasis correspondingly increased.

41

Natural systems are homeotelic to Gaia

~

Living beings are connected, so chained together, that they all aim at the same end, and to this end a vast number of intermediate ends are subservient.
Linnaeus

One cannot help being struck by the way in which the cells in an organism not only co-operate but co-operate in a specific direction towards the fulfillment and maintenance of the type of particular organism which they constitute.
Jan Smuts

We HAVE SEEN that co-operation is the primary Gaian inter-relationship. But natural systems can only co-operate *for the purpose of achieving a common goal*. If they did not have a common goal, they could not co-operate; the very term would be meaningless. Natural systems, as differentiated parts of the Gaian hierarchy, share the common goal of maintaining its critical order or stability, for only in this way can they maintain *their own critical order and hence their own stability*. It is significant that there is no word in the English language that makes explicit the essential goal-directed and whole-maintaining character of co-operation, or for that matter of competition, so I have had to coin a new word—homeotely, from the Greek *homeo* (same) and *telos* (goal)—to apply to both.

At the level of a biological organism, the operation of this principle is clear. Cuenot notes how birds that fly can do so because a thousand details converge; long wing and tail feathers, pneumatic bones, airsacs, breast bone and pectoral muscles, design of the ribs, necks, feet, spinal column, pelvis, automatic hooking of feather barbules etc. All the features of a bird, in fact, conspire to enable it to fly. All are homeotelic to its flying activities, while flying itself is homeotelic to the maintenance of the critical order of avian populations within the Gaian hierarchy.

The same principle applies to a community and a society. Anthropologists of the "functional" school saw cultural behavior as ensuring the integrity and stability of social systems. For Radcliffe-Brown the function of a behavioral trait is the contribution it makes "to the total activity of which it is part," while "the function of a particular social usage is the contribution it makes to *the total social life as a functioning unit of the total social system*."[1]

The principle of homeotely must clearly apply to all natural systems. Thus von Bertalanffy accentuates the "whole-maintaining character" of life processes, at the level of the biological organism:

The most convinced representative of an ateleological point of view must admit that actually an enormous preponderance of vital processes and mechanisms have a *whole-maintaining* character; were this not so the organism could not exist at all. But if this is so, then the establishment of the significance of the processes for the life of the organism is a necessary branch of investigation.[2]

He cites E. Ungerer as being so impressed by the "whole-maintaining" function of life processes that he decided to replace the biological "consideration of purpose" with that of "wholeness"[3] (see chapters 5 and 27).

If we accentuate the temporal rather than the spatial aspect of a natural system, seeing it as a process rather than an entity, it is apparent that it is a strategy made up of a number of closely associated steps which must occur in the right order (see chapter 51). *Only when these successive steps are seen in terms of their specific contributions to the process as a whole do they have any meaning.* Thus the development of an embryo in the womb is not a series of *ad hoc* moves, but part of a carefully co-ordinated strategy designed to give rise to an end-product, the human child. Every step in an ecological succession contributes to the achievement of the ecosystem's goal, a climax state. Each of these different steps can be seen superficially as co-operating *with each other* —but in reality, it is *with the process as a whole* with which they are co-operating, and such co-operation only makes sense if it is seen teleologically as a homeotelic process serving to promote the integrity and stability of the whole.

The co-ordination of homeotelic processes is particularly impressive. The processes occurring within an organism, for instance, clearly cannot interfere with each other's functioning. Thus food cannot be properly digested if the blood does not circulate adequately, nor can the circulation of the blood take place in an organism that is no longer capable of digesting its food and which, as a consequence, is wasting away from starvation. In other words, the sort of trade-offs encountered in a fragmented modern society cannot occur.

It is not so obvious but it is equally true that this coordination of homeotelic activities occurs in all natural systems, whether they be stable societies, climax ecosystems or Gaia herself. This was fully understood by Radcliffe-Brown. He saw the essential "functional unity" of a society as "a condition in which all parts of the social system work together with a sufficient degree of harmony or internal consistency, i.e. *without producing persistent conflicts which could neither be resolved nor regulated.*"[4] He notes that this view of society is in direct conflict with the view that culture is no more than a collection of "shreds and patches" for which there are "no discoverable significant social laws." However, without the co-ordination required to prevent "persistent conflicts," life processes could not conceivably achieve their common goal of maintaining the critical order of the Gaian hierarchy.[5]

Competition as well as co-operative behavior serve in different conditions to maintain the critical order of the cosmos, and can therefore be regarded as homeotelic. Thus the competitive activity that serves to eliminate randomness within any natural system must be homeotelic to that system and to the hierarchy of natural systems of which both are part. Competitive strategies that serve to space out populations and increase diversity are similarly homeotelic.

Predators have an obviously homeotelic function to fulfill within an ecosystem. Their role is to apply qualitative and quantitative controls on the prey populations, maintaining their optimum size, organization and viability, and helping to maintain at the same time, the optimum structure of the ecosystem of which they are part. An individual zebra does not see the lion that is stalking it as a benefactor, yet its behavior is undoubtedly beneficial to the zebra population as a whole. It is thus only if one sees predator/prey relations holistically that their homeotelic nature becomes apparent. Significantly, predatory behavior is encouraged by the prey species itself. Thus, behind a herd of cape buffalo there is often a much smaller herd of stragglers, made up of the old and weak. If one of the stragglers tries to join the main herd, it is pushed out. It is on the stragglers, of course, that the lions will concentrate, for to attack the main herd would be too daunting a prospect. In a sense, both predator and prey co-operate to ensure that it is the old and weak—one might say the random elements—that are eliminated, so as to maintain the viability of prey populations required to assure the critical order of the ecosphere (see chapter 40).

The homeotelic nature of normal predatory behavior becomes clearer still when one is faced with the ecological consequences of removing predators from the ecosystems in which they would normally live. In Bangladesh, for instance, frogs were being caught in vast numbers and exported to satisfy the very considerable market for frogs' legs in France and elsewhere. The result was a population explosion of the insects on which the frogs fed, leading to a massive increase in the use of pesticides required for controlling them. Eventually, it is said that the cost of the pesticides became greater than the income derived from selling the frogs.

The removal of predators has also led to a reduction in the ecological diversity required to maintain an ecosystem's stability. Putman and Wratten note that the removal of the starfish *Pisasta ochracens* in the intertidal ecosystem in California caused a dramatic ecological change. Instead of the original fourteen species, only eight remained of which only four were among the eleven species preyed upon by the starfish. They admit that predators therefore seem to "enhance production of individual prey populations" and "create and maintain diversity within a community."[6] The "exploitation" of prey populations by predators is optimal when it is homeotelic, i.e. when it is that which applies those quantitative and qualitative controls on them that *are required* to help maintain the critical order of the ecosystem of which they are part. When there is a breakdown in the balance between predators and their prey populations, these conditions are no longer satisfied and predation becomes heterotelic.

Why do living things normally behave homeotelically to the Gaian hierarchy of natural systems? One reason must be that they are the differentiated parts of such systems in isolation from which they have no meaning, cannot survive or, in the case of a loosely integrated system, can survive only imperfectly and precariously. As Eugene Odum writes, "because each level in the biosystem's spectrum is integrated or interdependent with other levels, there can be no sharp lines or breaks in a functional sense, not even between organism and population. The individual organism, for example, cannot survive for long without its population, any more than the organ would be able to survive for long as a self-perpetuating unit without its organism."[7]

From another perspective, they must behave homeotelically because the hierarchy of larger systems provides them with their field, i.e. with the environment to which they have been adapted by their evolution and upbringing and which, as Boyden points out, must best satisfy their most fundamental needs. For these reasons, one can go so far as to say that *in a stable ecosphere, behavior that satisfies the requirements of the whole must also be that which best satisfies the requirements of its differentiated (as opposed to random) parts.* I refer to this as the principle of hierarchical mutualism.

The dependence of the parts on the whole cannot be better illustrated than by the tendency of the parts of a natural system to reorganize themselves after separation, and even after having been shuffled like a deck of cards, into something approaching their original configuration. Monod notes how this is true of a virus, the bacteriophage T4. When its parts are mixed *in vitro*, they reassemble of their own accord and the reconstituted virus is quite capable of fulfilling its normal functions.[8] Weiss has noted too how freely floating cells from disassociated embryonic skins, cartilage and kidney tissue, if thrown together at random, reassociated themselves to form "higher stages of the tissue in question."

The same of course would be true if one were to shuffle the members of a family or of a climax community in such a way as to create a random assemblage of individuals. Like the parts of the bacteriophage or the embryonic kidney tissue, they would quickly reorganize themselves into their natural groupings. Indeed, one can imagine the frenzied efforts that mothers would make to locate their children; children to find their mothers; fathers to search for their wives and children; elderly grandparents to reintegrate themselves into their families.

Members of different lineage groups and village communities also seek each other out when they migrate to big cities that, in Africa, tend to be clearly divided up into distinct tribal areas. Much the same thing occurs in Western cities. In New York for instance, different ethnic groups such as the Jews, Irish, Italians, Germans, Puerto Ricans and Afro-Americans, live very largely in separate ethnic communities, even when, as is usually the case, the state is committed to integrating them into the anonymous mass-society that best suits its heterarchic purposes.

42

When Gaian control breaks down behavior becomes heterotelic

———

Nature has placed man under the governance of two sovereign masters, pain and pleasure. It is for them alone to point out what we ought to do, as well as to determine what we shall do.
Jeremy Bentham

We have lived to see a time without order
In which everyone is confused in his mind.
One cannot bear to join in the madness
But if one does not do so, one will not share in the spoils.
Modern Javanese Song

Homeotelic behavior is normal behavior serving the purpose for which it was designed phylogenetically and ontogenetically, which is to maintain the critical order of the ecosphere (see chapter 61). Heterotelic behavior (from the Greek, *hetero*—different, and *telos*—goal) is behavior *that is misdirected*, satisfying up to a point the needs of the individual but not those of the Gaian hierarchy as a whole. The critical distinction between homeotelic and heterotelic behavior, between normal and abnormal behavior, is foreign to the paradigm of science. If behavior is looked at reductionistically, there is no way in which its purposive and "whole-maintaining" function can be established and hence no way of determining whether it is fulfilling a homeotelic or a heterotelic function.

Behavior can be misdirected if it is based on faulty information. It can also be misdirected if, in new and unpredictable conditions, behavior based on what has hitherto been sound information ceases to be adaptive. Heterotelic behavior often occurs when new environmental conditions mimic conditions to which a system is capable of adapting homeotelically, but differ from them in at least one very important respect. Thus when a developing organism is exposed to the radionuclide Strontium 90, that is chemically very similar to calcium, it treats it as a raw material for building up bone. This may serve the immediate requirements of the process in question but it does not serve its long-term purposes, and hence those of the organism as a whole, since its chances of contracting cancer and other degenerative diseases are considerably increased.

The Australian ecologist Stephen Boyden establishes the difference between adaptation and what he refers to as "pseudo-adaptation."[1] In Scotland today, there is a very high consumption of refined white bread, margarine, sweets and other junk foods, to the point that nearly forty percent of people who reach the age of twenty-five have already lost all their natural teeth. The homeotelic, adaptive or normal response would be to improve the Scottish diet. Only such a response could conceivably *solve* the problem. The heterotelic or pseudo-adaptive or abnormal response, on the other hand, consists in providing the victims with false teeth. Even if we regard false teeth as a real substitute for real teeth for the purposes of mastication, to provide them does nothing for all the other symptoms of a faulty diet—such as diabetes, diverticulitis, peptic ulcers, appendicitis, varicose veins, various forms of cancer, and the other diseases of civilization most of which have been very convincingly linked with the consumption of junk foods.

On the contrary, because the provision of false teeth makes one particular symptom of a bad diet more tolerable, it will encourage people to pursue their poor eating habits, perpetuating the other resulting afflictions. Because each of them in turn will be dealt with heterotelically: their symptoms being suppressed by various patented medicines all of which have more or less serious side-effects, the victims will be subject to further afflictions and the cycle of heterotelically treated illnesses will widen until the unfortunate people are consigned to hospitals. There, their symptoms are likely to be suppressed by even more drastic methods such as surgical operations, causing still more serious side-effects etc.

There are, of course, exceptions to this rule. Enlightened doctors may well put their patients on a healthier diet, and in general cause them to lead healthier lives that minimize the incidence of disease, but this is likely to be the exception, since for medical practitioners health is a man-made commodity, one that is provided by hospitals and modern medicines.

The heterotelic use of heterotelic medicines on the present scale assures above all the perpetuation of a massive medical industry, increasingly known as the medical-industrial complex, whose sales in the USA account for some fourteen percent of gross national product. The medical industry also consumes its share of non-renewable resources generating a corresponding amount of pollution, and other forms of social and ecological destruction.

The same principle applies in almost every other field of activity in the modern world. In no case are the causes of our problems seriously addressed. All such problems as floods, droughts, epidemics, crime, delinquency, poverty and unemployment are dealt with heterotelically, largely by technological means which our society is geared to providing and which satisfy the immediate economic interests of the corporations and institutions into which it is organized.

Let us consider another example. A man in a stable society will have been designed by his evolution and his cultural upbringing to fulfill those functions within his family that will assure its stability and survival. He fulfills them spontaneously, because it is by doing so that he best satisfies his own individual needs. Thus the husbandly behavior he displays towards his wife, which, indeed, he must display if the family is to survive, will also satisfy his basic individual needs such as sex and companionship. In aberrant conditions however, these same needs may be satisfied by displaying similar behavior towards a woman who is external to the family unit and who may be regarded as *mimicking* his wife. In this way, one or more husbandly needs are satisfied—*but in a way that does not lead to the satisfaction of the needs of his family nor of the hierarchy of larger systems of which it is part.* This means that a mechanism designed to hold together the key family unit has been mobilized to do exactly the opposite. We are then left with a one parent family, a highly unstable entity that does not provide a satisfactory environment for the children's upbringing, and which can break down still further, leading to the abandonment of the children, as is happening on such a scale in the slums of the major South American cities.

If a man needs a family, so does he need a community. However, with economic development, the community like the family breaks down and becomes correspondingly atomized, to be replaced by big corporations or other institutions (gesselschaften), which can be regarded as surrogate social groupings that mimic real communities (gemeinschaften). This is particularly so in Japan, where the large corporations usurp most of the functions normally fulfilled by the community—paying for their employees' education, looking after them when they are sick, and securing their retirement. While this is in many ways admirable, and elicits on the part of the employees a great feeling of loyalty towards the corporation for which they work, it remains true that such behavior is strictly heterotelic, for though it may serve the interests of the corporations themselves, and for a time, those of their employees, it does not serve the interests of society as a whole, still less those of the natural world, to whose rapid destruction Japanese corporations are making such a singular contribution.

If the corporation mimics the family and the community so does the state. This means that the behavior of modern man towards the state upon whose many bureaucratic services he has become increasingly dependent is also heterotelic. For the state is no more a natural constituent of the Gaian hierarchy than is the corporation. It does not seek to provide that environment for its citizens which is required to satisfy their fundamental needs both biological, psychological and social but rather that which best satisfies its own immediate political requirements.

Modern man's religion is also heterotelic since it diverts human religiosity from fulfilling natural homeotelic religious functions towards the natural world, thus making the latter correspondingly more vulnerable towards exploitation and destruction (see chapter 63).

Heterotelic behavior there will always be. It could be regarded as little more than biological, social and ecological randomness. However, in a stable society, it is the exception rather than the rule, and all sorts of social mechanisms exist for reducing its incidence to a minimum. It becomes the rule rather than the exception once a society disintegrates and the biosphere is replaced by the technosphere. As this occurs, behavior ceases to be capable of self-regulation, or homeostasis, and thereby loses its capacity for counteracting randomness or heterotely. The society is then out of control as is our modern society today and set on a course towards social and ecological disaster. All that can save it then, is a cultural "mega-mutation"—an ecologically-based revitalist movement (see chapter 66) giving rise to a society committed, as were the vernacular societies of the past, to a homeotelic behavior pattern.

43

Natural systems can only behave homeotelically within their tolerance range

⸻

Nuclear tests have increased radiation fallout and now the nuclear industry is increasing background levels of radiation which could conceivably exceed our level of tolerance. Our various industrial activities too, are modifying water tables, contaminating groundwater, eroding and desertifying our arable land and in general modifying our environment to a point that many of its essential features will no longer fall within our tolerance range.
Eugene Odum

It is true that a system in homeostasis is forgiving about disturbance, but only when it is healthy and well within the bounds of its capacity to regulate. When such a system is stressed near the limits of its capacity to regulate, even a small jolt may cause it to jump to a new stable state or even to fail entirely.
James Lovelock

THE ECOLOGICAL "principle of tolerance" states that natural systems can only function adaptively within an environment whose basic features have not diverged too far from the optimum. As their environment diverges, so adaptive behavior becomes more difficult and eventually impossible. For each particular feature of the environment there are limits beyond which, in the words of McIntosh, organisms "cannot grow, reproduce, or the ultimate extreme, survive."[1] The same of course can be said for any other natural systems, whether they be ecosystems or human communities. Today, with global economic development, environments almost everywhere are either reaching these limits or have already passed them.

Diversions can occur in both directions—a living thing can be subject to too little as well as too much of anything. They can thus have "an ecological minimum and maximum." Significantly, most animals in their natural habitat live in the middle of their "tolerance range." Thus according to Odum, the eggs of the brook trout can develop in water with a temperature of between 0°C and 12°C, with an optimum at about 4°C; frog eggs can develop in water with a temperature of between 0°C and 30°C with an optimum at about 22°C, "while the upper temperature tolerance for hot spring bacteria is about 88°C and for blue green-algae about 80°C compared to 50°C for the most tolerant fish and insects."[2]

The principle of tolerance can be stated in a more subtle way. To begin with, it must be noted—though it rarely is—that the environment most friendly to the needs of living things, that within which their behavior is most fulfilling and adaptive, can only be that to which they have been adapted by their evolution and upbringing.[3] Common sense tells us that this must be so. Thus a tiger has been adapted by its evolution and upbringing to living in the jungle, which clearly provides its optimum environment. It is the activities in which it is capable of indulging in the jungle that best satisfy its physical and psychological requirements; it is the food that it finds there that it has best been adapted to eating and digesting and it is the smells encountered there that it has best been adapted to detecting, interpreting, reacting to adaptively and enjoying. There is no reason for supposing that man is in any way exempt from the operation of this fundamental principle.

But what is man's natural environment? To answer this, we must consider that man is by nature a hunter-gatherer. As S. Washburn and C. Lancaster write,

> The common factors that dominate human evolution and produced homo sapiens were pre-agricultural. Agricultural ways of life have dominated less than 1 percent of human history and there is no evidence of major biological changes during that period of time . . . the origin of all common characteristics must be sought in pre-agricultural times.[4]

As Wes Jackson puts it, if man were designed to be a farmer, "he would have longer arms."[5] If he had been designed by his evolution to be an industrialist, Jackson might have added, he would be a robot with no requirement for a family or a community, no feelings for the natural world, no morals and no emotions. He would also be equipped with a physical constitution that enables him to feed, with impunity, on devitalized and contaminated food, to drink polluted water, and breathe polluted air.

It must follow that the optimum environment for man can only be that in which his hunter-gatherer ancestors evolved: a climax society, living in a climax ecosystem. As we transform this environment to satisfy the requirements of economic development or progress, so it satisfies his basic needs ever less satisfactorily. This principle has been formulated very eloquently by Boyden:

> The important corollary to Darwinian theory that I wish to stress has not been given a name. I shall refer to it here as the principle of phylogenetic maladjustment [that he now refers to as evodeviance]. According to this principle, if the conditions of life of an animal deviate from those which prevailed in the environment in which the species evolved, the likelihood is that the animal will be less well suited to the new conditions than to those to which it has become genetically adapted through natural selection and consequently some

signs of maladjustment may be anticipated. Obvious though this principle is, and obvious though its importance, it is seldom referred to in the literature, and consequently its significance seems to have been largely overlooked. It relates not only to environmental changes of a physiochemical or material nature, such as changes in the quality of food or air, but also to various non-material environmental influences, such as certain social pressures that may affect behavior. Furthermore, signs of phylogenetic maladjustments may be physiological, behavioral or both.[6]

If many of us refuse to face this inescapable principle, it is above all because its implications are so far reaching. Among other things it makes nonsense of the very idea of progress and hence of economic development. Far from fulfilling its claim to improve our lives, economic development brings about changes that must increasingly cause our environment and our way of life to diverge from the conditions to which we have been adapted by our evolution, giving rise to conditions that lie increasingly outside our "tolerance range." It is thus a process which, if allowed to continue for long enough, must lead to the extinction of our species.

44

The tolerance range of living things is their field or ordered environment

—

The fate of a cell is a function of its position.
Hans Driesch

The Bantu cannot conceive man as an individual, and hence as a force
existing by itself, isolated from its relationships with other living things
and with the animate and inanimate forces that surround it.
Placide Tempels

One of the central elements of Buddhism is the concept of *sunyata* or
"emptiness." I had difficulty understanding the meaning of this at first,
but over the years, in talking to Tashi Rabgyas, things became clearer
to me: "It is something that is not easy to talk about, and impossible
to understand through words alone," he told me once. "It is something
you can only fully grasp through a combination of reflection and personal
experience. But I'll try to explain it in a simple way. Take any object, like a
tree. When you think of a tree you tend to think of it as a distinct, clearly
defined object, and on a certain level it is. But on a more important level
the tree has no independent existence; rather, it dissolves into a web of
relationships. The rain that falls on its leaves, the wind that causes it to
sway, the soil which supports it—all form a part of the tree. Ultimately, if
you think about it, everything in the universe helps to make the tree what
it is. It cannot be isolated; its nature changes from moment to moment—
it is never the same. This is what we mean when we say that things are
'empty,' that they have no substance."
Helena Norberg-Hodge

ONE OF THE MOST glaring deficiencies of both modern development theory and modern (neo-Darwinian) evolutionary theory is that the information determining these processes is seen to be exclusively contained within the genes. Such a view fits in with the notion of causality. The phenotype is seen as the product of a process controlled by an external agent, or manager, the genes. It fits in too with the mechanistic view of life processes, since machines are run in this way by their human operators, but it bears no relationship with what actually happens in the real world.

According to Weiss, the claim that the gene is "the sole ordering principle in organism . . . rests on sheer assertion, based on blind faith and unqualified reductionist preconception." He accuses the proponents of the genetic view of development of "glossing over the difficulty of the problem by bestowing on the gene the faculty of spontaneity, the power of 'dictating,' 'informing,' 'regulating,' 'controlling,' etc. the ordering process in its unorganized milieu, so as to mould the latter into the co-ordinated teamwork that is to culminate in an accomplished organism. But they never explain just how this is done."[1]

The organism is a particular type of natural system. It is organized in a specific way, and these qualities of the organism can neither be attributed exclusively to the action of the genes nor to the chromosomes of which they are part, nor even to the genome itself. Thus an essential feature of the development of an organism is the differentiation of the cells that compose it. These cells, regardless of whether they are liver cells, pancreatic cells, intestinal cells or cells from the muscles and other tissues, were originally endowed with the same genetic information, yet they have somehow learned to fulfill very different functions.

It became clear in the 1920s that this could not be explained in terms of mechanistic science, but only in terms of a totally new paradigm.

The original inspiration probably came from the New Physics of James Clerk Maxwell. Before Maxwell, as Albert Einstein noted, the physical world was seen as made up of little bullet-like atoms, or "material points, whose change consists exclusively of motion."[2] Maxwell's work led to the development of a new view of physical reality, which came to be seen as "continuous fields, not mechanically explicable." An atom could thus no longer be seen in isolation from other atoms, but was seen instead as a small area of an electric field where there is an intense concentration of field force. The French physicist Louis de Broglie saw particles as "wave fields." For the new physicists, the field, what is more, was not regarded in mechanical or even in material terms. It was "a concept of relation," as Jerome Ashmore puts it, and was seen as exerting an "organizing or co-ordinating action" on its constituents.[3]

In the 1920s, Paul Weiss and A. Gurwitsch sought to apply this new concept of the field to biology. Only in terms of this new paradigm, it seemed to them, could scientists explain the notions of form, organization, and the differentiation of the parts of any natural system. "To me," Weiss writes,

as an observer of nature the universe presents itself naively as an immense cohesive continuum. However, we usually do not look at it as such. We are used to looking at it as a patchwork of discrete fragments. This habit stems partly from a biological heritage, which makes focusing on "things," such as prey, enemies, or obstacles, a vital necessity; partly from cultural tradition; and partly from sheer curiosity, which draws our attention and interest to limited "objects."[4]

It is this "immense cohesive continuum" of which a natural system is part that Weiss and Gurwitsch referred to as its "field." Waddington also adopted this view of the living world. He defined a field as a "system of order such that the position taken up by unstable entities in one portion of the system bears a definite relation to the position taken up by unstable entities in other portions."[5] V. Hamberger, one of the original formulators of this view of the living world, saw a field as

a unit or a whole and not merely the sum of the cellular materials of which it is composed. The field with its organizing capacities remains undisturbed if the cellular material which it controls under normal

273

circumstances is diminished or enlarged. The unit character of the field finds its clearest manifestation in these regulative properties.[6]

In this way, the field controls or coordinates the action of the parts and can maintain its stability in the face of internal or external challenges.

The question we must then ask, is how a system interrelates with its "field" in order to assure its own differentiated development along a constellation of chreods. Weiss draws attention to the intimate nature of the cybernism's relationship with its specific environment at every level of organization up to that of the individual and the environment.

> Each cell's genes is, and always has been, a captive of an ordered environment. While the genome contributes to the specific properties of that environment in mutual interactions with it during the whole course of embryogenesis, it is only by virtue of the primordial frame of organization of the cytoplasm of the egg that an individual can maintain from the very start the unity of overall design.[7]

In other words instructions, in this case genetic instructions, are not designed to be transmitted *into a random environment*. Information, as Anatol Rapoport notes, is not something "that can be poured into an empty vessel like fluid or even energy." This is one of the most serious flaws in the neo-Darwinian theory of natural selection in which behavior is seen as determined by the genes *acting in a random environment*. The genes do not dictate, as Weiss puts it, but "interact in co-operation with the whole of which they are part."[8] The instructions they issue will only be obeyed by systems that have been designed by their evolution and upbringing to receive, understand and believe them. This must be true of the transmission of instructions in all living processes regardless of the level of organization at which it occurs (see appendix 2).

As Waddington writes,

> No transmission system can effectively carry information between a transmitter and a recipient *unless the recipient accepts the message as meaningful* . . . As the new born infant develops, for instance, it must be "moulded" into an information acceptor . . . and an entertainer of beliefs.[9]

But this is not enough. The receiver of a message must also be structured, and motivated in such a way as to be capable of acting on the information adaptively. "It is no use pushing the DNA of your sperm into an egg," as Waddington points out, "unless the egg contains the polymerases capable of transcribing it into a messenger and all the rest of the machinery for turning out a protein according to specification."[10] In the same way, the cries of a baby in distress provide an important message to its mother who is not only predisposed to hear them and understand their significance but also to respond to them effectively, otherwise there would be no advantage to be gained from the ability to detect them. In other words, the child's message *is only likely to be really effective within its immediate field, that of its family, within which the mother is the most essential member*. Outside this field the message is likely to lead to a defective response and, if the field is particularly inappropriate, to no response at all.

This is a clear indication of why a child needs to be brought up in its correct family environment that displays the appropriate degree of order and co-operation. This is all the more important in that the experiences of the very early years are the most critical, and if it does not occur in the appropriate conditions the child is likely to display aberrant psychological traits. Indeed, much of the delinquency and retreatism (drug addiction, alcoholism, schizophrenia) that is a feature of modern society seems to be at least partly due to the breakdown of the family and the community under the impact of economic development (see chapter 46). In spite of institutional education or government welfare services, the child deprived of a family is likely to remain emotionally and intellectually stunted. An extreme case is that of the children who have grown up in isolation such as Kasper Hauser or the wild boy of the Aveyron or those brought up by wild animals, who, in spite of all efforts on the part of those who sought to rehabilitate them, could never achieve a mental age of more than two or three.[11]

As children grow older and venture out into the world at large, they undoubtedly require adventure, stimulation, challenges that they had not previously encountered within the family unit. Indeed, living things can suffer not only from family deprivation but also from family saturation. Thus a young person brought up for too long in a womb-like family unit, whose every need is anticipated and who is allowed to take no initiative of any kind, is likely to be ill-adapted for dealing with the problems it will encounter when it leaves the family environment and ventures out into the world at large. Living things should develop within an environment or field that displays a specific "order gradient" or "gradient of co-operation," in which their insulation from the external world is reduced as they grow up, at a rate and to an extent that will vary in different social and ecological conditions.

It is clear that a natural system's "field" is nothing more than its ordered environment. Indeed, if it had been realized before that an environment had to be highly structured rather than random, then there would have been no need for the term "field" or for "field theory." A still more important point is that neither the term "field" nor the term "environment" tends to be seen in the context of the Gaian hierarchy in terms of which their structure and function alone make sense.

45

The behavior of a natural system is controlled homearchically by the hierarchy of larger systems of which it is part

~

Comparative embryology reminds us at every turn that the organism dominates cell formation, using for the same purpose one, several or many cells massing its material and directing its movements and shaping its organs, as if cells did not exist.
Charles Otis Whitman

W E HAVE SEEN (in chapter 44) that the environment or field controls the behavior of the natural systems subjected to it, but how, we might ask, can it conceivably do this?

Like most of the basic terms used by mainstream scientists today (complexity, organization, competition, hierarchy, stability), the term "environment" has never been properly defined. It is usually used loosely to refer to little more than "all that is out there," and no one seems interested in asking what exactly it is that is out there. The same can be said for the term "field."

Once we realize that every system is part of a larger system, it becomes clear that what is the environment of one system comprises, together with the system itself, the larger system of which it is part, to which it is homeotelic and to whose control it is subjected. This was clear to Woodger with reference to the cytoplasm, that provides the nucleus with its immediate environment:

> The word cytoplasm can be understood . . . simply in a topographical sense as meaning whatever is left after the removal of the nucleus. Now there is of course, *no such entity as this to be found in nature.* What is found in nature, is a certain recurrent mode of organization amid the flux of events. And it is to this important fact that the cell concept gives expression.[1]

Patten and Odum also complain that in ecology the term environment *is never defined.*

> The theory of ecology is not pat for us. We believe that to understand the organism in nature, the other half, environment, will have to be understood as well. At present "environment" means environment unspecified, but "ecosystem" is environment specified.[2]

Of course, it is not sufficient to see a living thing or a life process as part of a system that provides it with its immediate environment:

278

we must see it, as Weiss reminds us, in the context of its *total environment: the hierarchy of natural systems of which it is part.*

> What has confounded thinking has been that, due to inattention to the hierarchical structure of living beings . . . the term "environment" *has mostly been used indiscriminately without specifying the respective boundary.* Sometimes, it meant that natural outer environment of the individual (nutrition, meteorological and social climate, stress etc.) sometimes the "milieu interieur" of body fluids and tissue associations, sometimes the cytoplasm around the cell nucleus, whereas in reality, as far as the genes are concerned, it *comprises all of those to the extent to which they are in the last instance relevant for genic interactions.* From the earliest stages of development on, *every cell of the body constitutes an environment for all the others,* every cytoplasm for the nucleus and the cell organelles, every chromosome for the gene-strings in it.[3]

The same argument applies to other life processes, including the upbringing of a child, day-to-day behavior and the all embracing evolutionary process. All involve feedback interactions, directly or indirectly, with every part of their environments, and hence with every system that makes up the hierarchy of the ecosphere, or what Claude Bernard referred to as the "milieu cosmique."

To see the environment of a natural system in this way enables one to see one of the main defects of the neo-Darwinian theory of natural selection: the undefined and anonymous environment was, and still is, seen as having mysteriously acquired the capacity to "select," and what is more, with the most astonishing discrimination, those individuals that it judges to be the "fittest"—which is taken to mean the most individualistic and competitive. How it is capable of doing this and indeed why it should *want* to do so, has never been explained. It all makes much more sense, however, once we see the environment or field as the highly organized environment provided by the ecosphere itself which, like all its constituent sub-systems, *is endowed with the control mechanism required for controlling and coordinating the homeotelic behavior of its constituent parts.*

Such control I shall refer to as homearchic (from the Greek *homeo* meaning same and *archos* meaning government) as opposed to heter-archic (from the Greek *hetero* meaning different and *archos* meaning government) which I shall apply to control by an external agent such as the state.

Homearchy can be seen as a form of holistic as opposed to reductionist causation. The notion has been used in psychology among members of the "mentalist" school. Popper and Eccles refer to it as "downward causation" and Sperry as "emergent causation" or "holistic control."

Weiss points to the various mechanisms that multicellular organisms develop to control and coordinate the activities of their constituent cells: "the nervous system, the hormone system, the homeostatic maintenance of the composition of the body fluids." Eugene Odum also sees ecosystems as possessing very elaborate mechanisms for controlling their constituent parts (see chapter 24).

It is significant that the principle of the control of the parts by the whole is almost entirely ignored by modern cybernetics—the science of control. This is partly, at least, because cyberneticians are mainly concerned with the control of machines rather than of natural systems. When controlling a machine, such as a missile along its course towards its target, the environment can be assumed, for practical purposes, to be random. At the most, allowances must be made for the action of the wind and of other such strictly physical phenomena. However, this will not do when trying to understand the control of the behavior of a natural system, whose environment, provided as it is by the hierarchy of larger systems of which it is part, is highly organized, and exerts considerable control over the behavior of its constituent parts.

To understand the role of the controlling process we must realize that the sub-systems come into being as relatively homogeneous individuals with great potentialities, but unable to constitute viable, differentiated, orderly, natural systems, capable of maintaining their homeostasis within the Gaian hierarchy. Whether they be cells or human individuals, this they must learn, and the learning process (seen in its widest sense) must necessarily occur within the context of the larger whole of which they must become the differentiated, homeotelic constituents.

This sounds as if it is only the part that learns while the whole remains immutable. This is clearly not the case, but undoubtedly the whole is more conservative than the parts. The parts change, as I have already noted, and indeed must do so in order to prevent bigger and more destructive changes that could affect the whole or, more precisely, its overall pattern that must be preserved at all costs.

In the words of Paul Weiss, a natural system must display micro-indeterminacy but also macro-determinacy, in other words the parts are free to change within certain limits but not beyond these limits, and it is the role of the whole to make sure that they do not. Only in this way can their behavior remain homeotelic to the whole, i.e. to the Gaian hierarchy or the cosmos.

Homearchic control is really best seen as regulation rather than control. At the level of a vernacular society, rather than force people to behave contrary to their natural inclinations, it only regulates their natural behavioral tendencies—ensuring that their behavior remain homeotelic to the families, communities, societies and to the cosmos within which they have evolved, and to which it is normally perfectly adjusted, biologically, psychologically and cognitively.

In a vernacular society, it is largely internalized (see chapter 50). Thus to prevent heterotelic behavior, such as overhunting or the over-use of natural resources, the appropriate controls are built into the cultural pattern, which is unfortunately no longer the case in the fragmented mass societies of today.

Robert Nisbet[4] (and, of course, Weber) refers to such control as "exerted by 'traditional authority.'" He sees it as "so closely woven into the fabric of tradition and morality as to be scarcely more notice-able than the air we breathe." It is very much the sort of control that the Taoists referred to as "Wu Wei," that in the words of Wing-Tsit-Chan means "taking no action that is contrary to Nature."[5]

Without this traditional authority, human societies could not conceivably contribute to maintaining the critical order of the cosmos. Political power on the other hand has played a key role in disrupting this critical order. It is unnatural or heterarchic control that, instead of being exerted by the whole on its constituent parts, is imposed, on the contrary, by an external agent such as the State or a corporation at the level of a society, and is designed above all to satisfy their own interests that are usually in conflict with those of society, the natural environment and people as a whole.

46

As the environment diverges from the optimum, biological maladjustment increases

———

Almost all studies that attempt to reconstruct the history of infectious diseases indicate that the burden of infection has tended to increase, rather than decrease, as human beings adopted civilized life styles.
Mark Nathan Cohen

We are witnessing the decay of man—the decay of his teeth, his arteries, his bowels and his joints, on a colossal and unprecedented scale.
John Liverlees (general practitioner and
President of the McCarrison Society)

DAMAGE TO THE BIOSPHERE drastically brought about by economic development or progress is altering the environment of the living things that make up the Gaian hierarchy. Less and less does it resemble that to which we have been adapted by our evolution and ontogenetic development. For example, we now eat food that is grown by unnatural processes that make use of a host of chemical substances: hormones, antibiotics, biocides (including insecticides, herbicides, nematocides, fungicides and rodenticides) of which residues are to be found in nearly all the food commercially available today. Our food is then processed in vast factories with the result that its molecular structure is often totally different from that of the food we have been adapted to eat during the course of our evolution. It is further contaminated with other chemicals such as emulsifiers, preservatives and anti-oxidants designed to impart to it those qualities required to increase shelf-life and otherwise improve its commercial viability. We drink water contaminated with nitrates, heavy metals and synthetic organic chemicals, including pesticides, which no commercial sewerage works or water purification plants can entirely remove. We breathe air that is polluted with lead from gasoline, asbestos particles from brake-linings, carbon monoxide and nitrogen oxides from car exhausts, sulfur dioxides from chimney flues, radioactive iodine, caesium and a host of other radionuclides from the flues of nuclear installations.

It is not surprising that in such conditions we should suffer from a whole range of new diseases, nor that they should be increasingly referred to as "the diseases of civilization." Samuel Epstein of the University of Illinois and other scholars attribute a very high proportion of cancers to exposure to chemicals in the food we eat, the water we drink and the air we breathe—a thesis that is, needless to say, fervently contested by the chemical industry and the experts they sponsor.[1] Ischaemic heart disease, diabetes, peptic ulcers, diverticulitis, appendicitis, varicose veins and tooth caries, like cancer, are also diseases of civilization.

The incidence of these diseases is extremely low (in some cases, nil) among vernacular people living in their natural habitats, as Albert Damon and others have shown for the Solomon Islands,[2] and Ian Prior and his colleagues have demonstrated for Puka Puka in the Cook Islands and for the Tokelau Islands over a period of thirty years.[3] Such studies have also shown, however, that as people become exposed to the Western way of life, and in particular as they adopt the modern Western diet, the incidence of the same diseases increases dramatically. Infectious diseases too, become much more common. This should not surprise us; in many ways, development creates ideal conditions for their transmission.

Malaria is transmitted by the anopheles mosquito which was originally a parasite of monkeys living on the canopy of tropical forests. Well adapted to its hosts, it caused them only mild symptoms of the disease but once the forests were cut down, the mosquitoes had to find alternative hosts and the most generally available one was man. The cutting down of forests in Amazonia has also brought man into contact with the vectors of leichmanosis, previously a disease of sloths and armadillos. The present pandemic of AIDS, which may once have been a disease of green monkeys or chimpanzees, probably became a disease of man once we entered, in different ways, into closer contact with these animals. Modern agriculture has also put us into close contact with parasites that had previously established a stable relationship with the animals we have domesticated: one example is smallpox, probably a variant of cowpox; another is brucellosis.

Large-scale irrigation projects have also provided an ideal habitat for water-borne diseases like malaria and schistosomiasis, spreading them to parts of the world where they were previously unknown. Modern highly intensive livestock rearing, in particular the offensive but presumably "cost-effective" practice of feeding poultry on the carcasses of their fellows, or on their own excrement, has caused their meat and eggs to be increasingly contaminated with such pathogenic bacteria as salmonella. The equally offensive practice of incorporating offal and other animal wastes in the feed of dairy cattle has led to an increase in the contamination of milk products with another pathogenic bacterium, listeria, and to the contamination of beef offal and possibly also beef with the vectors of Bovine Spongiform Encephalopathy (BSE), which is probably transferable to man.

Ironically, the modern preoccupation with hygiene also gives rise to ideal conditions for the proliferation of pathogens. Pasteurized milk products can easily be colonized by micro-organisms, some of which could be pathogens, since in the sterile conditions provided they do not encounter any competition from other micro-organisms. This is the favored explanation for the epidemic of listeria poisoning in Switzerland a few years ago. Poliomyelitis is also a disease of hygiene. Vernacular people, who as children were exposed to the micro-organisms present in soil and perhaps to animal excrement, and who were at the same time fed on their mother's milk, do not get it—but they become vulnerable if on the contrary, they are brought up in a hygienic environment and fed on cow's milk.

Greatly increased human mobility has also contributed to the spread of diseases. In a matter of weeks, if not days, any new outbreak will reach the major population centers of the world. Under such conditions, it is not surprising that the incidence of just about every infectious disease, with the exception of smallpox and poliomyelitis, is increasing worldwide. Meanwhile new diseases, such as AIDS, are appearing and there will undoubtedly be more of them, especially once genetic engineering really gets into its stride, for it can only be a matter of time before our scientists release into the environment a genetically engineered pathogen of which our species has had no evolutionary experience, with potentially disastrous consequences.

As the depletion of the ozone layer increases over the next ten to fifteen years, which will happen even if we stop producing CFCs and other ozone-depleting chemicals today, we shall be subjected to increasing ultraviolet radiation that will not only dramatically increase the incidence of skin cancer, but also disrupt the functioning of our immune systems, making us correspondingly more vulnerable to both degenerative and infectious diseases. The health consequences of global warming are also likely to be serious for the inhabitants of temperate areas, who will now be exposed to the vectors and pathogens that transmit a host of tropical diseases that make life very much more difficult and more precarious in the tropics than in the cooler areas of our planet. Lacking evolutionary experience of these diseases, we are likely to be all the more seriously affected by them.

To these problems, there is no effective technological solution. Medicine can certainly do little to help since it is largely concerned with treating symptoms of diseases, while to control their incidence would mean taking measures that lie outside the brief of the medical profession (see chapter 65), and that would in any case be unacceptable both politically and economically, since it would mean reversing many of the essential processes of economic development or progress.

The molecular biologist and Nobel Laureate James Watson suggests that if man cannot adapt to the world that science is bringing into being, then he must be changed. A new genetically engineered man must presumably be mass-produced, one who can adapt to and perhaps even thrive in the polluted and ecologically degraded world that modern man is substituting for the world to which we have been adapted by our evolution. Such a suggestion can only demonstrate to what extent mainstream science has lost touch with the real world in which we continue to live so precariously.

47

As the environment diverges from the optimum, social maladjustment increases

---

We must reject the trendy thesis that crime is caused by socioeconomic factors.
Michael Howard, speaking while in office
as British Home Secretary (Conservative)

The tendency of unlimited industrialism is to create masses of men and women—detached from tradition, alienated from religion and susceptible to mass suggestion, in other words, a mob. And a mob will be no less a mob if it is well fed, well clothed, well housed, and well disciplined.
T.S. Eliot

Poverty in the black Puerto Rican neighbourhoods on the west side of Chicago is worse than any poverty I saw in West Africa. The people there are guided by strong traditional values. They do not live in constant fear of violence, vermin and fire. We don't find the same sense of desperation and hopelessness that you find in the American ghetto.
Robert Wurmstedt

ECONOMIC DEVELOPMENT causes our social as well as our physical environment to diverge from the optimum. Man evolved as an integral part of the extended family, the lineage group and the small community, together with a host of intermediary associations, such as age-grades and secret societies. In other words, he evolved within a highly structured social environment that we can regard as his social field (see chapter 44).

With economic development, however, the community and the intermediary associations disintegrate. Edward Banfield, who made a sociological study of a south Italian village, was particularly struck by the alienation and demoralization of its inhabitants, a phenomenon known locally as *la miseria*. This, he found, was not basically attributable to the lack of money or material goods—what is normally regarded as poverty—but to the isolation of the families from each other due to the absence of any wider social groupings. This, as we shall see (see chapter 60), he attributed to the usurpation by the state of the basic functions which the village should normally assume.[1]

With the development of modern industry, the extended family itself disintegrates until we get an atomized society of which all that is left of the original social structure is a truncated nuclear family. Even that is eventually subject to further degradation and we end up with the one-parent family, which in the worst case, disintegrates still further into its individual members (see chapter 60).

There is yet another form of social atomization. Families, communities and societies exist in time as well as in space. To be isolated from them thus makes of us temporal as well as spatial isolates—isolated from our ancestors and our children as we are from our contemporaries. This is reflected in our world-view. Whereas in a vernacular society a man sees his life as but a link in a long chain of being, a man in an atomized society such as ours, sees it as something unique. When a man dies, all is over. That is one of the reasons why we in the

West have so great a fear of death, a fear that is not shared by man in a vernacular society who sees himself as living on in the person of his children. In the former society, people are only concerned with the short-term. They are no longer interested in creating a good world for their children and grandchildren and great-grandchildren. "What has posterity done for me?" is a common refrain in the West today. The notion that we owe nothing to posterity seems to justify, in the eyes of many people, our terrible egotism and the deliberate pillaging of the world's natural resources to which our society is so committed in order to satisfy the requirements of the corporations that control it.

Not surprisingly, people in such conditions become increasingly unhappy and depressed. A study undertaken by the Alcohol, Drug Abuse and Mental Health Administration of the United States Government documented how people born after 1945 are ten times more likely to suffer depression than people born 50 years earlier;[2] a second study found that the people born after 1950 were twenty times more likely to suffer depression than those born before 1910. What is more, such depressions are afflicting much younger people than before.

Durkheim referred to the alienation suffered by people deprived of a satisfactory social environment as "anomie." Robert McIver sees people as suffering from anomie "when their lives are empty and purposeless, and deprived of meaningful human relations." The disintegration of the family is possibly the most serious source of alienation or anomie, and it is proceeding today at an unprecedented rate. In the USA one-parent families were a little more than ten percent of the total in 1970 but the figure was more than twenty-three percent in 1988.[3] In the UK, the proportion of babies born to unmarried mothers was twenty-eight percent in 1990, up from 12.8 percent in 1981. This is consistent with a 1990 report which predicted that by the end of the century, fifty percent of children in the UK would be brought up outside the family, which must inevitably bring about a further massive increase in social alienation. Significantly, the number of abandoned children in the UK is increasing. In South America it has already reached epidemic proportions, with about 10 million abandoned children at present roaming the streets of the major cities of Brazil and an estimated 30 million in South America as a whole, a figure that is expected to increase to 100 million by the end of the century.

There is increasing evidence that deprivation of a satisfactory family environment will affect children profoundly and color every aspect of their later lives. Such children are often referred to as emotionally disturbed. However bright they may be, they will tend to find it very difficult to fit into their social environment, the reason being that the early and most important stages of their socialization were badly impaired. As D.O.Hebb shows, the earlier family deprivation occurred, the more will this be the case. School education cannot do much for emotionally disturbed children. They tend to have a short concentration span and are particularly concerned with the present and the short-term, are loath to accept social constraints, and are predisposed to all pathological forms of behavior such as delinquency, drug addiction, alcoholism and schizophrenia. When these young people are forced, at the same time, to live in squalid modern housing estates and as adolescents are largely unemployed, as is increasingly the case today, their lot becomes hopeless. Theodore Dalrymple, a doctor on one such estate in the U K, describes the sheer hopelessness of the world in which he lives:

> I live in a wasteland. In the council estate the glass of many of the windows has been replaced by ply-wood; such gardens as there are have reverted to gray-green scrub, with empty beer and soft drink cans, used condoms and loose sheets of tabloid newspaper in place of flowers; and the people trudge through the desolation as disconsolately as in any communist city.[4]

Dalrymple refers to the young men of the housing estates as "bodily mature, but the with the minds and inclinations of juvenile barbarians." They

> eye the world with solemn hostility, which the tattoos on their knuckles, necks and forearms not infrequently express in words. They are unemployed and often profoundly unemployable; they are intolerant of any external restraint on their behavior, and cannot fix their minds upon anything for more than a few moments. What job could one give them?[5]

What makes matters even more hopeless is that these young people live in a moral and cultural void. "In the absence of a system of values," Dalrymple writes, "adolescent revolt has become a permanent state of mind. Lack of belief in anything is compensated for by shrillness, as if mere noise could fill the inner void."[6]

The same hopelessness has been a feature of the welfare-maintained ghettos of the larger American cities for decades. Oscar Lewis describes the inhabitants of such areas as having a

> strong feeling of fatalism, helplessness, dependence and inferiority. Other traits include a high incidence of weak ego-structure, morality and confusion of sexual identification, or reflecting internal deprivation, a strong present time orientation, with relatively little disposition to defer gratification and plan for the future, and high tolerance of psychological pathology of all kinds. There is widespread belief in male superiority, and among men, a strong preoccupation with machismo, their masculinity.[7]

He refers to this situation as "the culture of poverty" and sees it as a feature of the welfare-maintained slums of the industrial world. Today, however, it is spreading to other sectors of society and, at the current rate, *it could soon be the culture of industrial society as a whole*. That economic development would lead to this state of affairs was intuited by Adam Smith himself. According to Lawrence Dickey, "Towards the end of the 1780s, Smith was becoming increasingly alarmed by what he referred to as 'the depleting moral legacy' of commercial society."[8] His alarm was well-justified; indeed, a recent report by James Pattison and Peter Kim, *The Day America Told the Truth*, shows that Americans now live in a virtual moral vacuum. The authors of the report found

> that ninety-one percent of Americans lie regularly both at work and at home; sixty-eight percent believe there are no American heroes; forty-seven percent are not certain that they would marry the same person again; thirty-one percent of married people have had, or are having, an affair; twenty percent lost their virginity before the age of thirteen; and thirty-three percent of AIDS victims have not told their partners that they are infected.[9]

Equally illustrative is the aberrant behavior of people when the elaborate mechanisms of the law break down for some technical reason. In Montreal, during a twenty-four-hour police strike, shops were pillaged, women raped, and houses burgled. In London, during a power strike, theft increased to such an extent in shops and department stores that many had to close until the lights came on again. In

Saint Croix, the capital of the American Virgin Islands, members of the Police and National Guard were among those who took advantage of the chaos that followed a hurricane by looting stores and terrorizing island residents, many of whom barricaded themselves into their homes.

Crime is increasing at a record rate in the UK, in America and elsewhere. A study by Humberside Police Superintendent John Taylor predicts that by the year 2000 the number of recorded crimes in the UK will have increased from four to six million per year, and that only one in four is likely to be solved. Taylor considers that recorded crimes are merely "the tip of an iceberg," no more than a quarter of those actually committed.[10] If this is so, then in the UK by the end of this century, there would be 24 million crimes, nearly one for every two inhabitants. The crime rate in the USA is even higher and it is worse still in many South American countries, especially in the cities where frequently order has simply broken down.

Crime is closely connected with social alienation. The victims react in a number of different ways to their plight. One reaction among young slum dwellers is to organize themselves into street gangs—a rudimentary community that provides them at once with an identity, a goal structure, an embryonic cultural pattern and a means of achieving recognition and success, at least within their particular group. This gives rise to what Richard Cloward and Lloyd Ohlin refer to as the "violent gang sub-culture."[11]

Another reaction to social alienation, more common among middle-class youths, is to indulge in some form of retreatism, isolating themselves from a way of life and an environment that increasingly fails to satisfy basic psychological needs. For American sociologist Robert Merton,

> Defeatism, quietism and resignation are manifested in escape mechanisms, which ultimately lead him to "escape" from the requirements of the society. It is thus an expedient which arises from the continued failure to near the goal by legitimate measures and from an inability to use the illegitimate route because of internalized prohibitions, this process occurring while the supreme value of the success-goal has not yet been renounced.[12]

One obvious form of retreatism is alcoholism. Another is drug addiction, and the incidence of both these aberrations increases dramatically with social disintegration. Another form of retreatism is schizophrenia, which involves building up and seeking refuge in one's own world of fantasy. This and other forms of mental disease tend to increase with social disintegration, and are particularly in evidence among the members of a society undergoing acculturation (when a culture is breaking down under the influence of an alien one).

Durkheim regarded suicide as the ultimate manifestation of anomie. In one study he found that the suicide rate was particularly low in poor rural communities where social structures were intact and high in disintegrated affluent society, especially among the working classes and even more so among Italian immigrants to the cities of Lorraine. He goes so far as to say that "suicide varies in inverse proportion to the degree of integration of the social groups to which the individual belongs."[13]

The reaction of our political establishment to the increased incidence of all these social aberrations is to blame the victims. They are seen to be deficient in one way or another or "unfit" in the terminology of social Darwinism. Often this is seen as an inherited problem and attributed to a faulty gene; numerous studies have been conducted to explain why this should be so. Thus the U S A government study on depression cited above attributed its growing incidence to a genetic cause. Criminals are often made out to be men with an x and two y chromosomes, rather than single x and y chromosomes, which is a more normal arrangement. Another ploy is to attribute these social aberrations to purely economic factors. They are often seen to be caused by poverty, interpreted in purely economic and material terms, conveniently ignoring that the incidence of these social aberrations is extremely low in the "poorest" Third World countries where social structures have not yet disintegrated. One can wander, for instance, in total security through the worst slums of Calcutta where hundreds of thousands of people are condemned to sleeping rough on the pavements. For there the extended family is still largely intact.

Today such aberrations tend in particular to be attributed to unemployment and the present running-down of the Welfare State. These are undoubtedly important factors, but they do not provide a sufficient explanation since the incidence of these social aberrations was also increasing in the 1960s and early seventies when unemployment levels were low and the social services still highly funded.

Such interpretations *conveniently rationalize further economic development that is inevitably seen as providing the only means of combating any social or economic problem* (see chapter 65). That economic development has itself brought these problems into being is never suggested in political nor academic circles, for it remains the overriding goal of government policies throughout the world—a goal that above all, serves the immediate political and economic interests of politicians and their allies within the industrial community.

48

As the environment diverges from the optimum, cognitive maladjustment increases

Nature endowed us with the capacity to determine nutritional quality and safety of food so long as it was *natural*. For example, we can distinguish between corn fresh from the stalk and corn a day old. Colour, smell and texture are all sensations we use in assessing the nutritive value of food. But all this changes in the modern era of fabricated food. Bakery products and candy appear yellow because they have been treated with a coal tar derivative. Bread, soups and pickles seem tastier because they contain sugar. Meat appears fresher because it contains sodium nitrites to inhibit bacterial growth. Net result: *the taste of fabricated food is no reliable guide to freshness, nutritional quality, or whether the food will eventually kill you.*
Ross Hume Hall

Man has been driven out of the paradise in which he could trust his instincts.
Konrad Lorenz

How can man get into harmony with his surroundings when he is constantly altering them?
E.M.Forster

OUR PERCEPTIVE FACULTIES are admirably suited to providing us with the subjective knowledge of our relationship with our environment that we require for adaptive purposes, *so long as its basic features have not been allowed to diverge too much from those to which we have been adapted by our evolution and upbringing* (see chapters 14 and 43). As our environment moves beyond these limits, however, our perceptions become ever less useful for understanding it and for helping us to adapt to it; we cease, in fact, to be cognitively adjusted to it.

Ross Hume Hall points out that we are cognitively maladjusted to eating modern processed foods and, as a result, are incapable of behaving adaptively towards them.[1] It is not only our senses, but our very intuitive faculties that cease to provide us with the requisite adaptive knowledge. As a result, the solutions to the problems which confront us become increasingly "counter-intuitive," to use Jay Forrester's expression—though this is not because the environment is too complex, as he suggests, but because we have no evolutionary experience of it.[2]

Thus, whereas our ancestors had no difficulty in understanding their relationship with the living world, we have no means of understanding our relationship with the surrogate world we have created. What are the implications, for instance, of subjecting our children to x-rays, of permitting a nuclear power station to be built in the vicinity of our homes, of using CFC-emitting cosmetic sprays that erode the ozone layer which shields our planet from ultraviolet radiation, of cutting down the world's tropical forests, or indeed, of countenancing the industrialization process itself? We depend for counsel on experts who are rarely objective and, even if they were, are unlikely to have been trained to take into account all the relevant factors involved.

It is not only our senses and our intuitive faculties that fail us before the brave new world to which economic development is giving rise;

our very instincts cease to serve as a guide to adaptive behavior. The instinctive behavior of a child in a vernacular society is channelled as the child is socialized via the socialization process within its particular community so as to assure that it is homeotelic to the Gaian hierarchy (see chapter 53). Once social and ecological systems have disintegrated, however, socialization can no longer occur, and the child's behavior becomes heterotelic to what remains of the Gaian hierarchy.

A typical example is our instinctive aggressivity. In a vernacular society, like all other forms of competitiveness, it is highly ritualized and serves social, indeed cosmic, ends. Its destructiveness is also limited because vernacular technology is under social control, which means that wars are fought with traditional, and hence not particularly lethal, weapons (see chapter 57). All this changes dramatically with economic development when the associated social and cultural destruction deprives us of the means of controlling our aggression and of preventing the development of the most lethal and destructive armaments.

Thus we bring into being a world that has diverged so drastically from that to which we have been adapted by our evolution that the very mechanisms with which evolution has endowed us for maintaining the stability of our societies, and hence our own survival, *now serve to achieve the opposite end*. Wilson and other proponents of perpetual progress consider for that reason that "we must suppress our instinctive drives and our emotions," for they can lead to aggressive behavior that in the modern world is no longer tolerable.[3] But if we are to adapt to the brave new world that progress is creating for us, it is not just our aggressivity that must be suppressed but also those instinctive drives and emotions that make of us religious as well as social beings—for only in this way can we adapt to living in the atomized, competitive, secular, and psychically meaningless world that progress is creating for us. Even if this were possible it would mean depriving us of just about everything that makes us truly human. But if the Promethean enterprise we call progress requires that we be transformed into unfeeling and emotionless robots, then surely we have no alternative but to put it into reverse.

Undoubtedly the most alarming instance of cognitive maladjustment must be our failure to grasp the critical nature of the global environmental problems that confront us—deforestation, soil erosion, salinization and desertification, the general chemicalization of the environment, the depletion of the ozone layer and global warming. Only a tiny minority of our academics—not to mention our industrialists or politicians—show any concern at all for these daunting problems, and no measures of any consequence have been undertaken to solve them. At conferences held by the Conservative, Labour and Social Democratic Parties in the UK in 1991, politicians discussed the usual vote-catching topics, obstinately refusing even to mention (save perhaps in a most cursory manner) the real issues that must determine our future and that of our children.

It may not be irrelevant to note that even very modest forms of life, like earthworms, dung beetles and fiddler crabs, have no trouble identifying the real problems they must deal with if they are to survive.

49

Man is psychically maladjusted to the world as depicted by the paradigm of science

~

It is time that man awakens from his millennial dreams, to face the reality of his isolation and of his solitude. He must realize that, like the gypsy, he lives on the margins of the cosmos—cosmos that is deaf to his music and indifferent to his aspirations, as it is to his sufferings and to his crimes.
Jacques Monod

Scientific civilization has destroyed the soul of the world.
Alexis Carrel

Traditional man has a deep-seated need to live in a world that is both whole and organized, hence in a cosmos.
Mircea Eliade

Science has substituted for our world of quality and sense perception, the world in which we live and love and die, another world—the world of quantity, of rectified geometry, a world in which, though there is a place for everything, there is no place for man.
Alexandre Koyré

As MODERN SCIENCE progresses it depicts the world and our relationship to it in terms that have ever less meaning to the human psyche. The Austrian psychologist Victor Frankl regards as absolutely basic what he refers to as "the will to meaning," which he contrasts with Adler's "will to power" and Freud's "will to pleasure." For Frankl, one in four neuroses are of noogenic origin (originating in thought) and most of these, he believes, can be traced to our "existential vacuum," the meaninglessness of life in the world about us.[1]

This "existential vacuum" is deepened by the modern scientific view of man as no more than a machine, responding robot-like to environmental stimuli. His innermost feelings, values and beliefs are little more than illusions; his family, community, society, even the natural world itself, are no more than a seething mass of atoms and molecules —random, purposeless and uncaring. Frankl recalls his reaction as a child to being told by his science teacher that life is nothing but combustion—an oxidation process. On hearing this, he jumped indignantly to his feet. "Dr. Fritz," he asked, "if this is true, what meaning then does life have?" To which key question the teacher presumably had no better answer than have today's mainstream scientists.[2]

Man is psychically adjusted to entertaining the chthonic worldview, or the "old-Gnosis" as Roszak refers to it,[3] in terms of which all the constituents of the natural world—whether they be animal, plant or mineral—radiate meanings, are intelligible beings, integral parts of the cosmic hierarchy (see chapter 55, pp. 337-345). Vernacular man did not have to be cajoled or coerced into accepting such a world-view. It was the world-view of his ancestors and he was imbued with it as he learned to become a member of his society.

Monod admits that vernacular man, or "animistic man" as he refers to him, could see himself as an integral part of the natural world. "Animism," he writes, "established a covenant between man and nature, a profound alliance outside of which seems to stretch only terrifying solitude."[4] But today, science has revealed to us the terrible truth. "The ancient covenant has been broken, man knows at last that he is alone in the immensity of the universe—a universe in which he has no function, to which he has no duties and in which he emerged by pure chance." Monod nevertheless considers that we have no choice but to continue along our present path, however meaningless, however alien. But this is not the view of the German philosopher of science, Gunther Stent. "The dissolution of the covenant," he writes, "presages the end of science, since there is little use in continuing to push the limits of our knowledge further and further if the results have less and less meaning to man's psyche."[5]

50

The internalization of control
increases stability

~

The operation of rituals among the Tsembaga and other Maring helps to maintain an undegraded environment, limits fighting to frequencies which do not endanger the existence of original populations, adjust man-land ratios, facilitates trade, distributes local surpluses of pig throughout the regional population in the form of pork and assures people of high quality protein when they are most in need of it.

Roy Rappaport

Animals are metaphors for survival. By analysing animal behavior, the Indians try to discover an order in the physical world, a world order to which human activities can then be adjusted.

Gerardo Reichel-Dolmatoff

As NATURAL SYSTEMS DEVELOP towards their climax state, their homeostatic mechanisms become more sophisticated, their relationship with their environment more stable. In this process, controls become internalized. In the early stages of development, controls are crude and applied externally (heterarchically). The limit to the expansion of a population, for instance, is set directly by the resources of its environment. If it expands beyond that limit, the population will be reduced by starvation and disease to a level that the environment can support. This is the only sort of population control that is reconcilable with the paradigm of science, which sees living things other than modern man as passive and robot-like and manipulated by some external agent as they largely are in the aberrant conditions of today.

One method of internalizing behavioral controls is through ritualization, a principle alien to industrial society's emphasis on bringing about the maximum change with the minimum human effort. Ritualization does the opposite: it minimizes change and hence social and environmental damage with the maximum effort. Contrary to what we have all been taught, it is the latter strategy that, in normal conditions, is most adaptive.

Wynne Edwards describes in detail how different living things have internalized population control. He notes that external factors—disease, starvation, accidents—play an insignificant role in controlling animal populations and concludes that "they themselves must exercise the necessary restraints." It is thus "the threat of starvation tomorrow, not hunger itself today, that seems to be the factor that decides what the density of a population ought to be."[1]

The territorial system of birds, and also of some animals, helps to make this possible. Wynne Edwards notes that in the breeding season, the male of many species of birds

306

lays claim to an area of not less than a certain minimum size and keeps out all other males of the species; in this way a group of males will parcel out the available ground as individual territories and put a limit on crowding. It is a perfect example of an artificial mechanism geared to adjusting the density of population to the food resources. Instead of competing directly for the food itself, the members compete furiously for pieces of ground, each of which then becomes the exclusive food preserve of its owner. If the standard territory is large enough to feed a family, the entire group is safe from the danger of overtaxing the food supply.[2]

There are many variations on this theme. Wynne Edwards refers to them as "social conventions" and sees them as providing the "homeostatic machinery that prevents the growth of the population from departing too far from the optimal density."[3]

In vernacular human societies, these internal controls are even more sophisticated. Many societies have taboos against sexual activity during lactation, or during the first year of widowhood, or before taking part in all sorts of different rituals and ceremonies. In India, among the Brahmins and related castes, widow remarriage is not permitted. This was at one time of considerable significance, since it was customary for children to get married at the age of five or six and if the bridegroom were to die a few years later, his widow would never be allowed to remarry. Indeed, when the British first went to India they were horrified to find that there were literally hundreds of thousands of widows under the age of eight or nine. In Tibet, a considerable proportion of young men entered monasteries and young women became nuns.

Indeed, there is every reason to suppose that traditional man exploited a veritable constellation of population-control strategies that best fitted into his particular cultural behavior pattern. This was imposed homearchically by his society via public opinion and the council of elders (see chapter 57) and was justified by his mythological and religious beliefs. Malthus was obviously unaware that in climax societies population control is internalized in this way, or he would not have declared that populations necessarily expanded until they were reduced by food shortages.

Gerardo Reichel-Dolmatoff explains how the mythology of the Tukano Indians of Colombia serves to rationalize a whole system of prohibitions against such undesirable trends as "population growth, the exploitation of the physical environment and aggression in inter-personal relations," which could otherwise destroy their ecological balance and threaten their survival. In their mythology, the superior forces of the Earth frequently punish animal species that have become over-indulgent, aggressive or improvident. They serve as examples not only to other animal species but to humans as well.[4]

The prohibitions against overhunting, eating different types of food and indulging in different types of sexual activity are very elaborate. All animals are governed by the "Master of Animals" who jealously guards his flock of deer, tapir, peccary, agouti, paca, monkeys and other species that the Tukano rely on for food. Before anyone can go out hunting, he must first obtain permission from the Master of Animals, and this will only be granted if he undergoes a rigorous preparation that consists of sexual continence, a restricted diet and purification rites including cleansing the body by bathing and emetics. For some days before going on a hunting excursion, the man should not have had any dream with an erotic content. Moreover, it is necessary that none of the women who live in his household be menstruating. To make things even more difficult, a species can only be hunted after the constellation with which it is associated in the Tukano mythology has risen over the horizon. Even then, Reichel-Dolmatoff notes, the hunt is not a purely utilitarian affair devoid of internalized controls. Highly ritualized, it is best regarded as "a courtship in which the prey has to be seduced to submit to the hunter."[5]

When the game is scarce it becomes even more difficult to obtain permission. The prospective hunter must visit the Master of Animals "in a narcotic trance" and promise to send to the Master's abode the souls of the persons who, at their death, must return to this great storehouse to replenish the energy of those animals the supernatural gamekeeper gives to the hunters. In this way, the necessary controls for preventing overhunting and overfishing are built into the cultural pattern of the Tukano. What is more, fear of retribution from the superior powers of the Earth—that usually takes the form of illness or misfortune in hunting—further strengthens the prohibitions against overtaxing the environment (see chapter 65). It follows that it is not the ecosystem in which they live as a physical entity that is controlling them homearchically, but the ecosystem as a product of their own world-view, formulated as it is in the language of their mythology.

With the breakdown of traditional societies under the impact of economic development, culturally internalized constraints of this sort cease to be operative. Unfortunately, the external heterarchic controls applied by the state and its specialized agencies are no substitute. Behavior gets out of control and increasingly heterotelic. Only crude external controls—such as those exerted by the four horsemen of the apocalypse—can, in such conditions, bring population growth and environmental devastation to an end. Massive discontinuities become the order of the day as we move towards a social and ecological disclimax.

51

Life processes are sequential and tend towards the most stable state

＿＿

Pioneering species are replaced not just because the environment does not suit them but because they are poor competitors and competition is more intense in climax ecosystems.
S.D. Putman and R.J. Wratten

That ecological succession is a developmental process and not just a succession of species each acting alone is one of the most important unifying theories in ecology.
Eugene Odum

Development does not occur by chance through encounters with the physical and social environment but follows a certain direction; in the development of thought, particularly, there are sequences or stages of progressive structuration.
Jean Piaget and Bärbel Inhelder

ALL LIFE PROCESSES are sequential. This implies that their various stages must occur in the right order, so much so that if one stage is left out then the succeeding stages will not occur or will occur imperfectly. It also implies that each stage must occur in the spatio-temporal environment or field to which behavior at that stage is adaptive. Let me make this a little clearer.

All behavior must be seen as modifying the environment, not in a random way but as part of a wider strategy. Thus the new environment will be that which will best serve to elicit the behavior that leads to the next stage in the strategy. This does not mean that the whole process is predetermined in a precise way, for at each stage there may be a large number of variants of a basic behavioral response, the given conditions determining which of these (whether one or more) will be adopted.

Piaget was struck by the "sequential character of development" that exhibits "a series of stages, of which each one necessarily results from the preceding one."[1] Indeed that embryological development, occurring as it does within a highly protected and ordered environment, constitutes a planned and sequential strategy, is fairly obvious, but so is the learning process. Piaget and Bärbel Inhelder pointed out at Koestler's famous Alpbach symposium that

> learning is definitely dependent upon the subject's development level. Generally, in all this research, it has been shown that the child never manages to accomplish more than the passage from one sub-stage to the next without ever jumping a stage.[2]

An essential feature of sequential development is that it must occur at the appropriate rate. If it is speeded up or slowed down, the end product is unlikely to be optimum. The reason is that any behavioral process or strategy, because of the hierarchical nature of the biosphere, is likely to be part of a larger process or strategy with which it must be synchronized. Riedl refers to the inertia caused by the need to synchronize a process with a host of others as its "burden." Piaget and Inhelder note the impossibility of accelerating the passage from one stage to the next. Indeed,

> if mechanisms in mental development can be compared to what Waddington in embryology calls "chreods" or necessary paths with a "time-tally" it appears obvious that development always has an optimum rate, neither too slow nor too fast.[3]

For Piaget and Inhelder, cognitive development is governed by precisely the same laws that govern embryological development. This is not very surprising, since the development of a foetus within the womb and a child's upbringing within its family clearly form a single process. The notion that they should be governed by different laws is only conceivable because scientific knowledge is arbitrarily compartmentalized and those two sub-processes are thereby studied in terms of separate disciplines.

The sequential principle in ecology is known as "ecological succession." Succession was regarded by Frederic Clements, one of the founders of holistic ecology in academia, as fundamental to the developing science of ecology. Nature, he considered, did not move aimlessly but in a steady flow towards stability. In a specific environment, a clear progression could be plotted through what Clements called a "sere" that begins in the pioneering stages with an unbalanced and relatively unstable assemblage and ends with a complex and stable equilibrium community capable of sustaining itself indefinitely. Clements accentuated the role of climate in determining the nature of the sere and also established the principle that in any given habitat the sere could only end in a single climax (monoclimax). Both these positions later came under serious attack.[4]

Clements's theory of succession to the climax, as Worster notes, undoubtedly reflected his "underlying, almost metaphysical faith that the development of vegetation must resemble the growth process of an individual plant or animal organism."[5] This view is unacceptable to modern science and hence to modern scientific ecology on a number of counts. Firstly, it tends to confirm the scientifically unacceptable idea that an ecosystem is a "superorganism" as Clements maintained, or at least that it resembles an organism in a significant way. Secondly, it implies that the development of an ecosystem is not the result of random changes selected by an undefined environmental "invisible hand" in accordance with the neo-Darwinian thesis, but occurs instead according to an orderly strategy. Thirdly, it implies that this strategy is carefully coordinated by the ecosystem, which means that ecological development is at once teleological and holistic, which is doubly anathema to mainstream scientists and scientific ecologists for whom life processes are random and atomized.

It is unacceptable for another closely associated reason. It implies that the goal of ecological development is the achievement of stability, whereas our modern industrial society is committed to perpetual change in a single direction, one that requires the reversal of the successional process or sere in order to assure the artificial maintenance of an ecosystem at its most productive but highly unstable pioneering stage.

To accept the principle of ecological succession to a climax is thus to accept the destructive nature of economic development, and not surprisingly ecologists had to reject Clements's thesis. Of course, Clements may well have gone too far; for instance, climate is clearly not the only factor in determining the nature of the climax; nevertheless, his basic thesis must be regarded as correct. As ecology became increasingly perverted to make it conform to the paradigm of science, succession came to be seen, not surprisingly, as largely random. As Gleason, who first formulated the new view of succession, wrote in 1927: "In the center of an association we see only the fluctuations in structure from year to year." He even suggested that succession might be retrogressive.[6]

The whole question of succession to a climax came to a head during the debate over the great dustbowl in the late 1930s. Ecologists at the time showed that the crisis was man-made. Ploughing the delicate southern plains, ecologists maintained, should never have been undertaken. It caused the land to diverge from its climax state and the dustbowl was the inevitable consequence. During the debate that followed, the very notion of a "climax" came under attack. Tansley was particularly keen to discredit the concept. He insisted that man, with his great ingenuity, was capable of creating his own climax, an "anthropogenic climax" as he called it, that he insisted could even be superior to the natural variety.[7]

Clements's climax was also attacked very bitterly by the agricultural historian, James Malin. For him, the large-scale mechanized agriculture, which was seen by ecologists as responsible for the dustbowl, was another step in the march of progress. The plains had benefited from it, nature needed to be plowed up, and "blowing dirt around was necessary for it to remain vigorous and fertile."[8] Clements was the bogey man. His writings provided the rationale for the "hysterical" conspiracy against progress and had to be discredited. "The conventional and traditional concept of the state of nature—the mythical idealized conditions, in which natural forces, biological and physical, were supposed to exist in a state of virtual equilibrium, undisturbed by man"—must be abandoned. Malin never bothered to disguise his motives. The idea of a climax "assumed the end of change" and hence of economic development, which he and his colleagues saw as a panacea for every possible problem.[9]

Ironically, it is the anti-ecological ideas of Gleason, Tansley and Malin that have come to be regarded as the ecological orthodoxy. It is the view of Ricklefs that "in recent years the concept of the climax as an organism or unit has been greatly modified to the point of outright rejection by many ecologists, with the recognition of communities as open systems whose composition varies continuously over environmental gradients."[10] In line with current scientific dogma, ecological succession is now explained in terms of competition and related to the properties of populations rather than whole ecosystems. This is the view put forward today in most ecological text books such as that written by Putman and Wratten.[11]

It is difficult to see how scientific ecologists can really believe this. The operation of all sorts of internally generated negative-feedback mechanisms (Eugene Odum's "environmental hormones") which inhibit the growth of species that are displaced in the succession towards a climax is clearly visible to all but the most prejudiced eye. Ricklefs alludes to the operation of such a mechanism when describing the process of succession on abandoned farmland in the piedmont region of North Carolina. He describes how

> decaying horseweed roots stunt the growth of horseweed seedlings: this self-inhibiting effect, whose function and origin is not understood, cuts short the life of horseweed in the sere. Such growth inhibitors

presumably are the byproduct of other adaptations that increase the fitness of horseweed during the first year of succession. If horseweed plants had little chance of persisting during the second year, owing to invasion of the sere by superior competitors, self-inhibition would have little negative selective value.[12]

Putman and Wratten also refuse to accept that the development of an ecosystem towards a climax is part of a long-term strategy. This means that the climax cannot be taken to its logical outcome; instead it must be seen as *"thrust upon"* the system from the outside. For this reason, they suggest that we abandon the use of the term climax altogether and use instead the term "end community."[13]

How then does their version of succession occur? Putman and Wratten offer the sort of simplistic explanation that can be quantified and modeled by systems ecologists. They suggest that succession is the result of "an accumulation of biomass" that stops when the process comes up against gross features of the environment that are immutable, such as a shortage of resources for further growth. Alternatively, they see it in purely energetic terms as "an imbalance within the energy relations of the community resulting in the accumulation of biomass by the community."[14] Both these explanations are based on the notion that the behavior of an ecosystem is random, mechanistic and individualistic, and thereby uncoordinated, passive and externally controlled, like all the life processes that have been made to fit, Procrustean-like, into the paradigm of science.

Putman and Wratten go further. Productivity, they tell us, is often low in a climax compared to earlier stages in the succession: "Due to the complexity of web-design, cycling of materials through the system is extremely slow."[15] Such features of a climax have traditionally been regarded as beneficial. But Putman and Wratten wonder if they really are. They point out that there are "many examples of far more productive, indeed far more diverse communities characteristic of earlier pre-climax seral stages." They then ask whether a climax is, in fact, tantamount to over-maturity.[16] The argument assumes that productivity is the yardstick for judging ecosystems—the position taken by Tansley and Malin when they opposed the application of any constraints on man's ecologically destructive agricultural activities in the southern plains. Unfortunately, Putman and Wratten are thoroughly representative of modern ecologists whose work serves above all to rationalize technological progress. For Putman and Wratten, a biological explanation of succession towards a climax is not necessary. All we are witnessing, they tell us, is an example of a "statistical process known as a 'regular Markov chain,'" which as we have seen (Chapter 12) bears but the most superficial resemblance to the ecological strategy required to achieve a stable end-state or climax.[17]

Eugene Odum is one of the few modern scientific ecologists to retain a holistic view of succession. For him, the main features of the process are the *more or less directional and predictable sequence of populations*, its ability to correct divergences from its optimum course (Waddington's chreods) which will lead to the requisite climax, and its achievement of an increasingly sophisticated and stable state as it reaches its climax, thereby converting "an inorganic environment to a more organic one" (see chapter 64).[18]

In an earlier textbook, he is still more explicit. Succession, he tells us, is

(1) The orderly process of community changes: these are directional and, therefore, predictable. (2) It results from the modification of the physical environment by the community. (3) It culminates in the establishment of as stable an ecosystem as is biologically possible on the site in question.[19]

He also points out that ecological succession "is community controlled" and insists that "each set of organisms changes the physical substrata and the microclimate (local conditions of temperature, light, etc), thereby making conditions favorable for another set of organisms" and that "when the site has been modified as much as it can be by biological processes, a steady state develops—at least in theory."[20]

In the same book he accentuates the similarity between the development of an organism and that of an ecosystem. He also asks us to think of the temporary communities as developmental stages analogous to the life-history stage through which many organisms pass before reaching adulthood. At the same time, he notes that the mature community with its greater diversity, larger organic structure, and balanced energy flows is often able to buffer the physical environment to a greater extent than the young community, which however, is often the more productive. Thus, the achievement of a measure of stability or homeostasis rather than a mere increase in productivity in a fluctuating physical environment may well be the primary purpose (that is, the survival value) of ecological succession when viewed from the evolutionary standpoint.

It is unlikely that any other leading ecologist today would dare state this unfashionable principle quite so explicitly—yet if it is not faced, there is no way in which the behavior of an ecosystem can be understood—no way, either, in which we can realize just how unnatural and how destructive is the idea of economic progress that seeks to maximize production, regardless of its destabilizing effects on biological, social and ecological systems.

52

Increased complexity leads to
greater stability

~

The stability of complex continental ecosystems was no armour against
the Japanese beetle, the European gypsy moth or the Oriental chestnut
blight *Edothia Parasitica* in North America. It is trivial but not irrelevant
to observe that stability was hardly enhanced by the extra links added to
the trophic web in these instances.
Robert M. May

The term "complex" (as used by modern ecologists) need imply no more
than a haphazard conglomeration, whereas in the living system, we find
distinctive orderliness of the complexes.
Paul Weiss

Uɴᴛɪʟ ʀᴇᴄᴇɴᴛʟʏ ecologists have tended, along with the famous British ecologist Charles Elton, to assume that as a system becomes more complex, it also becomes more stable—though Eugene Odum considers that complexity tapers off some time before a climax, the most stable state, is achieved. Today, however, this link between complexity and stability is denied by most mainstream ecologists.

One of the books that has played an important role in changing this attitude, is R.M.May's *Stability and Complexity in Model Eco-systems.*[1] Underlying it is the assumption that a system's complexity can be measured by the number of its constituent parts without considering the way they are organized, let alone their wider role within the Gaian hierarchy. In other words, it does not distinguish between a system's *natural or homeotelic* parts and its *unnatural or hetero-telic* parts. This means that because a highly destructive ecological invasion, such as the introduction of the rabbit into Australia or the walking catfish into Florida, increases the number of the constituent parts of ecosystems in these countries, it is seen as increasing their complexity. The fact that it also tends to reduce their health, integrity and stability can be construed as confirming May's preposterous thesis that complexity reduces stability.

In reality, of course, all it does is confirm the indubitable principle that to introduce into an ecosystem a living thing that has been designed by its evolution to fulfill a very different role as a constituent of a very different ecosystem, can only increase the former's randomness and reduce its organized or real "complexity."

Prigogine also insists that increased "complexity" is associated with growing instability. This for him is confirmed by the fact that the world is becoming ever more complex, yet, at the same time, increasingly unstable. It is this instability that is reflected in the ever-growing fluctuations—floods, droughts, epidemics and wars—that are everywhere on the increase. In his particular scheme of things, however, such fluctuations are highly desirable because they give rise to economic development or progress.[2] The "complexity" that Prigogine refers to is again of the random kind. It offers no basis for distinguishing between the biospheric complexity required to maintain the integrity and stability of the real world and the technospheric complexity created by economic development which is heterotelic to the biosphere, necessarily disrupting its critical order and stability.

If neither Prigogine nor May can handle organized complexity it is because, among other things, it is *extremely difficult to quantify and hence to model*. Not surprisingly, the model that May builds to prove that complexity reduces stability bears little relationship to the real world. Among other things, the underlying assumptions are totally unrealistic (see chapter 12). Thus May admits that his model only applies to systems with an even number of species, a "disquieting" thought, he agrees, but not one that leads him to question its intrinsic value because, for his purposes, "whether or not the Lotka-Volterra equations (on which the model is based) are applicable to real-world situations is beside the point being made here, which is that simple mathematical models are in general less stable than the corresponding simple mathematical models with few species."[3] In other words, he is not concerned with the relationships between complexity and stability in the real world, *but only in his mathematical model*. In the real world, May admits (though only as an afterthought) that things may be different. "Natural ecosystems, whether structurally complex or simple," he writes, "are the product of a long history of co-evolution of their constituent plants and animals. It is at least plausible that such intricate evolutionary processes have, in effect, brought about those relatively tiny and mathematically atypical regions of parameter space which endow the system with long term stability."[4] However, as May himself states, such an ecosystem is "mathematically atypical" and hence, he intimates, of little relevance to a mathematical model; and to him, it is this that is important.[5]

In the real world, complexity must first be distinguished from diversity (see chapter 53). A natural system can increase the number of its constituent parts so as better to achieve two different and indeed rival strategies. The first is to seek to fulfill adaptive functions with greater accuracy, thereby increasing its homeostasis, *within a given environment*. The second is to increase the number of environmental challenges it can deal with adaptively. The first strategy is the most adaptive in an orderly and predictable environment; the second, in a disorderly and unpredictable environment. The first strategy has been referred to by the German biologist B. Rensch as "anagenesis," the second as "cladogenesis," terms that have been adopted by a number of theoretical biologists such as Julian Huxley and Waddington.

Natural systems that organize their differentiated parts so as best to achieve the first strategy we can refer to as displaying complexity. Those that organize their differentiated parts so as best to achieve the second strategy we can refer to as displaying diversity.

Let us first consider the former. Complexity is organized and purposive. The different parts of a complex system do not come into being by accretion but by differentiation. Differentiation implies integration. For the constituent parts of a natural system to be mobilized to act in conjunction with each other so as to achieve a particular adaptive function, they *must* be differentiated and hence integrated. Thus in a simple ecosystem, for instance, different species of herbivores are relatively undifferentiated eaters. A mountain goat must be able to eat practically anything if it is to survive in its inhospitable habitat, so much so that a slight increase in the population of other species is sufficient to cause a shortage of the basic foodstuffs they have in common. Complex ecosystems, however, are far less vulnerable to such discontinuities. Impala and eland in the African savannah, for instance, have a much more specific diet. They will not only eat different plants but often different parts of the same plants. This means that they make the best use of their environment which will thereby support a greater diversity of herbivores without being degraded. An increase in the number of predator species must also further differentiate and hence further refine the quantitative and qualitative controls applied on prey populations. In these, and a host of other ways, a system becomes more stable as it becomes more complex.

There is a cost however: the greater the specialization and the commitment to specific environmental conditions, the smaller the range of possible responses that a system is capable of mediating, and hence the fewer the environmental challenges to which it can respond adaptively (unless cybernismic complexity is increased). This means that the more highly integrated a complex ecosystem, the less capable it is of tolerating improbable internal or external challenges.

Thus a tropical rainforest is a highly integrated ecosystem judged by the standard of other ecosystems (though clearly it displays nothing like the degree of integration of a biological organism). For this reason it does not withstand improbable external disturbances. Cut down its trees, for instance, and it does not readily recover, whereas a simpler and less integrated system such as a savannah can recover from similar treatment much more readily. The human organism, being still more highly integrated, is correspondingly more vulnerable to a disturbance. Deprive it of the organs that ensure essential metabolic functions, such as the liver or the kidneys, and it too will fail to recover.

Natural systems can only function adaptively (maintain their homeostasis) within specific conditions (see chapter 43). In the case of complex integrated systems, these conditions are often very specialized. For this reason, certain ecologists have maintained that such systems are non-persistent. But this is not so, for on the basis of a very long experience such living things can predict, usually with justification, that these specialized conditions will be maintained (see chapter 30).

What is more, why such conditions have been maintained can very easily be explained. A system together with its environment constitute a larger system. This larger system, by maintaining its own stability, assures the orderliness of the environment to which its sub-systems are submitted and hence the stability of their relationship with their environment. Thus an embryo will tolerate only minor changes to the highly ordered environment or field it requires. However it cannot, on this account, be regarded as unstable. The requisite orderliness of its environment is assured *by virtue of being an integral part of the hierarchy of natural systems whose goal it is to maintain overall stability* which must include, of course, that of its internal environment. Similarly, a child can only flourish in an environment or field displaying a certain measure of order—that of the family. This does not mean that it is unstable, or non-persistent, as this orderly environment is preserved by the normal behavior of the various members of the family unit. The family itself is designed to live in an environment or field that also displays a certain measure of order though less so than that required by its individual members, and this is provided by the community and so on, all the way up the hierarchy of the biosphere. In other words, though a complex integrated system may only be able to adapt to a limited range of environmental conditions, *changes that are outside this range are unlikely to occur* because of the orderly and predictable environmental conditions provided by the hierarchy of natural systems of which it is part. In other words, it displays high resistance stability (see chapter 22).

A less complex and less integrated system may be able to adapt to a wider range of environmental conditions, but it is not insulated in the same way from these conditions, which are correspondingly more likely to occur. For this reason it must be more capable of dealing with them, displaying the requisite level of *resilience* stability. In both cases, the system's capacity to deal with change in the environment to which it has been adapted by its evolution, seems commensurate with the probability of the occurrence of such change. It clearly must be if the system is to maintain its stability and hence survive.

53

By increasing its diversity
a system increases the range of
environmental challenges with which it
is capable of dealing

~

No single organism can make use of all forms of energy and nutrient resources, attack all host genotypes, survive in all temperatures and moisture conditions, or self resist all forms of predation.
David Pimentel

Monocultures are almost invariably prone to disease.
Miguel Altieri

THE TERM "diversity" is used by mainstream ecologists to denote the number of different species that inhabit a complex ecosystem. Diversity is generally considered as having two components. The first is "species richness," also referred to as "species density," a measure of the total number of species present in an ecosystem. The second is "species evenness," a measure of the relative abundance of the different species present and of the extent to which the most abundant ones dominate. It is difficult to see what is to be gained by including these two different and not necessarily connected notions under the same heading of "diversity." How can such a concept help us to understand the role of natural systems within the ecosphere, let alone their role in maintaining its critical order?

Eugene Odum sees diversity as a measure of redundancy. There is considerable apparent redundancy in the natural world. Flies, ticks, herrings and many other forms of life produce a vast number of offspring, of which but a minute fraction will survive and reproduce. Only a very small proportion of the genes that make up the human genome are made use of in protein-synthesis. The others, often referred to as "junk-genes," are regarded as redundant. A human can lead an apparently normal life even when deprived of half of the neurons that make up his neo-cortex. The rest might also be regarded as redundant or "junk neurons." A population, too, can be reduced drastically without its ability to survive being impaired, at least in the short-term.

It would be presumptuous to suppose, however, that the systems involved have not been affected in some way by the reduction in the number of their constituents. Eugene Odum obviously thinks they have, for he considers that to increase an ecosystem's redundancy must also increase its stability, for there would then be more than one species capable of fulfilling a specific function, and hence if one were to become extinct, the others could take over.

326

However redundancy is a misleading term to use. One of the basic techniques used in biotechnology is cloning, which means growing large numbers of plants or other forms of life that are all genetically identical. However, for Pat Mooney genetic uniformity in crops amounts to an invitation for an epidemic to destroy that crop. The world has already experienced the terrible consequences of an agricultural system's dependence on too narrow a genetic base. The best known example is the fate of Ireland's nineteenth century potato economy. The bulk of the population of that country lived off the potato, cereals being produced largely for export to England. Since the potatoes were of a single variety, it was only a matter of time before the whole crop would be struck by a disease. When this happened, some two million people died and several million more were forced to seek a new life in North America. In 1970, the world was reminded of this danger when the USA lost fifteen percent of its maize crop to corn-blight. Fortunately, the superpower did not depend on maize for its sustenance; but in many Third World countries, such a blight would have been a catastrophe.

Genetic uniformity also reduces a population's adaptive capacity. Thus D.J. Merrell and J.C. Underhill failed to induce resistance to DDT among inbred strains of the fruit-fly *Drosophila Melanogaster* after two and a half years exposure to that poison.[1] In contrast to this, resistance to DDT was induced in normal wild populations in less than six months. Waddington also found that genetic assimilation (see appendix 4) "fails completely, at least over periods of fairly small numbers of generations, in in-bred strains lacking genetic variability."[2]

Not surprisingly, "uniform redundancy" does not occur in the natural world. It is not part of the strategy of nature. Natural redundancy is *highly diversified* and the ecosphere's capacity to create this diversity is stupendous. We all know just how many different words can be constructed by using an alphabet of twenty-six letters. Similarly, it would seem that an almost limitless number of instructions can be issued by using the genetic code of four basic nucleotides; and an almost limitless number of different forms of life can be generated from the twenty different amino acids required to make proteins. Not surprisingly, the ecosphere is not only capable of generating an incredible number of different species, but also of different sub-species, varieties and individuals.

This organized diversity enables a natural system to deal with a very wide range of both internal and external challenges—not a random but a specific range—that which, in the light of the system's phylogenetic and ontogenetic experience, is most threatening and most likely to materialize. The more diversity a system displays, the more unthreatening and the more improbable the challenges it is capable of dealing with. This means that the sub-systems must be able to act very much more on their own. Each must be specialized in dealing with different possible challenges. On the other hand, a complex system, displaying very little diversity and organized to adapt with great accuracy to very specific environmental conditions, would only be capable of dealing with the most threatening and the most probable challenges—unless it had developed the requisite cybernismic diversity as in the case of man and other sophisticated mammals.

It might be useful to think of the role of diversity as one of insurance against discontinuities. Thus the most significant feature of tribal agriculture is the incredible diversity of the crops (and varieties of the same crop) that are grown. According to Jurion and Henry, among Central African farmers

> fields of sorghum and millet are commonly composed not only of different varieties, but even of different species of the same genera. As for rice, maize, groundnuts and voandzu, it is more a matter of mixtures of different types than of varieties distinguished one from another.[3]

In peasant societies the same principle applies. Peasants are imbued with what has been termed the "subsistence ethic." Their concern is not to maximize yields but to reduce vulnerability and hence discontinuities such as droughts, floods or plant epidemics. As James Scott writes,

> the local tradition of seed varieties, planting techniques and timing was designed over centuries of trial and error to produce the most stable and reliable yield possible under the circumstances . . . Typically, the peasant seeks to avoid the failure that will ruin him rather than attempting a big, but risky, killing.[4]

Such prudence, however, is inimical to the development of the market and hence to the interests of industrialists and politicians.

To satisfy them, production and consumption must be maximized and insurance sought via market mechanisms. This motivates farmers to adopt precisely those biologically, socially and ecologically disruptive methods that will maximize rather than minimize risk. The results can only be disastrous for, in the long-term, there is no effective substitute for diversity as an insurance against discontinuities.

It is often very difficult to determine which of the constituents of a natural system contribute to its complexity, and which contribute to its diversity. The planting of a large number of different crops by traditional agriculturalists increases not only the diversity but also the complexity of the agricultural ecosystem. In a well planned intercropping system, early established plants tend to reduce soil temperature and produce the appropriate micro-climate for other plants. Plants also complement each other in terms of nutrient cycling; thus deep-rooted plants can act as "nutrient pumps," bringing up minerals from deep down in the sub-soil. Minerals released by the decomposition of annuals are taken up by perennials. The nutrient intensity of some plants is compensated for by the addition of organic matter to the soil by others. Thus cereals benefit by being grown in conjunction with legumes, that have deeper roots, permitting a better use of nutrients and soil moisture, and whose root nodules host bacteria specialized in fixing nitrogen. All these crops thereby play a significant role in the metabolism of an agricultural ecosystem and hence contribute to its complexity. On the other hand, such crops retain their ability to react individually to many environmental challenges. They can thus fulfill two roles, contributing both to the ecosystem's complexity and to its diversity.

It is interesting to note that some natural systems that are organized to display great diversity can, if required to deal with new environmental changes, transform this diversity into complexity and vice versa. A typical example is the slime mould, a small ameba-like creature which normally lives in colonies that display considerable diversity. When there is a shortage of *Enterechia coli*—the bacteria on which they feed—they undergo an impressive metamorphosis, joining together to form a highly differentiated multi-cellular organism displaying a corresponding degree of complexity. As soon as their food supply increases this organism breaks down once more into its constituent parts, complexity yielding once more to diversity.

329

The same occurs among vernacular human communities. When faced with an external challenge, they organize themselves to form larger social groupings—as did the Bushmen in their struggle against the Bantu invaders and as occasionally did the Indians of North America in their struggle against the colonial invaders. There is every reason to suppose that had these native peoples won their struggle, and kept out the invaders, they would afterwards have resumed their normal lifestyles in the traditional social groupings within which such lifestyles are best led—complexity once more giving way to diversity.

54

In a vernacular society education is homeotelic to Gaia

~

Education is the cultural process . . . the way in which each new born individual is transformed into a full member of a specific human society, sharing with the other members a specific human culture.
Margaret Mead

By definition children are pupils and learning is a human activity which least needs manipulation by others. Most learning is not the result of instruction. It is rather the result of unhampered participation in a meaningful setting.
Ivan Illich

Education in a vernacular society is but another word for socialization, a process whereby a child born with a potential for becoming a member of almost any family, community or society, learns to become a member of a specific family, community, society and ecosystem (see chapters 41 and 45). In other words, from the point of view of the society itself, it is the means of renewing itself, or progressively reproducing itself by integrating successive generations into its critical spatio-temporal structure.

A functionally similar process occurs at all levels of organization. Thus a cell, immediately after division, is endowed with the potential for becoming a member of a large number of possible tissues or organs, and slowly learns to fulfill its specialized functions within that tissue or organ in which it is situated (see chapters 41 and 45). The process of cell development or differentiation is also the means whereby the organ or tissue, and indeed the organism itself, can reconcile the necessarily short life-span of its constituent cells with its overall goal of maintaining its stability and that of the biospheric hierarchy of which it is part.

Not surprisingly, the educational process is governed by precisely the same general laws that govern the differentiation of a cell, the development of an embryo and indeed all other homeorhetic life processes (see chapter 25) at different levels of organization. One such law is that behavior proceeds from the general to the particular. It is during the earlier phases that the generalities of a child's behavior pattern will be determined. It is these earlier stages that are the most important and that is why the mother is the most important educator and the quality of the family environment the most significant factor in determining a child's character and capabilities. Another complementary law is that behavioral processes are sequential, their various stages occurring in a specific order. If one is left out, it must follow then the subsequent ones will either not be able to occur at all, or will occur at best imperfectly.

Thus what a child learns during its formal institutionalized education cannot make up for any deficiency in the earlier phases of its upbringing. This is the conclusion that most serious studies have revealed. J.S.Coleman for instance, whose massive study led him to examine the career of 600,000 children, 6,000 teachers and 4,000 schools, reported in 1966 "that family background differences account for much more variation in achievement than do school differences."[1]

This is also the conclusion to the u.s. Government study *Equality of Education Opportunities* published in 1964, which concluded that "variations in the facilities and curriculum of the schools account for relatively little variation in pupil achievement," the most important factor measured being the home background of the individual child. If their educational upbringing is deficient then the incidence of the symptoms of faulty socialization—emotional instability, delinquency, drug addiction and alcoholism—are likely to increase correspondingly.[2]

Like all life processes, education in a vernacular society is highly dynamic, the child being an active participant rather than a consumer of educational merchandise. In such conditions, institutions are largely unnecessary. It suffices to introduce a child into the dynamic social process so admirably described by O.F.Raum, author of that seminal book *Chaga Childhood*, for him to be properly socialized or educated. "The child is not a passive object of education," Raum writes,

> He is a very active agent in it. There is an irrepressible tendency in the child to become an adult, to rise to the status of being allowed to enjoy the privileges of a grown up . . . The child attempts to force the pace of his "social promotion."[3]

Homeorhetic life processes such as education are closely integrated. Waddington emphasizes the close integration of individual chreods within the constellation of chreods that make up the epigenetic landscape, noting that "the sequence of changes by which the fertilized egg becomes an adult animal always involves considerable interactions between neighbouring parts of the embryo."[4] The development of a child into an adult, in a vernacular society, proceeds in the same way. The child develops a close interrelationship with the different members of different social groupings, its lineage group, its age grade, its clan, the secret society to which it may belong and hence with the community that these different social groups constitute.

If education is identified with socialization, then each society must require a different type of education. Thus the program which will transform a Chaga child into an adult member of its society, capable of fulfilling its specific functions within a very distinctive African tribe, cannot conceivably be the same as that which will enable a baby Eskimo to learn its equally specialized but very different functions as a member of a family and small community geared to survival in the inhospitable Arctic regions. A Chaga with the education of an Eskimo is, from the point of view of his society, uneducated, as he would be were he to have been exclusively educated in a Western school or university.

The Colonial powers sought to destroy the cultural pattern of traditional societies largely because many of their essential features prevented traditional people from subordinating social, ecological and spiritual imperatives to the short-term economic ends served by participation in the Colonial economy. There is no better way of destroying a society than by undermining its educational system. Thus as Margaret Read tells us

> the learning of genealogies of the families and clans as among the Ashanti and the Baganda, the recognition of social groupings in hierarchical tribal settings and of their reciprocal relationships, the hearing of tribal history in praise songs and legends told at tribal gatherings —none of these essential socializing activities were deemed worthy of figuring in the curriculum of institutionalized western schools.[5]

Indeed they had little contribution to make towards the achievement of the overriding economic goals of the Colonial regimes or for that matter of Third World governments today, geared as they are to economic development under the tutelage of the World Bank and the IMF. Unable to renew themselves, traditional societies on whom the Western educational system was imposed are doomed to annihilation and their citizens to becoming isolates in an anonymous mass society.

In the modern world, we have lost sight of the true role of education. The main reason is that our society has disintegrated—and if there is no society, then of course, there can be no socialization. In these conditions education must mean something quite different.

Among other things, it requires that children be educated in special-ized institutions instead of in their families and communities; and the isolation of education from the social process has dramatic con-sequences. For one thing, it ceases to be a spontaneous vernacular process and becomes instead an institutional one. The results are dramatic. As Coleman writes,

> this setting-apart of our children in schools which take on ever more functions, ever more extra-curricular activities, for ever longer periods of training, has a singular impact on the child of high school age. He is "cut off" from the rest of society, forced inward towards his own age group, made to carry out his whole social life with others of his own age. With his fellows, he comes to constitute a small society, one that has most of its important interactions within itself, and maintains only a few threads of connections with the outside adult society. Consequently, our society has within its midst a set of small teenage societies, which focus teenage interests and attitudes on things far removed from adult responsibilities and which may develop standards that lead away from those goals established by the larger society.[6]

The child is cut off from society for another reason. It is that modern education is concerned with training people for a career in the predominantly urban industrial world. It is said in India that when a young person gets a high school diploma, he leaves his ancestral village for the nearest town; when he gets a university degree he moves to the city; and when he gets a PhD, he leaves the country for Europe or America. Instead of providing the village with a means of renewing itself, education thereby provides instead a means of assuring its inevitable demise.

Education is one of the many key social functions that the state has usurped and that, in an ecological society, must once again be fulfilled at the level of the family and the community, so that young people should learn once again to fulfill their social, ecological and cosmic roles within the context of their specific culture.

55

In a vernacular society settlements
are homeotelic to Gaia

~

A house is a machine for living in.
Jean Le Corbusier

In vernacular societies, every dwelling is seen as an image of the cosmos,
for every house or tent "contains" and "envelops" man on the model of
the great world.
Titus Burkhardt

We need our *marae* [the traditional Maori meeting compound] for a host
of reasons:
that we may rise tall in oratory,
that we may weep for our dead,
that we may pray to God—
that we may have our feasts,
that we may house our guests,
that we may have our meetings,
that we may have our weddings,
that we may have our reunions,
that we may sing,
that we may dance,
and there know the richness of life,
and the proud heritage that is truly ours.
Maori saying

Vᴇʀɴᴀᴄᴜʟᴀʀ sᴇᴛᴛʟᴇᴍᴇɴᴛs through the ages were designed to satisfy the needs of the whole Gaian hierarchy. To begin with, they were small. Vernacular man usually lived in communities of between fifty and a thousand people. Aristotle considered that a city should not be of more than 5,400 people—the number that could comfortably gather in the Athens market-place.

Ecologically, the temporary settlements of nomads are the most desirable because, among other things, they have the smallest impact on the environment. Stanner goes so far as to say that Australian aborigines probably had less impact on their environment than do many non-human animals. Unlike beavers, who build dams, and termites, who construct huge nests, an aborigine encampment, a year or so after its abandonment, is almost impossible to identify.[1]

Even among sedentary people the needs of small settlements for timber and firewood can be met without annihilating local forests; their need for food does not overtax the soil and their wastes can be absorbed by the local ecosystem without degrading it.

This clearly cannot be said of even the cities of antiquity. The decline and fall of these cities has been attributed to a number of factors, but among them must surely be reckoned the fatal impact of these massive conurbations on fragile ecosystems. Thus in about 1500 BC the great Indus civilization drew to an end. Its principal city, Mohenjo Daro, was built of kiln-baked bricks. Its demise could have been predicted on purely ecological grounds: among other things, it has been estimated that four hundred square miles of forest would have had to be cleared just to fire the bricks for a city of this size.

If this process had continued for centuries, as Sir Mortimer Wheeler notes, it would have led to such serious soil deterioration that the area would no longer have been able to support the city. It is not surprising that the sites once occupied by most of the great cities of antiquity are now deserts. The impact of our modern industrial cities on their environment is, of course, very much greater and correspondingly more destructive.[2]

From the health point of view, the small settlement is also desirable. Its inhabitants will be exposed to relatively low levels of pollution and it does not provide the niche required to sustain a viable population of some of the principal pathogens affecting human populations. George Armelagos considers that

> Small, isolated populations are incapable of the continuous trans-mission of disease, and outbreaks of endemic infectious disease, where they do occur, are likely to be periodic or sporadic. This is a con-sequence of the lack of potential hosts in a small population. If the disease pathogen cannot survive until it comes into contact with a new host, the disease will not be maintained in the population. Many infec-tious diseases, amongst them measles and influenza, require an inter-acting population of 500,000 individuals in order to be maintained.[3]

This thesis tends to be confirmed by paleoecological studies. For instance, R.F. Heizer and L.K. Napton studied fossilized dung of ani-mals from Lovelock Cave in Nevada. They found no eggs or larvae of parasitic helminths, but because of the extraordinary state of preser-vation of certain pseudoparasites—mites and nematodes—they were able to conclude, with what they regarded as a fair degree of certainty, that the ancient people represented by these specimens were free of a whole range of intestinal helminths, including flukes, tapeworms, and many nematodes such as hookworm and Ascaris. This conclusion did not altogether surprise them. They saw it as consistent with our present knowledge of helminthiasis in modern Bushmen and other hunter-gatherers of arid regions.

The American historian William McNeill has shown how infec-tious diseases, throughout the historical period, have spread in one direction: from the urbanized countries of the West to areas where people still lived in small and much healthier settlements.[4]

Settlements must also be small so that each person can have contact with nature. Man has evolved as part of the world of living things. It is doubtful if he can live in the totally artificial environment that we have created in our cities with biological and psychological impunity. Dubos went so far as to question whether man can retain his physical and mental health if he loses contact with the natural forces that have shaped his biological and mental nature.[5] Not surprisingly, urban man often tries desperately to create something of nature in the concrete jungle in which he lives. Thus we see balconies in urban apartment blocks shrouded in vegetation, sprouting from rows of plastic pots. In the background, we can sometimes even hear recorded versions of the sounds of nature, the wind blowing through the trees, a bubbling brook, or the song of the humpback whale.

Settlements must also be small in order to satisfy social requirements, for the structure of human settlements must reflect that of the societies whose physical infrastructure they provide. The basic social unit is undoubtedly the extended family and it is this that must first of all be accommodated, but the settlement must also accommodate the lineage group and the community. Each of these social groupings, moreover, must have an element of privacy. In an Australian Aboriginal encampment, for instance, we find that each family has its own space—the area that the family sweeps several times a day. This place is protected by a windbreak (*wiltja*) and at the edge of it there is a fire. The family spaces are grouped around a larger central space. In the darkness of the night they cannot see each other and thereby have the privacy they require, further enhanced by the custom that once it is dark people do not leave their family space—for fear of malignant spirits that lurk around it.[6]

In a traditional Zulu village, according to Eileen Jensen Krige, the huts are arranged in a circle around the cattle kraal; the chief's hut is always situated in the same position and those of the wives arranged in order of seniority. The kinship group (whose blood relationship may be real or fictitious) that inhabits such a village also enjoys the necessary privacy, with considerable space between the grouped huts of each family.[7]

The Motilone Indians of the Amazon forests, according to Robert Jaulin, live in settlements called *bohios*, which accommodate ten to thirty families under a single roof. Inside the bohio there is semi-darkness. Each family has a space partitioned off from other families. Each too, has a fire in front of its space facing the central circular public space, which blocks the view from the central, circular, public space.[8]

According to Paul Sterling, the traditional Turkish village is made up of households organized into village groups that tend to occupy the same quarters or wards (*mohalle*). The cities of the Yoruba of

Western Nigeria are also divided into areas inhabited by different extended families, which are further organized into neighborhoods inhabited by closely related families. Those inhabiting adjoining areas are also related, although less closely. The traditional city is thus a hierarchical system of houses, compounds, neighborhoods and clusters of neighborhoods of related people: these are closely built and larger spaces separate less closely related groups. In this way the settlement pattern reflects the society's social structure.

The evidence suggests that it is by following these principles that social problems in modern conurbations are reduced to a minimum. Thus Valerius Geist points out that successful modern building designs have been those that

> limited people to social groups close in number to those found in primitive societies. We can recognize three limits, one of about eight persons mimicking the size of an extended family, one of about twenty-five, mimicking a hunting band; one of about two hundred which is the limit of people that any one individual can recognize . . .
>
> A successful building should have less than 200 inhabitants, and should be broken into units housing clusters of about twenty-five people of five families. Had architects designed public housing units keeping these "magic numbers" in mind, they would have taken one step towards reducing anonymity.[9]

Conversely, a number of anthropological studies have shown how disastrous is the modernization of the settlements of stable societies to satisfy market requirements. Jaulin has shown how such changes led to the disintegration of the society of the Motilone Indians. The French anthropologist Claude Lévi Strauss has also described the same process as it affected the Bori Indians of Brazil.[10]

A village or small town must also be arranged so as to confer on it a feeling of wholeness and oneness. In the South West of France, the two neighboring towns of Marmande and Villeneuve-sur-Lot are said to exert very different influences on their inhabitants. The former is stretched out along a main road, the latter, an ancient *bastide*, is built round a central square. Of the two, it is the latter which is known for its spirited community.

Cities, if we are to have them, should also be designed in the same way if they are to satisfy social needs. The central square is a very important feature, offering a place where the citizens can gather to run their affairs. The Greeks could not conceive of a city without its *agora*. Significantly, in the industrial cities of the West, as economic concerns take over from social ones, it is the new shopping precinct with its multi-storied car-park that is the focal point.

Houses and squares and other parts of the settlement should serve as many purposes as possible so as to maximize social contacts. As Nicholas Hildyard notes, it is when the whole spectrum of classes, ages, occupations and activities are concentrated into one localized area

> that the tight mesh of relationships, which form the basis of a community, can develop. Dissect the community, and like a dissected body, it eventually dies. Instead of one community, one gets a series of disjointed, fluid, and highly unstable groupings. By fragmenting activities, one quite simply fragments social relations.[11]

That is precisely what we are doing today. "Work belongs to the industrial estate, play to the playground, leisure to the leisure center, sleeping and eating to the housing estate, shopping to the shopping center, growing old to the old people's home, being ill and dying to the hospital, being rich to one area, and being poor to another."

A settlement should also be compact, the houses close together. Instead of expanses of lawn and concrete there should be narrow streets, maximizing social contact. As Peter Blake writes:

> What the city needs is not wide open spaces, but tightly structured spaces full of shops, restaurants, markets and all the rest. The one sure way to kill cities is to turn their ground floors into great spacious expanses of nothing—"into a sort of social no man's land."[12]

A society's monuments are also important in that they confer on a settlement its identity, as does its language and customs which help to differentiate it from its neighbors. More than that, they are associated with its heroes, its founders, its religious leaders, all those who symbolize the city and serve to sanctify it. This contributes to preserving its identity and its continuity, and helps make people proud of it—which they need to be if it is to be a real community.

A settlement must also be aesthetically satisfying, which means providing an interesting and also a diverse environment, which vernacular settlements invariably succeed in doing. Psychologically, this diversity is as necessary as its absence in the faceless conurbations, where increasingly more people are condemned to live, is intolerable. Indeed, as Lewis Mumford writes

> If man had originally inhabited a world as blankly uniform as a "high-rise" housing development, as featureless as a parking lot, as destitute of life as an automated factory, it is doubtful that he would have had a sufficiently varied experience to retain images, mould language, or acquire ideas.[13]

The depressing effect of living in such conditions was brought home to me during an electoral campaign in Walsall, a suburb of Birmingham, some years ago. My wife Katherine and I, together with a number of our friends, had come from Cornwall to help Jonathan Tyler, then Chairman of the Ecology Party (now the Green Party), to contest that parliamentary seat. In a bar, Katherine met a group of young men with whom she tried to discuss the town in which they lived. They showed little interest in doing so: "We are ashamed of our town" they told her.[14]

This could not be in starker contrast with the attitude of young people in Siena towards their beautiful city. Their love for that city is intense, as is their pride in belonging to it. This could not be made more evident than after the Palio, when the young people of the winning *contrade* strut triumphantly through the streets all night, and indeed for several days and nights afterwards, singing the traditional Palio song:

> In the Piazza del Campo
> Where the verbena grows
> Long live our Siena
> The most beautiful of all cities.
>
> Long live our square
> The town and the chapel
> Long live our Siena
> the most beautiful of all cities.

Significantly, Siena is socially an ideal city, one with an extremely low incidence of crime and other social aberrations.

Finally, another essential feature of a settlement must be its sanctity. Vernacular man could not consider living in a house or settlement that had not been sanctified and hence ritually integrated into the cosmic hierarchy. Thus before a wild and uninhabited area could be inhabited, sacred rites had to be performed so as to "cosmicize" it. Ananda Coomaraswamy tells us that in the Rig Veda, the word *vima*, meaning to "measure out" or to "lay out," is used to refer to "the bringing into being of inhabitable space," or the laying out of "abodes of cosmic order."[15]

To build a new village or city meant first building a holy house or temple, on the cosmic model (see chapter 61). In this way, the settlement that surrounded it was integrated into the cosmic hierarchy. The traditional ceremony performed for that purpose was, as Eliade puts it, a re-enactment of the original act of creation, or cosmogenesis. Thus when Romulus founded Rome, he dug a small ditch in the form of a circle. He threw into it some sacred Earth that he brought with him from the town where his ancestors were buried, and each of his companions did likewise. In this way, Rome remained *terra patrum*. The ditch was always known as *mundus*, which apparently referred to the place the *manes* or ancestors lived, and which also meant the world or cosmos.[16]

Believing that he, his artefacts and his settlements were integral parts of the cosmic hierarchy, chthonic man saw them all as designed according to the same basic plan. According to Fred Eiseman, in Bali, man

> is a tiny part of the overall Hindu-Balinese universe but he contains its structure in microcosm. Man's body has three parts—head, body and feet—just as the universe, macrocosm, has three parts; the upper world of God and heaven, the middle world of man, and the underworld. Man is a kind of scale model of the universe, with exactly the same structure —as is the island of Bali and each village, temple, house, compound, building and occupant of it.[17]

Reichel-Dolmatoff shows how true this still is of the temples built by the Kogi Indians of Colombia.

> Kogi temples are meant to be Cosmic models, models that convey a sense of world order and, simultaneously, are interpreted as the body of

the Mother. Each post, beam or rafter, up to the smallest detail of roof constructions, thatch or vines, used in tying together the different parts, has its specific symbolic values. A temple construction can be read as an anatomical model, a geographical model, a model of social structure and organization, or priestly ritual, or of the upper—and netherworlds; it also is an instrument for astronomical observation.[18]

This was also true of the ancient Jewish temple. According to the Midrash Tanhuma it "corresponds to the whole world and to the creation of man who is a small world."[19] In an ancient Jewish legend, Yahveh orders Moses to build him the temple. "But how shall I know how to make it?" Moses asks. Yahveh answers,

> Do not get frightened; just as I created the world and your body, even so will you make the Tabernacle. You find in the Tabernacle that the beams were fixed into sockets, and in the body the ribs are fixed into the vertebrae and so in the world the mountains are fixed into the fundaments of the Earth. In the Tabernacle there were bolts in the beams to keep them upright and in the body limbs and sinews are drawn to keep man upright and in the world trees and grasses are drawn in the Earth. In the Tabernacle there were hangings to cover its top and both its sides, and in the body the skin of man covers his limbs, and his ribs on both his sides, and in the world the heavens cover the Earth on both its sides. In the Tabernacle the veil is divided between the Holy Place and the Holy of Holies, and in the body the diaphragm divides the heart from the stomach, and in the world it is the firmament which divides between the upper waters and the lower waters.[20]

By seeing his body, his house and his settlement as reflecting the same critical order, which is also that of his society, of the natural world and of the cosmos itself, it becomes clear to vernacular man that his life is subject to the same single law that governs the cosmic hierarchy, and that he is a participant in the great Gaian enterprise, whose goal is to maintain the critical order of the cosmos.

Needless to say, during the industrial age, those who have planned and built our cities have almost totally ignored such considerations. Over the last fifty years particularly, our settlements have been designed almost exclusively with purely economic and utilitarian ends in view, and the results, as we all know, have been catastrophic.

56

In a vernacular society economic activity is homeotelic to Gaia

~~~

Organize your actions for your own benefit. God implanted self-interest
in the human breast as a motive of progress. By following self-interest, we
follow God's will. Going against self-interest only inhibits God's plan.
Heinrich Gossens

I owe the public nothing.
John Pierpoint Morgan

The outstanding discovery of recent historical and anthropological research is that man's economy, as a rule, is submerged in his social
relationships. He does not act so as to safeguard his individual interest
in the possession of material goods; he acts so as to safeguard his social
standing, his social claims, his social assets. He values material goods only
in so far as they serve this end.
Karl Polanyi

Economics is based on *homo economicus* as a self-interested individual
who commends policies that inevitably disrupt existing social relationships. These social costs can be considered only as externalities and
are actually little considered even under that heading. For the most
part they are hardly noticed. We believe these social costs are of
enormous importance, that the increase of gross global product at the
expense of human well-being should cease. We believe human beings
are fundamentally social and that economics should be refounded on the
recognition of this reality. We call for rethinking economics on the basis
of a new concept of *homo economicus* as person-in-community.
Herman Daly and *John Cobb*

MODERN ECONOMICS is supposed to determine how scarce resources should be distributed within a society. Its basic assumption, which is never questioned, is that such resources should be distributed so as to maximize wealth. Wealth is measured in terms of per capita Gross National Product (GNP) which is the sum of all economic transactions within a nation state. This means that to maximize wealth means maximizing transactions, or trade.

Neither of these two assumptions can be accepted. If economics concerns itself with the distribution of scarce resources, this is largely because it is only when resources are scarce that they can be sold at a profit, which is when corporations find it worth their while to produce and distribute them. This is so much the case that much of their work involves creating artificial scarcities, firstly by creating a market that did not previously exist for goods that they have developed or plan to develop, and secondly by building into these goods what is generally referred to as "planned obsolescence." However, for thousands of years prior to the development of the formal economy, the food and artefacts that were required to satisfy human needs were not necessarily in short supply. Scarcity was not, in fact, a feature of the economy of vernacular man, as Lee and Devore, Laurens van der Post and Marshall Sahlins point out over and over again (see chapter 34).

For this reason, it would be more appropriate to adopt George Dalton's view of economics as dealing with the provision of material goods to satisfy biological and social needs. This is what Karl Polanyi refers to as the "substantive" use of the term economics as opposed to the "formal" use. I propose a still more general use of the term economics to refer simply to the study of how resources are distributed within a natural system. In this way we could expand our study to include the economics of biological organisms, ecosystems, vernacular societies and the ecosphere itself. Clearly all require resources of various sorts such as nutrients to ensure their sustenance and hence to preserve their critical order or stability. In addition, if we accept the thesis of General Systems Theory (see chapter 38), we may also suppose that the same fundamental laws govern the distribution of resources in all natural systems regardless of their level of organization.

The most fundamental of such laws—and this must be the basic Law of Economics—is that resources are distributed so as to maintain the integrity and stability of social and ecological systems within which they are distributed, which also means helping to maintain the integrity and stability of the Gaian hierarchy of which these systems are part.

That resources within a natural system are distributed for the purpose of maintaining its integrity and stability is clear at the level of a biological organism. Thus, oxygen is transported via the red corpuscles to all parts of the body in accordance with its requirements; so are the various nutrients that the body requires. This principle is even clearer when scarcity occurs. In such conditions, a natural system is perfectly capable of setting up its own very effective rationing system, and one that clearly reflects its priorities. Nutrients are provided to the parts in accordance with the importance of their contribution to the preservation and hence the stability of the living whole. As Gerard points out, "one can get along without a digestive system quite well under starvation conditions, a great wasting of muscles can be tolerated, the reproductive system isn't important, and so on; but if the heart stops pumping or the brain functioning, the whole system is gone."[1] In the same way, in cold weather, a rationing system becomes operative in preserving the necessary temperature of the critical parts of the body. To begin with, there is a reduction in the blood flow to the surface of the skin, reducing radiation and conduction. This may proceed so far that the skin is frozen and dies, the subordinate unit sacrificed "for the protection of the larger unit."[2] Such behavior is an essential part of an organism's homeostatic mechanisms. The same principle applies within a vernacular society. It is well known that in times of food scarcity, hunter-gatherer groups will make food available to the adults who are necessary for assuring the continuity of the society—the old, who are at least partly dispensable, and the very young, who can be replaced, being occasionally sacrificed.

This has many implications. Thus because our planet's resources are finite (for the biosphere is a closed system from the point of view of materials though it is an open system from the point of view of energy) materials must be constantly recycled, the waste products of one process serving as the raw materials of other processes. Recycling materials is necessary too, in order to avoid their accumulation in any part of the system which would give rise to randomness or pollution. Thus during photosynthesis, carbon is extracted from carbon-dioxide in the atmosphere and the oxygen is released. Oxygen is a waste product of this particular process, but it is the essential raw material for another process, that of breathing by animals. Oxygen is thereby recycled from one living process to another, as are all the chemicals required to sustain the living systems that make up the ecosphere and to maintain its critical chemical composition.

Another essential cyclic process is the food chain, that should really be referred to as the "food cycle": the primary producers (grass, algae and phytoplankton), which alone can harness the energy of the sun, are eaten by herbivores, who in turn are preyed on by carnivores, their dead bodies together with other dead matter being eaten by scavengers, and what remains being broken down by micro-organisms into the nutrients required by the primary producers so that the cycle can renew itself. All living things co-operate in assuring the success of this cycle, without which life would not be possible.

The need to recycle all materials was built into the cultural pattern of all traditional peoples. It was not seen as a scientific requirement but as a moral one. Interestingly enough, the principle is formulated in the sole surviving fragment of the writings of Anaximander. "Things perish into those things out of which they have their birth," he writes, "according to that which is ordained; for they give reparation to one another and pay the penalty of their injustice according to the disposition of time."[3] Anaximander intimates here that the development of living things is an injustice—a violation of both fate (*Moira*) and righteousness (*Dike*) or morality. "Birth was seen as a crime," as Cornford puts it, and growth "an aggravated robbery."[4] It must follow that reparations had to be made to the natural world and the living things that committed the offence must return to the dust from which they came. The same notion is also reflected in the following lines that are always recited by the disciples of that remarkable British social philosopher and guru, John Bennett, before settling down to a meal.

> All life is One.
> And everything that lives is Holy.
> Plants, animals and men,
> All must eat to live and nourish one another,
> We bless the lives that have died to give us food:
> Let us eat consciously,
> Resolving by our Work
> To pay the debt of our existence.[5]

Martin Von Hildebrand shows that a very similar notion is built into the cultural pattern of various Amazonian Indian tribes of Colombia.[6]

Modern man violates this fundamental law of natural economics in everything he does and in doing this, he is spelling his own doom. Human waste, instead of being carefully returned to the soil—the practice of endless generations of traditional farmers—is simply consigned to the nearest waterway; twenty billion tons of it every year, depriving the soil of its fertility, poisoning our waterways and correspondingly reducing their capacity to support fish life. Furthermore agricultural produce, instead of being consumed locally by those who produce it, is exported as systematically as the timber from our woodlands—a one-way process stripping the land of its essential minerals and organic matter. The American agronomist F. H. King noted in his classic *Farmers of Forty Centuries* (1904) how traditional farmers in Japan, Korea and China—countries which he visited at that time—meticulously returned all organic matter to the soil, as a result of which its fertility had been maintained for more than 4,000 years. In his words, he had traveled "from practices (in the USA) by which three generations had exhausted strong virgin fields . . . to others still fertile after thirty centuries of cropping."[7]

The economic activities of modern man are also interfering ever more dramatically with the most fundamental Gaian cycles—such as the water, carbon, sulfur and phosphorus cycles—thus disrupting the critical order of the ecosphere and reducing its capacity to support life. All this is unfortunately inevitable if economic development remains modern man's overriding goal. For economic development is a one-way process in which the biosphere is systematically transformed into the technosphere and technospheric waste—a process that cannot continue indefinitely.

If the economic system of vernacular society is subject to the same laws that govern the economics of other self-regulating, natural systems, then it cannot at the same time be governed by the laws that our modern economists have formulated on the basis of their experience of modern market economies, and that they assume to be of universal application. As the economic historian Karl Polanyi showed so convincingly, in the vernacular world, *homo economicus* is conspicuous by his absence, and economic activities are largely conducted *to satisfy social rather than commercial goals*.[8]

Polanyi also notes that, in behaving in this way, vernacular man was serving his own immediate interests, for vernacular society

> keeps all its members from starving unless it is itself borne down by catastrophe, in which case interests are again threatened collectively, not individually. The maintenance of social ties, on the other hand, is crucial. First, because by disregarding the accepted code of honor, or generosity, the individual cuts himself off from the community and becomes an outcast; second, because in the long run, all social obligations are reciprocal, and their fulfillment serves also the individual's give-and-take interests best.[9]

The embeddedness of the vernacular economy in social relationships is clear, if one considers that its units of economic activity are not corporations, but families and communities.

The family is a social, religious, ceremonial, but also an economic unit of behavior. That is why, once institutions and corporations begin to usurp its economic functions, it tends to disintegrate. Economic functions fulfilled at the level of the family, the lineage group, the community, occur without any external inducement; a mother looks after her children; a father provides for his wife and also helps bring up the children. Both look after their aged parents and other relatives, as they must do if they are to assure the stability of the family and of the community, that, because it is but an association of families, cannot otherwise exist.

In such a society, a man does not act as a purely economic animal. As Sahlins writes, "He produces in his capacity as a social person, as husband and father, brother and lineage mate, member of a clan and village." He works as an integral member of these social groups, as *a whole man*.[10]

So alien is the modern concept of "work" to those living within stable societies, that there is no word for it in their vocabularies. Jean Liedloff tells us that the Yequana Indians of Venezuela, with whom she lived for two and a half years, did have a word for work—*tarabajo* —which obviously came from the Spanish word *trabajo*, pointing to its relatively recent origin.[11] Mungo Park wrote, towards the end of the eighteenth century, that "paid service is unknown to the negro, indeed, the African language ignores the word."[12]

Primitive economic behavior is, to quote Sahlins, "largely an aspect of kinship behavior and is thereby organized by means completely different from capitalist production and market transactions"[13] and also, one might add, from socialist production and distribution via a state bureaucracy. That in a vernacular society there is sufficient motivation to perform "work" with enthusiasm and skill is attested by many anthropologists. Richard Thurnwald notes for instance, that among tribes "labor always tends beyond that which is strictly necessary"[14] and again that "work is never limited to the unavoidable minimum but exceeds the absolutely necessary amount, owing to a natural or acquired functional urge to activity."[15] Neither is vernacular man alienated from the product of his work as Karl Marx saw the worker to be in a capitalist economy. As Sahlins tells us,

> the tribesmen's relation to productive means and finished products often exceeds ownership as we understand it, moving beyond mundane possession to a mystic attachment. The land is a spiritual value, a beneficent source—the home of his ancestors, "the plain of one's bones," Hawaiians say. And the things man makes and habitually uses are expressions of himself, perhaps so imbued with his genius, that their ultimate disposition can be only his own grave.[16]

It is hardly surprising that members of vernacular societies strongly resisted being transformed into mere units of wage-labor. Thus Agwu Akpala describes the difficulties encountered by the Enugu coal-mining industry in Nigeria in obtaining labor for its mines. Laborers, it appears, could only be obtained by press-gangs. Every day 700 of them disappeared never to be seen again, unless they had the misfortune to be "grabbed" a second time. Eventually, the chiefs were employed to force their subjects into working for the mining company, and paid for each wage-laborer they provided. At first, those who refused to obey their chiefs were fined; eventually it became necessary to sentence them to varying periods of hard labor.[17] This gives some idea of how difficult it is to persuade people leading a fulfilling vernacular life, to leave their families and communities for monotonous, soul-destroying work in some large enterprise. Ironically, such enterprises have often been justified on the grounds of relieving unemployment in tribal areas.

Homeotelic economic behavior is well demonstrated by vernacular horticulture and agriculture, family and community activities to which people contribute largely in accordance with their status within the society—the produce being then distributed by individual farmers and gardeners according to their obligations to different members of the family and community. The anthropologist Peter Huber, who has studied the agriculture of the Anggor people of New Guinea, goes so far as to argue that they do not just organize themselves in order to produce food; on the contrary, they *produce food in order to organize themselves.* He sees "the problems of creating and maintaining sociality" as being "the central element" in their agricultural system.[18] Social organization is mainly produced among the Anggor by the hunting and communal distribution of feral pigs. "These pigs are not valued simply as meat," he writes,

> or even simply as pigs, but rather in terms of a complex system of association which links religion, land tenure, daily life and social classification. It is because of these associations that the Anggor can produce organization by killing and distributing feral pigs.[19]

This is not an isolated example: on the contrary, Huber tells us that the ethnographic record "is replete with instances in which agricultural production is quite explicitly linked—directly and/or indirectly—with ritual events which organize communities on various levels."

Polanyi sees the distribution of food and other products in a vernacular society as governed by two basic principles: reciprocity and redistribution. When a hunter kills a game animal he will not sell it or even store it for a rainy day; instead, he will give a feast. In a sense this will provide him with all the advantages he could have derived from selling or storing it, because he knows that his hospitality will one day be reciprocated. Giving a feast is like putting money in the bank or using one's friends as a deep freeze, but it enables one to get fresh food instead of frozen food in exchange and a party to boot. At the same time, the system creates a *veritable network of mutual obligations which help knit together the members of his society, and increase its cohesion and viability.*

Once people are provided with the equipment for storing perishable food, much of the apparent need for holding feasts is removed. In one of the Pacific islands administered by New Zealand, deep freezes have apparently been installed at the main population centers. As a result, reciprocity has ceased to be the favored means of storing surplus food; there are far fewer feasts and so of course social cohesion has suffered.

Phyllis Kaberry describes what reciprocity involves among the Lunga of Australia:

> The husband must from time to time give kangaroo to his wife's parents and brothers; besides this, he always distributes a little among his blood relatives. Most of what the woman has obtained is consumed by herself, husband and children; if she has a little extra, she takes some to her mother, sister, mother's mother, father, in fact to any close relative. She on another occasion receives similar offerings from them, and also meat from her male relatives, which she shares with her husband and children. These gifts are not compulsory as are her husband's to her people. They are dictated by tribal sentiment and her own affection for these individuals; by a kinship system that finds concrete expression not only in attitudes and linguistic usage but also in exchange of the limited food resources and the material and ritual objects that are found in the community.[20]

Kaberry regards such behavior as motivated by "enlightened self-interest." The donor may not get anything material in exchange, as elderly relatives do not go hunting and may not have enough strength to do much gathering, but he benefits from their esteem and also from that of the community at large. He is thereby building up "social wealth" for which, in many cases, money in the bank may be but a poor substitute.

There is also a redistributive element in many apparently reciprocal transactions. In the Comores for instance, gifts of oxen and food-stuffs (*djelileo*) are made to a young man by members of his age grade on the occasion of his "grand marriage"—the most important ceremony of his life—on the lavishness of which his subsequent status within the community will, in great measure, depend. When a lender subsequently prepares his "grand marriage" he will expect repayment of any loans he previously made. He will not, however, get goods of exactly the same value. Some previous borrowers may return less than they borrowed; most, however, will try desperately to return goods whose value will be as much as possible in excess of that of the goods that they themselves once borrowed. The reason is obvious; their status will depend on their generosity. The more the value of the goods they return exceeds that of the goods they borrowed, the greater the prestige they thereby acquire and the more social wealth they build up.

This brings us to redistribution proper, as the term is normally used. In some societies, important men (big men, as they are referred to in Melanesia) give large feasts which other members of the society may never be in a position to reciprocate. It is social prestige that they obtain in exchange. The best known example of this sort of redistribution is the legendary *potlatch* of the Indians of the North West coast of North America, a practice that satisfies many social requirements. As Malinowski writes, "the chief everywhere acts as a tribal banker, collecting food, storing it, protecting it and then using it for the benefit of the whole community."[21] At the same time, it contributes, as does reciprocity, to the building up of social bonds. An economic system based on reciprocity and redistribution also prevents the accumulation of goods that might otherwise be translated into capital leading to the development of large-scale economic enterprises that are *no longer subject to effective social control*, and also to the development of the market with the corresponding reorganization of the biosphere to satisfy market requirements.

Economic behavior in a stable society does not interfere with social and ecological priorities as it does in our modern industrial society; instead it serves to fulfill essential social and ecological functions. Malinowski came to this conclusion after his exhaustive study of the life of the Trobriand Islanders. He regarded their elaborate system of reciprocity and redistribution as "one of the main instruments of social organization, of the power of the chief, of the bonds of kinship and of relationships in law."[22]

That the vernacular economy was "embedded"—to use Polanyi's expression—in "social relationships" is critical.[23] What this means is that such an economy is under *social control*, hence designed to satisfy the society's basic requirements, and in particular the maintenance of its integrity and stability. Once economic life ceases to be embedded in social relationships, and worse still, once social relationships actually become "embedded in the economic system" then the economy ceases to be under control, becoming random to the society and to the ecosphere, and disrupting their critical order.

57

In a vernacular society technology
is homeotelic to Gaia

———

At the heart of the Industrial Revolution of the eighteenth century there was an almost miraculous improvement in the tools of production, which was accompanied by a catastrophic dislocation of the lives of the common people.
Karl Polanyi

Technology, as we know it today, is a historical phenomenon born of a certain idea of nature, of a certain idea of progress, of a certain preconception about the deterministic structure of the world and also related to specific social ideals and specific visions of the ends of human life.
Henryk Skolimowski

Appropriate technology reminds us that before we choose our tools and techniques we must choose our dreams and values, for some technologies serve them, while others make them unobtainable.
Tom Bender

High technology is merely an instrument for making the plundering of our planet more effective.
Paul Blau

The Chang Thang is a ferocious place. One minute the air is calm and the sun is shining, the next it is hailing. It isn't possible to try and alter the Chang Thang. We don't try: instead we use our knowledge to adjust to it.
Tibetan nomad

359

In a vernacular society, technology is "embedded" in social relations—in other words, it is under social and hence ecological control. The technology used by a vernacular society in the production of its artefacts or in the cultivation of its fields is not that which maximizes productivity, but that which best suits the strategies that the society exploits for achieving its goal of maintaining its homeostasis and hence the homeostasis of the ecosphere itself. This technology is also rationalized and legitimized by its mythology.

All economic activities in vernacular society are highly ritualized. Every stage in an economic activity is marked by a ceremony that endows it with a cosmic meaning enabling it to contribute to maintaining that wider critical order on which the survival of every society depends.

That this was the case among the ancient Greeks is made clear by Hesiod in his *Works and Days* (see chapter 61). The art of agriculture, in order to be effective, he tells us, must above all be in keeping with the *Nomos*, or the traditional law, and hence with nature's course. As Cornford puts it, "Man must keep straight upon the path of custom (*Nomos*) or right (*Dike*) or else the answering processes of natural life would likewise leave the track."[1]

Thus the technology of vernacular man was not designed to transform or master the environment, but rather to enable him to live with it. Reichel-Dolmatoff notes how the Tukano Indians of Colombia have

> little interest in new knowledge that might be used for exploiting the environment more effectively, and there is little concern for maximizing short-term gains or for obtaining more food or raw materials than are actually needed. But there is always a great deal of interest in accumulating more factual knowledge about biological reality and, above all, *about knowing what the physical world requires from man.*

> This knowledge, the Indians believe, is essential for survival because man must bring himself into conformity with nature if he wants to exist as part of nature's unity, and must fit his demands to nature's availabilities.[2]

He notes how highly developed is the Indians' knowledge of ecology and animal behavior. "Such phenomena as parasitism, symbiosis, commensalism and other relationships between co-occurring species have been well observed by them and are pointed out as possible methods of adaptation." They are also well aware of what would be the consequences for them of violating basic ecological laws. Thus their mythology describes how various animal species have been punished and occasionally made extinct

> for not obeying certain prescribed rules of adaptive significance. Thus, gluttony, improvidence, aggressiveness and all forms of over-indulgence are punished by the superior forces to serve as examples not only to the animal community, but also to human society. Animals, then, are metaphors for survival. By analysing animal behavior the Indians try to discover an order in the physical world, *a world-order to which human activities can then be adjusted.*[3]

It follows that a society's technology is very much its own, an integral and often sacred part of its cultural heritage. For this reason there is very little "technology transfer" among vernacular people. Mary Douglas describes how the Lele, who live on one bank of the Kasai river in Zaire, persist in making use of their own relatively simple technologies, although they are well acquainted with the more sophisticated technologies made use of by the Bushong who live on the opposite bank of the river. It does not occur to the Lele to make use of Bushong technology because it *does not fit in with their own cultural pattern*, nor is its use rationalized and validated by their metaphysical beliefs and mythology.[4]

Similarly, according to Igor de Garine, the Massa of the North Cameroons and of Chad have refused to cultivate sorghum during the dry season even though to do so would enable them to double their food production. This is not because they do not know about its cultivation, since their neighbors the Tupuri cultivate sorghum very successfully. It is simply that the Massa regard it as *more important to maintain their cultural identity than to increase their food production.*[5]

When the Portuguese introduced the musket into sixteenth century Japan, its use was frowned upon and it took a very long time before it was allowed to replace traditional weapons. Its efficacy as an instrument of war was unquestioned, but it simply did not fit in with the Japanese cultural traditions in terms of which the use of a device which enabled a small child to kill an experienced samurai who had devoted his life to mastering the martial arts was totally unacceptable. The musket had no part to play in their traditional lifestyle.

Similarly the wheel, that we regard as one of the most basic of technologies, was not seen by the Yequana Indians of Venezuelan Amazonia as capable of playing any useful role in their lives. Jean Liedloff, who lived among them for two and a half years, claims that she has seen the wheel being invented at least eleven times. Children played with it and it was a source of great amusement for all, but it never occurred to them that it could be put to any other use, and once they got bored with it, it was unceremoniously relegated to the rubbish heap.[6] It was no different in the Golden Age of ancient Athens when, as Henryk Skolimowski notes, all sorts of ingenious gadgets were developed, not for utilitarian purposes but purely for entertainment.[7] According to Plutarch, even Archimedes attached little importance to technological innovations and did not bother to leave any commentary on his inventions.

Robert Fernea, who describes the traditional irrigation system of the El Shabana tribe of Mesopotamia, accentuates its sustainability and contrasts this with the non-sustainability of modern irrigation methods. He believes that all the ancient tribal societies who once practiced irrigated agriculture in Mesopotamia achieved a "congruence of fit" between their methods of cultivation, their land-tenure systems and "the nature of land, water and climate" which modern society cannot begin to emulate.[8]

It is among other things because vernacular society *adapted its technology to its environment* that it was sustainable, which modern industrial society *by seeking to adapt its environment to its technology* cannot conceivably be.

It is often assumed that sustainability can only be achieved at the cost of reduced efficiency, but this is untrue. At the turn of the century, the British government sent an agricultural expert, Augustus Voelcker, to study Indian agriculture with a view to modernizing it. He was surprised and extremely impressed by what he saw:

> I do not share the opinions which have been expressed as to Indian agriculture being, as a whole, primitive and backward, but I believe that in many parts there is little or nothing that can be improved . . . I make bold to say that it is a much easier task to propose improvements in English agriculture than to make really valuable suggestions for that of India . . .[9]

He was particularly impressed by their traditional technology.

> Anyone who has watched the clever devices of the native cultivators in the implements which they use, for harrowing, leveling, drilling, raising water, etc. will see that if anything is to replace the existing implements it must be simple, cheap and effective. He will indeed be a clever man who introduces something really practical.

A. O. Hume, another British agronomist of that period, formed the same impression:

> I believe that the implements in ordinary use are entirely suitable for the conditions of Indian agriculture. To those who are sceptical I can show in parts of the Bombay Presidency cultivation by means of indigenous tillage implements only, which in respect of neatness, thoroughness and profitability cannot be excelled by the best gardeners or the best farmers in any part of the world. That statement I deliberately make and am quite prepared to substantiate.[10]

The same is true of African agriculture. For example, Robert Mann considers that the Ethopian ard plow cannot be improved upon for the conditions under which it has been designed to work:

> It produces a ridged tilth, does not invert the soil, leaves dead vegetation on the surface, and the unique pivot action between furrow-openers and beam enables the plow point to be lifted up and over obstacles. Yet there have been many attempts to introduce plows of foreign origin into Ethiopia contrary to that accumulated local wisdom.[11]

If traditional agriculture was so eminently satisfactory, one might ask, why then has it been systematically abandoned and replaced by obviously non-sustainable modern agricultural methods? The answer is that there is no place for it in the atomized, corporation-dominated consumer society that economic development has brought into being. Its existence is not compatible with the achievement of such a society's overall goal, the maximization of economic activity and hence of economic growth. The World Bank, which had a hand in financing economic development in Papua New Guinea, is quite honest about its motives:

> over much of the country, nature's bounty produces enough to eat with relatively little expenditure of effort . . . Until enough subsistence farmers have their traditional lifestyles changed by the growth of new consumption wants, this labor constraint may make it difficult to introduce new crops.[12]

And new crops must be introduced—the new hybrids in particular that are particularly responsive to inputs of fertilizer, pesticides and irrigation water. Their introduction is required to satisfy the needs of the powerful agrochemical industry and the dam builders. They are specifically designed for export to the industrial world to enable Third World governments to earn the foreign exchange required to finance the purchase of still more of our manufactured products and to pay the interest on the loans that were contracted to modernize agriculture in the first place.

Even in the World Bank's iniquitous Berg report, it is acknowledged that smallholders "are outstanding managers of their own resources —their land and capital, fertilizer and water." However, the dominance of this type of agriculture or "subsistence production" "*presented obstacles to agricultural development. The farmers had to be induced to produce for the market, adopt new crops and undertake new risks.*"[13]

However, economic development rapidly puts the small farmers out of business as it does the artisans, and they are replaced by ever bigger, ever more powerful corporations. As this process occurs, so is technology disembedded from its social and ecological context and grows increasingly out of control.

Nowhere is the socially destructive nature of modern technology more apparent than when we introduce it into vernacular societies in the Third World. Lauriston Sharp tells a story that has been repeated over and over again in the anthropological literature. It shows how a minute and seemingly inoffensive technological innovation—in this case the substitution of the use of steel axes for stone axes in an Australian Aboriginal tribe—is sometimes enough to spell a society's rapid disintegration. The elders of the tribe in question had a virtual monopoly of the use of stone axes and only lent them out in accordance with a very strict set of rules which ensured that they returned into their possession. The power of the elders and indeed the whole structure of the society is shown by Sharp to have depended on the maintenance of these arrangements. However missionaries eager to modernize this tribal society introduced steel axes that were distributed indiscriminately within the tribe; in this way, the elders were deprived of one of the most important means at their disposal for maintaining the critical order of their society. It soon disintegrated, and it was not long before its now alienated members began to drift to the shanty towns and the mission stations.[14]

Wolfgang Sachs also notes the social implications of the generalized use of as seemingly innocent a technological device as the electric mixer:

> Whirring and slightly vibrating, it makes juice from solid fruit in next to no time. A wonderful tool! So it seems. But a quick look at cord and wall-socket shows that what we have before us is rather the domestic terminal of a national, indeed, worldwide system.
>
> The electricity arrives via a network of cables and overhead utility lines, which are fed by power stations that depend on water pressures, pipelines or tanker consignments, which in turn require dams, offshore platforms or derricks in distant deserts. The whole chain only guarantees an adequate and prompt delivery if every one of its parts is staffed by armies of engineers, planners and financial experts, who themselves can fall back on administrations, universities, indeed, entire industries (and sometimes even the military) . . . Whoever flicks a switch on is not using a tool. He or she is plugging into a combine of functioning systems. *Between the use of simple techniques and that of modern equipment lies the reorganization of a whole society.*[15]

"Disorganization" may, of course, be a more appropriate term. As Ralph Keyes notes, "Our household conveniences—our whole drive for a convenient life—has cut us off from each other. The co-operation and communication that used to accompany life's chores is being built out of our social system."[16] Technologies, as J.C. Mathes and Donald H. Gray put it, "make us independent of community and social restraints and tradition, but dependent on the technological system."[17] Patrick McCully refers to Western technology in the Third World as "a Trojan Horse of Western economics and social values and beliefs."[18]

It may well be, as Mathes and Gray insist, that the engineer, rather than the bureaucrat, the politician, or the economist is the true architect of our brave new world. Indeed, no government edict could possibly have changed society as drastically as did the introduction of the automobile or the television set. There is irony in this, for the engineer tends to be a conservative in the true sense of the term, who cherishes such institutions as the family, the community and their traditional values—all of which his professional activities must inevitably destroy.

It is the gross irresponsibility and indeed the unprecedented immorality of many of today's high technology undertakings that are particularly striking. Ravetz, the well-known philosopher of science, considers that even Bacon and Descartes retained some moral sense. For them the development of science and technology would still be subjected to moral constraints. Thus, the sages of "Solomon's House" in Bacon's *New Atlantis* decided which knowledge should be revealed to the state and which should remain secret, while Descartes took a "scientist's oath" not to engage on projects which could be useful to some, only by harming others. Galileo, however, was uncompromising. He saw himself as having the right to state what he took to be the philosophical truth without any concern for its possible social consequences, and denied any responsibility for his actions.[19]

This has increasingly become the standpoint of today's scientists in spite of the terrifying nature of the new technologies they have unleashed on the world. Nuclear power is a case in point. When nuclear fission was discovered in 1938, its military applications were rapidly understood. Some of the atomic scientists—Leo Szilard for example—wanted to keep the discovery a secret; but others, such as Jean Joliot-Curie, refused. For him, one could not stop scientific progress. Besides, he insisted, scientists were not responsible for the use to which their discoveries were put. Most mainstream scientists join him in protesting that science and technology are neutral. Medawar for instance insists that "it is the height of folly to blame the weapon for the crime."[20] As Dorothy Nelkin notes, many scientists feel that "freedom of scientific enquiry is a constitutional right—like freedom of speech."[21]

In 1973, Arthur Tamplin and John Goffman resigned their important posts at the Lawrence Livermore Laboratories in Berkeley, California. They had reached the conclusion that there was no peaceful atom, and that the building of nuclear installations to provide electricity was just as much a threat to human survival as the building of nuclear weapons. Very few members of the nuclear establishment have since displayed that degree of responsibility.

Molecular biologist James Shapiro and his colleagues also refused to participate any further in what is perhaps the most threatening of all technological enterprises so far—genetic engineering, the creation of evolutionary new forms of life. Even if this technology were neutral, they argued, the basic control over scientific work in the United States was in the hands of a small minority of industrialists and bureaucrats who have always exploited science for harmful purposes so as to increase their own power. They believed that scientists, and everyone else for that matter, should actively work for radical political changes and that if this means that the progress of science itself may be interrupted that is something they would have to accept.[22] Shapiro resigned from his post, but few have followed his lead. So far, all attempts to bring genetic engineering under social control have failed. To quote the Nobel laureate David Baltimore,

> Contemporary research in molecular biology has grown up in an era of almost complete permissiveness. Its practitioners have been allowed to decide their own priorities and have met with virtually no restraints on the types of work they can do.[23]

A few eminent scientists have continued to warn us of the terrible perils of genetic engineering. Erwin Chargaff of Columbia University, writes of the

> awesome irreversibility of what is being contemplated . . . You can stop splitting the atom, you can stop visiting the moon; you can stop

using aerosols; you may even decide not to kill entire populations by the use of a few bombs, but *you cannot recall a new form of life* . . . An irreversible attack on the biosphere is something so unheard-of, so unthinkable to previous generations, that I could only wish that mine had not been guilty of it.[24]

Liebe Cavalieri of Cornell University, warns that "a single unrecognized accident could contaminate the entire Earth with an ineradicable and dangerous agent that might not reveal its presence until its deadly work was done."[25] But Chargaff and Cavalieri represent only a small minority of the scientists involved in genetic engineering which provides the basis of an increasingly big and powerful industry whose irresponsible activities are now totally out of control.

Our inability to control technological intrusions into the workings of the ecosphere constitutes an ever growing threat to human survival as the scale of the interventions increases. Already, scientists have exploded a nuclear bomb in the Van Allen belt without bothering to find out its exact function in assuring the habitability of our planet. In the mid 1960s, nearly a hundred million dollars were spent on the Mohole project, that consisted of drilling a hole through the Earth's crust—a project which, fortunately, came to naught. Pentagon officials also talked seriously, some years ago, of using the moon as a missile-testing target.

They were outdone, however, by Alexander Abian, a professor at Iowa State University. The learned professor considers the moon to be responsible for the bad weather on our planet. It apparently exerts a pull on the Earth that helps tilt it on a 23° axis which alters the angle at which it is hit by the sun's rays. This is seen as causing hot summers in parts of the world and stormy winters elsewhere. If only the moon could be got rid of, the Earth would rotate more smoothly and then the sun would warm the planet more evenly, which would enable us to enjoy what the professor refers to as "eternal spring." Abian seriously proposes that the moon be blasted with nuclear rockets. If certain romantics really wanted the moon back again, he assures us that this could easily be arranged. "Once human beings learn the secrets to re-arranging the Universe, scientists will be able to pluck moons from other planets and bring them closer to Earth—but not so close that they interfere with the weather." The professor is shocked that no one has yet sought to do so. "From the earliest traces of primate fossils, some 70 million years ago," he writes, "no-one—but no-one —has ever raised a finger of defiance at the celestial organization."[26] To defy the "celestial organization" of the universe is obviously the duty of technological man. God obviously did a bad job—it is clearly incumbent on our scientists to re-arrange the universe according to their vastly superior design. What is particularly terrifying is that Abian's suggestion is apparently being taken seriously by various scientific bodies—the Czechoslovak Academy of Sciences for instance (1991).

These and similar tales should make it clear just how urgent it is that science and technology be brought back under social control —embedded once again in social relations. To those who fear that this might compromise our ability to solve our problems, it must be pointed out that technology, though it has many uses, cannot solve the real problems that confront our society today. The root of our crisis is the disruption of natural systems, whose proper functioning no technology can restore. There is no technology for instance that will recreate a tropical rain-forest; none that will bring back into being the tens of thousands, if not hundreds of thousands, of species that are made extinct every year and of which only a fraction have even been catalogued by our scientists. There is no gadgetry that will reconstitute a disintegrated family or community, or restore its degraded cultural pattern. Only nature can do this, and the most our technologists can do is develop, as a matter of urgency, less destructive technologies that exert a much smaller impact on our environment, creating conditions in which nature can once more do its work.

58

In an ecological economy, money is homeotelic to Gaia

~

(General purpose) money is one of the shatteringly simplifying ideas of all time, and like any other new and compelling idea, it creates its own revolution.
Paul Bohannan

Our money is impersonal and commercial while primitive money frequently has pedigree and personality, sacred uses, or moral and emotional connotations.
George Dalton

Only when the last tree has been cut down,
only when the last river has been poisoned,
only when the last fish has been caught,
only then will you learn that money cannot be eaten.
Plains Sioux

In OUR WORLD, money is a medium of exchange in terms of which the value of all commodities designed for exchange on the market can be expressed. It is thus general purpose money. It clearly serves to facilitate trade in goods and services but it does so regardless of whether such trade is desirable on social, ecological, spiritual or moral grounds. Money, in this sense of the term, does not exist in a vernacular society. In the first place, goods are not produced for exchange except in special circumstances, but for use; secondly, the system of valuation is different: things are not valued in accordance with what they can be exchanged for, but for their importance in maintaining the stability of the social system, the ecosphere and the cosmos itself.

Some form of money is used in vernacular societies; but rather than being designed, as is our money, to facilitate economic exchange, it is designed instead to *serve social ends*: to maintain social structures, strengthen social bonds and hence build up social wealth. Not surprisingly, modern economists criticize what they regard as the irrational nature of primitive money. They find it too bulky and difficult to carry about; worse still, it is not divisible in the way pounds can be divided into pence. Thus the Rossel Islanders use two different types of shells, *Ndap* and *Nka*. There are actually twenty-two different classes of the *Ndap* and only a limited number of actual shells in each class, probably no more than a thousand in each of the first thirteen classes. Each shell is known and has a veritable identity of its own and a different value. There is no means of changing a shell of one class into one of another. This means that something which is priced in terms of shells of class twenty for instance, must be paid for in shells of that class. Thus under the existing arrangements, if a man wants to buy an object priced in terms of number twenty class *Ndap* shells, he has to borrow an object also priced in terms of this currency.

W.E. Armstrong, an economist who studied Rossel Island money, was keen to show the islanders how their currency could be "rationalized" so as greatly to facilitate the conduct of their commercial transactions. He pointed out that this elaborate borrowing could be avoided, or much reduced if the value of the different shells could be related to each other as dollars are to cents. What he completely failed to grasp was that their unsuitability for use in a modern market economy was irrelevant, for *they were designed to fulfill a very different purpose.*[1]

The Kula armbands used in the famous Kula trade described by Mauss[2] and Malinowski,[3] the coppers (great ceremonial copper disks) used by north-west coast Indian chiefs at a *potlatch*, Rossel Island shells and all the other currencies in use in tribal societies may not be convenient, portable or divisible, but neither, as Dalton points out, are they the media of commercial exchange. Instead, as Malinowski suggests, they should be regarded as treasure items or heirlooms, crown jewels or sport trophies. According to Dalton

> such treasures can take on special roles as non-commercial money; their acquisition and disposition are carefully structured and regarded as extremely important events; they change hands in specified ways, in transactions which have strong moral implications. Often they are used to create social relationships (marriage; entrance into secret societies), prevent a break in social relationships (bloodwealth; mortuary payments), or keep or elevate one's social position (potlatch). Their "money-ness" consists in their being required means of (reciprocal or redistributive) payment.[4]

Mary Douglas regards primitive money as more closely resembling coupons than modern commercial money. Their role "is not to expedite the transformation of goods and services, as is money," but instead to control the drive to satisfy individual wants:

> The essence of money is to be transferable. It circulates, but coupons (like primitive money) when spent, return to an issuing point and their acquisition is continually under survey and control. Admittedly, there is a big difference between modern and primitive coupons. In a modern economy, paper coupons once spent are returned to the office of issue, counted and destroyed. But primitive commodity coupons

simply return at each transfer into the hands of the senior members of the community who become by this fact to all intents and purposes the issuing authority. This makes it almost impossible to acquire coupons without being acceptable to the senior old men who hold them. Coupons do not circulate; they are continually issued and returned and re-issued.[5]

Going further, she suggests that they provide a means of licensing rather than rationing. The object of rationing is to assure equal distribution of scarce resources. The object of licensing on the contrary is protective. One of its uses is

> to ensure the responsible use of possibly dangerous powers, so we have licensing of guns and liquor sales. Licensing pins responsibility so we have marriage licenses and pet licenses, licensing protects vulnerable areas of the economy so we have import licensing etc.

But licensing, of course, creates monopoly advantages both for those who issue them and those to whom they are issued, both parties becoming "bound in a patron/client relation sustained by the strong interest of each in the continuance of the system."

Mary Douglas shows that this is precisely what occurs among the Lele of Zaire. The old men of the tribe, by the workings of the system, obtain a monopoly of the issue of raffia cloth, which is the currency used for paying bridewealth. Because of their monopoly, the older men establish a patron/client relationship with the younger men who acquire the raffia from them if they wish to get married. This serves at once as a means of licensing marriage, and hence of controlling population, whose increase can lead to the degradation of the biotic environment; as a means too of maintaining the society's basic structure and hence its stability or continuity that, among other things, depends on maintaining the power and prestige of the elders —the custodians of the traditional wisdom—thereby permitting its transmission to succeeding generations.

59

The vernacular economy is localized
and hence largely self-sufficient

——

Whenever the timber trade is good, permanent famine reigns in the
Ogowe region.
Albert Schweitzer

Free trade for a country which has become industrial, whose population
can and does live in cities, whose people do not mind preying upon other
nations and, therefore, sustain the biggest navy to protect their unnatural
commerce, may be economically sound (though, as the reader perceives,
I question its morality). Free trade for India has proved her curse and held
her in bondage.
M.K. Gandhi

The charkha (the spinning wheel) is the symbol of the nation's prosperity
and, therefore, freedom. It is a symbol not of commercial war, but of
commercial peace. It bears not a message of ill-will towards the nations
of the Earth, but of goodwill and self-help. It will not need the protection
of a navy threatening a world's peace and exploiting its resources, but it
needs the religious determination of millions to spin their yarn in their
own homes as today they cook their food in their own homes.
M.K. Gandhi

Let goods be homespun whenever it is reasonably conveniently possible;
and above all, let finance be preferably national.
John Maynard Keynes

Free traders, having freed themselves from the restraints of community at
the national level and having moved into the cosmopolitan world, which
is not a community, have effectively freed themselves of all community
obligations.
Herman Daly and *John Cobb*

As EVOLUTION PROCEEDS, so do natural systems become increasingly self-sufficient, reducing their dependence on forces outside their control. This is an essential strategy for increasing their capacity for homeostasis and hence their stability. Thus Eugene Odum notes how in the case of ecological succession, ecosystems as they develop become increasingly self-sufficient and less dependent for their maintenance on resources derived from the outside. Food chains become more complex, with detritus providing an increasingly important source of nutrients. "In a mature forest less than ten percent of annual net production is consumed (that is, grazed) in the living state: most is utilized as dead matter (detritus) through delayed and complex pathways involving as yet little understood animal-microorganism interactions." Similarly, inorganic nutrients which were originally derived from outside the ecosystem slowly become "intrabiotic," being constantly recycled within it.[1]

This is an essential strategy for increasing an ecosystem's ability to maintain its homeostasis and hence its stability. Similarly, with the development of a vernacular community, self-sufficiency increases as dependency on outside sources decreases. Food and artifacts become largely distributed via procedures that observe the rules of reciprocity and redistribution and that are entirely under social control. In many vernacular societies, what appear to be commercial transactions are in reality highly ritualized exchanges embedded in social relations. Thus certain goods are often traded with goods of another sort and even with socially valuable objects which closely resemble what we would regard as money. But even such trade is not conducted for "economic" motives, as Malinowski insists, with reference to the Trobriand Islands, for

> there is not even a trace of gain, nor is there any reason for looking at
> it from the purely utilitarian and economic standpoint, since there is

no enhancement of material utility through the exchange . . . Thus it is quite a usual thing in the Trobriands for a type of transaction to take place in which "A" gives twenty baskets of yams to "B," receiving for it a small polished blade, only to have the whole transaction reversed in a few weeks time.[2]

The same applies to trade with other related social groups. Thus both Mauss and Malinowski have described the large trading expeditions periodically undertaken by the same people. They transported certain types of valuable objects to people living in distant islands visited in a clockwise sequence, while other expeditions carried other kinds of valuable objects to islands lying counter clockwise. The object of these expeditions was not an economic one. "We describe it as trade," Polanyi writes, "though no profit is involved; either in money or in kind."[3]

Even in the vernacular Indian village where social structure has diverted somewhat from the tribal norm, what one might regard as commercial transactions were, until recently, under social control. A farmer obtained his pots from the village potter and his tools from the village blacksmith, giving them an amount of food in exchange at a rate established by tradition, rather than by blind market forces. What is more, if the local potter were an indifferent craftsman and better pots could be bought elsewhere, this was not regarded as a sufficient reason for abandoning him.

Judged by the values of modern economics, such a system provided no inducement to potters to increase production, or indeed, improve the quality of their produce, but this objection misses the point. The trading relations between the different members of a traditional Indian village were primarily designed to satisfy *social* rather than economic goals. After all, the quality of the available pots is not the primary consideration. The maintenance of social cohesion and stability is *much more important.*

Mahatma Gandhi understood this well. One of the basic concepts of his philosophy was that of *swadeshi*, which he describes as that "spirit in us which restricts us to the use and service of our immediate surroundings to the exclusion of the more remote."[4] Sunderlal Bahuguna, the leader of the Chipko movement in the Himalayas, regards *swadeshi* as the most fundamental of Gandhi's teachings.

Economic development, of course, totally undermines the practice of *swadeshi* since it is based on the very principle that all considerations, whether moral, social or ecological, must be ruthlessly subordinated to short-term economics. The village community is thereby sacrificed to the overriding ideal of churning out ever greater quantities of bigger and better pots, and of influencing villagers by every possible means to increase their consumption of pots way beyond what they need and without any concern for whether there is enough clay for producing them, the effect on the environment of digging up the clay or whether the villagers can, in fact, afford them. Production and consumption, in such circumstances, are no longer subject to any controls, social or ecological. Pots simply proliferate like cancer cells.

In tribal societies, it is only when dealing with complete strangers that the laws of the market are allowed to operate free of social constraints and exclusively market transactions are allowed to occur. For Bohannan,

> A "market" is a transaction which in itself calls up no long-term personal relationship, and which is therefore to be exploited to as great a degree as possible. In fact, the presence of a previous relationship makes a "good market" impossible. People do not like to sell to kinsmen since it is bad form to demand as high a price from a kinsman as one might from a stranger. *Market behavior and kinship behavior are incompatible in a single relationship and the individual must give way to one or the other.*

This is very much in keeping with the Old Testament precept that "unto a stranger thou mayest lend upon usury; but unto thy brother, thou shalt not lend upon usury."

Sahlins shows that it is possible to distinguish between the economic relations within different sectors, such as the house, the lineage, the village, the tribe and those outside the tribe. As we proceed from the former to the latter so reciprocity and solidarity are slowly replaced by haggling and profit-making, and so do economic relations become increasingly commercial. That is why the development of the market system within a society could only occur once solidarity and reciprocity within the inner social groupings had waned and the essential difference between social relations within and without these groupings had become sufficiently blurred; in other words, before economic wealth could become man's principal preoccupation, *he had first to be deprived of his social wealth.*

Though all societies have possessed an economy of some sort, no economy previous to our time, as Karl Polanyi notes, "has ever existed that, even in principle, was controlled by markets."[5] This is not surprising, since only by resisting the power of market forces could "the integrity of our social and ecological systems . . . be maintained for so long." Once markets became more than incidental to economic life, the societies in which they operated, together with the ecosystems in which the society existed, were condemned to rapid disintegration.

During the Middle Ages in Europe, only resources of secondary importance—spices, candle-wax, oriental silks and luxury articles primarily of interest to the Church and aristocracy—were traded via the market at annual fairs, held at a few major European cities. In the twelfth and thirteenth centuries, however, an economic revolution occurred: the market expanded rapidly until it came to dominate the economic life of many European societies. Essential to this revolution was the transformation of the key resources—labor and land—into commodities. This was of key significance, for as Polanyi points out, "Labour is only another name for human activity that goes with life itself, which is not produced for sale but for entirely different reasons, nor can that activity be detached from the rest of life, be stored or mobilized: land is only another name for nature."[6]

In medieval Europe, neither labor nor land had previously been exchanged via the market. Medieval serfs were bound to their land, but their relationship to their lord was one of mutual obligations rather than of sheer economic expediency, and in exchange they normally had security of tenure. The occupation of land was thus determined by "status" rather than "contract." However, once human life came to be treated as a mere commodity, work ceased to be embedded in social relations, and the "whole man" was replaced by the worker, a new human category. Whereas vernacular man—the whole man—is a member of a family and community, and has access to land on which to grow his food, the worker lives in a largely atomized society, has been deprived of his land, and can be mobilized to fulfill any function —however socially and ecologically disruptive or morally repulsive— so long as it provides the wage on which he has now become dependent for the satisfaction of his most basic biological and social needs.

The transformation of land into a commodity also had enormous social and economic implications. Contract, established via the market system—rather than status established by tradition and reflecting the society's social structure—now determined where individual families lived and worked the land (see chapter 60). The resulting pattern of land-ownership may well have satisfied the requirements of the new economic system but it set in train the disintegration of society into mere congeries of strangers. The disintegrated community, what is more, was often deprived of its livelihood, since food was sold via the market, and bought by whoever paid the most for it, regardless of the community or society to which he belonged.

Indeed, Polanyi attributes the severe famines that occurred in India under the British Raj to the operation of the newly established market system which destroyed the Indian village community. "While under the regime of feudalism and of the village community, *noblesse oblige*, clan solidarity and the regulation of the corn market checked famines; under the rule of the market the people could not be prevented from starving according to the rules of the game."[7] It is the very basis of the market system, once freed of social constraints, that goods should be bought as cheaply as possible and sold at the highest price. This means that there must be one-way traffic of the essentials of life to the rich from the poor, who are thereby condemned to malnutrition and famine. Thus Redcliffe Salaman notes how, in Ireland, during the great famine, corn continued to be exported to England even though millions of people were dying of hunger. "If it was not available to the local people, it was partly because it was being shipped to England at the rate of 16,000 quarters a week and also because, even if it were not, the Irish could not have afforded it."[8]

Today, this traffic is one of the major causes of malnutrition and famine in the Third World, where a high proportion of the arable land —up to seventy percent in certain countries—is used for export crops, marginalizing the staple food crops on which the local population depends for its sustenance. What is more, according to the rules established by the General Agreement on Tariffs and Trade (GATT), the crops that a country produces must be exported so long as a market demand exists. Only when malnutrition and hunger prevail can an exception be made, and US delegates at the current Uruguay Rounds of the GATT insist that even in such dire circumstances, food must continue to be exported. If they have their way, it will thus become "GATT-illegal" for a country to feed its starving people rather than export its goods to the already over-fed. For as cynical as this may seem, it is by doing so that it can maximize its expenditure on the manufactured goods of the industrial countries that control GATT, no human considerations of any kind being allowed to compromise the achievement of this sordid goal. This illustrates the principle that production, governed by "market forces," is not designed to satisfy biological, social or ecological needs.

Kenneth Lux points out that economists must deny the very existence of such needs if modern economic theory is to make any sense at all. The market is seen as catering only for our "wants" which are reflected in "effective demand," and a country is seen as becoming "self-sufficient" once this "effective demand" is satisfied. Thus the modernization of agriculture through the adoption of the "Green Revolution" is said to have enabled India to achieve food self-sufficiency. This sounds very impressive, because it suggests that all the citizens of that country are now properly fed; but nothing could be further from the truth.[9] A recent report by the United Nations Children's Fund (UNICEF) reveals that about eighty-five percent of India's children are now affected by malnutrition and many will be stunted physically and mentally as a result. To state that India is self-sufficient in food merely means that to put more food in the shops would not lead to further sales, for those who are malnourished do not have the money to buy it—their biological needs not being reflected in the pathetic "effective demand" that they can exert.

Once the market rules our economic life, the natural world is seen to be no more than a source of resources to be commoditized and transformed into cash on the global market. The process is a malignant one. By means of it—everywhere, forests, wetlands, coral reefs, rivers, estuaries and seas, together with all the living things that inhabit them —are systematically cashed in. What happens when all these are gone and the countries are transformed into virtual deserts does not seem to concern either our politicians, industrialists or economists.

To preserve any resource at all that is capable of being commoditized and cashed-in is only possible by keeping it outside the orbit of the global market. In New Zealand, it is illegal to sell trout in shops. They are reserved for anglers and it is for this reason that there are still trout to be caught in the country's lakes and rivers. Only by setting up National Parks in which living things are kept out of the orbit of the market can many species be preserved, though one can unfortunately predict that if economic development proceeds for very much longer, the pressures on many of these parks will become irresistible. Significantly, in certain parts of Tanzania where the economy has largely collapsed and there is not enough money to repair the roads, people are once again beginning to eat properly for, no longer able to export their food on the global market, they are free once more to eat it themselves.

The export process, what is more, is often as destructive to the importer as it is for the exporter: it is, in E.F.Schumacher's phrase, "a process of mutual poisoning." For, the import of cheap food from areas where it can be grown particularly cheaply, or is heavily subsidized by the state, to areas where, for various reasons, it is more expensive to produce, has ruined farmers throughout the Third World. The adoption of modern agricultural methods—imposed by international agencies such as the IMF on its debtor countries—increases the dependence of farmers on imported farm machinery, hybrid seeds, fertilizers and pesticides, which they can ill afford, especially as the prices of these off-farm inputs continue to increase, and farmland becomes increasingly degraded. Such farmers are condemned to becoming ever more impoverished until eventually they must leave their land and seek refuge in the slums that surround the nearest conurbation, a fate which on current trends awaits the bulk of the Third World's rural population.

The lot of the traditional craftsman or artisan is very similar. Mahatma Gandhi's constant theme was how Lancashire's mass-produced textiles had destroyed India's artisanal, village-based textile industry, causing the degradation of rural life. Carders, dyers, spinners and weavers—droves of them, who kept the village economy going— were ruined and the Indian village was deprived of its economic and social life.

It is for the same reasons that the small farmer and the artisan have been virtually eliminated in Britain and North America and are rapidly disappearing in the rest of Europe. Even the medium-sized farmer and the medium-sized company are everywhere under stress. During the present recession (1991), the European agricultural community is in a state of near bankruptcy and only the biggest farms have any prospect of survival. In the USA, agriculture is in similar straits. The plight of small to medium businesses is scarcely better, with nine hundred or so going bankrupt every week in the UK at the time of writing.

That the future (temporarily at least) lies with the large corporations —in particular the transnational corporations—no one familiar with current trends can doubt. As the market expands to encompass the entire world and becomes progressively "freer," the greater must be the niche it provides them. Free trade sounds highly desirable; its proponents make it appear that it frees the oppressed individual from yet another set of shackles previously imposed on him and on his ancestors by tyrannical customs and governments. But the transnational corporation is the "individual" that benefits from free trade; and the freedom it provides is the freedom to cut down virgin forests in order to produce plywood, lavatory paper and the Sunday edition of the *New York Times*. It is the freedom to erode, salinize, waterlog, compact and desertify agricultural land so as to produce the cheap raw materials for the food-processing industry; it is the freedom to pillage the oceans with vast trawlers that literally annihilate fish populations with "wall of death" drift nets that are often sixty miles long. It is the freedom to grub up the world's remaining coral reefs that protect vulnerable islands from the waves and that are among the most productive of all ecosystems, in order to provide specimens for souvenir shops. It is the freedom to drain the pathetic remains of the world's once extensive wetlands in order to provide more pastureland for the world's over-inflated livestock population, or to make available ever more building land for the developers. It is the freedom to churn out ever greater amounts of ever-more toxic chemicals to spread on our fields, release into our rivers and ground waters, dump into holes in the ground, or inject under pressure into deep bore-holes— from where they find their way into our food and drinking water. It is the freedom to destroy the ozone layer, which protects us from lethal ultraviolet radiation, in the interests of using patented CFCs in cosmetic sprays, refrigerators, and air conditioners, rather than non-patentable substitutes that would reduce the profits of the main producers, Du Pont and ICI. It is the freedom to increase poverty and misery, malnutrition and disease, to extinguish tens of thousands, if not hundreds of thousands of species of living things every year, all in order to satisfy the short-term financial interests of a few utterly irresponsible industrialists and the bureaucrats and politicians who live off them. This is the freedom that free trade provides, and those are the interests that the current GATT proposals are designed to serve. If approved, they will have delivered the world to its pillagers on a plate, to do with it as they like.

What is required is just the opposite—a transition to a world of largely self-sufficient communities, carrying out their economic activities at the level of the family, of the small artisanal enterprise and the community itself, largely to satisfy local needs via local markets. Only in this way can economic activity be subordinated to biological, social, ecological and moral imperatives, as indeed it must if we are to survive for long on this beleaguered planet.

60

The vernacular community is the
unit of homeotelic behavior

~

Men may make kingdoms, but the community seems to come from the
hand of God.
Alexis de Tocqueville

It is not by the wax and parchment of lawyers that the independence
of men can be preserved. Such things are the mere externals; they set
off liberty to advantage; they are as its dress and paraphernalia, its
holiday-suit in times of peace and quiet. But when the evil days set
in, then the invasions of despotism have begun, liberty will be retained,
not by those who can show the oldest deed and the largest charters, but
by those who have been most inured to habits of independence, most
accustomed to think and act for themselves, and most regardless of that
insidious protection which the upper classes have always been so ready
to bestow that, in many countries, they have now left nothing worth the
trouble to protect.
T.H. Buckle

The state in important matters is an instrument of the industrial system.
J.K. Galbraith

The ideal of a future based on ecological principles must have, as a
fundamental prerequisite, the re-emergence of *Gemeinschaft* in social
relationships.
Alwyn Jones

In the light of the world-view of modernism the State is the only possible instrument of government. It is seen as normal, and indeed desirable, that people should be but the individualistic, competitive, aggressive and disorderly units of an atomized society. The notion that society is a natural system, capable of governing itself and assuring its own homeostasis, is foreign to modern sociologists, let alone modern politicians. Margaret Thatcher, when Prime Minister, stated quite explicitly that a human society is no more than the sum of the individuals and families that inhabit it. Such a society, or rather non-society, cannot govern itself and must depend on the State and its specialized services to maintain any semblance of order—a situation we are taught to regard as normal. Indeed, we are told, where there is no State there can only be "a war of everyone against everyone" and life must necessarily be in Hobbes's consecrated phrase "solitary, nasty, brutish and short."

This distorted view of human society can only be entertained by one who has had no experience of a vernacular society of the type within which our ancestors once lived, and which still survives somewhat precariously in those areas that have succeeded in remaining, partly at least, outside the orbit of international trade.

A succession of scholars have noted the essential difference between these two types of society. Sir Henry Sumner Maine in his *Ancient Law* traced the transition from the "familial" to the "individuated" society, from one governed by personal and sacred law to one governed by impersonal and secular law. For him, behavior in the former society was based on "status," while in the latter it was based on "contract."[1]

Locke's "social contract," entered into by the citizens of an originally chaotic and disorderly non-society in order to set up a government that would provide them with order and security, is still a generally accepted notion. It fits in perfectly with the world-view of modernism, since the contract is seen as having been entered into *consciously* and *rationally* by *individual* people; and implicit to it is also the idea of *management by an external agency* just as labor is managed within a corporation.

On the other hand, the notion of a society as a natural and spontaneous biospheric creation is unacceptable to the modernist worldview. Such a society could only be held together by irrational forces such as *emotion* or *sentiment* that, in Sumner's view, have no role to play in public affairs and should be limited to the field of personal relations.

The French historian and social philosopher, Fustel de Coulanges, in his seminal *La Cité Antique*, stressed the religious nature of the family, community and larger society, which he saw as providing their cohesion and stability. Of the ancient Greek city state, he wrote: "This State and its religion were so totally fused that it was impossible not only to imagine the conflict between them, but even to distinguish one from the other." For him, the ancient society died once its law was separated from its religion.[2]

The early American ethnographer Lewis H. Morgan published his *Ancient Society* in 1877. He distinguished between *societas* and *civitas*, the former based on kinship and the latter on territorial connection.[3] This is an important distinction. Real vernacular communities are based on consanguinity, real or fictitious. With the development of trade and industry however, normal rules of residence reflecting the kinship structures of communities, and their relationships with other key groupings such as the clan were subordinated to new economic considerations. Thus among the Hebrews, as Adolphe Lods writes,

> the early groupings, based originally on consanguinity (natural or artificial), tended to become territorial aggregations. The clan finally became synonymous with the population of a town . . . Membership of a tribe consisted not in descent from a particular individual but in belonging by birth to a particular territory.[4]

As this change occurred, contiguity became the main bond holding together the members of a community. Today, even this bond has been eroded; people live wherever they can find a job and in the USA it is said that less than fifteen percent of people now live where they were born. In this way, a country's population is shuffled like

387

a deck of cards to satisfy the requirements of the economy, and the community is transformed into a mere congeries of strangers incapable of governing themselves or fulfilling their other homeotelic functions.

Perhaps the best-known distinction between these two types of society is that proposed by the German sociologist Ferdinand Tonnies in *Gemeinschaft und Gesellschaft* (1920). He saw the *gemeinschaft* or community as constituting a single coherent social unit whose members are bound together by intimate social bonds and common values, whereas the members of a *gesellschaft*, on the contrary, are linked by superficial and self-motivated considerations.[5] F. Pappenheim states this very clearly:

> Individuals who enter a *Gesellschaft* do so with only a fraction of their being, that is, with that part of their existence which corresponds to the specific purpose of the organization. Members of a tax-payers' association, or individuals who own stock in a company, are related to each other, *not as whole persons, but with only that part of themselves which is concerned with being a taxpayer or shareholder* . . . Thus they remain loosely connected and essentially remote from each other . . . So deep is the separation between man and man in *Gesellschaft* that . . . it becomes a social world in which latent hostility and potential war are inherent in the relationship of one to another.[6]

Roy Rappaport contrasts the community with what he calls the "special purpose" association. Whereas the community seeks to satisfy social and ecological requirements, the special purpose association —in which category he includes corporations and governmental institutions, and which corresponds very closely to Tonnies's *gesellschaft* —only seeks to achieve the purpose for which it was set up. Even then it is rapidly subject to what he calls "goal displacement," at which point its one preoccupation is to perpetuate itself and if possible, increase its power and influence, which can often mean becoming an obstacle to the realization of its original goal.[7]

In the case of government agencies set up to control the activities of unscrupulous industrialists, goal-displacement occurs very rapidly. They are nearly always subverted, indeed often completely taken over by the industrialists whose activities they have been set up to control —a process known as "regulatory capture" or "agency capture." In the UK, the Advisory Committee on Pesticides which is supposed to advise the government on the control of the use of pesticides is largely made up of representatives of the agrochemical industry and various academics whose research grants they pay or otherwise control. The UK's Ministry of Agriculture, Fisheries and Food (MAFF), like the United States Department of Agriculture (USDA), is dominated by the agrochemical industry, the thousands of agricultural extension offices throughout the USA being little more than agencies for the sale of fertilizers and pesticides. The same can be said of the Food and Agriculture Organization of the United Nations (FAO), to which subject *The Ecologist* recently devoted a special issue.[8]

When the Reagan administration came to power in the USA, Anne Gorsuch, an attorney specialized in defending polluting industries against litigation by the Environmental Protection Agency (EPA), was actually made head of that agency and proceeded to dismiss the scientists engaged during the Carter administration—not, on her own admission, because they were incompetent, but because they were "their scientists" (or scientists with real environmental concerns) and had to be replaced by "our scientists" (or scientists representing the interests of the polluters).

In general, governments will take no measures that go against the interests of any important industry, however destructive its activities, unless forced to do so by public opinion. The main reason is that governments have an insatiable appetite for money. In a "democracy" it is money that will enable them to get re-elected by providing material advantages to those sectors of society whose electoral support they particularly require, and it is money that will enable them to sell themselves to the electorate through elaborate publicity campaigns at election times. In a dictatorship, money will buy the arms and pay the police and troops that maintain the dictator in power. Unfortunately, big corporations have a virtual monopoly of money—hence the inevitable alliance between government and industry. The inevitable result is that virtually no important policies are adopted today because they are desirable on human, social or ecological grounds, but rather because they serve the purpose of powerful special-purpose associations; and it is these heterotelic policies that are rapidly making out planet uninhabitable.

For the French anthropologist Pierre Clastres the most basic feature of the vernacular society is probably its capacity to run its own affairs without the aid of formal State institutions.

> There is on the one hand the primitive society, or the society without the State, and on the other, the society with the State. It is the presence or absence of the State (that can take many forms) which separates these two fundamentally different types of society from each other.[9]

That the vernacular society can run itself without the aid of formal State institutions is well documented. As the classical American anthropologist Robert Lowie writes,

> the legislative function in most primitive communities seems strangely curtailed when compared with that exercised in the more complex civilization. All the exigencies of normal social intercourse are covered by customary law, and the business of such governmental machinery as exists is rather to exact obedience to traditional usage than to create new products.[10]

The power of public opinion, reflecting traditional values, is enough to bring disorderly elements to heel. Often a miscreant is simply laughed at; if this is not enough, people will no longer attend his feasts and his company will be avoided. This is usually sufficient; if it is not, he will be ostracized—the worst possible penalty, since a man in a vernacular community cannot conceive of life outside it, away from the land where his ancestors are buried and where alone he can perform his essential religious rites. As British anthropologist Sir Edward Tyler puts it, one of the most essential things that we can learn from the life of crude tribes is how society can function without the policeman to keep order.

A vernacular society is also fully capable of bringing up its own children, looking after the sick and the old, and dealing with any psychiatric disorders. The social psychiatrist Marvin Opler has shown that a vernacular society will automatically provide a cathartic outlet for the particular tensions that, by its specific nature, it must inevitably generate.

Vernacular society co-ordinates all those activities that contribute to maintaining its stability in the face of change. Above all, this means maintaining the critical order of the hierarchy of larger systems of which it is part and on whose preservation its stability must ultimately depend. For this to be possible, the vernacular community, together with the families and individuals that compose it, must co-operate in the achievement of this goal, seeking among other things, to avoid interfering with each other's activities (see chapter 41). As a result, the conflict of interests with which we are often faced in the modern world—say between the use of land for agriculture or for urban development—tend not to occur.

A member of a vernacular society, in Stanley Diamond's words, is

> an integrated person. His society is neither compartmentalized nor fragmented and none of its parts is in fatal conflict with the others. Thus he does not perceive himself as divided into *homo economicus*, *homo religiosus*, *homo politicus* and so forth. On the contrary, he performs his various economic, religious and political tasks as part of a coordinated strategy that is embodied in the cultural pattern with which he has been imbued, and which has regulated his relationship with his fellow men and with his natural environment from time immemorial.[11]

In such conditions, there is clearly no need for the State. The intrusion of such a foreign body into a society's affairs would usurp its most fundamental functions and prerogatives, generating initiatives beyond the control of traditional law as laid down by the ancestors. In a vernacular society, as Clastres puts it, "there is no State because the State is an impossibility."[12]

The State can only come into being once social structures have been destroyed. This is a central theme of Aristotle's *Politics*. He notes that tyrants like Pisistratus of Athens and Dionysius of Syracuse could only come to power once the social structures of their respective cities had broken down with the emergence of an anonymous proletariat incapable of governing itself. This explains the title of Clastres's seminal essay *La Societé contre L'Etat*. Indeed, society and the State cannot coexist. In every country, the State seeks purposefully to destroy the vernacular institutions of society. In India, it wages war against the caste system which, in spite of its obvious abuses, provides the very basis of Indian social structure. It also attacks "linguism," the preservation of the languages spoken by the different ethnic groups which inhabit modern India and even rounds on "statism" where this refers to the residual autonomy of largely ethnically-based Indian States.

In Africa, the governments of the artificial Nation-States, whose arbitrary boundaries have been inherited from the colonial period, strive to eradicate "tribalism" in the interest of creating "national unity," which really means bringing into being vast homogeneous masses of anonymous and alienated people totally dependent, as we in the West have become, on the specialized services provided by an increasingly powerful State.

The close relationship between the development of the State and the disintegration of a self-regulating community is described by Banfield in a study of peasant society in southern Italy. The village, he finds, has been relieved of responsibility for organizing its own religious life by the centralized bureaucracy of the Vatican. It has also lost control of its own educational system, since its school has been built for it and teachers are appointed by the State. It no longer maintains law and order; the State's police are supposed to do that. As a result, the community has begun to disintegrate, the largest unit of organization now being the family, with no effective co-operation above that level. In such a society, Banfield writes,

> no-one will further the interests of the group or community except as it is to his private advantage to do so. In other words, the hope of material gain in the short run will be the only motive for concern of public affairs . . . the law will be disregarded when there is no reason to fear punishment . . . an office holder will take bribes when he can . . . but whether he takes bribes or not, it will be assumed by society that he does.[13]

Clearly, such a society can only exist because the State provides it with all the services it once provided itself. "Except for the intervention of the State," Banfield writes, "the war of all against all would sooner or later erupt into open violence, and the local society would either perish or produce new cultural forms"—precisely the state of affairs that Hobbes and later the Social Darwinists took to be the norm.[14]

A peasant society is still only in the early stages of disintegration, since the extended family is still intact. But as economic development proceeds, the extended family breaks down into the very unstable nuclear family with which we are all acquainted today. Eventually, even that disintegrates until, in the growing slums of the industrial world's conurbations, the one-parent family becomes the rule. In such a society, there is still less co-operation. It is each one for himself, and individualism and competition are the rule (see chapter 47). People are so alienated that they are no longer capable of looking after their own affairs and the State takes over more and more of the functions that they are no longer capable of fulfilling. As a Pomo Indian pointed out to a white North American,

> the police and soldiers take care of protecting you, the courts give you justice, the Post Office carries messages for you, the school teaches you. Everything is taken care of, even your children, if you should die, but with us the family must do all that. Without the family, we are nothing, and in the old days, before white people came, the family was given first consideration by anyone who was about to do anything at all. That is why we got along.[15]

Unfortunately, we have been taught to regard the proliferation of a country's State services as a sign of social and economic progress. The more of them a government provides to its citizens, the higher their perceived standard of living. This notion is consistent with the dogma that all benefits are man-made, the product of economic development or progress (see chapter 34). It is consistent too with the modern belief in scientific and technical expertise and professionalism, for the services provided by the State are seen to be superior in these terms to those provided by the family and the community in a vernacular society. In Sweden, according to David Popenoe, the bourgeois family is seen as a major cause of social problems and "in order to destroy it, some Welfare State ideologues are eager to promote alternatives not only to the bourgeois family, but to the nuclear family, and to turn over most child-rearing to the State."[16] Even parents in Sweden are apparently succumbing to this propaganda, and coming to accept that care is best provided by government-employed professionals. After all, they are scientifically trained to look after children and must therefore be capable of doing so better than their ignorant and amateurish parents.

As people delegate their prerogatives to experts, John McKnight notes they act less as citizens and more as clients.[17] This is occurring in just about every field of activity—in medicine, in education, and in the care of old people—and it is affecting every aspect of social policy. At the same time, normal people are prevented from fulfilling the basic functions for which they were equipped by their evolution and which *they must fulfill* to maintain the integrity and stability of the families, communities, societies and ecosystems that make up the Gaian hierarchy.

The State is foreign to society. It is a *gesellschaft*—a special purpose association—concerned almost exclusively with its own short-term interests and almost invariably oblivious of the real needs of those it has been called upon to govern. There is no place for the State or its specialized institutions in a society that seeks to recreate for itself a sustainable existence on a sustainable planet. In its place, we must recreate the extended family and the vernacular community within which we have evolved and which, throughout our evolutionary experience, have been the effective units of homeotelic social and ecological behavior.

61

Vernacular man follows the Way

——

Tao is like Dike, the Way, the way of nature; and man's whole religion,
his whole moral effort is to bring himself into accordance with Tao.
Jane Harrison

When the world has the Way,
ambling horses are retired to fertilize fields.
When the world lacks the Way,
war horses are reared in the suburbs.
Lao Tzu

Man follows the Earth
The Earth follows Heaven
Heaven follows the Tao
The Tao follows what is natural.
Lao Tzu

LIKE THE DEVELOPING embryo in the womb, each life process must follow an appointed constellation of chreods or path if it is to achieve its end-state and thereby contribute to maintaining the critical order of the cosmos. Thus one can talk—as does Rupert Sheldrake—of "behavioral chreods" and also of "cultural chreods," in that a society, by means of its specific cultural pattern, is capable of maintaining itself on its path by correcting any diversions from it —so long as they occur within its tolerance range and hence its field.[1] The Way a society must follow is that which conforms to its traditional law (see chapter 2) which the ancient Greeks referred to as the *Nomos*. The Way was also referred to by them as *Dike*, which meant justice, righteousness or morality. Jane Harrison tells us that *Dike* was also "the Way of the world, the way things happen."[2]

The Way was also referred to as *Themis*, which Jane Harrison regards as "that specialized way for human beings which is sanctioned by the collective conscience."[3] *Themis* was also taken to be the Way of the Earth, and sometimes the Way of the cosmos itself, that which governed the behavior of the gods. Later, when these concepts were personalized, *Themis* became the goddess of law and of justice, and hence of morality. The Way was also seen to coincide with *Moira*, the path of destiny or fate. The chthonic gods were subordinated to *Moira*, as they were to *Dike*, the two actually coinciding with each other. Thus for Anaximander, all basic things are attributed to different provinces that provide the basis of the critical order of the natural world "according to what is ordained,"[4] a concept in which, according to Cornford, "necessity and right are united."[5] In Homer, the gods are seen as subordinate to *Moira*, and indeed to *Dike*— cosmic forces that are older than the gods themselves and that are moral. Against fate, and hence against the moral law, the gods can do nothing. As Homer tells us in the *Odyssey*, the gods cannot even save a man whom they love, if the "dread fate of death" is upon him.

Herodotus tells us that "it is impossible even for a god to avoid the fate that is ordained."[6]

The Way to be followed by all human beings was the same as that which must be followed by society as a whole, by the natural world, by the cosmos and therefore by the gods themselves. There is thus a single law which governs the behavior of the whole cosmic hierarchy. "Themis in the world of Zeus," as Pythagoras writes, "and *Dike* in the world below, hold the same place and rank as Nomos in the cities of men; so that he who does not justly perform his appointed duty may appear as a violator of the whole order of the universe."[7] The higher the status of an individual, and hence the greater the vital force with which he was endowed (see chapter 62), the more important it was that he should rigorously follow the Way. Thus Odysseus tells us that when a blameless King maintains the *Dike*, "The black Earth bears wheat and barley, and the trees are laden with fruit, and the sheep bring forth and fail not, and the sea gives store of fish and all out of his good guidance, and the people prosper under him."[8]

The concept of the Way was probably entertained, explicitly or implicitly, by all vernacular societies. Thus in ancient China the *Tao* refers at once to the order and to the Way of the cosmos. The term is applied to the daily and yearly "revolution of the heavens" and of the two powers of light and darkness, day and night, summer and winter, heat and cold.[9] J.J.M. de Groot tells us that

> It represents all that is correct, normal or right (*ching* or *twan*) in the universe; it does, indeed, never deviate from its course. It consequently includes all correct and righteous dealings of men and spirits, which alone promote universal happiness and life.[10]

Tao represents the natural course of things. It was considered, Joseph Needham writes, "not only as vaguely informing all things, but as being the naturalness, the very structure of particular and individual things."[11] Feng Yu-Lan sees the *Tao* as "the all-embracing first principle of things."[12] All living things, including humans, are part of this all-embracing natural order, subject to the *Tao* which is its governing principle. "*Tao*, as the order of nature," Feng Yu-Lan writes, "governs their very action."[13] Humans follow the *Tao*, or Way, by behaving *naturally*. In Taoist terms, this means abiding by Lao Tzu's principle of *Wu Wei*, for "when all things obey the laws of the *Tao*," as Wing-Tsit Chan writes, "they will form a harmonious whole, and the universe will become an integrated organism."[14]

In ancient Egypt, we learn from Siegfried Morenz that the concept of *Maat* fulfilled a similar role. *Maat* meant "the right order in nature and society as established by the act of creation . . . what is right, what is correct, law, order, justice and trust"—not only in society but in the cosmos as a whole. Significantly, Re was at once Lord of the cosmos, Lord of the judgment of the dead and Lord of *Maat*. Later, when Osiris came into his own, he also became the Lord of *Maat*. Though *Maat* came into being with creation, nevertheless it had to be renewed and preserved. It follows that "*Maat* is . . . not only right order but also the object of human activity. *Maat* is both the task which man sets himself and also, as righteousness, the promise and reward which awaits him on fulfilling it."[15]

Because ancient Egypt was a centralized kingdom, run by a divine king, it was his role in particular to maintain *Maat* and hence the order of the cosmos. Thus we read in contemporary texts edited by Morenz that "the sky is at peace, the Earth is in joy, for they have heard that (the deceased king) will set right (*Maat*) in the place of disorder (*Isft*),"[16] and again, Tut-ankh-amun "drove out disorder (*Isft*) from the two lands and *Maat* is firmly established in its place: he made lying (*Grg*) an abomination and the land is as it was at the first time." It was the king's close association with *Maat* that gave authority to his edicts. What he ordered was necessarily part of the *Maat* that his subjects must follow.

A similar concept existed in Vedic India. It was referred to as *R'ta*. "The processes whose perpetual sameness or regular recurrence," writes Maurice Bloomfield, "give rise to the representation of order, obey *R'ta* or their occurrence is *R'ta*."[17] We read in the Vedas that

> The rivers flow *R'ta*. According to *R'ta* the light of the heavenborn morning has come . . . The year is the path of *R'ta*. The Gods themselves are born of the *R'ta* or in the *R'ta*; they show by the acts that they know, observe and love the *R'ta*. In man's activity, the *R'ta* manifests itself as the moral law.

R'ta also stands for the truth, though in a philosophical context truth is usually *Satya*. Untruth, though it is sometimes *Asatya*, is usually expressed as as *An-R'ta*, hence as a divergence from *R'ta* or the Way.

The Vedic poet, as Krishna Chaitanya notes, fully realizes that to obtain nature's bounty, man must obey *R'ta*: "for one who lives according to eternal law, the winds are full of sweetness, the rivers pour sweets. So may the plants be full of sweetness for us."[18] The great Vedic *Hymn to Earth* clearly expresses the belief in man's dependence on the order of the cosmos and in man's role in maintaining it by observing the ancient law. In it the poet expresses his faith in the eternal order and in man's duty to preserve it. It is this order that has bound "rock, soil, stone and dust" in such a way that "trees, lords of the forest, stand very firm." It is this order that maintains in "unfailing flow, day and night, the waters that are common to all" and nurtures "cornfields that nourish quadrupeds and bipeds." In all this the poet displays a respect that unites the spiritual and the practical: "Whatever I dig from thee, Earth, may it have quick growth again. O purifier, may we not injure thy vitals or thy heart."[19]

Later, the concept of *Dharma* was also used by the Hindus in the same way. "That regularity, that normality of the universe, which produces good crops, fat cattle, peace and contentment," A.M. Hocart writes, "is expressed by the word *Dharma* which means etymologically 'support,' 'upholding'."[20] It describes the way in which animals, men or things are expected to behave; it is natural law. The sun is sometimes identified with Dharma because it regulates the seasons; sometimes it is considered to be regulated by it. Among the Gods, Varuna is the Lord of Right, who lays down ordinances for the universe. The king on his accession is seen to have become to his people what Varuna is to the gods. For that reason, he too is known as the "lord of Right." In Balinese Hinduism, Eiseman writes, *Dharma* is seen as "the organizing force that maintains order, the organization that governs the universe as a whole, the relationships between various parts of the universe and actions within the various parts of the universe."[21]

The concept of *Dharma* was also taken up by the Buddhists who brought it to China where the *Dharma* of Mahayana Buddhism was identified with the *Tao*. De Groot describes the Buddhist *Dharma* as the universal law that embraces the world in its entirety. "It exists for the benefit of all beings, for does not its chief manifestation, the light of the world, shine its blessing on all men and all things?"[22] When a Buddhist Lama sets his prayer-wheel turning, he is performing a ritual that has deep meaning both in terms of the *Dharma* and the *R'ta*. Not only are the prayers printed on it repeated by his audience, but as Jane Harrison notes,

> He finds himself in sympathetic touch with the Wheel of the Universe; he performs the act, "Justice-Wheel-Setting in motion." He dare not turn the wheel contrariwise; lest that were to upset the whole order of nature.[23]

In the Persian *Avestas*, the Way is referred to as *Asha*, the celestial representative of justice on Earth. According to Chantepie de la Saussaye, "Justice is the rule of the world's life, as *Asha* is the principle of all well-ordered existence and the establishment or accomplishment of justice is the end of the evolution of the universe."[24]

In ancient Judaism the terms used are *Mishpat*, which means justice or right judgment and *Sedeq* which also means righteousness. These virtues are attributed to God, but in the words of Robert Murray, "the overarching vision is of human society in harmony with heaven."[25] This harmony is *Shalom* which means peace, but is in reality a wider term standing for harmony between Earth and Heaven, also cosmic or moral order or "the right functioning of all nature as God created it."[26] As in other ancient societies, the king had a big role to play in the maintenance of *Shalom*. As Murray writes, "if the king acted according to the divine gift of *Sedeq*, his Kingdom would be blessed with it in the senses of social justice, victory over enemies and the fruitfulness of the land, and would enjoy *Shalom*."[27] Traces of this key aspect of ancient Jewish religion are to be found in some of the Psalms, in Isaiah and more explicitly in 1 Enoch.

Significantly enough, when the Hebrew Bible was translated into Greek, the *Sedeq* words such as *Sedaqah* were translated by the Greek *Dike* and its derivatives such as *Dikaios* and *Dikaiosyne*. The same concept was taken up by the early Christians for whom the term *Dikaios* or Justice was, through the relationship to Jesus, still imbued with a cosmic dimension. Needless to say, the term gradually lost this cosmic dimension, especially with the Reformation.

If to follow the Way is to maintain the critical order of the cosmos —then a society can be seen as doing so when its behavior pattern

400

is homeotelic. When, on the contrary, it is heterotelic, then a society must be seen as following the anti-way, that which threatens the order of the cosmos and must thereby give rise to the worst possible discontinuities. Thus in the Vedas, as Chaitanya notes, we read that *R'ta*, though benign, can also be "stern and fierce" when it comes to transgressions. "Brihaspati rides a fearsome chariot of *R'ta* for destroying the wicked," meaning those who violate the eternal laws and so threaten the critical order of the cosmos.[28] The latter are best seen as following the Anti-Way, or in Vedic India, the *An-R'ta*, the opposite to the *R'ta*, and later, among the Buddhists, the *adharma*, the opposite to the *Dharma*.

Among the ancient Egyptians, the anti-way was referred to as *Isft*. Among the Greeks, it was often called *ou Themis*, the opposite to *Themis* (which occasionally was used to mean "social order" and occasionally the order of the pantheon as well as the path to be followed to achieve such order).

To follow the *ou Themis* could not be done with impunity. Among the Greeks, *Themis* (or *Dike*) was seen on such occasions as taking on the form of Nemesis, which is seen by Cornford as related to *Nomos*—in turn related to Nemos, the sacred grove that was almost certainly the original place of worship of the Ancient Greeks as it was of the Celts. Nemos, or Nemesis, inhabited such a grove. She may originally have been the woodland goddess, identified with Artemis, or Diana of the woods. She was also a goddess of fertility, closely allied with Fortuna, "the Lady who brings forth the fruits of the Earth." However, as Cornford notes, "She who dispenses good things can withhold them or dispense blights instead of blessings, the awful power which haunts the nemos may blast the profane invader of her sanctuary."[29]

In the earliest times, when Nemos was a sacred grove, Nemesis, as Donald Hughes notes, would have wrought vengeance on those who trespassed.[30] Eventually, once the sacred groves fell into disuse, Nemesis would have become the guardian of the law, that is of *Nomos* and hence of *Dike*.

Classical mythology abounds in stories of the Earth taking her revenge on those who destroy the natural world. Thus Erysichthon, whose name means "tearer of Earth," cut down a tree inhabited by a dryad in spite of the tree-spirit's protests. She complained to Mother

Earth, who afflicted him with insatiable hunger. Orion boasted that he would kill all the animals in the world. This too was reported to Mother Earth, who sent a monstrous scorpion to sting him to death. Today they are constellations opposite one another in the sky.[31]

Our modern society has quite clearly set out systematically to diverge from the Way. Its overriding goal is economic development or progress, the supreme heterotelic enterprise, which can only be achieved by methodically disrupting the critical order of the ecosphere so as to replace it with a totally different organization—the technosphere that derives its resources from the ecosphere and consigns to it its ever more voluminous and more toxic wastes. Technospheric expansion is thereby but another way of looking at ecospheric disintegration and contraction and the pattern of behavior that must be adopted to achieve this fatal goal is the anti-Way (see chapter 64).

62

For vernacular man, to increase his stock of "vital force" is to follow the Way

—

The ultimate goal of the Bantu is to possess as much vital force as possible, while what he fears most is to see a reduction in his stock of this inestimable commodity. Every disease, wound or suffering or depression, every injustice and every failure is interpreted by the Bantu as a sure sign that there has been a reduction in his stock of vital force.

Father Placide Tempels

A vast old religion which once swayed the Earth lingers in unbroken practice there in New Mexico. . . . In the oldest religion, everything was alive, not supernaturally but naturally alive. There were only deeper and deeper streams of life. . . . So rocks were alive, but a mountain had a deeper, vaster life than a rock. . . . For the whole life-effort of man was to get his life into direct contact with the elemental life of the cosmos, mountain-life, cloud-life, thunder-life, air-life, Earth-life, sun-life, to come into immediate *felt* contact, and so derive energy, power and a dark sort of joy. This effort into sheer naked contact *without an intermediary or mediator* is the root meaning of religion.

D.H. Lawrence

What is required is restoring the category of the sacred, the category most thoroughly destroyed by the scientific establishment.

Hans Jonas

VERNACULAR MAN follows the Way even in those societies in which the concept has not been clearly articulated. Most vernacular societies have developed another key concept, that of "vital force," which one can identify with the better-known concept of the sacred. Cornford tells us that in the classical world, a place was regarded as sacred because of the presence in it of a dangerous power that made it sacrosanct—"not to be set foot on by the profane."[1] Thus things that were sacred had to be treated with great respect, indeed with trepidation. They were the source of every benefit and also of all misfortunes, for sacred things contained this dangerous energy or "vital force." Every traditional society had its word for it: *Mana* for instance among the Melanesians and Polynesians; *orenda* among the Sioux and *muntu* among the Baluba.

Durkheim regards vital force as "the source of all religiosity." He sees "the spirits, demons, genii and gods of every sort" as "the concrete forms taken by this energy."[2] It is partly, at least, because they are endowed with this vital force that they are sacred and have become objects of religious cults. The sun, the moon and the stars are also worshiped for this reason. "They have not owed this honor to their intrinsic nature or their distinctive properties but to the fact that they are thought to participate in this force which alone is able to give things a sacred character, and which is also found in a multitude of other beings even the smallest."[3] Lods considers that "the very ancient term which is found in all Semitic languages to express the idea of 'god,' one of the various forms of *el* (Hebrew), *ilu* (Babylonian), *ilah* (Arabic), originally denoted the vague force which was the source of all strength and life."[4]

Vital force is seen as powering the whole living world. To acquire it personally is the only sure avenue to success. Placide Tempels, in his seminal work on Bantu philosophy, tells us that for the Bantu "supreme happiness, the only form of good fortune is to possess the greatest possible amount of vital force, while the worst adversity and indeed the only real misfortune is to see a reduction in one's stock of this power."[5] Among the Baluba, vital force is referred to as *muntu*. A powerful man is described as *muntu mukulumpe*, a man with a great deal of *muntu*, whereas a man of no social significance is referred to as a *muntu mutupu*, or one who has but a small amount of *muntu*. A complex vocabulary is used to describe all the changes that can affect a man's stock of *muntu*. All illnesses, depressions, failures in any field of activity are taken to be evidence of a reduction in this vital force and can be avoided only by maintaining one's stock of it. A man with none left at all is known as *mufu*. He is as good as dead.[6]

Tempels considers the same to be true of the Bantu in general. "The goal of all efforts among the Bantu," Tempels tells us, "can only be to intensify this vital force." And indeed, their customs only make sense if one interprets them "as a means of preserving or increasing one's stock of vital force."[7] Leopold Senghor, the poet, philosopher and former President of Senegal, considers that the goal of all religious ceremonies, all rituals and indeed of all artistic endeavor in Africa, is but "to increase the stock of vital force."[8] The same is true in Melanesia, so much so that according to Codrington "all Melanesian religion consists in getting this *mana* for oneself, or getting it used for one's benefit."[9]

Vital force was not just accumulated by individuals; it is usually seen as flowing through the cosmos and concentrating in certain things and beings, and in so doing, forming a pattern of power and hence of sanctity—a philosophy known as Hylozoism. Paul Schebesta tells us that for the Pygmies of the Ituri forest in Zaire, vital force or *megbe*

> is spread out everywhere, but its power does not manifest itself every-where with the same force nor in the same way. Certain animals are richly endowed with it. Humans possess a lot more of some types of *megbe* but less of other types. Able men are precisely those who have accumulated a lot of *megbe*: this is true of witch-doctors.[10]

For the Comanches of the Nevada Desert, according to Ralph Linton, the constituents of the natural world are imbued with different sorts of vital force. The greatest is personified by the eagle, the Earth, the sky and the sun. The highest force is God. After him come the first fathers who founded various clans, and next comes the head of the tribe. The living also form a hierarchy in accordance with the vital power that they possess, and animals, plants and minerals are also organized in the same way.[11]

For the Bantu, according to Senghor, "All the forces are organized hierarchically: first come the demi-gods or genii, then the original mythical ancestors, then the ordinary ancestors, then living men, in order of primogeniture, then animals, plants and minerals."[12] It seems that this pattern of power and hence of sanctity faithfully reflects what was taken to be the *hierarchical structure* of the cosmos.

In this way, the distribution of vital force *serves to sanctify the cosmic hierarchy and hence to preserve it against human depredations.* Significantly, the amount of vital force residing at the different levels of social organization reflects the extent to which the society is integrated or centralized. Thus in a very loose society, individuals and families are endowed with a considerable proportion of the society's vital force. On the other hand, in highly centralized traditional kingdoms such as ancient Egypt or Benin (now part of Nigeria) the vital force becomes concentrated in the person of the divine king, who is divine precisely for that reason. In such a society, what is more, the welfare of all the inhabitants is regarded as totally dependent on the fulfillment of the important rituals and ceremonies designed to preserve and increase the king's stock of vital force, and on the observance of the many taboos surrounding his person.

It is only if one realizes this that the practice of killing the king at regular intervals, as described by Frazer in *The Golden Bough*, can possibly make sense. The king was killed because, for reasons that varied from one society to another, he was no longer seen as being a fit repository for the society's stock of vital force which, if society is to avoid the most terrible calamities, must thereby be transferred to a more appropriate repository.

The relationship between things and beings at different echelons in the hierarchy of the cosmos is not symmetrical. Vital power flows downwards to vitalize and hence sanctify things and beings at the lower echelons, though it will only do so if the latter fulfill their obligations towards the higher echelons and hence towards the cosmos as a whole. It is thus understandable that so many of the rituals and ceremonies of a traditional people—and indeed, their whole way of life—should be designed to maintain the correct distribution of vital force at each level in the cosmic hierarchy. In this way they can maintain the critical order and stability of the cosmos, and thereby follow the Way.

To neglect the performance of these sacred rituals and ceremonies —worse still, to break the sacred laws that govern their performance —is to violate a taboo. This can only lead to a disastrous change in the distribution of vital force within the cosmic hierarchy. An act is taboo, according to Roger Caillois, because it disrupts "the universal order, which is at once that of nature and society" and as a result, "the earth might no longer yield a harvest, the cattle might be struck with infertility, the stars might no longer follow their appointed course, death and disease could stalk the land."[13]

This all-pervading fear of disrupting the critical order of the cosmos is reflected in the taboos set up in all tribal societies against mixing things that belong to the different classes or provinces into which the cosmos is seen to be divided. This goes a long way towards explaining food taboos. If it is taboo to eat pork among the Hebrews, this is because the pig, as Mary Douglas notes,

> is put into the class of abominable, unclean creatures, along with the hare, the hyrax and the camel. The grounds alleged are that these creatures either cleave the hoof or chew the cud, but do not do both. In other words, they don't quite make it into the class of ungulates.[14]

To eat water creatures that do not have fins and scales is also taboo for they do not fall into natural cosmic categories either. Nor do air creatures that do not fly or hop on the Earth, and do not have wings and two legs. To eat such creatures can only reduce a person's vital force and simultaneously threaten the critical order of the cosmos. Mixed marriages between people from naturally exogamous social groups are seen in the same light; they threaten the critical order of society and thereby that of the cosmos of which it is part.

Among the Igbo of Nigeria, according to Emefie Ikenga Metuh "deviations which disrupt the natural order are called *Aru*; literally, abominations." The word *Aru*, however, also means "crime against nature."[15] Such crimes include a number of unnatural acts that defy normal behavioral categories, such as a man having sexual intercourse with his father's wife or with an animal. The birth of twins and a hen hatching but one chick also fall into this category. These taboo events are *Aru* because the Igbo believe "that they transgress the laws guiding the ontological order and will therefore bring disaster to the community."[16]

The naïve and irresponsible tampering with the inner processes of the natural world by scientists, technologists and industrialists would be impossible in such a society.

For instance, feeding chickens on their own excrement, cows on offal derived from their fellows, or worse still, as has recently been reported in Switzerland, on human placentas acquired from the maternity wards of local hospitals, would undoubtedly be classified as "crimes against nature," and would be subject to the most stringent taboos. More so still would be the transplant of human genes into pigs in order to make them fatter, or the transformation of these unfortunate creatures into living factories, churning out "human milk" to be fed to our babies as a substitute for the real human milk that would otherwise be provided by their mothers. Built into the cultural pattern of vernacular society was the knowledge that such sordid practices are violations of the moral laws governing the cosmic order and that this can only lead to catastrophes on an unimaginable scale.

63

For vernacular man, to serve his gods is to follow the Way

In the stillness of the mighty woods, man is made aware of the divine.
Richard St Barbe Baker

There is no better way to please the Buddha than to please all sentient beings.
Ladakhi saying (quoted by *Helena Norberg-Hodge*)

The religious behavior of man contributes to maintaining the sanctity of the world.
Mircea Eliade

And God saw everything that He had made, and found it very good. And He said: This is a beautiful world that I have given you. Take good care of it; do not ruin it.
Jewish Prayer

And as to love: Love God. He is rock, earth and water, and the beast and stars, and the night that contains them.
Robinson Jeffers

THE DEITIES OF CHTHONIC MAN were above all the guardians of the critical order of the cosmic hierarchy. As such, they personified the laws that were seen as governing the cosmos and that man had to observe if he was to assure the preservation of its critical structure. This meant that by observing those laws man was also fulfilling his obligations to the appropriate deities. Thus to follow the Way in Vedic India was to fulfill one's obligations to Varuna, the God who personified the *R'ta*; in ancient Egypt to Re, who personified the *Maat*; in Greece to *Themis*, once the cosmic force bearing that name came to be represented by that Goddess.

The Gods also personified the vital force that flowed through the living world, reflecting its critical structure and sanctifying it. Jane Harrison notes that, originally, the gods of the Romans were impersonal and ill-defined, and that rather than being referred to as *dei* or gods, they were seen as *numina*, the plural of *numen* which meant vital force, suggesting along with Marrett and later Durkheim and Lods that the notion of vital force preceded that of the gods and spirits.

Whether this is so or not, the two concepts are complementary. It is probable that, as the gods grew in importance, so did they in turn reinforce the sacred nature of the vital force with which they were imbued. In this way, they sanctified each other as well as the structure of the living world which their organization faithfully reflected.

The role of the gods of vernacular man in sanctifying and hence in preserving the critical order of society is particularly well documented. 'Ancestor Worship' seems to be common to all known tribal peoples throughout the world, though the term is misleading, for the ancestors were not worshiped as modern man worships his god. His relationship with them was rather one of mutual obligations. Thus, rather than pray for favors, tribal man reminded his gods instead that he had fulfilled his obligations towards them and expected them to do likewise. He would even curse them if they did not reciprocate. Jomo

Kenyatta prefers to refer to this relationship as "communion with the ancestors."[1]

The relationship between chthonic people and their gods was one of mutual obligations. The gods had needs, and their principal need was for the living to fulfill their ritual and ceremonial obligations, observing the laws that the ancestors had enacted *in illo tempore*. For their part, the living and their families, clans and tribes, needed the gods to protect them from malnutrition, disease, enemy invasions and other disasters. In Japan, as Lafcadio Hearn puts it, "The happiness of the dead depends upon the respectful service rendered them by the living; and the happiness of the living depends upon the fulfillment of their pious duty to the dead"—a clear case of hierarchical mutualism.[2]

Underlying this form of religion is the principle that a dead ancestor, or a deity, remains a member of his family, his community and his society, rather than gravitating to some distant paradise—a concept unknown to chthonic man.

In this way, the ancestral gods in chthonic society are as much part of society as are the living. As William Robertson Smith pointed out many years ago in a famous passage:

> The circle into which a man was born was not simply a group of kinsfolk and fellow-citizens, but embraced also certain divine beings, the gods of the state, which to the ancient mind were as much a part of the particular community with which they stood connected as the human members of the social circle. The relationship between the gods of antiquity and their worshippers was expressed in the language of human relationship, and this language was not taken in a figurative sense but with strict literality. Thus a man was born into a fixed relation to certain gods as surely as he was born into a relation to his fellow-men; and his religion, that is, the part of conduct which was determined by his relation to the gods, was simply one side of the general scheme of conduct prescribed for him by his position as a member of society. There was no separation between the spheres of religion and of ordinary life. Every social act had a reference to the gods as well as to men, for the social body was not made up of men only, but of gods and men.[3]

Significantly, the gods of vernacular man, like his vital force, were seen as faithfully reflecting the hierarchical structure of his society. Thus Lafcadio Hearn writes of Japan:

> The three forms of the Shinto worship of ancestors are the Domestic Cult, the Communal Cult and the State Cult; or, in other words, the worship of family ancestors, the worship of clan or tribal ancestors and the worship of imperial ancestors. The first is the religion of the home; the second is the religion of the local divinity, or titular god; the third is the national religion.[4]

E. Driver shows how the differences in the organization of the gods among North American Indian societies could be explained in terms of their degree of integration or centralization:

> There was a strong tendency to arrange gods in a ranked hierarchy in areas where people were ranked in a similar manner, and to ignore such ranking where egalitarianism dominated human societies. Thus the people of Meso-America carefully ranked their gods, while those in the Sub-Arctic Plateau and Great Basin believed in large numbers of spirits of about equal rank. Other areas tended to be intermediate in this respect. Among the Pueblos where many spiritual personalities were widely recognized to be designated as gods, there was little tendency towards ranking, just as there was more equality among human beings.[5]

The people of Alor, as described by Cora Dubois, have a very loosely organized society. Few constraints are applied at a level higher than that of the family, and the family itself is very weak. The average Alorese is undisciplined and self-indulgent, and has little regard for authority of any kind. Not surprisingly, the Alorese pantheon reflects this disorderly state of affairs. "They have a culture hero and a supreme deity," writes Cora Dubois,

> but these play a very small part in their thought. Ancestral spirits are more important, but behavior to them is loose and undisciplined, just as it is towards their parents . . . The dead are merely pressing and insistent predators who can enforce their demands through supernatural powers. This is precisely the experience of the child with his parents, whom he obeys reluctantly and grudgingly.[6]

The Swazi, on the other hand, have developed a cohesive and hierarchically organized society and, according to Hilda Kuper, their gods are organized in exactly the same way:

> In the ancestral cult, the world of the living is projected onto a world of spirit (emadloti). Men and women, old and young, aristocrats and commoners, continue the patterns of superiority and inferiority established by Earthly experiences. Paternal and maternal spirits exercise complementary roles, similar to those operating in daily life on Earth; the paternal role reinforces legal and economic obligations; the maternal exercises a less formalized protective influence. Although the cult is set in a kinship framework, it is extended to the nation through the king, who is regarded as the father of all Swazi. His ancestors are the most powerful of all the spirits.[7]

The ancestral gods and thus the vital force which they personify are organized in such a way as to *reflect the critical order of vernacular society*. In this way, the critical structure of society is sanctified and its members forced, for fear of incurring the most terrible penalties, to preserve it, come what may. By sanctifying the critical order of society, the ancestral Gods simultaneously sanctify the natural world of which it is an integral part and which, as we have seen, is organized along the same basic plan. Significantly, the original chthonic gods had animal forms. For instance, among the Greeks, according to Jane Harrison, Zeus Ktesios was once a snake, while "Zeus Olbios in local worship long preserved his bull's head . . . the Sun god of Crete in bull form wooed the Moon Goddess, herself a cow; their child is a young bull-god, the Minos-Bull, the Minotaur."[8]

Because chthonic man made no radical distinction between himself and other animals, there was no reason in his scheme of things to distinguish between himself and his gods and the animals and the spirits that represented them, for all were part of the same cosmos. Significantly, among the Ancient Greeks and Romans, the original worshipping place was the sacred grove, known to the Greeks as the *temene* and to the Romans as the temple. "The woods," as Pliny writes, "were formerly temples of the deities, and even now simple country folk dedicate a tall tree to a God with the ritual of olden times; and we adore sacred groves and the very silence that reigns in them no less devoutly than images that gleam in gold and ivory."[9] Nor could the sacred groves be desecrated with impunity. It was Agamemnon's crime not just to kill a deer, but to do so in a *temene*. Trees, as Hughes tells us, were sacred to the Gods: "The Oak to Zeus, the Laurel to Apollo, the Willow to Hera, the Pine tree (or perhaps the oak) to Pan."[10]

Robert T. Parsons, writing on the Kono of Nigeria, sums up the nature and function of vernacular religion: it is "not only an organization of human relationships, but it includes also the relationships of people with the earth as a whole, with their own land and with the unseen world of constructive forces and beings in which they believe. *Religion brings them all into a consistent whole.*"[11] However, chthonic religion dies as society disintegrates. The Olympian Gods were the products of this social disintegration. Whereas the behavior of the original chthonic deities was subjected to the great powers that governed the cosmos (the *Moira*, or fate, which once also referred to the spatial order of the cosmos, and *Dike*, or justice, which was responsible for assuring its temporal order), the Olympian Gods were set above these cosmic powers. Their behavior and indeed that of the disintegrating society whose organization they reflected was no longer subject to the constraints that previously served to maintain the critical order of the cosmos.

Jane Harrison sees the shift from the chthonic to the Olympian gods as a move from the holistic view of society and of the cosmos to the individualized view. "The Olympian has clear form," she writes,

> he is the *principium individuationis* incarnate; . . . the mystery (or chthonic) god is the life of the whole of things, he can only be felt—as soon as he is thought and individualized, he passes, as Dionysos had to pass, into the thin, rare ether of the Olympian. The Olympians are of conscious thinking, divided, distinct, departmental; the mystery god is the impulse of life through all things, perennial, indivisible.[12]

As social disintegration proceeded still further, the Olympian gods ceased to have any relationship with society, for society was no more. The accent was then on the cult of a national God and eventually on that of the universal God. As society further disintegrated, the only remaining vernacular social grouping was the nuclear family and, not surprisingly, the universal god acquired a wife and a child so that the now truncated pantheon reflected the newly atomized society.

The Christian Trinity finds its counterpart in the religion of other disintegrated societies. The cult of Osiris and Isis and the baby Horus, for example, developed during the breakdown of ancient Egyptian society and was most popular during the Ptolemaic age. As the role of religion ceases to be social, it serves instead to provide solace to the individual and his nuclear family, beyond which lies but an undifferentiated mass of humanity from which he feels increasingly alienated, as he is from the natural world and from the cosmos. It is then only to the Universal God who, like him, is a temporal as well as a spatial isolate, that he feels any duty. As Roszak puts it, such a God having become "infinitely removed from falling nature, becomes that cosmic bouillon cube, in which all holiness is now to be concentrated for safe keeping."[13]

The "revealed" religions of today such as Christianity, Islam and modern Judaism, have desanctified society and the natural world, leaving them open to exploitation and destruction. For Nicholas Berdyaev, "Christianity alone made possible both positive science and technique. The reason is that it severed man from nature emotionally."[14] But the same is true of the other revealed religions that developed to satisfy the psychological needs of atomized societies.

As society disintegrates and religion becomes increasingly "other-worldly," as man is severed from nature and indeed from the entire Gaian hierarchy, so his behavior towards his gods ceases to occur within its correct field, that provided by the Gaian hierarchy of which he is part. Instead, it becomes heterotelic to this hierarchy, ceasing to fulfill its true social, ecological and cosmic role, which leads man even further along the anti-Way.

64

Progress is anti-evolutionary
and is the anti-Way

—

. . . Such is my awful Vision:
I see the Four-fold Man, The Humanity in deadly sleep
And its fallen Emanation, The Spectre and its cruel Shadow.
I see the Past, Present and Future existing all at once
Before me. O Divine Spirit, sustain me on thy wings,
That I may awake Albion from his long and cold repose;
For Bacon and Newton, sheath'd in dismal steel, their terrors hang
Like iron scourges over Albion: Reasonings like vast Serpents
Infold around my limbs, bruising my minute articulations.
I turn my eyes to the Schools and Universities of Europe
And there behold the Loom of Locke, whose Woof rages dire,
Wash'd by the Water-wheels of Newton; black the cloth
In heavy wreathes folds over every nation: cruel Works
Of many Wheels I view, wheel without wheel, with cogs tyrannic
Moving by compulsion each other, not as those in Eden, which
Wheel within Wheel, in freedom revolve in harmony and peace.
William Blake

We have not stumbled into the arms of Gog and Magog, we have
progressed there.
Theodore Roszak

Do you think you can take the world and improve it?
I do not think it can be done.
The world is sacred.
You cannot improve it.
If you try to change it, you will ruin it.
If you try to help it, you will lose it.
Lao Tzu

In terms of the world-view of modernism and of the associated paradigm of science—the changes brought to the ecosphere in the name of progress by modern man, with the aid of science, technology and industry—are part and parcel of the evolutionary process. No distinction is made between the process which leads to the development of the world of living things, or the ecosphere, and that which leads instead to the development of the technosphere.

On the contrary, these two obviously very different and indeed conflicting processes are seen as one and the same. If they differ at all, it is only insofar as one type of evolution is seen as "endosomatic," in that it involves the modification of organs and of behavior, or the emergence of new organs and behavior; while the other, referred to as technical or "exosomatic" evolution, proceeds largely by the making of new "organs" *outside* of the organism.

Sir Peter Medawar makes fun of a student who asks if humans "might not evolve to possess wings and so make it possible to fly." "This is a foolish question," he insists, since "it is obvious that human beings have already acquired some of the capabilities of both birds and fish—capabilities which they owe to their own special style of evolution, the 'exosomatic.'"[1]

Julian Huxley actually believed that the historical and particularly the industrial age have created a heightening of human evolution in psychological and social terms. Even ecologists see things in this way. Ramon Margalef, for instance, tells us that "industrialization has brought mankind a marked acceleration of evolutionary processes."[2] Jantsch goes further. For him, progress or economic development "forms a meaningful and integral part of a universal evolution," and he sees mankind as "an agent of this universal evolution, and even an important one."[3]

Another ardent supporter of this view is Peter Russell who invites us to "sit here and wonder at the whole evolutionary process, which has, step by step, resulted in me and you, in farms, automobiles and computers, in men walking on the moon, in the Taj Mahal, the Emperor Concerto and the Theory of Relativity."[4] For Russell, one of the most powerful tools that modern science makes available to this version of evolution is genetic engineering. This will enable us to create "completely new species" and, as a result, evolution will no longer have to follow "the slow process of trial and error, and natural selection." Instead, new species will be "consciously designed and created within a matter of months." Atomic physics, he assures us, will also contribute to our further evolution. It already has, for

> with the advent of particle accelerators, scientists once again became more than just passive observers. They were now able to change some elements into others, or even create completely new elements, by bombarding the nucleus with atomic particles and thereby changing its structure.[5]

The invention of the solar cells, he also insists, "represents an evolutionary development as significant as that of photosynthesis 3.5 billion years ago."[6] Moreover, we shall soon be able to influence our evolution by means of our growing ability to colonize space, "a development as significant as the colonization of land by the first amphibians 400 million years ago."[7] Russell is so impressed by all these technological developments that he is led to ask whether "the rapid acceleration so characteristic of today is heading us towards an evolutionary leap."[8] Indeed he asks: "Could we be on the threshold of a leap as significant as the evolution of life from inanimate matter?"[9]

Those who support the notion that economic and technological progress is part and parcel of the evolutionary process usually regard the early stages of evolution as instinctive, while the later stages that we associate with technological progress are seen to be conscious and purposive. This seems to be the standard position of today's mainstream scientists.

Indeed some of our most brilliant theoretical biologists, among them Julian Huxley and Waddington, see progress in this way. For them "human evolution," as they refer to it, is the latest phase of evolution and it is principally the product of the development of *mind, consciousness and reason*. Because they considered man to be endowed with these three unique attributes, *he is free to determine his*

own evolution—unencumbered, they clearly intimate, by any obliga-
tion to subject his progressive activities to any social, ecological or
cosmic constraints (see chapter 33).

In the light of the analysis provided in this book, however, what
they call human evolution or progress is the very negation of evolution or the Gaian Process, and is best referred to as anti-evolution.
Since evolution can be equated with the Way, serving as it does to
maintain the critical order and hence the stability of the ecosphere,
progress or anti-evolution can be equated with the anti-Way—serving to disrupt the critical order of the ecosphere and to reduce its
stability.

To neo-Darwinists who see evolution as a random process heading
in no particular direction, and hence just as capable of giving rise to
a climax ecosphere as to a highly developed industrial technosphere,
the very notion of anti-evolution is meaningless; but this is not so if
we view evolution in terms of an ecological world-view, in the light
of which it is a goal-directed process tending towards the increased
stability of the Gaian hierarchy. It then suffices to show that economic development or progress tends in the opposite direction—
towards ever greater ecospheric instability—to justify regarding it as
anti-evolutionary or as corresponding to the anti-Way. Let us see why
this must be so.

As biological, ecological and social systems develop, they become
more complex and also more diverse; though in ecosystems, complexity and diversity tend to stop increasing shortly before a climax
state is reached. Increasing complexity enables a system to assure
its homeostasis in the specific conditions in which it lives, whereas
increasing diversity enables it to hold its own in a wide range of
conditions, dealing with challenges that are less probable in terms
of its evolutionary experience. Biological evolution has led to the
development of highly complex forms of life, such as man, and also
to the most complex ecosystems. It has also given rise to some thirty
million different plant and animal species and countless varieties of
these species. Social evolution has led to the development of complex
social groupings and to a wide diversity of different ethnic groups,
each perfectly adapted to the specialized environment in which it lives.
There are said to have been at least 120 different tribes in California
alone and possibly 700 in New Guinea.

With progress, the culture of all these ethnic groups is disrupted and their members transformed into a homogeneous mass of alienated people, most of whom today are condemned, within a decade or two, to living in the growing slums that will soon accommodate most of humanity. In the meantime, climax forest ecosystems are destroyed and replaced by a series of ever less complex and diverse systems: secondary forests, then plantations of fast growing exotics, and then pasture—and they are eventually paved over to accommodate urban development.

Increasing complexity and diversity that accompany evolution are closely associated with increasing co-operation between the constituents of the ecosphere. Indeed, with evolution, competition gives way to co-operation, or what ecologists call mutualism. However, as the anti-evolutionary process gets under way, and complexity is dramatically reduced, so mutualism gives way to competition. In a human society, the same is true. The co-operation that obtains among the members of an extended family and the vernacular community of which they are part is so great, and contributes so much to the quality of their lives and indeed to their survival, that it is best regarded as "social wealth." With progress, on the other hand, social wealth is rapidly dissipated as social co-operation is replaced by interpersonal competition and aggression. The social wealth lost in this way cannot be compensated for by state services or economic wealth, which can only satisfy a small proportion of human needs—and heterotelically at that.

As evolution proceeds, there is a reduction in randomness and a corresponding increase in order. This order is maintained by the homeotelic behavior of the parts towards the whole. Thus, in a climax society, education is homeotelic to society, to the natural world and to the cosmos itself. So are settlement patterns, technology, economic activities, religion and government itself. The efforts of the differentiated parts to maintain the integrity of the whole, outside of which they have no meaning, is complemented by the efforts of the whole to maintain the integrity of its parts, without which it would not survive.

The units of homeotelic activity are the natural social units within which human beings evolved: the family, the community and the society. When these units disintegrate under the impact of economic development or progress they are replaced by corporations and institutions, whose behavior is increasingly heterotelic or random to the goal of maintaining the critical order of society and of the Gaian hierarchy. Thus education no longer serves its basic function of socializing young people so they can become homeotelic members of their families and communities; settlement patterns cease to be designed to reflect social structure and the structure of the cosmos; technology and economic activities in general cease to be embedded "in social relations," and rapidly spin out of control, eventually becoming the principal agents of social and ecological destruction. Religion becomes universal and otherworldly and no longer serves to sanctify social structure or the structure of the natural world, leaving them open to exploitation and destruction. Government, instead of being a normal communal function, is fulfilled by the state, an external body that is only pre-occupied with its own short-term interests which are necessarily in conflict with both those of the society it is called upon to govern and of the natural world.

As evolution proceeds, systems also become increasingly self-sufficient: Eugene Odum notes that the perfecting of a system's recycling mechanisms is an essential means of increasing self-sufficiency.[10] As ecosystems develop, they are endowed with ever more elaborate methods for recycling materials: this is particularly true of tropical rainforests. A vernacular society, too, becomes increasingly committed to the careful recycling of all materials.

Again, progress or anti-evolution puts this process into reverse. The waste products of one process, rather than serving as the raw material for the next, are being simply released into the environment in the cheapest possible way, without any regard for the pollution, and the shortages to which they must inevitably give rise. Worse still, xenobiotic materials of which the biosphere has had no experience, and cannot recycle homeotelically, are released to it in ever greater amounts, further reducing its critical order.

Societies, as they evolve, also learn to produce for themselves the basic necessities of life. Trade (and hence dependency on external sources of supply as well as on external markets for the sale of their produce) is limited to products that are of secondary importance to them. It is only in this way that they can insulate themselves against external changes that could deprive them of their livelihoods.

Once again, with economic development or progress, this evolutionary process is also put into reverse, until the world eventually becomes one vast free-trade zone in which all the social and ecological imperatives to which economic activities are normally subjected, are now systematically subordinated to the short-term interests of the transnational corporations that control the world market—the most fundamental cause of the social and ecological devastation that is fast making this planet uninhabitable for complex forms of life.

Also, with evolution, living things become increasingly adapted biologically, socially, cognitively and psychically to their respective environments, just as societies and ecosystems are to theirs. As economic development or progress occurs, however, they become, on the contrary, ever less well adapted to their respective environments. The result is an increase in discontinuities of all sorts, such as crime, delinquency, alcoholism and drug addiction at the level of the alienated individual; social chaos at the level of society, which is ever less capable of running itself and falls increasingly into the hands of dictatorships; floods, droughts and epidemics, at the level of the ecosystem; global problems such as climate change and the erosion of the ozone layer, at the level of the ecosphere itself.

Significantly, both Margalef and Odum note that the changes brought about by industrial man are unquestionably *reversing ecological succession*. Margalef also points out that man's interference with the functioning of ecosystems must return them to a lower and more unstable successional stage—one Odum refers to as a "disclimax" (a disturbance climax) or an "anthropogenic sub-climax." This is difficult to reconcile with Tansley's notion of the superiority of the anthropogenic climax over the natural climax; it is also incompatible with the very notion of economic development or progress as a means of improving human welfare.

Today, with the globalization of progress, we are rapidly heading towards a global ecospheric disclimax in which modern man will have effectively reversed three thousand million years of evolution to create an impoverished and degraded world that is ever less capable of sustaining complex forms of life. Medawar admits that our hopes have not worked out: "every folly, every enormity we look back on with repugnance can find its equivalent in contemporary life." But still, for him, this does not invalidate the principle of progress. "There is no need," he writes, "to be dismayed by the fact that we cannot yet envisage a definitive solution of our problems, we can obviously do better than this."[11] In any case, "it is a bit too early to expect our grander ambitions to be fulfilled." We must remember that "human history is only just beginning." We have known that "there has always been room for improvement; now we know that there is time for improvement too."[12]

But is there really time? Is history only just beginning, or is it coming to an end? Is there really any reason to suppose that "we can do better" if we continue to misinterpret our ever more terrifying problems, as we must do, if we insist in continuing to see them in the light of the highly flawed paradigm of science and the world-view of modernism that it so faithfully reflects? The argument put forward in this book is that we can only conceivably do better if, among other things, we set out to re-interpret our problems in the light of a very different world-view —the world-view of ecology—inspired as it must be by the chthonic world-view entertained by our remote ancestors who knew, as modern man no longer knows, how to live on this planet.

65

To keep to the Way society must be able to correct any divergence from it

———

The lower doctor heals the illness,
The medium doctor heals the whole person,
The higher doctor heals human society.
Sun Sze-Ma, Chinese physician, eighth century AD

Man has lost his way in the jungle of chemistry and engineering and will have to retrace his steps, however painful this may be. He will have to discover where he went wrong and make his peace with nature. In so doing, perhaps he may be able to recapture the rhythm of life and the love of the simple things of life, which will be an ever-unfolding joy to him.
Richard St Barbe Baker

DEVELOPING NATURAL SYSTEMS can only maintain themselves on their course or along their constellation of chreods if they can deal effectively with any external or internal challenges that might divert them from it. To do this, they must either isolate themselves from such challenges (resistance stability) or, alternatively, correct diversions from their path or Way (resilience stability) which requires that they interpret the problems caused by such divergences correctly.

Vernacular man in the classical world understood, as Hughes notes, that "hunger, ill-health, erosion, poverty and general ruin" were only different forms "that the earth's revenge could take for the terrible mistreatment meted out to her by man"—punishments for having diverted from the Way in pursuit of the anti-Way or what the ancient Greeks would have called the *ou Themis*.[1] The only way to combat these ills, therefore, was to treat the Earth with greater care, which meant to return to the Way of the ancestors who lived in the Golden Age when such ills were unknown.

Vernacular people invariably interpreted disease in this way. Thus among the Tukano of Colombia, as Reichel-Dolmatoff notes,

> Illness is taken to be the consequence of a person's upsetting a certain aspect of the ecological balance. Overhunting is a common cause and so are harvesting activities in which some relatively scarce natural resource has been wasted. The delicate balance existing within the natural environment, between nature and society, and within society itself, is bound to affect the whole.

To restore this "delicate balance,"

> The shaman as a healer of illness does not so much interfere on the individual level, but operates on the level of those supra-individual structures that have been disturbed by the person. To be effective, he has to apply his treatment to the disturbed part of the ecosystem. It

426

might be said then that a Tukano shaman does not have individual patients: his task is *to cure a social malfunctioning.*[2]

He does this by re-establishing the rules that "will avoid over-hunting, the depletion of certain plant resources and unchecked population increase."[3]

Quite clearly then, the shaman is more than a medical practitioner. He is a "truly powerful source in the control and management of resources," for he can really affect the incidence and severity of diseases over which the modern medical practitioner has no control whatsoever.

Victor Turner shows that among the Ndembu of East Africa, the doctor sees his task in very much the same way. It is

> less as curing an individual patient than *as remedying the ills of a corporate group.* The sickness of a patient is mainly a sign that "something is rotten" in the corporate body. The patient will not get better until all the tensions and aggressions in the group's interrelations have been brought to light and exposed to ritual treatment. The doctor's task is to tap the various streams of affect associated with these conflicts and with the social and interpersonal disputes in which they are manifested—and to channel them in a socially positive direction. The raw energies of conflict are thus domesticated in the service of the traditional social order.[4]

The philosophy underlying this interpretation of disease and means of curing it is even more explicit in the case of the Qollahuaya diviners of the community of Kaata in the Bolivian Andes. They see their community as an integral part of an *ayllu*—conceptualizing their mountainous territory as a human body, with communities living on the high ground, the central areas and in the lowlands. According to Joseph W. Bastien, the head of the *ayllu* is the "moist *puna* area . . ." where herders graze alpacas, llamas, sheep and pigs; the grasses that grow there are its hair; its eyes are the lakes of Apacheta. Its trunk is formed by the sloping terraced fields of potatoes, oca and barley.[5]

The *Kaata* also has a heart, and a liver, that produce blood and fat and are the "principles of life and power." They are circulated by the diviners throughout the community and in particular into the "Earth shrines" by means of rituals and ceremonies in which the sick people "eat with the mountain." For the people of Kaata, human health is thereby identified with the integrity of their *ayllu*: it follows that when people, their society and its environment "work together to form one body, the bodies of sick individuals become whole" and the sick are restored to health. The body metaphor provides in this way "a systemic model in which there is an analogy between the human body and the environmental and social bodies." Diseases are diagnosed as "signs of disorders between man and his land, or between his vertical *ayllu* and *Ayllu* Kaata." The disease is then combated "not by isolating the individual in a hospital away from his land" but instead by "gathering the members of his social group in ritual and together feeding all the parts of *Ayllu* Kaata."

Bastien sees this as being very much the approach to disease of the people of the Andes in general. For them disease

> is an organic, cultural, environmental and social phenomenon . . . By means of the body metaphor, diviners not only examine, but also interrelate the complex networks of environmental factors and social structure with physical distress. This often prevents subsequent illness because action is taken to change social and environmental causes of the sickness.[6]

In this manner, vernacular man correctly diagnoses heterotelic diseases as the symptoms of social and ecological maladjustments brought about by diverging from the Way, and thereby violating the laws of the cosmos and disrupting its critical order: maladjustments can only be eliminated by correcting the divergence and returning to the Way.

Modern man, on the other hand, interprets problems in terms of cause and effect relationships on the basis of which a disease is attributed to a discreet event such as the action of a bacterium, virus or other pathogen—which must be eliminated, usually by waging chemical warfare against it. To do this, we build factories for manufacturing the chemicals, shops in which to sell them, hospitals in which to administer them and universities in which to train the chemical engineers, pharmacists, doctors and other specialists involved in manufacturing, selling and administering them. Thus we put our faith in scientific, technological and industrial development, or progress—precisely what our society is organized to provide. This may occasionally serve to cure individual sufferers; it will always serve the interests of industrialists and their political allies; *but it will do nothing to reduce the incidence of the disease.*

All the other ever more daunting problems which confront our society today are interpreted in much the same way. Each one is made out to appear soluble by the expedients that science, technology and industry can provide and is rationalized and legitimized in terms of the world-view of modernism. Thus poverty is seen to be primarily a shortage of material goods and technological devices and of the money required to purchase them. Economic development can solve this problem, since it will enable us to build factories that can manufacture these commodities, and provide jobs to enable people to earn the money required to pay for them.

The World Bank and other Multinational Development Banks (MDBs) insist that the object of the destructive economic development that they finance is the eradication of poverty. Thus, in the President of the World Bank's 1987 address to his Board of Governors, he stated that his purpose that day was to

> outline the Bank's strategy for steady advance towards restored global economic growth, for steady progress in the fight against poverty.

Bilateral aid agencies seek to maintain the same fiction. "The principal purpose" of the United States Agency for International Development (USAID), a former US Secretary of State told his country's Senate Foreign Affairs Committee, is "to meet the basic needs of poor people in the developing countries"[7]—which is difficult to reconcile with the fact that about seventy-five percent of American bilateral aid is "tied" to the purchase of American manufactured goods, and serves principally to subsidize American exports.

The rapid degradation of the world's remaining agricultural lands is invariably attributed by governments and international agencies to traditional agricultural techniques. Thus USAID attributes the rapid deterioration of the "soil resource base" in arid lands to mismanagement, based on the use of "traditional technology and agricultural practices"—though in fact these techniques have been used sustainably for thousands of years. Broske G. Schoepf also notes how a scientist sent to Zaire to work on the Man and the Biosphere program (MAB) saw peasant cultivators as "enemies of the environment."[8] On the other hand, corporations operating large plantations were viewed

429

by him as "progressive in their contributions to development—as forces with whom alliance and accommodation are to be sought." Margaret Thatcher, in her 1989 address to the United Nations General Assembly, attributes the degradation of agricultural land to what she calls "cut and burn" agriculture, and recommends action "to improve agricultural methods—good husbandry, that plows back nourishment into the soil," a rather rosy view of modern agriculture.

Malnutrition and famine are also attributed to archaic agricultural practices and, in particular, to low inputs of fertilizer. A report based on a twenty-year study jointly undertaken by the Food and Agricultural Organization of the United Nations (FAO) and other organizations insists that the amount of food produced in the world is a direct function of fertilizer use, without mentioning the diminishing returns on successive applications of fertilizer experienced wherever farmers have adopted modern agricultural methods. According to the FAO, malnutrition and famine are also due to poverty. People starve because they do not have the money required to buy food; it follows that "the income of the poor must be increased so that their basic food requirements can be translated into effective demand."[9] Hence more economic development—even though, in spite of the unprecedented economic development of the post-war years, more people than ever before now lack the money to buy food.

The population explosion is also primarily attributed to poverty. Poor people are insecure, which leads them to produce more children who can be put to work to earn money for their parents. This means that to bring population growth under control requires rapid economic development that will provide them with the money they require to assure their security, assuring in this way "a demographic transition" as has already occurred in the industrial world. No mention is made of the fact that this transition only occurred in the industrial world once per-capita income had reached a much higher level than Third World people can conceivably hope to achieve. Nor is it noted that economic development, by destroying families and communities, annihilating their natural environment and forcing people off the land and into the slums, is the greatest source of their present insecurity.

The population explosion is seen above all to be the result of a shortage of family planning devices—so much so, that the World Bank estimates that to achieve "a rapid fertility decline goal" in sub-Saharan Africa, would mean increasing the amount of money spent on "family planning" twenty times by the end of the century—an extremely convenient approach to the problem from the point of view of the manufacturers of birth-control pills, condoms and IUDs.

So it is with all the other problems that confront us, whether it be unemployment, crime, delinquency, drug-addiction, alcoholism, pollution, resource depletion, global deforestation or global warming. Each is interpreted *in a way that rationalizes policies we have already decided to apply*: those that make the greatest contribution to economic development and hence best satisfy the requirements of the corporations and institutions that dominate our society. In other words, instead of interpreting our problems as the inevitable consequence of economic development or progress—that anti-evolutionary process that diverts us ever further from the Way—we interpret them instead as evidence that economic development *has not proceeded far or fast enough*—that, in effect, we have not deviated sufficiently from the Way.

This is the essence of the Great Misinterpretation—the ultimate manifestation of modern man's cognitive maladjustment to the industrial world that he has created. It draws us into a chain-reaction leading to ever greater social and environmental destruction, from which we must waste no time in extracting ourselves if we are to have any future at all on this planet.

66

The great reinterpretation requires a conversion to the world-view of ecology

~

Every social transformation . . . has rested on a new metaphysical and ideological base; or rather, upon deeper stirrings and intuitions whose rationalized expression takes the form of a new picture of the cosmos and the nature of man.

Lewis Mumford

The quest for a communal reality assumes the shape of a massive salvage operation, reaching out in many unlikely directions. I think this is the great adventure of our age and far more humanly valuable than the "race for space." It is the reclamation and renewal of the Old Gnosis. For those who respond to the call, what happens within the world of science, though still consequential in public policy, will have less and less existential meaning. The scientists and their many imitators will become for them an arcane priesthood carrying on obscure professional ceremonies and exchanging their "public knowledge" within the inner sanctum of the state temple.

Theodore Roszak

This generation may either be the last to exist in any semblance of a civilized world or that it will be the first to have the vision, the bearing and the greatness to say "I will have nothing to do with this destruction of life, I will play no part in this devastation of the land, I am determined to live and work for peaceful construction for I am morally responsible for the world of today and the generations of tomorrow."

Richard St Barbe Baker

Ultimately, reality matters.

James Michael Goldsmith

No amount of empirical or theoretical evidence is likely to persuade mainstream scientists or other protagonists of the world-view of modernism to accept any of the principles set out in this book. If eventually they are to be accepted, it will not be because they will by then have been "proved" to be true in the scientific sense of the term, but because the reigning paradigm or canonical knowledge will have changed to such an extent that they will have become consistent with it. Until this occurs these principles are, in the words of Gunther Stent, "premature," in that "their implications cannot be connected by a series of simple logical steps to 'canonical' or 'generally accepted knowledge' with the current paradigm."[1] In this way, Gleason's "individualistic concept of plant association" was rejected when ecology was still a holistic discipline, only to be adopted once it had been brought into line with the paradigm of science.

At the same time, no amount of empirical or theoretical "evidence" as to the untenability of a hypothesis can lead scientists to abandon it if it is part of current wisdom or canonical knowledge. However, once it has ceased to enjoy that status, because it has been transferred to another paradigm, then the hypothesis will simply die a natural death. In this way, hypotheses that have achieved the status of "scientific facts" have, in the space of a few years, been "completely discredited and committed to oblivion, without ever having been disproved or even newly tested." This is, as Polanyi points out, "simply because the conceptual framework of science had meanwhile, so altered that the facts no longer appeared credible."[2]

Clearly then, so long as we argue within the accepted "conceptual framework," or the reigning paradigm, or the canonical knowledge of the day, we can never dissuade people either to accept a new idea or to abandon an old one. "Demonstration," Polanyi insists, "must be supplemented . . . by forms of persuasion which can induce a conversion."[3] This is the crux of the matter. It is the conceptual

434

framework itself which must be changed, and this, as Polanyi suggests, means converting people to a new conceptual framework.

For people to accept the principles listed in this book, it is the paradigm of science itself that must be abandoned and hence the world-view of modernism which it faithfully reflects; and they must be replaced by the world-view of ecology. Such a conversion, or generalized paradigm shift, involves a profound rearrangement or recombination of the knowledge that makes up our world-view. It must affect its very metaphysical, ethical and aesthetic foundations. It must, in fact, involve a change akin to a religious conversion to which —as Kuhn, Polanyi and more recently Rupert Sheldrake have noted —a paradigm shift, even one occurring in a purely scientific context, can be realistically compared.

However, one must distinguish between a real religious conversion and a nominal one. All too often a religious conversion is of a very superficial nature; it is largely the terminology used in addressing the world of Gods and spirits that changes and little else. A real conversion seems to occur in quite specific conditions, which the psychologist William Sargant has compared with those that lead, more stressfully, to a nervous breakdown, and also to the brainwashing to which prisoners of war are often subjected in order to make them confess to crimes that they have not committed.[4] It seems probable too that the electric shock treatment often given to psychiatric patients fulfills a similar function. This explains why religious conversions are often preceded by physically and mentally exhausting ceremonies, the taking of alcohol and drugs and the achievement of trance-like states, as in the famous Dionysian rites. All this gives rise to a state of mind that may be functionally analogous to a nervous breakdown, a state of heightened suggestibility *in which people can be inculcated with a new world-view.*

It may be that the same process occurs—though in a less dramatic way—in new environmental conditions such as those created by economic development, to which a traditional cultural pattern proves to be unadaptive, causing people to question and eventually to abandon the world-view on which it is based and with which they and their ancestors have been imbued for centuries or even millennia. Such people pass through a highly stressful, indeed, psychically intolerable experience, for the human psyche abhors a cultural vacuum, as it does

435

the terrible social disorder to which it must give rise.

Such a situation occurred with the breakdown of paganism—as we refer to the traditional religion or world-view of early Roman society. In the chaos that ensued, there was a frantic search to replace the old world-view with a different one—one that could at least satisfy the psychic requirements of the increasingly atomized and alienated masses that inhabited the growing conurbations of the Roman Empire. Not surprisingly, they turned eastwards for inspiration, to where similar social conditions already existed. Franz Cumont describes the proliferation of eastern cults among the culturally deprived Roman masses. Eastern gods, such as Attis, Adonis, Mithra, Osiris and Isis, all had their devotees. But it was the religion preached by St Paul, the religion of Jesus Christ, that was to prevail.[5]

Anthony Wallace seeks to explain the process involved.[6] He sees every person in society as "maintaining a mental image of the society and its culture, as well as of his own body and its behavioral regularities, in order to act in ways which reduce stress at all levels of the system." This mental image or model, he refers to as "a mazeway." However, when a person under stress receives repeated information indicating "that his mazeway does not lead to action which reduces the level of stress, he must choose between maintaining his present mazeway and tolerating the stress, or changing the mazeway in an attempt to reduce the stress." This involves "changing his total gestalt, or his image of self, society and culture, of nature and body, and of ways of action"—in this way a new culture comes into being. Such a culture is generally referred to as millenarian. They proliferated in Europe during the tenth century, a period of socio-economic change that caused very serious social stresses. Many of the movements that sought to establish new cultural patterns during those troubled times were convinced that the year 1,000 presaged the end of the world and they called upon their adepts to prepare themselves spiritually for this momentous event.

Such movements are also referred to as "messianic" in that they are often led by a prophet who sees himself as divinely inspired— as a re-incarnation of a previous great religious figure, or in the case of movements of this sort occurring among the Jews, as the Messiah himself. These movements have proliferated throughout the Third World, during the colonial period in particular. In Lagos, there has been such a proliferation of messianic cults that their leaders have gone so far as to set up the world's first trade union of messiahs. Wallace refers to such cults as "revitalist," and defines a revitalization movement as

> a deliberate, organized, conscious effort by members of a society to construct a more satisfying culture. Revitalization is thus, from a cultural standpoint, a special kind of culture-change phenomenon: the person involved in a process of revitalization must perceive their culture, or some major areas of it, as a system (whether accurately or not); they must feel this cultural system as unsatisfactory; and they must innovate not merely discreet items, but a new cultural system, specifying new relationships as well as, in some cases, new traits.[7]

Wallace considers that both Christianity and Islam, and possibly Buddhism too, originated in revitalist movements. Indeed, it seems that all organized religions are "relics" of old revitalization movements, surviving in routinized form in stabilized cultures.

The increasing failure of all policies based on the world-view of modernism and its derivative paradigms—those of science and modern economics—to satisfy our most fundamental psychic needs or indeed solve any of the worsening problems that threaten our very survival on this planet gives rise to psychic conditions increasingly propitious to the emergence of revitalist movements. The chances are that such movements will be affected by ecological ideas that are increasingly in the air and whose relevance is becoming ever more apparent to even the blindest among us. There are signs, too, that such movements are likely to preach a return to the vernacular way of life. Thus while the rise of Islamic fundamentalism in the Moslem world and of Hindu fundamentalism in India can be seen as an unpleasant trend towards chauvinism, bigotry and intolerance, it is clearly also a reaction against Western economic imperialism and the disruption of the cultures and traditions of Moslems and Hindus by Western science, technology and industrial development.

Significantly, too, a considerable proportion of the revitalist movements that have so far sprung up in the Third World have been "nativistic"—which is to say that they have correctly attributed the ills against which they were reacting to the way of life imposed upon them by their colonial masters, and preached a return to the Way of their ancestors. Many such movements have been violent and unpleasant, of that there is no doubt. Usually too, they have been put down with equal violence and unpleasantness as their ideas were seen as a threat to the established order. However, there is reason to hope that the ecology-based revitalist movements of the future will seek to achieve their ends in the true non-violent Gandhian tradition. It could be that Deep Ecology, with its ethical and metaphysical preoccupations, might well develop into such a movement. So could the Earth First! movement in the USA, whose religious and metaphysical basis has recently been described by Bron Taylor.[8]

We cannot afford to wait and see whether such movements will develop into revitalist cults that are powerful enough to transform our society. Instead, we should work towards their development by helping to create the conditions in which they are likely to emerge. Let us remember that the world-view of ecology is very much that of the vernacular community-based society, whereas the world-view of modernism is that of industrial society. We must set out to combat and systematically weaken the main institutions of the industrial system— the state, the corporations—and the science and technology that they use to transform society and the natural world. At the same time, we must do everything to help recreate the family and the community, and above all a localized and diversified economy based on them, reducing in this way our increasingly universal dependence on a destructive economic system that, in any case, is in decline and may well be close to collapse.

As we multiply our efforts in these directions, so we must create the terrain in which ecological ideas can take root and flourish. May they inspire those who will lead us back to the Way, and thereby restore and preserve what still remains of the beautiful world we have been privileged to inherit.

Appendix One

Does the entropy law apply to the real world?

There is a set of laws that has a privileged status. They are the laws of thermodynamics, in particular the second law, usually referred to as the entropy law.

The term "entropy" was coined by Rudolph Clausius in 1868. He observed that within a closed receptacle, heat differences tended to even out. The evening-out continued until total heat uniformity was obtained. This uniformity could thus be regarded as a position of "equilibrium," at least from the thermodynamic point of view, and he referred to it as "entropy."

However, the concept itself is much older. Sadi Carnot, a French engineer, first made use of it in 1827. In trying to understand the workings of a steam engine, he realized that it was exploiting the heat difference between that part of the system which was hot and that which was cold. It was this difference in temperature that enabled it "to do the work." The difference tended to even out, however, reducing the system's ability to do the work. In such conditions, energy is said to have been dissipated, which means that it has degraded to a more homogeneous state identified with equilibrium or what Clausius called "entropy."

This, in essence, is the entropy law, and it would be quite acceptable if it were applied strictly to the field of thermodynamics. The trouble, however, is that its use has been extended to apply to fields of behavior that are very distant from thermodynamics and would appear to most sensible people to be governed by very different laws from those that govern the behavior of hot air in a closed receptacle or of steam in the boiler of a locomotive.

The entropy law has suffered the fate of many other scientific theories. It has become the object of a cult, worshipped as the key which will unravel the secrets of the universe. The same thing has happened to Claude Shannon and Warren Weaver's "Information Theory" (see appendix 2) which is also perfectly acceptable so long as it is applied to the field of communications for which it was designed, but has only served to confuse everybody after being hailed as a great scientific discovery that would, among other things, provide a means of measuring biospheric complexity or organization.

How then, do we know that the entropy law does not apply to behavior within the ecosphere? To begin with, it is easy to see that it does not. Life probably began on this planet three thousand million years ago and since then—that is, until the beginning of the historical era a mere ten thousand years ago—it has developed in complexity, diversity and stability. In other words it has behaved, over what most sensible people would regard as a sufficient sample of time, in a manner diametrically opposed to that in which it should have behaved had it been governed by the entropy law. This is a source of great embarrassment to our scientists. "How is it possible to understand life," asks Brillouin, "when the whole world is ruled by such a rule as the second principle of thermodynamics which points towards death and annihilation?"[1] Indeed, either we are all mad and there has not been such a thing as evolution, and the ecosphere with its myriad forms of life is an illusion, or else the entropy law does not apply to the behavior of living things—only to that of hot air in a closed receptacle or steam in the boiler of a locomotive.

Some of the more thoughtful philosophers of biology, such as Arthur Koestler, seem to realize this:

> The Second Law applies only in the special case of so-called "closed systems" (such as gas enclosed in a perfectly isolated container). But no such closed systems exist even in inanimate nature, and whether or not the universe as a whole is a closed system in this sense is anybody's guess. All living organisms however, are "open systems," that is to say, they maintain exchanges of energies and material with their environment. Instead of "running down" like a mechanical clock that dissipates its energies through friction, the living organism is constantly "building up" more complex substances from the substance it feeds on, more complex forms of energies from the energies it absorbs, and more complex patterns of information—perceptions, feelings, thoughts —from the input of its receptor organs.[2]

Brillouin makes the same point. "Both principles of thermodynamics," he writes, "apply only to an isolated system, which is contained in an enclosure through which no heat can be transferred, no work can be done and no matter nor radiation can be exchanged." The world, on the other hand, is not a closed system. "It is constantly receiving energy and negative entropy from the outside— radiant heat from the sun, gravitational energy from the sun and moon (provoking sea tides), cosmic radiation from an unknown origin, and so on." In this way, "the sentence to 'death by confinement' is avoided by living in a world that is not a confined and closed system."[3]

Waddington questions the applicability of the entropy law to ecospheric processes. He notes that the embryo increases its complexity as it develops and for this and other reasons he cannot believe that "any serious embryologists have considered that the second law of thermodynamics could be applied in any simple way to their subject matter in spite of what classical physicists might say." Indeed, Waddington assures us that the most creative physicists of his day would not have been tempted to impose the entropy law "as a rigid dogma of biology."[4]

However, it is not only because the Earth receives energy from the sun (and is therefore an open system) that the entropy law does not apply; there are other reasons. After all, other celestial bodies are also open systems. They are all bombarded with energy, "radiant heat from the sun, gravitational energy from the sun and moon, cosmic radiation etc.," yet this has not enabled them to develop life as our planet has done.

It is not altogether surprising that other conditions should have to be satisfied, for it is difficult to believe that the development of the ecosphere can be explained, as the entropy law implies, simply in terms of energy. This is an old myth that we can refer to as "energy reductionism." It originally appears to have come into being as a way of getting round the problems associated with the understanding of matter. The atomic theory of matter was controversial. Thermodynamics was supposed to be based on it. Carnot, however, showed that this science was independent of such a theory; it only involved energy changes. As Stephen Mason points out, this meant that "thermodynamics could proceed without the supposition that matter existed objectively."[5] Hence the development of the "Energetik" school which taught that the phenomena of nature were explicable in terms of the transformation of energy.

Of course, other writers have told us that everything is number, while atomic reductionists tell us that the world is exclusively made up of atoms. In reality, it is the way these atoms are organized that is critical, and there is no reason to believe that atoms have any greater reality than the tables, chairs, dung beetles or fiddler crabs into which they are organized. It is only possible to maintain these various forms of reductionism if we limit our study to very simple inanimate objects like gases and billiard balls. As soon as we look at the behavior of complex forms of life in the real world, the illusory character of these theories is quickly revealed. As Brillouin points out:

> For inert matter it suffices to know energy and entropy. For living organisms we have to introduce the "food value" of products. Calories contained in coal and calories in wheat and meat do not have the same function. Food value must itself be considered separately for different categories of living organisms. Cellulose is a food for some animals, but others cannot use it. When it comes to vitamins or hormones, new properties of chemical compounds are observed, that cannot be reduced to energy or entropy. All these data remain rather vague, but they all seem to point towards the need for a new leading idea (call it principle or law) in addition to current thermodynamics, before these new classifications can be understood and typical properties of living organisms can be logically connected together.[6]

It is easy to show that if a complex natural system is deprived of any of its basic constituents—energy, information or any of the basic chemicals of life—it will cease to function properly and will slowly disintegrate, moving in the direction of what we could refer to as "energy entropy." Georgescu-Roegen formulated such a law with regard to materials—the Fourth Law of Thermodynamics. We could, of course, go further and subdivide materials entropy into carbon entropy, phosphorous entropy, water entropy and so on, recognizing a different sort of entropy for each of the essential ingredients of living things. All such concepts would be as valid as that of energy entropy about which people make so much fuss, but they would be equally invalid once all the other conditions favoring ecospheric development were satisfied, for in normal conditions systems are either able to synthesize their own constituents or derive them from elsewhere in the quantities required.

The availability of these constituents leads to a very strange, indeed, apparently unique phenomenon. Systems tend to organize themselves not in a random or haphazard way, as is suggested by Lotka, Volterra, May, Prigogine and many others, but in a highly directive way, for random organization does not exist in the real world. What is more, as living things develop, successive thresholds are achieved which are referred to as levels of organization. Each time one is achieved, new "emergent" forms of behavior appear that display new characteristics. At the most sophisticated levels of organization, behavior displays those features we associate with life and is governed by a set of laws quite unknown to the physicist and the chemist whose knowledge is derived from the study of behavior at lower levels of organization. What is particularly relevant to the thesis of this appendix is that living things are capable of overcoming many of the constraints applying to the behavior of simpler things. "Consider a living organism," writes Brillouin,

> it has special properties which enable it to resist destruction, to heal its wounds, and to cure occasional sickness. This is very strange behavior, and nothing similar can be observed about inert matter. Is such behavior an exception to the second principle? It appears so, at least superficially, and we must be prepared to accept a "life principle" that would allow for some exceptions to the second principle. When life ceases and death occurs, the "life principle" stops working and the second principle regains its full power, implying demolition of the living structure. There is no more healing, no more resistance to sickness; the destruction of the former organism goes on unchecked and is completed in a very short time. Thus the conclusion or question: what about life and the second principle? Is there not, in living organisms, some power that prevents the action of the second principle?[7]

The notion that living things have some property that distinguishes them from inanimate things is referred to as "vitalism." This property was once taken to be of a supernatural nature as in the case of Aristotle's "entelechy" or Bergson's "*élan vital*." Vitalism is condemned because it implies that the world cannot be understood purely in terms of physics, which our physicists—who want to maintain their dominion over science, indeed over knowledge in general—cannot conceivably accept. But we do not have to appeal to vitalism to show that the second law is irrelevant to an understanding of the real world.

Because of the way living things are organized, they are capable of providing themselves with the energy they require to maintain their stability—green plants via photosynthesis and herbivores by consuming green plants. A physicist might tell us that the sun's energy has been dissipated, but the answer to this is "so what?" As far as the student of the ecosphere is concerned, this dissipation is required to power the development of living things and to increase their stability and that of the ecosphere. The case of Georgescu-Roegen's fourth law is, superficially at least, a stronger one than his case for the second law, since though the world is an open system from the point of view of energy, it is closed from the point of view of materials. But once more, living things can overcome this constraint by developing the means of recycling the materials they require, the waste products of specific ecospheric processes serving as the raw materials of the next.

The question we must now ask ourselves is why our scientists so stubbornly refuse to face both the theoretical and empirical evidence against the applicability of the entropy law to the world of living things? To understand their obstinacy, one must consider what was the world-view or paradigm of the physical sciences in the middle and towards the end of the nineteenth century. In terms of it, the world was seen as an enormous machine whose components behaved largely like planets and billiard balls. It was just the world-view required to rationalize the trend initiated by the industrial revolution towards materialism, individualism, utilitarianism and economism—the closely associated values of the industrial age. Science then was largely identified with physics, as indeed it is today. All other sciences were, and still are, considered very inferior, so much so that their practitioners are largely preoccupied with raising their status by slavishly imitating the methodology of the physical sciences. If physics was to be the fundamental science governing everything else, then the behavior of physical things—billiard balls and the like—*must be shown to provide a model for that of living things.*

The trouble was that in terms of the neo-Newtonian world-view it failed to do so on two counts. The first and most important problem was that Newtonian time was reversible. It could move backwards or forwards just as a billiard ball can, while in the real world, time is irreversible: one cannot eradicate experience nor restore the past exactly as it once was. As Brillouin puts it,

> One of the most important features about time is its irreversibility. Time flows on and never comes back. When the physicist is confronted with this fact he is greatly disturbed. All the laws of physics in their elementary forms are reversible.[8]

The Newtonian paradigm also failed to explain the direction of time. Newton formulated laws governing the movement of bodies but did not tell us that they moved in one direction rather than any other. This again did not tally with the behavior of living things.

The entropy law *remedied all this*. Since energy could only be degraded, it must follow that the time during which its degradation took place is irreversible. As Brillouin notes, "it is a very strange coincidence that life and the second law represent the two most important examples of the impossibility of time's running backwards."[9] All this was just what our physicists were looking for: incontrovertible evidence, as they saw it, that the entropy law underlay the behavior of living processes. This was further confirmed by the fact that, as in living processes, energy did not move in a random but in a specific direction.

Ludwig Boltzmann's formulation of the entropy law as a statistical law further confirmed the entropy thesis, since the behavior of living things was also held to be governed by such laws. Of course, a limitless number of processes can be shown to tend statistically in an irreversible direction. Even a game of snakes and ladders satisfies these conditions, yet nobody suggests that this great nursery game provides a model for life processes. Why the behavior of gas in a closed receptacle should provide a better model is not at all clear, but what is clear is the stake our aristoscientists have in proving that it does.

Another reason why our scientists are so keen to preserve the entropy law, contrary to all the theoretical and empirical evidence, is that it is *easily quantifiable* (see chapter 11). This is a critical consideration, for it is a dogma of aristoscience that only a quantifiable proposition can be regarded as scientific. The "statistical method" is, of course, very convenient. Indeed, if the entropy law can be seen only as a statistical law, then the development of the ecosphere over the last three thousand million years, rather than providing a clear violation of the entropy law, can be interpreted as nothing more than an exception to this law which does not invalidate it. Boltzmann has outdone Lakatos's pre-Einsteinian physicist (see chapter 18). Georgescu-Roegen realizes how unsatisfactory Boltzmann's compromise is. "According to this new discipline," he notes,

> a pile of ashes may very well become capable of heating the boiler. Also a corpse may resuscitate to lead a second life in exactly reverse order of the first. Only *the probability of such events is fantastically small.*[10]

In other words, once the entropy law is seen to be no more than a statistical law, it tells us nothing about the real world, nor about the biological social and ecological processes that brought it into being, for these are so statistically improbable as not to be worth considering, and the fact that the laws of thermodynamics are irreconcilable with them is of no importance whatsoever.

A second device for sustaining the entropy law in the face of all the evidence to the contrary, is to postulate that though the Earth may be an open system, the universe itself is a closed one, which means that life on Earth can only develop *at the cost of increasing the entropy of the universe.* The trouble with this argument is that there is no reason whatsoever for supposing that the universe is a closed system. Mark Braham points out that a completely closed system "is a theoretical construct" and that "we have no way of determining whether the universe is closed or not," while to say that the universe is an open system raises a number of difficult problems.[11] It would mean, for instance, that it is exchanging energy with its environment, but we know nothing about such an environment; if it exists, then it must be part of another universe, a "mega-universe" of which we are but a sub-system.

"What then," Braham asks, "are the limits to the other universe, or to the mega-universe and so on?"[12] Since we are quite incapable of answering such questions, it may be convenient to postulate that the universe is closed. But would this help us very much? As Braham points out,

To assume closure is to assume a boundary. By definition, a boundary is between something and something else; there must therefore be something on the "other side." If we were to speculate meaningfully about this boundary, we would require information about the "other side" and this would clearly require a leak in the system and hence no closure at all.[13]

But even if we can find a way round this objection and accept that the system is a closed one, and that one day the sun's energy will be entirely dissipated, is this consideration of any practical significance? The terrible problems we face today (such as global warming, the depletion of the ozone layer, the population explosion, social disintegration, deforestation, desertification, the chemical contamination of our groundwater, rivers, seas and estuaries) *have not been caused by any reduction in the amount of energy generated by the sun*. To preoccupy ourselves unduly with the possibility that such a reduction may eventually occur is to divert attention from these immediate problems to an exceedingly long-term one (for no one suggests that the sun is likely to stop shining for a few million years or so). It is also to misdirect precious time and energy from problems that can be solved to one about which we can do strictly nothing—for not even our most fanatical technomaniacs have yet offered to devise a substitute for the sun.

Appendix Two

What is information?

The term "information," in a scientific context, refers to Claude Shannon and Warren Weaver's concept of information, developed in 1948. Since then, other theories of information have been proposed, but they seem to constitute little more than minor variations on the original theme. In any case, they do not appear to have earned any general acceptance among scientists. They are listed, together with their most salient features, by Everett Rogers and Lawrence Kincaid.[1]

Both Shannon and Weaver, when they developed their theory, were working for the Bell Telephone Company. Their chief concern was to determine how to maximize the amount of "information"—not just the number of signs—that could be transmitted via a communications channel with limited capacity. They found it convenient to define information in such a way that it could be measured in terms of Boltzmann's mathematical formula for the measurement of entropy. Information is thereby equated with entropy, with the difference that whereas entropy is seen as the most probable arrangement of molecules in a particular energy state, information measures the most probable arrangement of signs in a message; probability, in both cases, being equated with randomness in accordance with the Second Law of Thermodynamics, or the entropy law.

It is difficult to understand this notion unless one realizes that, for the communications engineer, randomness (and thus the absence of any organization or constraints on the order in which the signs appear) is equated with the freedom he enjoys in choosing the message he wishes to send, and hence the order in which the signs must appear so as to satisfy his professional requirements. Randomness, or entropy, is thus for him the "ideal" and must therefore, for his purposes, be associated with the highest information. To quote Shannon and Weaver,

> Information is highest when the probabilities of the various choices are as nearly equal as circumstances permit—when one has as much freedom of choice, being driven as little as possible towards some certain choices which have more than their share of probability.[2]

449

On the other hand, when a "situation is highly organized, it is not characterized by a large degree of randomness or of choice" and in these conditions, "the information (or the entropy) is low."

The sort of constraints that Shannon and Weaver regard as reducing this freedom of choice (and hence the information content of a message) are linguistic constraints.[3] Each language has a particular structure or organization, in terms of which one can predict that certain words are more or less likely to follow other words. Thus, "after the three words 'in the event' the probability for 'that' as the next word is fairly high, and for 'elephant' as the next word is very low." These linguistic constraints reduce the information content of a message by forcing the sender to include signs in his message not because he wants to but because they are imposed on him by the structure of the language in which the message is formulated. These signs are regarded as redundant and each language is said to have a quantifiable built-in redundancy, that of the English language being about fifty percent. Thus one can say that the higher the organization, and hence the lower the entropy, the greater must be the constraints, the higher the redundancy and the less the information communicated.

The amount of information in a message is calculated in terms of the logarithm (Base 2) of the number of choices. The result is formulated in terms of "bits" (the term "bit" was first suggested by John W. Tukey, as an abbreviation for "binary digit"). When numbers are expressed in the binary system, there are only two digits, zero and one. These may be taken symbolically to represent any two alternative choices. In a situation in which there are only two choices, there is said to be one bit of information. The greater the number of free unconstrained choices, the greater the amount of information. If there are sixteen choices from among which we are equally free to choose, there are four "bits" of information.

The greater the freedom enjoyed by the sender in the selection of signs or messages for emission the greater must be the improbability that a particular sign or message will be sent. To illustrate this, I shall assume that Shannon and Weaver's "information" takes "meaning" into account. Thus a message that told us that a horse called Green Crocodile would win a race in which there were sixteen contestants of unknown breeding and with no previous form (all in theory having the same chance of winning) would communicate four "bits" of information. If we knew something about their breeding and form and, on this basis, could classify the horses in accordance with what appeared to be their chances of winning the race, the information communicated would be correspondingly reduced. If one horse were backed down to even money on the theory that it had one chance out of two of winning the race, then a message informing us that it would win would communicate still less information, in fact no more than one "bit"—the same amount of information as it would communicate were Green Crocodile to have but a single other contestant to deal with, rather than fifteen others. The greater the number of "bits" ascribed to a message the more valuable the information must be. This is clearly a very sensible way of calculating the value of the information communicated to both the bookmaker and the punters.

In reality, it does not quite work this way, since Shannon and Weaver are not concerned with the probability or improbability of a statement being true or false. This is the concern of the epistemologist not the communications engineer. The latter is not even preoccupied with the probability or improbability of a particular statement, nor even of a particular word, but only of particular signs being emitted —regardless of whether these signs make up intelligible words or whether such words make up intelligible sentences. In other words, the information content of a message, for them, *does not take into account its meaning*. "Information must not be confused with meaning," they write, and "the semantic aspects of communication are irrelevant to the engineering aspect." This means, as they freely admit, that their use of the term "information" *is very different from its normal use in the English language*.[4]

An essential feature of Shannon and Weaver's theory is that during the emission of a message, its information content is reduced. The reason is that as a message is spelled out along a channel, so does the probability or improbability of specific signs occurring become easier to calculate. Linguistic organization is seen to build up—as does "redundancy"—which means that "entropy" and "information" are correspondingly reduced. Another reason why the amount of information contained in a message must fall as it is spelled out, is that communication channels are subject to "noise" or "randomness." Noise, of course, increases uncertainty or improbability. One might think that it would thereby lead to increased (rather than decreased) information; however, Shannon and Weaver distinguish between that type of uncertainty that is caused by noise, which they regard as undesirable, and desirable types of uncertainty which they identify with "freedom of choice" and hence with information. The information content of a message is therefore not equal to uncertainty but to "desirable" uncertainty minus "undesirable" uncertainty or noise.

That the equations used to measure entropy and information are the same holds great significance for Shannon and Weaver. They point out that for Sir Arthur Stanley Eddington "the law that entropy always increases—the second law of Thermodynamics—holds, I think, the supreme position among the laws of Nature."[5] Thus, Shannon and Weaver note, when the engineer "meets the concept of entropy in communications theory he has a right to be rather excited—a right to suspect that one has hold of something that may turn out to be basic and important."

Another aspect of the Theory of Information that makes it so attractive to the scientist is its quantifiability. However, for quantification to be possible, as Michael Apter points out, we must know the exact number of possible messages that could be transmitted at any one time. This may well be possible in the field of communications, but not in the field of behavior. It is for this reason, as Anatol Rapoport points out, that

> the modest but, we think, significant applications of information theory to various psychological experiments have occurred in precisely those situations in which the set in question was strictly defined: a list of syllables to be memorized, associations to be formed, responses selected from etc. There was therefore no difficulty in quantifying the associated "amounts of information" and relating such amounts to certain aspects of performance.[6]

But, as he points out too, such situations are "banal." We can add that they do not normally occur in the living world.

In any case, the notion of a passive source of information (whether it displays order or disorder) from which messages are selected by an external agent does not correspond to anything that exists in the world of living things. The natural systems that make up the ecosphere are dynamic not static, active not passive; what is more, they are self-regulating, not regulated from the outside (heterarchically) by an external agent such as a communications engineer. The source of information and the sender of the message in the world of living things are, in fact, *part and parcel of the same self-regulating system.*

If we integrate Shannon and Weaver's sender of messages and the source of the messages as part of the same system, however, it must cease to display entropy—for one of the basic features of entropy is randomness and hence non-purposiveness, whereas the sender of messages acts purposefully since, as we are told, he selects for emission those messages that display the minimum redundancy and hence the maximum information content. What is more, if the system is to achieve its goal efficiently, then the information it contains must be organized in the manner most favorable to the achievement of that goal. This we can predict with confidence on the basis of our empirical knowledge of the way patterns of information or cybernisms (brains, genes, genomes, gene pools, etc.) are organized in the world of living things.

Another consideration is that the sort of improbability that Shannon and Weaver write about is not a useful concept for understanding the working of the ecosphere. For Shannon and Weaver, improbability is either improbability *vis-à-vis* the workings of the entropy law, that as we have seen does not apply to the world of living things, or else it is improbability on the basis of probability theory, that they wrongly take to be the same thing. In the world of living things, improbability, if we are to use this concept, means improbability *vis-à-vis* a system's model or image of its relationship with its environment. This reflects its experience and that of its cultural group (if a human animal) and its species for a specific purpose—that of assuring the system's stability in relation to its environment, and hence its survival.

Thus as living things evolve they develop the capacity to discriminate between an increasing range of different environmental situations, to interpret them correctly and to react to them adaptively. A very simple organism, such as the *Dyonea* flytrap that so fascinated Darwin, can do one of two things when something lands on its trap: close it or not, and it does so with the minimum powers of discrimination since it cannot discriminate between an edible insect and an inedible pebble. At the other end of the scale is a human animal that can handle a vast number of different signals and interpret them correctly, and thus has at its disposal an exceptionally large repertoire of adaptive responses. In the language of Shannon and Weaver, one can say that the human animal is capable of handling messages with a high degree of improbability and hence of high information value—thousands of bits of information in contrast to the mere one bit that the *Dyonea* flytrap can handle. The human animal cannot however, handle each of these messages with equal ease (see chapter 53).

The ease with which a living thing can handle messages seems to be a function of their *importance* or relevance to its behavior pattern and also of the probability, in terms of its own experience and that of its species, that such a message will actually be received. In other words, information in the brain and nervous system is not arranged at random and hence does not display entropy; on the contrary it is highly organized, as is all information used by natural systems within the ecosphere (genetic information, for instance).

If information is organized, partly at least, in accordance with the probability of its being required, then systems living in a protected environment, in which only probable things occur, will need to react adaptively to a correspondingly limited range of different environmental situations. Those that live in a less well-protected environment in which improbable things occur, however, will need to react adaptively to a wider range of ever more improbable environmental situations—and hence will have to make use of information displaying a greater diversity or organized redundancy.

Shannon and Weaver rightly regard a certain amount of redundancy as useful for counteracting the effects of noise. However, they take it to be otherwise undesirable in that it reduces the information content of a message by reducing the freedom of choice of the sender, and hence the variety of messages he can send. But in the world of living things, as already mentioned, organized redundancy, or diversity, has a positive value. It increases rather than reduces a message's information content since it determines the system's key ability to adapt to improbable events.

An even more serious criticism of the extension of Shannon and Weaver's concept of information to the world of living things is that information, as I have already intimated, is very much more than improbability. This is also the view of Donald Mackay:

> To dress improbability up as a definition of information, as some exponents do, seems the most unfortunate obscurantism. Unexpectedness is a measurable quality or attribute of information—not a definition of it.[7]

In the world of living things, a message is not emitted because it is improbable, or for that matter, probable. It is emitted because it is of some relevance to the relationship between the sender and the receiver. Shannon and Weaver, however, are not in the least concerned with whether the receiver is interested in receiving a message, let alone whether he can understand it or is likely to believe it. Again, this may make sense in the world of communications engineering, but not in the world of living things, where these considerations are critical.

As Waddington points out, information in the real world largely consists of instructions (programs or "algorithms").[8] Thus genes combine to provide instructions for protein-synthesis. A gene pool provides instructions for the renewal of a viable population. The brain and central nervous system provide instructions for the proper functioning of an individual's metabolism and day-to-day adaptive relationships with its environment. A culture provides instructions for the mediation of a society's adaptive behavior pattern.

Such instructions will only be obeyed by systems that have been designed by their evolution and upbringing to receive, understand and believe them. This must be true of the transmission of instructions and hence of information in all living processes. What is more, the receiver of a message must also be capable of acting on the information adaptively (see chapter 44). The cries of a baby in distress provide an important message to its mother, who is not only disposed to hear them and understand their significance, but also to respond to them effectively. Otherwise, there would be no advantage to be gained from the ability to hear and understand them.

The quality of a message that will determine whether it will be detected and interpreted by a natural system is its *relevance to the system's behavior pattern*. Since information in a natural system is organized hierarchically, from the general to the particular, the importance of a message can be determined in accordance with its relevance to the most general and important information contained within a pattern of information or cybernism. This in turn, will reflect its relevance to the most important or general phases of the system's behavioral strategy. As natural systems evolve, they develop the capacity to deal with messages of lesser importance as well. This enables them to develop a more subtle behavior pattern and thus adapt with greater precision to their specific environment. Nevertheless, the more important messages will remain their primary concern.

The final reason why Shannon and Weaver's theory is inapplicable to the world of living things is that they see the amount of information contained in a message as it is being emitted as decreasing (because of the accumulation of linguistic constraints and noise). In the world of living things, however, the opposite is true: the information content of a message can only increase. It is fairly evident, as Waddington points out, that an adult rabbit running around a field contains a very much greater "amount or variety" of information than a newly fertilized rabbit's egg. How then, Waddington asks, can one explain such a situation "in terms of an information theory whose basic tenet is that information cannot be gained?"[9]

That the information content of a natural system increases as it becomes more complex seems clear to a number of writers who have nevertheless sought to measure a system's complexity in terms of its information content using Shannon and Weaver's concept of information. Thus S.M. Dancoff and H. Quastler postulate that the larger the number of different components in a system, and hence the greater its complexity, the greater must be the amount of information it contains, since the higher must be the improbability of building up such a system by assembling its components in a random manner.[10]

Unfortunately, what Dancoff and Quastler actually measure has nothing in common with the sort of complexity encountered in the biosphere. This cannot be measured by adding up its component parts, because it derives its essential features above all *from the way these parts are organized* (see chapter 52). For Shannon and Weaver, however, organization and the constraints associated with it, reduce rather than increase information. Thus, unless increasing complexity is associated with reduced information and the nematode *Ascaris* is taken to contain more information than man, Dancoff and Quastler have to ignore the all-important organizational component of complexity.

Significantly, Dancoff and Quastler themselves admit that their work yields but "crude approximations and vague hypotheses" and that their estimates are "extremely coarse." Nevertheless, they insist that this is "better than no estimates at all."[11] I do not think this is so. Mathematical calculations based on false premises and making use of inappropriate concepts, by virtue of the impression of great scientific accuracy that they convey, can only serve to mislead people and to obscure the real issues at stake.

I have tried to show that the use of the communications concept of information for understanding behavior in the world of living things cannot conceivably be justified on either theoretical or empirical grounds. This is not altogether surprising, since it was not designed for this purpose—any more, for that matter, than was the associated concept of entropy. This is Waddington's view. "Information theory," he points out, "was developed in connection with a particular type of process and has limitations which make it extremely difficult if not impossible to use in many of the biological contexts to which people have been tempted to apply it."[12] Margalef makes much the same point. "Information theory based on statistical considerations," he writes, "is concerned with how data are transmitted, ignoring however, any human factors involved."[13] Brillouin, as we have seen, also criticized the extension of this theory to the study of the world of living things.

Yet in spite of these criticisms, all these writers, with the exception of Apter, still explicitly justify its use for this purpose. Waddington, for instance, argues that it allows the concept "to be clearly expressed" though what I think he really means is "quantified." But what, one might ask, is to be gained by quantifying a concept that corresponds to nothing in the world of living things to which it is supposed to apply? It can only serve to give an air of spurious accuracy to what is, in effect, little more than a fiction.

Rapoport's argument for the extension of Shannon and Weaver's theory is that if it is "to break out" of "its original habitat of bandwidths and modulation" then a proper beginning must be made "which usually means a modest beginning."[14] But why *not* allow the concept of information to remain "in its original habitat of bandwidths and modulation"? What evidence does Rapoport or anybody else provide that its use can profitably be extended to other fields for which it was not designed? The answer, I am afraid, is none whatsoever.

On the contrary, the only function that the extension of the theory is likely to serve is to perpetuate the myth that behavior is mechanistic, passive, atomized and random, since the theory attributes precisely such features to the information on the basis of which behavior is mediated. This can only serve to obscure the most important features of the behavior of living things, which is, on the contrary, dynamic, creative, organized and purposeful. Applied to the world of living things, this theory is simply an instrument of scientific obscurantism and mystification.

Appendix Three

The artificialistic fallacy

The best-known objection to a biospheric or naturalistic ethic is a logical one. In his *Treatise on Human Nature*, Hume wrote the now famous passage:

> In every system of morality which I have hitherto met with, I have always remarked that the author proceeds for some time in the ordinary way of reasoning, and establishes the being of a God, or makes observations concerning human affairs; whereon of a sudden, I am surprised to find, that instead of the usual copulations of proposition, "is" and "is not," I meet with no proposition that is not connected with an "ought" or "ought not."
>
> The change is imperceptible; but, however, of the last consequence. For this "ought" or "ought not" expresses some new relation or affirmation, it is necessary that it should be observed and explained; and at the same time, a reason should be given for what seems altogether inconceivable, how this new relation can be a deduction from others, which are entirely different from it.[1]

To argue in this way from "is" to "ought" is to be guilty of what G.E. Moore called the "naturalistic fallacy" which no philosopher or scientist wishes to be accused of. My aim is to show that Hume's argument is invalid. The reason is that though it may well be true that an "ought" statement cannot be deduced from an "is" statement, no one is in fact suggesting that it can.

In its widest sense, Hume's argument does little more than state the perceived division between knowledge and values that is still taken to be fundamental to modern science—though Popper, Michael Polanyi and many other modern epistemologists have shown that it is illusory and that there is no such thing as value-free knowledge. This finding is not altogether surprising since objective information (and knowledge is clearly some type of information) plays no role in the strategy of the natural world (see chapter 13).

Objective knowledge may be impossible but, as Roszak notes, the psychology of objectivism continues to wield its influence. It leads, above all, to a separation of man from the real world of nature of which he is an integral part and outside of which he is meaningless.

If man cannot entertain objective knowledge, he clearly cannot be motivated by it. It is thus not reason that motivates him, but his largely unconscious values—the non-plastic general instructions that reflect the long-term experience of our society and of our species, and which control those differentiated instructions that reflect our own short-term experience.

Man, as Anatol Rapoport puts it, is a rationalizing rather than a rational animal. He has always cherished values and then sought some authority to rationalize and hence, in his eyes, to legitimize them: so much so that, as Donald Worster puts it, "*ought* has been shaping *is*, not vice versa."²

Such an authority is science, which, in the modern world, is constantly appealed to in order to legitimize a subjective value. But such an appeal, as Whitehead puts it, follows rather than precedes the conviction of rightness, which is clearly derived from our emotions and our intuitions. In reality, an "is" proposition is little more than the explicit and seemingly objective and value-free tip of a vast implicit, quite clearly subjective and value-laden cognitive iceberg. It is this that Polanyi calls a "cognitive framework" and that Kuhn refers to (in the very much more restricted field of science) as a "paradigm."

It is only in terms of this implicit, subjective and value-laden world-view that an explicit, apparently objective and value-free proposition has any meaning. What is more, it is only in terms of its ability to fit into a world-view that the validity of a proposition can be established. This is undoubtedly Waddington's conclusion. "The validity of Hume's argument," he writes,

> depends entirely on what is the content of the notion conveyed by "is." If one conceives of existence as, to put it crudely, Newtonian space-time with some billiard balls flying round in it, then clearly neither "ought" nor "owed" nor many other concepts can be logically deduced. But if, to take another extreme, existence is considered as the manifestation of the nature of a beneficent deity, quite other consequences would follow. In fact, any invocation of "is" other than as a logical copula, *involves an epistemology, and it is impossible to reduce the relation of "is" to "ought" to a matter of pure logic.*³

Now, quite clearly, still "other consequences would follow" when we see Hume's statement in the light of the world-view of modernism that is clearly reflected in just about all the knowledge imparted today in our universities.

For modern man, the argument from "is" to "ought" when used to justify the naturalistic ethic is judged to be false, *not because it is deemed unverifiable, unfalsifiable, illogical or meaningless, but because it is incompatible with his world-view.* In terms of that world-view, an earthly paradise can be achieved with the help of science, technology and industry, by systematically replacing the natural world —that which has developed as a result of three thousand million years of evolution—with a totally different organization, the artificial world of human artefacts. This process is known as economic development and is equated with progress. This world-view reflects an ethic that is in total opposition to the naturalistic ethic—one that we could call the *artificialistic ethic.* This ethic and the world-view that it underlies serve above all to rationalize and hence legitimize the enterprise of economic development to which our society is geared.

It seems clear that the artificialistic ethic is implicit to mainstream science today. Thus Wilson warns against

> the trap of the naturalistic fallacy of ethics which uncritically concludes that "what is," "should be." The "what is" in human nature is the legacy of a long heritage as hunter-gatherers. Even when we can identify genetically determined behavior it cannot be used to justify a continuing practice in present and future societies. As we live in a radically new and changing environment of our own making, such a practice would invite disaster. For example, the tendency under certain conditions to indulge in warfare against competing groups may well be in our genes, having been advantageous to our Neolithic ancestors, but it would be global suicide now.[4]

Implicit in Wilson's warning is the admonition that we "ought" to adapt to the brave new world that science, technology and industry are conspiring to create for us—*even if this means behaving in a way that is contrary to our nature as determined by our genes.* This may or may not be possible. However, neither Wilson nor any other writers who preach this "anti-nature ethic" bother to determine whether it is.

Boyden has convincingly argued that it is not. As we have seen, he regards the diseases of civilization, whose incidence increases with per capita GNP (a measure of the extent to which our lifestyle and environment have diverged from those to which we have been adapted by our evolution), as the symptoms of "phylogenetic (or evolutionary) maladjustment." In his view, attempts by our modern society to combat such maladjustments by largely technological means do not constitute adaptations in the true sense of the term, but rather "pseudo-adaptations" (or heterotelic adaptations), whose role it is to mask the symptoms of these maladjustments at the cost of perpetuating them.

The strongest objection to Wilson's argument is that he is, in effect, arguing from "is not" to "ought." But why, we might ask, should this be more legitimate than to argue from "is" to "ought"? Is the "ought" logically contained in the "is not" in a way that it is not contained in the "is"? Clearly not. Indeed, if a legitimate argument must be one that observes the laws of deductive logic, then Hume, Moore and Wilson are not arguing legitimately. The artificialistic fallacy violates the laws of deductive logic, just as the naturalistic fallacy does, but its principal failing is quite different. To argue from "is not" to "ought" is to argue for the morality of economic development or progress, a process that can only occur by disrupting the critical order of the ecosphere; whereas to argue from "is" to "ought" is to argue for the preservation of the critical order of the ecosphere and hence for maximizing the welfare of humans and other forms of life—*the only true moral enterprise* (see chapter 17).

Appendix Four

The need for a feedback mechanism
linking behavior to evolution

Mainstream science sees evolutionary change as exclusively the result of changes affecting the genes of individual living things. No other processes—neither morphogenesis nor the development of a child into an adult, nor our physiological, nor our behavioral experience—are regarded as affecting the genetic material in any way. These processes are seen as external to evolution and hence unable to play an evolutionary role.

Darwin never said this. For him, natural selection from random mutations (or random variations as he referred to them) was not the only mechanism of evolution—only the principal one. Indeed, towards the end of his life, he actually accepted Lamarck's ideas on the inheritance of acquired characteristics in order to dispose of Fleeming Jenkin's criticism. It was not Darwin but Weismann who formulated the preposterous dogma that natural selection is the only mechanism of evolution, thereby denying that behavior could affect evolution through the inheritance of "acquired characteristics." This thesis, another of science's gratuitous dogmas, is based on no serious theoretical or ecological considerations. Weismann's main argument for it is that he could not conceive of a mechanism whereby acquired characteristics could be translated into the language of the gene, and it was for this reason alone that he insisted—as P. Wintrebert points out—that all biologists *had* to agree that it did not exist.

It can be argued that Weismann proved his point experimentally—but his experiments were little more than a farce. He cut off the tails of rats, let them breed, repeated the experience on their progeny and went on doing this on twenty-two generations of these animals. The fact that a tailless breed of rats did not arise he held to be proof that acquired characteristics were not transmitted. However, as Wintrebert notes, Lamarck never suggested that living things passed on their *mutilations* to their progeny but only the characteristics that they developed as a result of their *own efforts*. Indeed, the rats, as Arthur Koestler put it, were no more likely to transmit

463

their mutilated tails than a mutilated man is likely to transmit his wooden leg.[1]

Such experiments are, in any case, deeply flawed for another reason. Though the genetic material is indeed plastic—contrary to what we are told—it is only slightly so. As J.B.S. Haldane noted, it is always possible that such experiments will fail, because the effects of acquired characters may not become apparent at a rate that makes them observable, though they may be rapid enough to be significant in geological time.[2]

There are countless reasons why the genetic material in the genome cannot be isolated from the genes of the soma. To begin with, no life process can maintain its homeostasis without acquiring information concerning its relationship with its environment in order to monitor its actions and correct any divergences from the appropriate course on which it is set. The only possible sources of such information are morphogenesis and behavior (ontogeny). Secondly, genetic material is not external to a living system but part of it. The genes do not dictate epigenesis, which, as Commoner has shown so convincingly, can only be understood in terms of the interaction between the genetic material and the cytoplasm which forms its environment. Nor, for similar reasons, do the genes dictate evolution.

In addition, as Grassé points out, if we accept the Weismann-Crick thesis, how do we explain the creation of new genes?[3] The first living thing itself would have been endowed with all the genes which have made possible the evolution of plants and animals in their infinite variety. Since no information can have come from the outside, DNA must have been the unique source of information. This means, surely, attributing miraculous properties to this chemical substance, which is simply not a serious thing to do.

It has always been quite clear to serious students of evolution that there had to be a feedback between behavior, ontogeny and evolution. In 1896 the American psychologist J.M. Baldwin published the famous article in which he described his principle of "functional and organic selection."[4] In adapting to its environment, Baldwin maintained, an organism can affect its congenital characteristics by "accommodating" them to new environmental conditions. These accommodations, he argued, can eventually become fixed genetically. Forty years later, Richard Goldschmidt suggested that information contained in the

464

phenotype which is acquired by a living thing during the course of its life, can, in certain conditions, be "copied" by the genome and then become fixed genetically as a "phenocopy."[5]

Waddington proposed an analogous mechanism that he referred to as "genetic assimilation."[6] He saw organisms as being able to respond to stress by changing their behavior and sometimes by bringing about corresponding structural changes. To do this, they must be able to defy the pressure on them to resist divergences from their pre-ordained course or constellation of chreods. This can only mean affecting, in some way, the genes that control the stability or flexibility of these chreods and eventually—perhaps after a few generations—modifying them. Once this has happened, the altered phenotype can occur with or without the environmental stress, and it would then be said to have been "assimilated by the genotype."

At the same time as Waddington developed the theory of genetic assimilation, the Russian theoretical biologist I. L. Schmalhausen worked out a slightly different way in which negative feedback could occur.[7] He referred to it as "stabilizing selection." Later, Piaget revived Goldschmidt's phenocopy, which he modified considerably. The resulting mechanism is the most interesting, in that it diverges the most from the neo-Darwinian position, as the acquired changes are not seen to be the product of natural selection.[8]

In any case, recent experiments conducted by Cairns and others now seem to have established empirically that information flows in both directions. This means that mainstream scientists no longer have any argument for opposing the essential and inescapable principle that morphology, physiology and behavior are integral parts of the evolutionary process, providing it with highly effective feedback mechanisms to ensure that it remain adaptive to changing environmental conditions, without sacrificing its stability or continuity.

Glossary

ANTHROPOGENIC CLIMAX. A term coined by the British ecologist Sir Arthur Tansley. An anthropogenic climax, as opposed to an ecological climax, was for him and his followers the product of economic development or progress rather than of ecological succession (see chapter 50). Unfortunately, economic development or progress reverses the evolutionary process and hence ecological succession, giving rise to an ecological disclimax (qv).

ARISTOSCIENCE. The term is used more particularly by John Passmore, the Australian philosopher of science, to refer to physics, the aristocrat of the sciences. Its great success is attributed to its methodology rather than to the relative simplicity of its subject matter. Other disciplines whose subject matter is often very much more complex have systematically sought to ape the methodology of physics, with absurd results.

ASSOCIATION. Or ecological association—see "community," or "ecological community."

BEHAVIOR. This term is used in two ways, firstly to refer to day-to-day behavior, as it is usually used in the English language, hence to distinguish it from other life processes such as ontogeny (qv), morphogenesis (qv) and evolution (qv). Alternatively, it is used synonymously with the more general term "life process" (qv). The context should make clear in which of these two senses the term is used.

BEHAVIORISM. A theory developed by Watson and Skinner, and other psychologists, which seeks to explain behavior in purely mechanistic and reductionist terms. Behavior rather than being dynamic and creative is seen instead in terms of robot-like responses or "reflexes" that are switched on by specific stimuli and "reinforced," if successful, by pleasurable rewards. This is the theory of behavior that best fits in with the paradigm of science. It has been at least partly discredited by the mentalist (qv) or cognitive school of psychology.

BIOSPHERE. Used by James Lovelock and others to apply to the world of living things, seen as an organization, the overall association (qv) or community. Lamarck, Vernadsky, Grinwald, Polunin and others apply the term to the world of living things together with its geological substrate and atmospheric environment, which Lovelock refers to as Gaia (qv), and which is also referred to in this book as the ecosphere (qv). After much hesitation, I have decided, for the sake of convenience, to adopt Lovelock's use of the term (see chapter 19).

CHREOD. From the Greek *chre*, it is necessary, and *odos*, a root or path. The term was coined by the great theoretical biologist and embryologist C.H. Waddington. It refers to the path along which a developing organ or tissue must travel in order to achieve its appropriate end-state. The total constellation of chreods along which an organism develops, Waddington refers to as its "epigenetic landscape" (see chapter 25). I extend the use of the term chreod to apply to all homeotelically (qv) developing natural systems, i.e. to all normal and viable life processes including human behavior and the culturally determined behavior of human vernacular social groups, whose chreods or epigenetic landscape I identify with the Way (see chapter 61).

CHTHONIC RELIGION. The religion of the Earth. Chthonos was the Greek god of the Earth. Chthonic religion could also be referred to as Gaian religion. It is still the popular and indeed the effective religion of tribal and peasant societies that have largely remained outside the orbit of the modern world. That this is so in Orissa, is testified by Frederique Appfel Marglin, and in many other parts of India by Vandana Shiva. I identify Chthonic religion with the world-view of ecology.

COMMUNITY or "ecological community." That organization of living things that inhabit the same area.

COMPLEXITY. The term is used by mainstream ecologists as a measure of the number of an ecosystem's constituent parts, without any regard for the way they are organized or whether they contribute to its stability and integrity, i.e. whether they should be there in the first place. Complexity also tends to be used practically synonymously with diversity—though in the latter case it is the number of different species that is measured rather than its unspecified parts. I reject the present use of complexity. Instead I take complexity to be a measure of its organized and hence differentiated parts which can act in conjunction with each other to maximize its stable relationship in predictable environmental conditions. To make this clearer, a simple system like an ameba, with its one cell, fulfills all those functions which are required to maintain its stability with its environment, but it does so in a rudimentary manner, so much so that it can only survive because of its numbers. A complex multi-cellular organism fulfills very much the same functions, but it does so with far greater sophistication, and thereby succeeds in maintaining a far more stable relationship with its environment, the individual's chance of survival being correspondingly increased.

COSMOS. From the Greek, originally meaning "order" as opposed to "chaos." I use the term loosely as it was used by vernacular (qv) man to refer to his subjective view of the ecosphere (qv) or of the universe.

CYBERNISM. An organization of information that is an essential part of a natural system's control mechanism. A cybernism provides a natural system with a set of instructions for the achievement of its goal and an associated model of its relationship with its environment or more precisely of the path it must take to achieve its goal and of the challenges that might prevent it from doing so. I take all information in the living world to be organized to constitute cybernisms. I consider a genome (qv), a gene pool, a fertilized egg, the nucleus of the cell, the very diffuse information organized in an ecosystem, in Gaia herself and in the mind of living things, including man, as falling into this category. Since there is no word that corresponds to it in the English language, I have been forced to coin one.

CYBERNISMIC COMPLEXITY. The more complex (see "complexity") a cybernism, the more complex the adaptive strategies that it can help mediate, and the greater the associated system's stability in predictable environmental conditions.

CYBERNISMIC DIVERSITY. The more diverse (see "diversity") a cybernism, the greater the range of different adaptive strategies that can be mediated and the greater the stability of the associated systems in the face of unlikely environmental conditions.

DARWINISM. Darwin put forward two associated theses. The first, originally referred to as "transformism," tells us that living things have slowly evolved from very simple organisms to more and more complex ones. This is certainly true of many living things. Darwin also proposed a mechanism for explaining how evolution has occurred. It is this mechanism that is contested in this book. Darwin was impressed by the great store of variations displayed by living things. He took these to be of a purely random nature. He was also struck by the competitiveness of living things, as a result of which he saw them as subjected to "natural selection." Those which displayed those variations which enabled them to be the victors in the struggle for survival, he described as "fit." They would procreate and transmit their characteristics to their progeny so that surviving living things became increasingly "fit." This means that evolution, rather than occurring as a result of the efforts of living things—as suggested by Lamarck—was seen instead as stage-managed by the environment, and living things, rather than being seen as dynamic and creative, were instead seen as passive and robot-like.

DIVERSITY. Used by mainstream ecologists to denote the number of different species that make up a complex ecosystem. It has two components: "species richness" and "species evenness" (see chapter 53). Eugene Odum sees it as a measure of an ecosystem's redundancy. I accept this, but it is not enough. Redundant parts could all be the same or their differences could be of a random nature. Diversity is *organized redundancy*. A single, non-diversified system can adapt to the most probable and the most threatening challenges. As it increases its diversity so is its capacity for dealing with ever less probable and ever less threatening challenges correspondingly increased.

The more disorderly and hence unpredictable a system's environment the greater the diversity required.

ECOLOGICAL ASSOCIATION. A group of interacting plants, animals and micro-organisms, inhabiting a given area and constituting a natural system (qv), also known as an ecological community (see "ecosystem").

ECOLOGICAL CLIMAX. An ecosystem that has reached maturity, or adulthood. The end state of the process of ecological succession (see chapter 50) and the most stable state in the existing ecospheric conditions. Once such a state has been achieved no further development is required and energy and resources are only used for maintenance and repair.

ECOSPHERE. The biosphere (qv) together with its geological substrate (the lithosphere) and its atmospheric environment. The term was first coined by the contemporary US ecologist Lamont Cole. I use the term ecosphere to correspond exactly to James Lovelock's Gaia. The relationship between the biosphere and the ecosphere is thus the same as that between an association (qv) or community and an ecosystem (qv).

ECOSYSTEM. An association (qv) or community together with its geological substrate and atmospheric environment. The term was originally coined by Sir Arthur Tansley, and has largely replaced "association" or "community" in the ecological literature.

EPISTEMOLOGY. From the Greek *episteme*, knowledge, and *logos*, discourse. The theory of knowledge, which is what philosophy, once divorced from metaphysics, is largely about. Because today, only scientific knowledge is regarded as valid, epistemology is unacceptably difficult to distinguish from the philosophy of science.

EQUIFINALITY. The ability of life processes to achieve the same end-state even though they may set off from very different starting points.

EUKARYOTE. A cell with a nucleus. The cells of all plants and animals fall within this category.

FIELD. The concept of the "field" was developed as the world came to be seen more as a continuum than as a collection of small bullet-like particles. The term was first used in physics, but was applied to biology by Weiss and Gurwitsch in the 1920s. Living things are seen by those who use this concept as living within their "field," and as making little sense outside of it. I identify a system's field with its ordered environment. I also take a system's field or ordered environment to correspond to the larger system, more accurately to the hierarchy of larger systems of which it is but a differentiated part, and outside of which it has no meaning (see chapter 45).

GAIA. The ecosphere (qv), i.e. the biosphere (qv), together with its geological substrate and atmospheric environment. The term was first used in this sense by James Lovelock at the suggestion of the novelist William Golding. Gaia was the Greek goddess of the Earth.

GENOME. That organization of genetic information that is in turn organized into its chromosomes and their genes (see "genotype").

GENOTYPE. The genetic basis of an organism. The genetic information as organized into a fertilized egg. The phenotype or mature organism as it was at the beginning of its ontogenetic development. The term is not altogether satisfactory: it suggests that the adult form can be seen entirely as a product of the information contained in the fertilized egg, which is not the case since information is derived from its ordered environment throughout the developmental process. However, I shall continue to use the term for the sake of convenience.

HETERARCHY. From the Greek *hetero*, different, and *archos*, to rule. I use the term to mean the control of the parts of a system by an agent that is external to it, just as people are controlled by corporations and state institutions, as opposed to the families, communities and societies of which they are the homeotelic constituents (see "homearchy").

HETEROTELIC BEHAVIOR. From the Greek *hetero*, different, and *telos*, goal. A term coined by the author—abnormal or misdirected behavior which, though it may, partly at least, satisfy the requirements of the individual, does not satisfy those of the larger systems of which it is part, i.e. of the Gaian hierarchy as a whole, and which thereby reduces its stability and integrity (see chapter 41).

HIERARCHICAL MUTUALISM. There is a mutualistic relationship between a natural system and the larger natural system of which it is a differentiated part (as opposed to a random part) and hence of the Gaian hierarchy as a whole.

This must be so since the larger systems (as opposed to external controlling agents such as the State) can only maintain their homeostasis if the smaller systems that compose them are also stable, while the latter in turn can only maintain their homeostasis if the larger systems of which they are a part provide them with their appropriate fields, i.e. with the environments to which they are capable of behaving adaptively (homeotelically).

Hierarchical mutualism is but another way of stating the principle that both homeotely and homearchy are prerequisites of homeostasis.

HOMEARCHY. From the Greek *homeo*, same, and *archos*, to rule. I use the term to mean the control of differentiated natural systems by the hierarchy of larger systems of which they are part. For instance, the control of people (much of which is likely to be internalized—see chapter 50) by their families, communities, and ecosystems (see Heterarchy).

HOMEORHESIS. A term coined by Waddington, from the Greek *homeo*, same and *rhesis*, flow. Homeostasis applied to a developing system—one seeking to maintain itself along its chreods (qv) or epigenetic landscape or, in the case of a human or human social system, along the Way, and to correct diversions from it caused by internal or external challenges (see chapters 25 and 64).

HOMEOSTASIS. From the Greek *homeo*, same and *stasis*, stoppage. A term coined by the physiologist Walter Cannon in the 1920s. A homeostatic machine is a machine with feedback that is able to return to a ground position after a disturbance. In the living world, behavior is largely irreversible and living things after a disturbance do not return to a ground position but to a slightly new position that is as close as possible to the previous one. Thus it is best to see a natural system as displaying homeostasis when it is able to reduce discontinuities to a minimum in the face of internal or external challenges. It is essential to the thesis of this book that a system can only maintain its homeostasis by maintaining that of the hierarchy or larger systems of which it is part. In other words, homeotely is a precondition of homeostasis.

HOMEOTELIC BEHAVIOR. From the Greek *homeo*, same and *telos*, goal. A term coined by the author—normal behavior that serves to maintain the critical order of the whole, more precisely of the Gaian hierarchy. Such behavior can be co-operative in that it serves at the same time the immediate interests of the constituent parts. It can also be competitive, serving the interests of the whole, but to the detriment of the less well differentiated and less adaptive parts that may fall victim to such competition.

HYLOZOISM. From the Greek *hyle*, matter, and *zoe*, life. The theory that a vital force flows through the living world, settling and accumulating in different places and in different beings and spirits. It is to the extent that the latter are imbued with vital force that they are sacred. This was an essential part of the belief systems of vernacular people and in particular chthonic people. It still is among many vernacular societies that have remained outside the orbit of the modern world. I try to demonstrate in this book that the organization of vital force in a society and in an ecosystem and within the Gaian hierarchy itself is seen in the vernacular society as reflecting their critical order (see chapter 62).

INDUCTION. Knowledge acquired by accumulating observations of specific phenomena and in particular cause and effect relationships—without necessarily seeking to explain them in terms of any theoretical considerations. Empiricists consider this to be the only way of acquiring knowledge about the world (synthetic knowledge) as opposed to *a priori* knowledge that is true by definition (analytic knowledge).

INEFFABLE KNOWLEDGE. Knowledge that cannot be articulated. A term used in particular by Michael Polanyi.

LIFE PROCESS. I use this term in a general way to include evolution and its constituent processes such as morphogenesis, ontogeny (qv) and behavior proper (qv). Evolution is regarded by neo-Darwinists as distinct from these processes, a thesis which I regard as untenable (see chapter 21).

MECHANISM. Or mechanomorphism. The thesis that living things are like machines, or indeed are machines, was first put forward explicitly by Galileo, Newton and later by Descartes. The thesis remains fundamental to the paradigm of science. The alternatives are seen to be vitalism (qv) and organicism (qv).

MENTALISM. A theory developed in the 1970s by Sperry and others, as a reaction to the behaviorism (qv) of Skinner and Watson. Its thesis was that you cannot explain behavior without reference to the mind and understanding.

MUTUALISM. The term is normally used in the ecological literature for co-operation.

NATURAL SYSTEM. Must first of all be distinguished from the sort of system that engineers deal with, which is only superficially similar. A natural system I take to be a unit of behavior in the wider sense of the term. It includes cells, organisms, non-human animal societies and human societies, (so long as the latter are of a vernacular nature—see chapter 60), and also ecosystems and indeed Gaia herself. The generalities of the structure and function of all these natural systems are taken to be the same, which justifies the use of the term. Of all the different definitions of the natural system proposed so far (see chapter 38) I shall adopt that of Paul Weiss, for whom a system is "a complex unit in space and in time, whose sub units co-operate to preserve its integrity and its structure and its behavior and tend to restore them after a non-destructive disturbance." The term "system" sounds a little mechanistic and alternative terms have been proposed. Koestler proposes the term holon, which I very much prefer. However, I feel that the term "system" is too well-established to be abandoned. I may be wrong.

NEO-DARWINISM. A new version of Darwinism developed in particular by August Weissmann in Germany and William Bateson in Britain, towards the end of the 19th century. It differed from Darwinism in that it took on board Mendel's genetic theories, with which Darwin was not acquainted. This enabled Darwin's followers to answer a particularly embarrassing objection to his theory—that put forward by Fleeming Jenkins—which had reduced the credibility of Darwinism. Neo-Darwinism was in many respects a hardening of Darwinism. For instance, whereas Darwin saw selection from random variations as one of the mechanisms of evolution, they insisted it was the only one. Neo-Darwinism slowly went out of favor in the 1920s and 1930s, until it was again revived in a slightly different form (see the synthetic theory of evolution).

ONTOGENY. From the Greek *ontos*, a being and *genos*, to give birth to. The development of a fertilized egg into an adult. I shall take it to include morphogenesis, the individual's upbringing and adult life, as well as his behavior (qv) during the course of his life. Ontogeny is often contrasted with phylogeny (qv). I shall take ontogeny to be an essential part of phylogeny (see chapter 21).

ORGANICISM. The thesis that living things are above all living organizations or natural systems which, by their very nature, must behave differently from inanimate things or machines. The great theoretical biologists of the 1940s and 1950s, such as Needham, Waddington, von Bertalanffy, Weiss, etc. adhered to the organicist thesis. It is an alternative to both mechanism (qv) and vitalism (qv).

PARADIGM. The term was brought into fairly general use among philosophers of science by Thomas Kuhn, who has since then given it up in favor of the term "theory." In spite of that, it is still used by many authors. I use the term to refer to a theory or model developed by like-minded scholars to explain a particular set of phenomena within their field of study. Thus one can talk about the paradigm of neo-Darwinism, the paradigm of science and the paradigm of economics. I take a paradigm as faithfully reflecting the world-view with which specialists, who entertain it as members of their particular cultural group, have been imbued.

PARADIGM SHIFT. An expression also coined by Thomas Kuhn. Scientists do not abandon a paradigm as a result of being confronted with objective evidence that it is wrong and that a rival paradigm is right, but because, for reasons that are largely unconscious and ineffable (qv), they have undergone what is in effect a conversion to a new paradigm.

PHYLOGENY. From the Greek *phylon*, a tribe and *genesis*, origin. The term "phylon," or rather "phylum," has been taken over by zoologists to apply to a species, rather than to a tribe, so phylogeny now means the evolution of species. I argue in this book that evolution can only be understood if one takes Gaia herself rather than an individual species, let alone individual organisms, as the unit of evolution. For this reason, I refer to evolution as the Gaian Process.

PROKARYOTE. A cell without a nucleus. Only microbes have prokaryote cells.

SOCIOBIOLOGY. This is seen as a new field of study, though it is in reality a school of thought or even more so, a movement among theoretical biologists headed by Edward O. Wilson. He and his disciples see society as having a biological basis, which is difficult to deny. The trouble is that it is difficult to accept their view of biology, still less their view of society, which are both desperately mechanistic and reductionist and that faithfully reflect the paradigm of science in its most extreme form.

STABILITY. This must not be mistaken for equilibrium which is *static*. Stability in the natural world is *dynamic*. A stable system is one whose behavior is marked by the smallest possible discontinuities. Such a system will, by the same token, seek to preserve the basic features of its critical order or "integrity," or its wholeness. Many different types of stability have been proposed by ecologists. I accept Eugene Odum's distinction between "resistance" stability and "resilience" stability (see chapter 22).

SYMBIOSIS. Co-operation between organisms of different species.

SYNTHETIC THEORY OF EVOLUTION. Biologists tended to lose interest in neo-Darwinism in the 1920s and 1930s. It was revived by Julian Huxley, Dobzhansky, Simpson, Mayr and others in the early 1940s. This still newer version of Darwinism took into account population genetics, which had been developed in the meanwhile, and also sought to express the theory in more quantitative terms, making it correspondingly more respectable in scientific circles. This meant defining the "fit"—until then a vague term—as those who best succeeded in proliferating their genes.

TECHNOSPHERE. The world of human artefacts, or the surrogate world, as contrasted with the biosphere, the world of living things or the natural world. The distinction between the two, as far as I know, was first made by Max Nicholson in his book *The Environmental Revolution*.

VERNACULAR. From the Latin *vernaculus*, a household slave, but also from the Latin *vernare*, to sprout, hence vernal, appearing in Spring. More appropriately, something that springs out of a local culture. The term is usually applied to a social group's local dialect or architecture. Ivan Illich has extended the use of the term to refer to all features of a society's culture that have not been imposed on it by the State or some other external agent. I apply the term vernacular to a society and to the various features of such a society that are self-organizing and self-governing, rather than being organized externally by the State and its institutions, or by commercial corporations.

VITALISM. The theory that life processes cannot be explained without reference to some supernatural principle, such as the "entelechia" of Aristotle, the "entelechy" of Driesch, or the "élan vital" of Bergson. The alternatives to vitalism are seen to be mechanism (qv) or mechanomorphism and organicism (qv).

Bibliography

Abian, Alexander, 1991, "Hate Winter? Here's one man's solution: Blow up the moon," *Wall Street Journal, Europe,* April 22nd.

Ackoff, Russell L., 1963, "General systems theory and systems research: contrasting conceptions of systems science," *General Systems Yearbook* Vol. VIII.

Adams, C.C., 1917, "The new natural history ecology," *American Museum Journal,* 27th April.

Akpala, Agwu, 1973, "Problems in initiating industrial labor in a pre-industrial community," *Cahiers d'Etudes Africaines,* Spring.

Allee, W.C., Emerson, W.C.E.A., Park, O., Park, T., Schmidt, K.P., 1949 *Principles of Animal Ecology,* Philadelphia, W.B. Saunders.

Anaximander, fragment, quoted by Cornford, F.M. (qv).

Apter, Michael, 1966, *Cybernetics and Development,* Pergamon Press, Oxford.

Armelagos, George, and McArdle, Alan, 1976, "The Role of culture in the control of infectious diseases," *The Ecologist,* Vol. 6, No. 5, June.

Armstrong, W.E., 1925, "Rossel Island money. A unique monetary system," *The Economic Journal,* 34.

Asch, S.E., 1955, "Opinions and social pressure," *Scientific American,* November.

Ashmore, Jerome, 1966, "Technology and the humanities," *Main Currents in Modern Thought,* Vol. 22.

Atlan, Henri, 1979, *Entre le Cristal et la Fumée,* Editions du Seuil, Paris.

Augros, Robert and Stanciu George, 1987, *The New Biology: Discovering the Wisdom in Nature,* New Science Library, Boston, Mass.

Ayala, F.J. and Dobzhansky, Theodosius, eds., 1971, *Studies in the Philosophy of Biology,* University of California Press, Los Angeles.

Bacon, Francis, *Novum Organum,* 1878, Ed. Thomas Fowler, Clarendon Press, Oxford.

Bajaj Jatinder, 1988, "Francis Bacon, the first philosopher of modern science: a non-western view" in Nandy ed., *Science, Hegemony and Violence.*

Bakeless, John, 1977, "Our land as it was," *The Ecologist,* Vol. 7, No. 2.

Baldwin, J.M., 1896, "A New factor in evolution," *American Naturalist.*

Baltimore, David, 1979, "Limiting science: A biologist's perspective," in Holton and Morison, eds., *Limits of Scientific Inquiry.*

Banfield, Edward C., 1958, *The Moral Basis of a Backward Society,* The Free Press, New York.

Barcroft, Joseph, 1938, *The Brain and its Environment,* Yale University Press, New Haven.

Barker, Jonathan ed., 1984, *The Politics of Agriculture in Tropical Africa,* Sage, London.

477

Barker, Margaret, 1988, *The Lost Prophet. The Book of Enoch and its influence on Christianity*, S.P.C.K., London.

Barry, D.G., 1965, "Art in Science."

Bartlett, Frederic C., 1977, *Remembering. A Study in Experimental and Social Psychology*, Cambridge University Press, Cambridge.

Bastien, Joseph E., 1981, "Metaphorical relations between sickness, society and land in Qollahuaya ritual," *American Anthropological Association Bulletin*, No. 12.

Bean, William B., 1980, quoted by Graham, "The Witch-hunt of Rachel Carson," *The Ecologist*, Vol. 10, No. 3.

Beer, Stafford, 1969, "Beyond the twilight arch," *General Systems Yearbook*, Vol. v.

Begon, Michael, Harper, John L., Townsend, Colin R., 1986, *Ecology*, Basil Blackwell, Oxford.

Berdyaev, Nicholai Aleksandrovich, 1936, *The Meaning of History*, trans. Geoffrey Bles, The Centenary Press, London.

Bergson, Henri, 1981, (original edition 1911), *L'Evolution Créatice*, Presses Universitaires de France, Paris.

Berman, Morris, 1981, *The Re-Enchantment of the World*, Cornell University Press, Ithaca.

Bernal, J.D., 1969, *The World, The Flesh and The Devil*, Indiana University Press, Bloomington.

Bernard, Claude, *Leçons sur les Phenomenes de la Vie communs aux Animaux et aux Vegetaux*, ed. A. Dastre, Cours de Physiologie Generale du Museum d'Histoire Naturelle, Paris.

Bernardin de St. Pierre, Jacques Henri, S.H.B., 1976 (original edition 1784), *Studies of Nature*, translated by H. Hunter, London.

Bernier, Francois, 1699, *Voyages de Francois Bernier*, ["Contenant la Description des Etats du Grand Mogul, de l'Hindoustan, du Royaume de Kachemire"] Paul Marret, Amsterdam (ed. in English: Archibald Constable, London, 1941).

Bertalanffy, Ludwig von, see Von Bertalanffy.

Bethwell, A. and Ogot, A., eds. 1976, *Ecology and History in East Africa*, Nairobi.

Bettelheim, Bruno, 1979, *Surviving and Other Essays*, Knopf, New York.

Binet, A. and Simon, T.H., 1916, *The Development of Intelligence in Children*, Williams and Williams, London.

Blake, Peter, 1975, "Can technology solve the housing crisis?," *The Atlantic Monthly*, October.

Bloomfield, Maurice, 1908, *The Religion of the Veda, The Ancient Religion of India from Rig-Veda to Upanishads*.

Bodenheimer, F.S., 1957, "The Concept of Biotic Organization, in Synecology," in Bodenheimer, F.S., ed., *Studies in Biology and its History*, Biological Studies Publishers, Jerusalem.

Bohannan, Paul, 1959, "The impact of money on an African economy," *Journal of Economic History* Vol. xix, No. 4.

Bohannan, Paul, ed. 1967, *Law and Warfare*, Natural History Press, New York.

Bohannan, Paul and Laura, 1968, *Tiv Economy*, Longmans, London.

Bolen, Jean Shinoda, 1979, *The Tao of Psychology, Synchronicity and the Self*, Harper and Row, New York.

Boucher, D.H., James, S., and Keeler, K.H., 1982, "The ecology of mutualism," *Annual Review of Ecology and Systematics*.

Boucher, D.H., "The Idea of Mutualism" in D.H. Boucher, ed., 1985, *The Biology of Mutualism*, Croom Helm, London.

Boucher, D.H., and Vandermeer, J.H., 1978, "Varieties of mutualistic interactions in population models," *Journal of Theoretical Biology*, 74.

Boucher, D.H. and Risch, S., 1976, "What ecologists look for," *Bulletin of The Ecological Society of America*, 57.

Bowles, B.D., 1976, "Underdevelopment in agriculture in colonial Kenya. Some ecological and dietary aspects" in Bethwell and Ogot eds., *Ecology and History in East Africa*.

Boyden, Stephen, 1973, "Evolution and health," *The Ecologist*, Vol. 3, No. 8.

Boyle, Robert, Stewart, M.A., ed., 1979, *Selected Philosophical Papers of Robert Boyle*, Manchester University Press, Manchester.

Braham, Mark, 1973, "A General theory of organization," *General Systems Yearbook*, Vol. XVIII.

Bridges, Bryn, 1971, "Environmental genetic hazards. The impossible problem?" *The Ecologist*, Vol.1, No. 12, June.

Brillouin, L., 1968, "Information, communication and meaning," in Buckley and Rapoport eds., *Modern Systems Research for the Behavioral Scientist*, Aldine, Chicago.

Brillouin, L., 1968, "Life, thermodynamics and cybernetics" in Buckley, ed., *Modern Systems Research for the Behavioral Scientist*, Aldine, Chicago.

Brindle, David, 1990, "Rate of divorce and births outside marriage increases," *The Guardian*, July 5th.

Broadhurst, Anne, and Ramsay, W.R., 1968, "The non-randomness of attempts at random responses: relationships with personality variables in psychiatric disorders," in *British Journal of Psychology*, Vol. 59, August.

Brown, Harold I., 1979, *Perception, Theory and Commitment*, University of Chicago Press, Chicago.

Buckley, Walter and Rapoport, Anatol, 1968, *Modern Systems Research for the Behavioral Scientist*, Aldine, Chicago.

Bunyard, Peter and Goldsmith, Edward, eds. 1988, *Gaia—the Thesis, the Mechanism and the Implications*, Wadebridge Ecological Centre, Wadebridge.

Burckhardt, Titus, 1967, *Sacred Art in East and West*, Trans. Lord Northbourne, Perennial Books, London.

Caillois, Roger, 1988, *L'Homme et le Sacré*, Gallimard, Paris.

Calow, Peter, 1976, *Biological Machines: A Cybernetic Approach to Life*, Edward Arnold, London.

Cannon, Walter, 1932, *The Wisdom of the Body*, Norton, New York.

Carnap, Rudolph, 1936 and 1937, "Testability and meaning," *Philosophy of Science*, Issue 3 and Issue 4.

Carson, Rachel, 1962, *Silent Spring*, Houghton Mifflin, Boston.

Cattel, Cohen and Travers, eds. 1937, *Human Affairs: Essays on the Application of Science to the Study of Society*, Macmillan, London.

Cavalieri, Liebe F., 1981, *The Double-Edged Helix. Science in the Real World*, Columbia University Press, New York.

Césaire, Aimé, 1972, *Discourse on Colonialism*, Monthly Review Press, New York.

Chaitanya, Krishna, 1972, *The Physics and Chemistry of Freedom*, Somaiya Publications, Bombay.

Chaitanya, Krishna, 1975, *The Biology of Freedom*, Somaiya Publications, Bombay.

Chaitanya, Krishna, 1976, *The Psychology of Freedom*, Somaiya Publications, Bombay.

Chaitanya, Krishna, 1983, "A Profounder ecology: the Hindu view of man and nature," *The Ecologist*, Vol. 13, No. 4.

Chan, Wing-Tsit, ed. 1963, *A Source Book in Chinese Philosophy*.

Chantepie de la Saussaye, Pierre Daniel, 1904, *Manuel d'Histoire des Religions*, Paris.

Chargaff, Erwin, 1976, "Letter to Science" June 4th, in Culliton 1978, "Science's restive public" in Holton and Morrison eds. 1979, *Limits of Scientific Inquiry*.

Clastres, Pierre, 1976, *La Societé contre L'Etat*, Les Editions de Minuit, Paris.

Clements, Frederic, 1916, *Plant Succession*, Washington. D.C.

Clements, Frederic and Shelford, Victor, 1930, *Bio-Ecology*, Wiley, New York.

Cloward, Richard A., and Ohlin, Lloyd E., 1959, "Illegitimate means, anomie and deviant behavior," *American Sociological Review*, 24th April.

Cloward, Richard A., and Ohlin, Lloyd E., 1961, *Delinquency and Opportunity*, Free Press of Glencoe, New York.

Codrington, Robert Henry, 1891, *The Melanesians, Studies in their Anthropology and Folklore*, Clarendon, Oxford.

Cody, M.L. and Diamond, J.M., eds. 1975, *Ecology and the Evolution of Communities*, Belknap Press, Cambridge, Mass.

Cole, Lamont, 1958, The Ecosphere, *Scientific American*, 198, April.

Coleman, J.S., 1968, *The Adolescent Society*, The Free Press of Glencoe, New York.

Colinvaux, P.A., 1973, *Introduction to Ecology*, Wiley, New York.

Commoner, Barry, 1964, "DNA and the chemistry of inheritance,"
  American Scientist, Vol. 52.

Concern, 1981, *The Times*, September 6th.

Connell, J.H., 1980, "Diversity and the co-evolution of competition, or the
  ghost of competition past," *Oikos*, 35.

Coomaraswamy, Ananda, 1983, *Symbolism in Indian Architecture*, The
  Historical Research Documentation Centre, Jaipur.

Cornford, F.M., 1957, *From Religion to Philosophy*, Harper Brothers,
  New York.

Craik, J.W.,1966, *The Nature of Psychology*, ed. S.L. Sherwood,
  Cambridge University Press, paper no.24.

Craik, Kenneth, 1952, *The Nature of Explanation*, Cambridge University
  Press, Cambridge.

Crawford, C.C. and Leitzell, F.M., eds. 1932, *Learning a New Language*,
  University of Southern California Press, Los Angeles.

Crawford, O.G.S., 1951, *The Fung Kingdom of Sennar*, John Bellows,
  Gloucester.

Crick, Francis, 1966, *Of Molecules and Men*, University of Washington
  Press, Seattle.

Cuenot, Lucien, 1941, *Invention et Finalité en Biologie*, Flammarion, Paris.

Cuenot, Lucien, 1951, *L'Evolution Biologique*, Masson, Paris.

Culliton, Barbara J., 1978, "Science's restive public," in Holton and
  Morrison eds., 1979, *Limits to Scientific Inquiry*.

Cumont, Franz, 1956, *Oriental Religions in Roman Paganism*, Dover
  Publications, New York.

Curtis, J.T., 1959, *The Vegetation of Wisconsin*, University of Wisconsin
  Press, Madison.

Dalrymple, Theodore, 1991, "Nasty, British and Short," *Spectator*,
  September 21st, London.

Dalton, George, 1961, "Economic theory and primitive society," *American
  Anthropologist*, Vol. 63.

Dalton, George, 1965, "Primitive money," *American Anthropologist*,
  Vol. 67.

Dalton, George, ed. 1967, *Tribal and Peasant Economics*, University of
  Texas Press, Austin.

Dalton, George, ed. 1968, *Primitive, Archaic and Modern Economics:
  Essays of Karl Polanyi*, Anchor Books, New York.

Dalton, George, ed. 1971, *Economic Development and Social Change*, The
  Modernization of Village Communities, the Natural History Press,
  New York.

Daly, Herman E. and Cobb, John B., 1990, *For the Common Good:
  Redirecting the Economy Towards Community, the Environment and
  a Sustainable Future*, Beacon Press, Boston.

Damon, Albert, 1974, "Human ecology in the Solomon Islands,"
  Biomedical observations among tribal societies, Human Ecology, Vol.
  2, No. 3, July.

Dancoff, S.M. and Quastler, H., "The Information content and error rate of living things," in Quastler, ed. 1953, *Information theory in Biology*.

Darwin, Charles, p. 490 MS, Darwin Archives, Cambridge University Library in Vol. 30.1.

Darwin, Charles, 1952 (original edition 1839), *Diary of a Voyage on the Beagle*, J.M. Dent, Guildford.

Darwin, Charles, 1971 (original edition 1859), *On the Origin of Species*, J.M. Dent, Guildford.

Darwin, Charles, 1974 (original edition 1887), *Autobiographical Sketch*, as a section of Darwin, Francis, *The Life and Letters of Charles Darwin*, Oxford University Press, Oxford.

Darwin, Francis, ed. 1887, *The Life and Letters of Charles Darwin*, John Murray, London.

Darwin, F. and Seward A.C., eds. 1903, *More Letters of Charles Darwin*, London.

Dawkins, Richard, 1989, *The Selfish Gene*, Oxford University Press, Oxford.

Day, W.R., 1929, "Environment and disease. A discussion on the parasitism of armillaria mellea," *Forestry*, Vol. 3.

de Beer, Sir Gavin, 1958, *Embryos and Ancestors*, Clarendon Press, Oxford.

de Groot, Jan Jacob Maria, 1910, *The Religion of the Chinese*, Macmillan, New York.

de Haan, J.A. Bierens, 1966, *Animal Psychology*, Hutchinson's University Library, London.

Dermon, William, "U.S. Aid in the Sahel, development and poverty," in Barker ed. 1984, *The Politics of Agriculture in Tropical Africa*, Sage Publications, London.

Descartes, René, 1946 (original edition 1637), *Discourse on Method*, Everyman, London.

Diamond, Stanley, 1974, *In Search of the Primitive*, Transaction Books, New Brunswick.

Dickey, Lawrence, 1986, "Historicising the Adam Smith problem," *Journal of Modern History*, No. 58, September.

Dixon, M. and Webb, E.C., 1964, *Enzymes*, Longmans, London.

Dobzhansky, Theodosius, 1962, "Mankind evolving," *The Evolution of the Human Species*.

Dobzhansky, Theodosius, 1975, "Studies in the philosophy of biology" in van Dobben and Lowe McConnell, eds. *Unifying Concepts in Ecology*.

Douglas, Mary, 1966, *Purity and Danger*, Routledge and Kegan Paul, London.

Douglas, Mary, 1967, "Raffia cloth distribution in the Lele economy," in Dalton ed., *Tribal and Peasant Economics*.

Douglas, Mary, "Lele economy compared with the Bushong," in Dalton 1971, *Economic Development and Social Change*.

Driesch, Hans, 1908, *The Science and Philosophy of the Organism*, Black, London.

Driver, E., 1961, *Indians of North America*, University of Chicago Press, Chicago.

Dubois, Cora, 1945, "The Alorese," in Kardiner, *The Psychological Frontiers of Society*.

Dubos, René, 1967, *Man Adapting*, Yale University Press, New Haven.

Dubos, René, 1970, "Will man adapt to megalopolis?," *The Ecologist*, vol.1, No. 4, October.

Durkheim, Emile, 1964 (original edition 1915), *The Elementary Forms of the Religious Life*, George Allen & Unwin, London.

Durkheim, Emile, 1964 (original edition 1933), *The Division of Labour in Society*, trans. George Simpson, Macmillan, Free Press Paperback edition, London.

Durkheim, Emile, 1966 (original edition 1897), *Suicide: A Study in Sociology*, Routledge and Kegan Paul, London.

The Ecologist—1991 Special Issue: The UN Food and Agricultural Organization (FAO), 1991, "Promoting World Hunger," *The Ecologist*, March-April.

Eden, Murray, 1965, "Mathematical Challenges to the Neo-Darwinian Interpretation of Evolution," Wistar Institute Symposium Monograph, No. 5.

Egerton, Frank, 1973, "Changing concepts of the balance of nature," *Quarterly Review of Biology*, Vol. 48.

Eibl-Eibesfeldt, Ireneus, 1961, "The fighting behavior of animals," *Scientific American*, Dec.

Eiseman, Fred, 1989, *Bali: Sekala and Niskala*, Vol. 1, ed. David Pickell, Pickell-Periplus, Berkeley.

Eliade, Mircea, 1959, *The Sacred and the Profane*, Harcourt and Brace, New York.

Eliade, Mircea, 1971, (original edition 1949) *The Myth of the Eternal Return, or Cosmos and History,* Princeton University, Princeton.

Ellul, Jacques, 1977, *Le Système Technicien*, Calman Levy (French Edition).

Engels, Friedrich, 1858, *The Condition of the Working Class in England*, London.

Epstein, S.S., 1978, *The Politics of Cancer*, Sierra Club, San Francisco.

Evans-Pritchard, E.E., 1937, *Witchcraft, Oracles and Magic Among the Azande*, Oxford University Press, Oxford.

Evans-Pritchard, E.E. ed. 1970, Introduction to Hocart, *Kings and Councillors*, University of Chicago Press, Chicago.

Eyre, Edward John, 1945, *Journal of an Expedition of Discovery into Central Australia and Overland from Adelaide to King George's Sound in the years 1840-41*, 174.

Fantz, Robert L., 1961, "The Origin of form perception," *Scientific American*, May.

Farrington, Benjamin, 1973, *Francis Bacon, Philosopher of Industrial Science*, Macmillan, London.

Feng, Yu-Lan, 1984, *A Short History of Chinese Philosophy*, Macmillan, New York.

Fernea, Robert A., 1970, *Shayk and Effendi: Changing Patterns of Authority Among the El Shabana of Southern Iraq*, Harvard University Press, Cambridge, Mass.

Fischer, Claude, 1990, *L'Homnivore*, Odile Jacob, Paris.

Fisk, E.K., ed. 1978, *The Adaptation of Traditional Agriculture: Socio-economic Problems of Urbanisation*, Development Studies Centre Monograph, No. 11, Australian National University, Canberra.

Flew, Anthony, 1968, *Evolutionary Ethics*, Macmillan, London.

Food and Agricultural Organization of the United Nations (FAO), 1984, *Land, Food and People*, Development Series, No. 30, FAO, Rome.

Food and Agricultural Organization of the United Nations (FAO), 1987, *Agriculture; Towards 2000*, FAO Social and Economic Development Series, No. 27, FAO, Rome.

Forbes, S.A., 1880, "On some interactions of organisms," *Bulletin of the Illinois State Laboratory of Natural History*, I.

Forrester, Jay W., 1971, "Alternatives to catastrophe: Understanding the counterintuitive behavior of social systems," Part 1, *The Ecologist*, Vol. 1, No. 14, August.

Frankl, Viktor E., 1972, "Reductionism and nihilism," in Koestler and Smythies eds., *Beyond Reductionism*.

Frazer, Sir James George, 1935, *Creation and Evolution in Primitive Cosmogonies*, Macmillan & Co., London.

Fredericq, Leon, 1885, in Archeologie de Zoologie *Exp. et Gen.* iii, xxxv.

Freeman, Peter, 1971, Unpublished report for the World Bank, *Subsistence Agriculture, An exploration of environmental and development problems*, The Conservation Foundation, Washington, DC.

Freud, Sigmund, 1970, *Inhibitions, Symptoms and Anxiety*, Hogarth, London.

Fuller, Robert W. and Putnam, Peter, 1966, "On the origin of order in behavior," *General Systems Yearbook*, Vol. XI.

Fustel de Coulanges, Numa Denis, 1927, *La Cité Antique*, Hachette, Paris.

Gandhi, M.K., 1949, *An Autobiography*, trans. M. Desai, Phoenix Press, London.

Gaud, William S., Price, Peter W., and Slobodchikoff, C.N., 1984, *A New Ecology, Novel Approaches to Interactive Systems*, John Wiley, New York.

Geist, Valerius, 1974, "About natural man and environment design," *Proceedings of the Third International Conference on the Unity of the Sciences*, International Cultural Foundation, New York.

Georgescu-Roegen, Nicholas, 1971, *The Entropy Law and the Economic Process*, Harvard University Press, Cambridge, Mass.

Georgescu-Roegen, Nicholas, 1972, "Economics and Entropy," *The Economist*, Vol. 2, No. 7, July.

Georgescu-Roegen, Nicholas, "Afterword" in Rifkin and Howard, eds. 1980, *Entropy*.

Gerard, Ralph W., 1949, "Physiology and psychiatry," *American Journal of Psychiatry*, Vol. 106.

Gerard, Ralph W., "The biological basis of ethics," *Philosophy of Science*, 9.92.

Gerard, Ralph W., "Hierarchy, entitation and levels," in Lancelot Law Whyte et alia, ed. 1969, *Hierarchical Structures*.

Gesell, Arnold, 1936, "Studies in child development," in *Cell and Psyche*, New York.

Gleason, H.A., 1926, "The Individualistic concept of the plant association," *Bulletin of the Torrey Botanical Club*, 53.

Goldschmidt, Richard, 1935, "Gen und Aussenergenschaft induktive Abstammungs," *Vererbungslehre*, 69.

Goldschmidt, Richard, 1940, *The Material Basis of Evolution*, Yale University Press, New Haven.

Goldsmith, Edward, 1988, *The Great U-Turn*, Green Books, Hartland.

Graham, Frank Jr. 1980, "The Witch-hunt of Rachel Carson," *The Ecologist*, Vol. 10, No. 3, March.

Granit, Ragnar, 1974, "Adaptability of the nervous system and its relation to chance, purposiveness and causality," *Proceedings of the Third International Conference on the Unity of the Sciences*, Vol. 2, International Cultural Foundation, New York.

Granit, Ragnar, 1977, *The Purposive Brain*, MIT Press, Cambridge, Mass.

Grassé, Pierre-P., 1973, *L'Evolution du vivant*, Albin Michel, Paris.

Grene, Marjorie, "Hierarchy: one word, how many concepts?," in Whyte et alia eds., *Hierarchical Structures*.

Grey, Sir George, 1945, quoted by Eyre, Edward John, in *Journal of an Expedition of Discovery into Central Australia and Overland from Adelaide to King George's Sound in the years 1840-41*.

Grinewald, Jacques, 1988, "Sketch for a history of the idea of the biosphere," in Bunyard and Goldsmith eds., *Gaia—the Thesis, the Mechanisms and the Implications*.

Haeckel, Ernest, 1903, *Histoire de la Création des Etres Organisés D'Après les Lois Naturelles*, Paris, Librarie C. Reinwald.

Haldane, J.B.S., 1940, *Possible Worlds*, London.

Hall, A.D., and Fagen, R.E., 1956, *Definition of System*, General Systems Year Book, Vol. 1.

Hall, Ross Hume,1976, in "Beware of those fabricated foods," *Executive Health*, Vol. XII, No. 7, April.

Hamberger, V., 1935, "Regeneration," *Encyclopedia Britannica*, Vol. XIX, London.

Hammond, Peter Boyd, 1971, *An Introduction to Cultural and Social Anthropology*, Macmillan and Collier Macmillan, London.

Harding, Thomas G., 1960, "Adaptation and stability," in Sahlins and Elman eds., *Evolution and Culture*.

Hardy, Sir Alister, 1965, *The Living Stream. A Restatement of Evolution Theory and its Relation to the Spirit of Man*, Collins, London.

Harlow, H.F., "The Evolution of learning" in Roe and Simpson eds., 1964, *Behaviour and Evolution*.

Harrison, Jane, 1927, *Themis: A Study of the Social Origins of Greek Religion*, Cambridge University Press, Cambridge.

Head, H., 1920, *Studies in Neurology*, Oxford University Press, Oxford.

Hearn, Lafcadio, 1904, *Japan: An Attempt at Interpretation*, Macmillan, New York.

Heatwole, H. and Levins, R., 1972, "Trophic structure stability and faunal change during recolonization," *Ecology*, 53.

Hebb, D.O., 1949, *The Organization of Behaviour*, John Wiley, New York.

Heim, A.W., 1970, *The Appraisal of Intelligence*, National Foundation for Education Research, London.

Heller, Eric, 1957, *The Disinherited Mind*, New York.

Herodotus, 1875, *The Histories*, ed. Rawlinson, George, John Murray, London.

Herrick, C. Judson, 1961, *The Evolution of Human Nature*, Harper & Brothers, New York, 163.

Hesiod, 1718, *The Works*, translated by M. Cooke, London.

Hildyard, Nicholas, 1977, "Building for collapse," *The Ecologist*, Vol. 8, No. 2, March.

Hildyard, Nicholas, 1978, "There is more to food than eating," *The New Ecologist*, No. 5, Sept-Oct.

Hingston, R.W.G., 1928, *Problems of Instinct and Intelligence among Tropical Insects*, Edward Arnold, London.

Hobbes, Thomas, 1968 (original edition 1651), *Leviathan*, Penguin, Harmondsworth.

Hocart, A.M., 1970, *Kings and Councillors*, University of Chicago Press, Chicago.

Holling, C.S., "Resilience and stability of ecosystems" in Jantsch and Waddington eds., 1976, *Evolution and consciousness*.

Holst, Erich von, 1937, "Vom Wesen der Ordnung in Zentral-nervensystem," *Die Naturwissenshafter*, 25.

Holton, Gerald and Morrison, Robert S., 1979, *The Limits of Scientific Inquiry*, Norton, New York.

Homer, *The Odyssey*, 1854, translated by Alexander Pope, Cooke, London.

Horn, F.S., 1975, "Markovian prospects of forest succession" in Cody and Diamond eds., *Ecology and the Evolution of Communities*.

Horowitz, Norman H., 1956, "The Gene," *Scientific American*, October.

Huber, Peter B., 1978, "Organizing production and producing organization. The sociology of traditional agriculture," in Fisk ed., 1978, *The Adaptation of Traditional Agriculture*, Australian National University, Canberra.

Hughes, J. Donald, 1981, "Early Greek and Roman environmentalists," *The Ecologist*, Vol. 11, No. 1, Jan-Feb.

Hughes, J. Donald, and Thurgood, J.V., 1982, "Deforestation in ancient Greece and Rome; a cause of collapse?," *The Ecologist*, Vol. 12, No. 5, September-October.

Hughes, J. Donald, 1983, "Gaia: an ancient view of the planet," *The Ecologist*, Vol. 13, No. 2-3.

Hull, C.L. 1952 (original edition 1927), *A Behaviour system: an introduction to behavior theory*, Yale University Press, New Haven.

Humboldt, Alexander von, 1849, *Cosmos: A Sketch of the Physical Description of the Universe*, 5 Vols. trans. Otte, E.C. and Paul, B.H., Bohns Scientific Library, Henry A. Bohn. London.

Hume, A.O., 1878, *Agricultural Reform in India*, W.H. Allen & Co., London.

Hume, David, 1969 (original edition 1740), *A Treatise on Human Nature*, Penguin, Harmondsworth.

Hungerford, T.A.G., 1956, *Australian Signposts*, ed. F.W. Cheshire, Melbourne.

Hutton, James, 1788, "Theory of the Earth; investigation of the laws observable in the composition, dissolution and restoration of land upon the globe," *Transactions of the Royal Society of Edinburgh*, I, Part 2.

Huxley, J.S., 1953, *Evolution in Action*, Harper Bros, New York.

Huxley,T.H. and Huxley, Julian, 1947, *Evolution and Ethics, 1843-1943*, The Pilot Press, London.

Iamblichus, *Life of Pythagoras*, quoted by Cornford, 1975, *From Religion to Philosophy*.

International Cultural Foundation, 1972, *Proceedings of the Third International Conference on the Unity of the Sciences. Science and Absolute Values*, International Cultural Foundation, New York.

Isutzu, Toshihiko, 1971, *The Conception and Reality of Existence*, the Keio Institute of Culture and Linguistic Studies, Tokyo.

Jantsch, Erich, 1976, "Evolution: Self-Realization through Self-Transcendence" in Jantsch, Erich and Waddington, Conrad H. eds., *Evolution and Consciousness: Our Human Systems in Transition*, Addison-Wesley, Reading, Mass.

Jantsch, Erich and Waddington, Conrad H. eds., 1976, *Evolution and Consciousness: Our Human Systems in Transition*, Addison-Wesley, Reading, Mass.

Jantsch, Erich, 1980, *The Self-Organizing Universe*, Pergamon Press, Oxford.

Janzen, D.H., 1986, "The natural history of mutualism," in Boucher ed., *The Biology of Mutualism*.

Jaulin, Robert, 1971, "Ethnocide. The theory and practice of cultural murder," *The Ecologist*, Vol. 1, No. 18, Dec.

Jeffers, Robinson, 1959, *The Selected Poetry of Robinson Jeffers*, Random House, New York.

Johnson, C.G., 1963, "The aerial migration of insects," *Scientific American*, Dec.

Jones, Alwyn, 1983, "Beyond industrial society: towards balance and harmony," *The Ecologist*, Vol. 13, No. 4.

Jones, W.H.S., 1946, "Philosophy and medicine in ancient Greece," *Bulletin of the History of Medicine*, Supplement 8.

Jungk, Robert, 1958, *Brighter than a Thousand Suns*, Penguin, Harmondsworth, quoted by Visyanathan, *Atomic physics: the career of an imagination*.

Kaberry, Phyllis Mary, 1939, *Aboriginal Women, Sacred and Profane*, Routledge and Kegan Paul, London.

Kalmus, H., ed., 1967, *Regulation and Control of Living Systems*, John Wiley, New York.

Kardiner, Abraham, 1945, *The Psychological Frontiers of Society*, Columbia University Press, New York.

Katz, S.H. and Young, M.V., 1978, "Biological and social aspects of breast-feeding," *The Ecologist Quarterly*, Spring.

Keyes, Ralph, 1972, "We, the lonely people," *Intellectual Digest*, No.4.

Kiev, Ari, ed. 1967, *Magic, Faith and Healing*, The Free Press, New York.

King, F.H., 1904, *Farmers of Forty Centuries*, Rodale Press, Emmaus, Pennsylvania.

Kline, Morris, 1972, *Mathematics in Western Culture*, Penguin, Harmondsworth.

Koestler, Arthur, et al. 1950, *The God that Failed—Six Studies in Communism*, Hamish Hamilton, London.

Koestler, Arthur, 1967, *The Ghost in the Machine*, Hutchinson, London.

Koestler, Arthur and Smythies, J.R. eds., 1972, *Beyond Reductionism*. Hutchinson, London.

Koestler, Arthur, 1972, "Beyond Atomism and Holism," in Koestler and Smythies eds., *Beyond Reductionism*.

Koestler, Arthur, 1978, *Janus—A Summing Up*, Hutchinson, London.

Kohler, Wolfgang, 1947, *Gestalt Psychology: An Introduction to New Concepts in Modern Psychology*, Liveright Publications, New York.

Kothari, Manu L., and Mehta, Lopa A., "Violence in modern medicine," in Nandy ed. 1988, *Science, Hegemony and Violence*.

Koyré, Alexandre, 1965, *Newtonian Studies*, University of Chicago Press, Chicago.

Krechevsky, I., "Hypothesis versus chance in the pre-solution period in sensory discrimination," in Crawford, C.C. and Leitzell, F.H., eds., 1932, *Learning a New Language*.

Krige, Eileen Jensen, 1936, *The Social System of the Zulus*, Longman Green, London.

Kropotkin, Peter, 1914 (original edition 1902), *Mutual Aid: A Factor in Evolution*, Horizon Books, Boston.

Kuhn, Thomas S., 1970, *The Structure of Scientific Revolutions*, University of Chicago Press, Chicago.

Kuhn, Thomas, 1979, "Logic of discovery or psychology of research?," in Lakatos and Musgrave eds. 1979, *Criticism and the Growth of Knowledge*.

Kuper, Hilda, 1963, *The Swazi. A South African Kingdom*, Holt, Rinehart and Winston, New York.

La Barre, Weston, 1954, *The Human Animal*, University of Chicago Press, Chicago.

Laflesche, F., 1905, "Who was the Medicine Man?," New York.

Lakatos, Imre, and Musgrave, Alan eds., 1979, *Criticism and the Growth of Knowledge*, Cambridge University Press, London.

Lakatos, Imre, 1979, "Methodology of scientific research programs" in Lakatos and Musgrave eds., *Criticism and the Growth of Knowledge*.

Lamarck, J.B., 1873 (original edition 1809), *Philosophie Zoologique*, 2 vols., ed. C. Martins, Savy, Paris.

Lamarck, J.B., 1964 (original edition, Paris, 1802), *Hydrogeology*, trans. Albert V. Carozzi, University of Chicago Press, Chicago.

Lashley, Karl, 1958, "Persistent problems in the evolution of mind," *Quarterly Review of Biology*, 24.

Lee, R.B. and Devore, I. eds., 1968, *Man the Hunter*, Aldine Publishing Co., Chicago.

Leopold, Aldo, 1953, *A Sand County Almanac*, Oxford University Press, Oxford.

Lévi Strauss, Claude, 1955, *Tristes Tropiques*, Plon, Paris.

Lewis, Oscar, 1966, "The culture of poverty," *Scientific American*, October.

Lichnerowicz, A. et alia, 1976, *Structure et Dynamique des Systèmes*, Maloine, Doin, Paris.

Linnaeus, Carl, 1964 (original edition 1753), *Systema Naturae*, B. de Graaf, Newkoop.

Linton, Ralph, 1945, "The Comanches" in Kardiner, *The Psychological Frontiers of Society*.

Lods, Adolphe, 1932, *Israel: From its Beginnings to the Middle of the Eighth Century*, trans. S.H. Hooke, Routledge and Kegan Paul, London.

Lorenz, Konrad, 1943, "Die Angeborenen Forman moglicher Erfahrung," *Z. Tierpsychologie* 5.

Lorenz, Konrad, 1962, "Gestalt perception as fundamental to scientific knowledge," in *General Systems Yearbook*, no.7.

Lorenz, Konrad, 1963, *On Aggression*, Harcourt, Brace, New York.

Lovelock, J.E., 1979, *Gaia: A New Look at Life on Earth*, Oxford University Press, Oxford.

Lovelock, J.E., "Gaia: A Model for Planetary and Cellular Dynamics," in Thompson, William Irwin ed., 1987, *Gaia: A Way of Knowing. Political Implications as a New Biology*.

Lovelock, J.E., "The Gaia Hypothesis," in Bunyard and Goldsmith eds., 1988, *Gaia—the Thesis, the Mechanism and the Implications*.

Lovelock, J.E., 1991, *Gaia: The Practical Science of Planetary Medicine*, Gaia Books, London.

Lowie, Robert, 1921, *Primitive Society*, G. Routledge and Sons, London.

Lundberg, George A., 1961, quoted by Herrick, *The Evolution of Human Nature* (qv).

Lux, Kenneth, 1990, *Adam Smith's Mistake: How a Moral Philosopher Invented Economics and Ended Morality*, Shambhala, Boston.

Mackay, Donald, 1964, "Communication and Meaning: A Functional Approach," eds. Northrop and Livingstone, *Cross-cultural Understanding*.

MacKinnon, Flora, ed., 1925, *The Philosophical Writings of Henry More*, Oxford University Press, Oxford.

Macko, D. and Mesarovic, M.D., "Foundations for a scientific theory of hierarchical systems," in Whyte et alia eds., 1969, *Hierarchical Structures*.

MacLean, Paul, 1964, "Man and his animal brains," *Modern Medicine*.

Maine, Sir Henry Sumner, 1905 (original edition 1861), *Ancient Law: Its Connection with the Early History of Society and its Relation to Modern Ideas*, John Murray, London.

Malin, James, 1953, "Soil, animal and plant relations of the grassland, historically reconsidered," *Scientific Monthly*, 76.

Malinowski, Bronislaw, 1937, "Anthropology as the basis of social science," in Cattel et alia eds., *Human Affairs*.

Malinowski, Bronislaw, 1961 (original edition 1922), *Argonauts of the Western Pacific*, E.P. Dutton, New York.

Malinowski, Bronislaw, 1965 (original edition 1945), *The Dynamics of Cultural Change*, Yale University Press, New Haven.

Mann, R.B., 1990, "Time Running Out: The urgent need for tree-planting in Africa," *The Ecologist*, Vol. 20, March/April.

Marett, R.R., *The Threshold of Religion*, Methuen & Co. Ltd., London.

Margalef, Ramon, 1958, "Information theory and ecology," in *General Systems Yearbook*, Vol. III.

Margalef, Ramon, 1963, "On certain unifying principles in ecology," *The American Naturalist*, Nov/Dec., No. 897.

Margalef, Ramon, "Diversity, stability and maturity in natural ecosystems," in van Dobben and Lowe-McConnell eds. 1975, *Unifying Concepts in Ecology*.

Marsh, George Perkins, 1965 (original edition 1864), *Man and Nature*, The Belknap Press of Harvard University, Cambridge, Mass.

Mason, Stephen F., 1956, *Main Currents of Scientific Thought*, Routledge and Kegan Paul, London.

Masterman, Margaret, "The nature of the paradigm," in Lakatos and Musgrave eds., 1979, *Criticism and the Growth of Knowledge*.

Mathes, J.C. and Gray, Donald H., 1975, "The Engineer as social radical," *The Ecologist*, vol.5., No. 4.

Mattson, W.L. and Addy, N.D., 1972, "Photophagous insects as regulators of forest primary production," in *Science* 190, 4214: 515-521.

Mauss, Marcel, 1954, *The Gift. Forms and Functions of Exchange in Archaic Societies*, Cohen and West, London.

May, Robert M., 1973, *Stability and Complexity in Model Ecosystems*, Princeton University Press, Princeton.

McCully, Patrick, 1991, "The case against climate aid," *The Ecologist*, vol. 21, No. 6.

McIntosh, Robert P., 1975, "H.A. Gleason, individualistic ecologist: his contribution to ecological theory," *Bulletin of the Torrey Botanical Club*, Vol. 102.

McIntosh, Robert P., 1980, "Some problems of theoretical ecology," in Saarinen ed, *Conceptual Issues in Ecology*.

McIver, Robert, 1964, *The Ramparts we Guard*, Macmillan, New York.

McKinney, H.L. 1966, "Alfred Russel Wallace and the discovery of natural selection," *Journal of the History of Medicine and Allied Sciences*, 21.33.

McKnight, John, 1978, "The politics of medicine," *The Ecologist*, No. 6, July/August.

McNaughton, S.J., 1979, "Grazing as an optimization process: grass ungulate relationships in Serengeti," *The American Naturalist*, May, Vol. 13, No. 5.

Meadows, Donella and Dennis, 1972, *The Limits to Growth*, Earth Island, London.

Medawar, P.B. 1974, *The Hope of Progress*, Wildwood House, London.

Medawar, P.B., & J.S., 1977, *The Life Science*, Wildwood House, London.

Medawar, P.B., 1982, *Plato's Republic* Oxford University Press, Oxford.

Merrell, D.J. and Underhill, J.C., 1956, "Selection for D D T resistance in inbred laboratory and wild stocks of Drosophila Melanogaster," *Journal of Economic Entymology*, 49.

Merrell, David J., 1985, *Ecological Genetics*, Longman, London.

Merton, Robert, 1951, *Social Theory and Social Structure: Toward the Clarification of Theory and Research*, The Free Press of Glencoe, New York.

Metuh, Emefie Ikeng, 1981, *God and Man in African Religion*, Geoffrey Chapman, London.

Meyerson, Emile, 1921, "De L'Explication dans les Sciences," Paris, Tome 1.

Middleton, John, ed. 1970, *From Child to Adult*, The Natural History Press, New York.

Monboddo, Lord, 1784, *Ancient Metaphysics*. Vol. III, James Burnet, London.

Monod, Jacques, 1970, *Chance and Necessity*, London.

Monod, Jacques, 1970, Discussion following Delattre, Pierre, "Langage Interdisciplinaire et théorie des systèmes," in A. Lichnerowicz et alia, 1976, *Structure et Dynamique des Systèmes*.

Mooney, Patrick Roy, 1979, *Seeds of the Earth: A Private and Public Resource*, Inter Pares, Ottawa.

Moore, Barrington, 1917, *Presidential Address to St. Louis Branch of the* U.S. Ecological Society.

More, L.T., 1944, *The Life and Works of the Honourable Robert Boyle*, Oxford University Press, London.

Morenz, Siegfried, 1973, *Egyptian Religion*, trans. by Ann E. Keep, Methuen, London.

Morgan, Lewis H., 1878, *Ancient Society*, H. Holt, New York.

Morgan, Thomas, quoted by Worster, 1977, *Nature's Economy*.

Morin, Edgar, 1977 and 1980, *La Méthode*. Vol. 1 *La Nature de la Nature* and Vol. 2 *La Vie de la Vie*, Seuil, Paris.

Morin, Edgar, 1980, "Answer to René Thom," *Les Débats*, November.

Mumford, Lewis, 1967, *The Myth of the Machine*, Secker and Warburg, London.

Murray, Robert, 1991, "The Biblical Vocabulary of Justice," unpublished notes for a lecture at a summer school for Jewish and Christian lay people reading Amos together.

Murray, Robert, 1992, *The Cosmic Covenant*, Sheed & Ward, London.

Nandy, Ashis, Personal communication.

Nandy, Ashis, 1981, *Traditions, Tyranny and Utopia: Essays in the Politics of Awareness*, Oxford University Press, New Delhi.

Nandy, Ashis, 1983, "The pathology of objectivity," *The Ecologist*, Vol. XIII, No. 6.

Nandy, Ashis, 1988, *Science, Hegemony and Violence*, Oxford University Press, New Delhi.

National Academy of Sciences, 1991, *Policy Implications of Greenhouse Warming*, National Academy Press, Washington DC.

Ndaw, Alassane, 1983, *La Pensée Africaine*, Les Nouvelles Editions Africaines, Dakar.

Needham, Joseph, 1936, *Order and Life*, MIT Press, Cambridge, Mass.

Needham, Joseph, 1956, *Science and Civilization in China*, Vol. 2, Cambridge University Press, Cambridge.

Needham, Joseph, 1969, *The Grand Titration*, George Allen and Unwin, London.

Nelkin, Dorothy, 1979, "Threats and promises. Negotiating the control of research," in Holton and Morrison eds., *The Limits of Scientific Inquiry*.

Nesbit, Robert, 1970, *The Sociological Tradition*, Heinemann Educational Books, London.

Nicholson, A.J., 1933, "The Balance of animal populations," *Journal of Animal Ecology*.

Noel, Emile, ed. 1979, *Le Darwinisme Aujourd'hui*, Le Seuil, Paris.

Northrop, F.S.C. and Livingston, Helen H. eds. 1965, *Cross-cultural Understanding*, Harper and Row, New York.

Oatley, Keith, 1978, *Perceptions and Representations*, Methuen, London.

Odum, Eugene, and Patten, B.C., 1981, "The Cybernetic nature of ecosystems," *American Naturalist*.

Odum, Eugene, 1975, *Ecology*, Holt, Rinehart and Winston, New York.

Odum, Eugene P., 1953, *Fundamentals of Ecology*, W.B. Saunders, Philadelphia.

Odum, Eugene P., 1969, "The strategy of ecosystems development," *Science*, 164, pp. 260-270.

Odum, Eugene P., 1983, *Basic Ecology*, Saunders College Publishing, Philadelphia.

Odum, Howard, 1971, *Environment, Power and Society*, John Wiley and Sons, New York.

Orians, G.H., 1975, "Diversity, stability and maturity in natural ecosystems," in van Dobben and Lowe McConnell eds., *Unifying Concepts in Ecology*.

Ospovat, Dov, 1981, *The Development of Darwin's Theory*, Cambridge University Press, Cambridge.

Owen, D.F. and Wiegert, R.G., 1981, "Mutualism between grasses and grazers: an evolutionary hypothesis," *Oikos*.

Pantin, C.P.A., 1968, *The Relations Between the Sciences*, Cambridge University Press, Cambridge.

Pappenheim, F., 1968, *The alienation of modern man*, Modern Reader paperbacks, 1968.

Park, Mungo, 1984 (original edition 1799), *Travels in the Interior of Africa*, Folio Society, London.

Parsons, Robert T., 1964, *Religion of an African Society*, E.J. Brill, Leiden.

Passmore, John, 1978, *Science and its Critics*, Duckworth, London.

Patai, Raphael, 1947, *Man and Temple in Ancient Jewish Myth and Ritual*, Thomas Nelson, London.

Pattee, Howard H., 1973, *Hierarchy Theory: The Challenge of Complex Systems*, George Braziller, New York.

Patten, B.C. and Odum, E.P., 1981, "The cybernetic nature of ecosystems," *American Naturalist*, p118.

Pattison, James and Kim, Peter, 1991, "The Day America told the truth," New York, quoted by Tisdall, Simon, 1991.

Payer, Cheryl, 1982, The World Bank, Monthly Review Press, New York, 1982.

Peerenboom, R.D., 1991, "Beyond naturalism: a reconstruction of Taoist environmental ethics," *Environmental Ethics*, Vol. XIII, Spring.

Piaget, Jean, 1967, *Biologie et Connaissance*, Gallimard, Paris.

Piaget, Jean, 1968, *The Child's Conception of the World*, Adams & Co., Littlefield, New Jersey.

Piaget, Jean, 1971, in Ayala and Dobzhansky eds. 1974, *Studies in the Philosophy of Biology*.

Piaget, Jean, 1976, *Le Comportement, Moteur de l'Evolution*, Gallimard, Paris.

Piaget, Jean, and Inhelder, Barbel, 1972, "The Gaps in empiricism," in Koestler and Smythies eds., *Beyond Reductionism*.

Pirie, N.W., 1969, "Gardyloo," *The Listener*, 82.

Pittendrigh, Colin, 1958, "Adaptation, natural selection and behavior," in Roe and Simpson eds., *Evolution and Behaviour*.

Plato, *Menexemus*, quoted by Hughes 1983, "Gaia, An ancient view of our planet," *The Ecologist*, Vol. 13, Nos. 2-3.

Pliny the Elder, *Natural History*, ed. Newsome, J., 1964, Clarendon Press, Oxford.

Polanyi, Karl, 1957 (Original edition 1944), *The Great Transformation*, Beacon Press, Boston.

Polanyi, Karl, "Societies and economic systems" in Dalton ed., 1968, *Primitive, Archaic and Modern Economics*.

Polanyi, Karl, "The self-regulating market" in Dalton ed., 1968, *Primitive, Archaic and Modern Economics*.

Polanyi, Michael, 1978 (original edition 1958), *Personal Knowledge. Towards a Post-Critical Philosophy*, Routledge and Kegan Paul, London.

Pollard, Nigel, 1981, "The Gezira scheme: A study in failure," *The Ecologist*, Vol. 11, No. 1.

Popenoe, David, 1991, "Family decline in the Swedish welfare state," *The Public Interest*, Winter.

Popper, Karl, 1963, *Conjectures and Refutations*, Routledge and Kegan Paul, London.

Popper, Karl, 1973 (original edition 1972), *Objective Knowledge*, Clarendon Press, Oxford.

Popper, Karl, 1983 (original edition 1959), *The Logic of Scientific Discovery*, Hutchinson, London.

Pound, R., 1893, "Symbiosis and mutualism," *American Naturalist*.

Price, Peter W., "Alternative paradigms in community ecology," in Gaud, Price and Slobodchikoff eds., 1984, *A New Ecology*, 206.

Prigogine, Ilya and Stengers, Isabelle, 1979, *La Nouvelle Alliance*, Gallimard, Paris.

Prior, Ian, et alia, 1987, "Migration and gout: The Tokelau Islands Migration Study," *British Medical Journal*, 22 August.

Putman, S.D. and Wratten, R.J., 1984, *Principles of Ecology*, Croom Helm, Beckenham, Kent.

Quastler, H. ed. 1953, *Information Theory in Biology*, University of Illinois Press, Urbana.

Radcliffe-Brown, A.R. 1965, *Structure and Function in Primitive Society*, Cohen and West, London.

Ramon-y-Cajal, Santiago, quoted by Sherrington, 1940, *Man on his Nature*.

Rapoport, Anatol, 1956, "The Promise and Pitfalls of Information Theory," *Behavioural Science*, 1.

Rappaport, Amos, 1978, "Culture and environment," *Ecologist Quarterly*, No. 4, Winter.

Rappaport, Roy A., 1967, *Pigs for the Ancestors*, Yale University Press, New Haven.

Rappaport, Roy A., 1979, *Ecology, Meaning and Religion*, North Atlantic Books, Richmond,Calif.

Raum, O.F. 1967, *Chaga Childhood*, Oxford University Press, Oxford.

Raum, O.F. 1978, "Some aspects of indigenous education among the Chaga" in Middleton ed., 1978, *From Child to Adult*.

Ravetz, Jerome R., 1971, *Scientific Knowledge and its Social Problems*, Oxford University Press, Oxford.

Read, Margaret, 1978, "Education in Africa. Its pattern and role in social change" in Middleton ed., 1978, *From Child to Adult*.

Reichel-Dolmatoff, Gerardo, 1977, "Cosmology as ecological analysis: a view from the rainforest," *The Ecologist*, Vol. 7, No. 1.

Reichel-Dolmatoff, Gerardo, 1983, "The Kogi Indians and the environment: impending disaster," *The Ecologist*, Vol. 13, No. 1, Jan-Feb.

Ricklefs, R.E., 1973, *Ecology*, Nelson, London.

Ricqles, Armand de, 1979, "Darwinisme, paleontologie et anatomie comparée," in Emile Noel ed. *Le Darwinisme Aujourd'hui*.

Riedl, Rupert, 1978, *Order in Living Organisms*, John Wiley, New York.

Rifkin, Jeremy and Perlas, Nicanor, 1983, *Algeny*, The Viking Press, New York.

Robertson Smith, W., 1914, *Essays on the Religion of the Semites*, Adams and Charles Black, London.

Roe, Anne and Simpson, George Gaylord eds., 1958, *Behaviour and Evolution*, Yale University Press, New Haven.

Rogers, Everett M., and Kincaid, D. Lawrence, 1981, *Communications Networks: Toward a New Paradigm for Research*, Collier Macmillan, London.

Roszak, Theodore, 1972, *Where the Wasteland Ends*, Faber and Faber, London.

Russell, Peter 1982, *The Awakening Earth*, Routledge and Kegan Paul, London.

Ryle, Gilbert, 1949, *The Concept of Mind*, Hutchinson's University Library, London.

Saarinen, Esa ed., 1982, *Conceptual Issues in Ecology*, D. Reidel, Dordrecht.

Sachs, Wolfgang, 1990, "Six essays on the archaeology of development," *Interculture*, 109,4, Fall.

Sagan, Dorion and Margulis, Lynn, 1983, "The Gaian perspective of ecology," *The Ecologist*, Vol. 13, No. 5.

Sahlins, Marshall, "Tribal economics" in George Dalton ed., 1971, *Economic Development and Social Change*.

Salaman, Redcliffe N., 1949, *The History and Social Influence of the Potato*, Cambridge University Press, Cambridge.

Sampson, R. Neil, 1981, *Farmland or Wasteland*, Rodale Press, PA.

Sargant, William, 1957, *The Battle for the Mind*, Heinemann, London.

Schebesta, Paul, 1940, *Les Pygmées*, Gallimard, Paris.

Schillp, P.A., 1959, ed. *Albert Einstein, Philosopher Scientist*, Harper and Row, New York.

Schmalhausen, Ivan, 1949 *Factors of Evolution: The Theory of Stabilizing Evolution*, trans. Isadore Dordick, ed. Theodosius Dobzhansky, Blakiston (McGraw-Hill), New York.

Schoepf, Broske Grundfest, "Man and biosphere in Zaire," in Barker ed., 1984, *The Politics of Agriculture in Tropical Africa*.

Scott, James, 1978, "The Subsistence ethic," *The New Ecologist*, No. 3, May/June.

Senghor, Leopold, 1983, Preface to Alassane Ndaw, *La Pensée Africaine*.

Shannon, Claude E. and Weaver, Warren, 1949, *The Mathematical Theory of Communication*, University of Illinois Press, Urbana.

Shapiro, J., Eron, L., and Beckwith, J., letter in *Nature*, December 27, 1969, p1337.

Sharp, Lauriston R. 1952, "Steel Axes for Stone Age Australians" in Hammond ed. 1966, *An Introduction to Cultural and Social Anthropology*.

Sheldrake, Rupert, 1988, *The Presence of the Past*, Collins, London.

Shelford, Victor, 1913, *Animal Communities in Temperate America*, University of Chicago Press, Chicago.

Sherrington, Sir Charles, 1947 (original edition 1906), *The Integration of the Nervous System*, Cambridge University Press, Cambridge.

Sherrington, Sir Charles, 1940, *Man on his Nature*, The Gifford Lectures, 1937-8, Cambridge University Press, Cambridge.

Sherrington, Sir Charles, 1906, *The Integrative Action of the Nervous System*, London.

Simberloff, D.S., 1980, "A succession of paradigms in ecology," in Saarinen ed., *Conceptual Issues in Ecology*.

Simberloff, D.S. and Wilson, E.O.L., 1969, "Experimental zoogeography in islands: the colonization of empty islands," *Ecology*, 50.

Simpson, George Gaylord, 1950, *The Meaning of Evolution. A Study of the History of Life and of its Significance for Man*, Oxford University Press, London.

Singh, Rev. J.A.L. and Zing, Robert M., 1942, *Wolf Children and Feral Man*, Harper and Bros, New York.

Sinnott, Edmund W., 1961, *Cell and Psyche*, Harper and Row, New York.

Skinner, B.F., 1957, *Verbal Behaviour*, New York.

Skolimowski, Henryk, "Problems of rationality in biology," in Ayala and Dobzhansky, 1974, *Studies in the Philosophy of Biology*.

Skolimowski, Henryk, 1983, *Technology and Human Destiny*, University of Madras, Madras.

Spengler, Oswald, 1939, *The Decline of the West*, Alfred Knopf, New York.

Sprigge, T.L.S., "The definition of a moral judgment," in Wallace and Walker eds., 1970, *The Definition of Morality*.

Stallnecht, Newton, 1958, "Strange Seas of thought," Studies in William Wordsworth's *Philosophy of Man and Nature*, Bloomington, Indiana.

Stanner, W.E.H., 1956, "The dreaming," in Hungerford, *Australian Signposts*.

Steinberg, L., 1905, "Die religion der Gijaken," *Archiv für Religionswissenschaft*, viii.

Stent, Gunther, 1978, *Paradoxes of Progress*, W.H. Freeman, San Francisco.

Stewart, M.A., ed., 1979, *Selected Philosophical Papers of Robert Boyle*, Manchester University Press, Manchester.

Suess, Edouard, 1875, *Die Entstehung der Alpen*, W. Braumuller, Vienna.

Sumner, William Graham, 1963, *Social Darwinism: Selected Essays of William Graham Sumner*, Prentice-Hall, Englewood Cliffs.

Tansley, Arthur, 1920, "Classification of vegetation or the concept of development," *Journal of Ecology*, 2.

Tansley, Arthur, 1935, "The use and abuse of vegetational concepts and terms," *Ecology*, 16, July.

Taylor, Bron, 1991, "The religion and politics of Earth First," *The Ecologist*, Vol. 21, No. 6, Nov-Dec.

Taylor, John, 1990, "50% Crime Rise Forecast 2000," *Daily Telegraph*, September 26th.

Tempels, Placide, 1948, *La Philosophie Bantoue*, Présence Africaine, Paris.

Thatcher, Margaret, 1989, Speech on the global environment to the United Nations General Assembly, New York, 8th November, typescript only, The Prime Minister's Office, London.

Thompson, William Irwin ed., 1987, *Gaia: a Way of Knowing. Political Implications as a New Biology*, Lindisfarne Press, Hudson, New York.

Thoreau, Henry David, 1906, *The Writings of Henry David Thoreau*, 20 Vols, Houghton Mifflin, Boston.

Thorpe, W.H., 1956, "Some implications of the study of animal behavior," *The Advancement of Science*, Vol. 13, No. 50.

Thorpe, W.H., 1965, *Science, Man and Morals*, Methuen & Co., London.

Thorpe, W.H., 1969, "Why the brain is more than a mere computer," *The Times*, London, January 25th.

Thorpe, W.H., Discussion following presentation of Ludwig von Bertalanffy's "Chance or Law?" in Koestler and Smythies eds., 1972, *Beyond Reductionism*.

Thorpe, W.H., Discussion after Waddington, "Theory of evolution today," in Koestler and Smythies, 1972, *Beyond Reductionism*.

Thurnwald, Richard, 1931, *Die Menschliche Gesellschaft*, Berlin.

Tillich, Paul, 1952, *Systematic Theology*, Chicago University Press, Chicago.

Tinbergen, N., 1951, *The Study of Instinct*, The Clarendon Press, Oxford.

Tisdall, Simon, 1991, "America loses moral values," *The Guardian*, May 2nd.

Tolman, E.C., 1962, *Purposive Behaviour in Animals and Men*, Century Psychology Series, New York.

Tonnies, Ferdinand, 1955 (original edition 1920), *Community and Association*, Routledge and Kegan Paul, London.

Toynbee, Arnold J., 1934, *A Study of History*, Royal Institute of International Affairs, London.

Trivers, R.L., Foreword to R. Dawkins, 1976, *The Selfish Gene*, Oxford University Press, Oxford.

Turner, Victor, "A Ndembu doctor in practice," in Kiev ed., 1967, *Magic, Faith and Healing*.

Tyler, Edward, 1903, *Primitive Culture*, John Murray, London.

Ungerer, E., 1930, "Der Aufbau des naturwissens," *Pedagogische Hochschule* ii, quoted by von Bertalanffy, 1962, *Modern Theories of Development*.

U.S. Dept. of Education, 1964, *Equality of Education Opportunities*, Washington DC.

van der Post, Laurens, 1958, *Venture into the Interior*, Hogarth, London.

van Dobben, W.H. and Lowe-McConnell, R. eds., 1975, *Unifying Concepts in Ecology*, Funk, The Hague.

Vayda, Andrew P., "Maori Warfare" in Bohannan ed., 1967, *Law and Warfare*.

Vayda, Andrew P., 1969, *Environment and Cultural Behaviour*, American Museum of Natural History, New York.

Vernadsky, V.I. 1945, "The biosphere and the noosphere," *American Scientist*, 33.

Visvanathan, Shiv, "Atomic physics: the career of an imagination," in Nandy ed. 1988, *Science, Hegemony and Violence*.

Voelcker, John Augustus, 1893, *Report on the Improvement of Indian Agriculture*, Eyre and Spottiswoode, London.

von Bertalanffy, Ludwig, 1962 A, (original edition 1933), *Modern Theories of Development: An Introduction to Theoretical Biology*, trans. J.H. Woodger, Harper Torchbook, New York.

von Bertalanffy, Ludwig, 1962 B, "General systems theory: a critical review," *General Systems Yearbook*.

von Bertalanffy, Ludwig, "Chance or Law?," in Koestler and Smythies eds., 1972, *Beyond Reductionism*.

von Bertalanffy, Ludwig, 1973, "Theorie Generale des Systèmes," Dunod, Paris.

von Bertalanffy, Ludwig, 1973, *General Systems Theory: Foundations, Development, Applications*, Allen Lane, London.

von Hildebrand, Martin, 1981, "An Amazonian tribe's view of cosmology" in Bunyard and Goldsmith eds., *Gaia: The Thesis, the Mechanisms and the Implications*.

Waddington, C.H., 1934, "Morphogenetic fields," a review of the elements of experimental embryology," *Science Progress*, Vol. 29, No. 114.

Waddington, C.H., 1952, *The Listener*, 13th November.

Waddington, C.H., 1960, *The Ethical Animal*, University of Chicago Press, Chicago.

Waddington, C.H., 1969, *Towards a Theoretical Biology*, 2 Vols. Edinburgh University Press, Edinburgh.

Waddington, C.H., 1970, "Basic ideas of biology," in Waddington ed., 1969, *Towards a Theoretical Biology*.

Waddington, C.H., "The theory of evolution today," in Koestler and Smythies eds., 1972, *Beyond Reductionism*.

Waddington, C.H., 1975, *The Evolution of an Evolutionist*, Edinburgh University Press, Edinburgh.

Wallace, A.F.C., 1956, "Revitalization movements: some theoretical considerations for their comparative study," *American Anthropologist*, Vol. 58, April.

Wallace, A.F.C., 1963, *Culture and Personality*, Random House, New York.

Wallace, G. and Walker, A.D.M. eds., 1970, *The Definition of Morality*, Methuen, London.

Ward, Lester, 1893, *The Psychic Factors of Civilization*.

Warming, Johannes Eugenius, 1909, *The Oecology of Plants: An Introduction to the Study of Plant Communities*, trans. Percy Bloom and Isaac Bailey Balfour, Clarendon Press, Oxford.

Warren, W.W., 1885, "History of the Ojibways," *Collection of the Minnesota Historical Society*, St. Paul.

Washburn, S. and Lancaster, C., "The evolution of hunting," in Lee and Devore eds., 1968, *Man the Hunter*.

Watkins, John, "Against normal science," in Lakatos and Musgrave, 1979, *Criticism and the Growth of Knowledge*.

Watson, John B., 1925, *Behaviourism*, Kegan Paul Trench Trubner, London.

Weiss, Paul, 1956, *Proceedings of the National Academy*, 42.

Weiss, Paul, 1971, *Hierarchically Organized Systems in Theory and Practice*, Hafner, New York.

Weiss, Paul, "The living system, determinism stratified," in Koestler and Smythies eds., 1972, *Beyond Reductionism*, Hutchinson, London.

Weiss, Paul, 1972, Discussion after presentation of his paper "The Living system," Koestler and Smythies eds., *Beyond Reductionism*.

Weiss, Paul, 1973, *A Science of Life*, Futura Publishing Co., New York.

Wheeler, Sir Robert Eric Mortimer, 1959, *Early India and Pakistan*, A. Praeger, New York.

White, Gilbert, 1902 (original edition 1789), *The Natural History of Selborne*, John Lane, London and New York.

Whitehead, A.N., 1958, *Science and the Modern World* (text of the 1925 Lowell lectures), Mentor, New York.

Whittaker, R.H., 1964, "Gradient Analysis of Vegetation," *Biological Reviews*, 42.

Whittaker, R.H., 1975, "Communities and Ecosystems," Collier Macmillan, London.

Whitten, N.E. Jr., 1978, "Ecological imagery and cultural adaptability," *American Anthropologist*, Vol. 80, No. 4, Dec.

Whorf, Benjamin Lee, 1956, *Language, Thought and Reality*, MIT Press, Cambridge, Mass.

Whyte, A.F., 1927, *China and the Foreign Powers*, Humphrey Milford, London.

Whyte, Lancelot Law, Wilson, Albert G., Wilson, Donna eds.,1969, *Hierarchical Structures* (Proceedings of the symposium held Nov. 18-19, 1968 at Douglas Advanced Research Laboratories, Huntington Beach, Calif.), American Elsevier, New York.

Wilson, Carroll, et alia, 1971, *Man's Impact on the Global Environment. A Study of Critical Environmental Problems*, MIT Press, Cambridge, Mass.

Wilson, Edward O., 1976, "Sociobiology: A new approach to understanding the basis of human nature," *New Scientist*, 13 May.

Wing-Tsit Chan, 1963, *A Source Book in Chinese Philosophy*, Princeton University Press, Princeton.

Wintrebert, P., *Le Développement du Vivant par lui-même*, Vol. 1, Masson et Cie, Paris.

Wiseman, Stephen ed., 1966, "Intelligence and Ability," *Modern Psychology*, Harmondsworth, London.

Woodger, J.H., 1967, *Biological Principles*, Routledge and Kegan Paul, London.

World Bank, 1981, *Accelerated Development in Sub-Saharan Agriculture*, Washington, DC.

Worster, Donald, 1977, *Nature's Economy*, Sierra Club, San Francisco.

Wynne-Edwards, V.C., 1962, *Animal Dispersion in Relation to Social Behaviour*, Oliver Boyd, Edinburgh.

Wynne-Edwards, V.C., 1964, "Population control in animals," *Scientific American*, August.

Young, L.Z., 1950, *The Life of Vertebrates*, Oxford University Press, Oxford.

Zuckerman, S., 1932, *The Social Life of Monkeys and Apes*, Kegan Paul Trench Trubner, London.

Zuckerman, S., *Address to the UN Conference on the Environment*, Stockholm, June 1972.

References

Chapter 1

1. Shelford 1913, pp. 302-3 *cit.*
   Worster 1977, p. 204
2. Tansley 1920, pp. 118-149
3. Odum E. 1953, pp. 192-3
4. Odum E., personal
   communication
5. Moore B. 1917, see also
   1920 pp. 3-5
6. Woodger 1967, p. 22
7. Ackoff 1964, pp. 117-122
8. Craik J.W. 1966, *cit.* Granit
   1977, p. 9
9. Ackoff 1964, pp. 117-122
10. Georgescu-Roegen 1972,
    pp. 13-18
11. Daly and Cobb 1987, p. 37

Chapter 2

1. Boyle, *cit.* Mason 1956, p. 136
2. Prigogine 1979, p. 193
3. Prigogine 1979, p. 64
4. Morin 1980, p. 78

Chapter 3

1. Weiss 1973, p. 75
2. Zuckerman 1932, pp. 94-97
3. Oatley 1975, p. 158
4. Chaitanya 1976, p. 214

Chapter 4

1. Adams 1917, pp. 491-1169
2. Simberloff 1980, p. 73
3. Bodenheimer, in Bodenheimer
   1957, pp. 75-90
4. Pirie 1969, p. 331
5. Passmore 1978, p. 53
6. Rutherford, *cit.* Passmore
   1978, p. 53
7. Crick F. 1966, p. 10

8. Koyré 1965, p. 23
9. Tansley 1920, pp. 202-204
10. Gleason 1926, pp. 1-20
11. McIntosh 1975, p. 102
12. Gleason 1926, pp. 1-20
13. McIntosh 1975, p. 102
14. Colinvaux 1973, p. 621, *cit.*
    McIntosh 1975, p. 14
15. Curtis, p. 657, *cit.* McIntosh
    1975, p. 265
16. Whittaker 1967, pp. 207-264
17. Kohler 1947, p. 168
18. Chaitanya 1972, p. 249
19. von Bertalanffy 1962
20. Passmore 1978, p. 53
21. Odum E. 1969, pp. 262-270
22. Thorpe 1956, p. 55

Chapter 5

1. Granit 1977, p. 7
2. Fuller and Putnam 1966,
   pp. 99-112
3. Granit 1977, pp. 18-19
4. Lovelock, 1987, p. 87
5. Gerard 1940, pp. 161-173
6. Huxley J.S. 1953
7. Merrell 1981, pp. 18-
   19
8. Calow 1976, pp. 13-
   14
9. Calow 1976, pp. 13-
   14
10. Atlan 1979, p. 21
11. Grassé 1973, p. 216

Chapter 6

1. Marsh 1965, p. 96
2. Dubos 1967, pp. 163-
   195
3. Margulis, personal
   communication
4. Day 1929, p. 95

Chapter 7

1. Fantz 1961, pp. 66-84
2. Fantz 1961, pp. 66-84

Chapter 8

1. Polanyi M. 1978, p. 88
2. Koestler 1975, p. 287
3. Frankl, in Koestler & Smythies 1972, p. 401
4. Polanyi M. 1978, p. 56
5. von Humboldt 1849, pp. 1848-58
6. Weiss, *cit.* Chaitanya 1972, p. 30
7. Jeffers 1959, p. 594

Chapter 9

1. Ryle 1949, p. 50
2. Watson 1925, *cit.* Koestler 1978, pp. 166-167
3. Tolman 1937, p. 372
4. Watson 1925, p. 198 *cit.* Koestler 1978, pp. 166-167
5. Lundberg 1961, *cit.* Herrick 1961 p. 19
6. Watson 1925, *cit.* Koestler 1978, p. 168
7. Hume 1969, p. 137
8. Hume, p. 189
9. Polanyi M. 1978, p. 168
10. Popper 1973, p. 259
11. Concern 1981
12. Polanyi M. 1978, p. 168
13. Popper 1973, p. 259
14. Darwin, *cit.* Medawar 1982, p. 88
15. Darwin 1861, in Darwin, F. 1903, p. 195
16. Medawar 1982, p. 88
17. Polanyi M. 1978, p. 167
18. Thorpe 1969, p. 9

Chapter 10

1. Horowitz 1956, pp. 78-90
2. Oatley 1978, p. 135
3. Bartlett 1977 p. 197
4. see Herrick 1961, pp. 302 also 403-4
5. Craik K. 1967, p. 61
6. Polanyi M. 1978, p. 74

Chapter 11

1. Kline 1972, p. 217
2. Pantin 1968, *cit.* Weiss, in Koestler & Smythies 1969, p. 44
3. Weiss 1972, p. 25
4. Woodger 1967, p. 123
5. Singer *cit.* Kothari and Mehta in Nandy 1988, p. 184
6. Merrell 1982, p. 425
7. Masterman, in Lakatos and Musgrave 1979, pp. 59-89
8. Margalef, in van Dobben and Lowe McConnell 1975, p. 51
9. Waddington, in Koestler and Smythies 1969, p. 360
10. Putman and Wratten 1984, p. 69
11. Robert Mann, personal communication

Chapter 12

1. Nicholson 1933, pp. 132-178, *cit.* Putman and Wratten 1984 p. 166
2. Putman and Wratten 1984, p. 103
3. Putman and Wratten 1984, p. 104
4. Piaget 1968, p. 56
5. Rappaport 1979, p. 98
6. Reichel-Dolmatoff 1977, pp. 4-11
7. Whitten 1978, pp. 830-900

Chapter 13

1. Rappaport 1979, pp. 97-98
2. Bacon, *cit.* Bajaj in Nandy 1988, p. 44
3. Farrington 1973, *cit.* Bajaj ibid. p. 45
4. Worster 1977, p. 30
5. Nandy 1983, p. 207
6. Izutsu 1983, *cit.* Nandy 1981, p. 207
7. Herrick 1961, adapted from pp. 334-335
8. Asch 1955, pp. 31-35
9. Kuhn 1970, p. 118
10. Popper 1973, p. 109

11. Polanyi M. 1978, p. 295
12. Popper 1973, p. 112
13. Whorf 1986, see p. 58
14. Spengler 1939 Vol 1. pp. 369-373, *cit.* Rifkin & Perlas 1983 p. 107

Chapter 14

1. Heller 1952, *cit.* Worster 1977, p. 6
2. Thoreau 1906, *cit.* Heller p. 30, *cit.* Worster ibid. p. 89
3. Tillich 1952, *cit.* Chaitanya 1972, p. 29
4. Darwin C. 1971
5. Trivers foreword to Dawkins 1976 p. VIII
6. Waddington 1975, p. 36
7. Lorenz 1943, p. 235
8. Piaget 1971 *cit.* Skolimowski in Ayala & Dobzhansky 1974, p. 221

Chapter 15

1. Darwin C. 1952, p. 39 *cit.* Worster 1977, p. 137
2. Worster 1977, p. 137
3. Polanyi M. 1978, p. 134
4. Carson 1962, *cit.* Graham, 1980, p. 75
5. Bean *cit.* Graham 1980, pp. 75-77
6. See Meadows 1972
7. See Zuckerman 1972
8. Brown 1979 p. 162
9. See Koestler 1967 pp. 267-312
10. Freud 1953, *cit.* Nandy 1983 p. 202
11. Nandy 1983, p. 206
12. Bettelheim, B. 1979, *cit.* Nandy 1983, p. 206
13. Césaire 1972, *cit.* Nandy, 1983, p. 206
14. Jungk 1958, *cit.* Visvanathan in Nandy 1988, p. 13
15. Polanyi, M. 1978

Chapter 16

1. Polanyi M. 1978, p. 266
2. Polanyi M. 1978, p. 286
3. Polanyi M. 1978, p. 266

4. Popper 1983, p. 38
5. Whitehead 1958, p. 405
6. Passmore 1978, p. 57

Chapter 17

1. Cornford 1957, p. 13
2. Hesiod, *cit.* ibid. 1957, p. 5
3. Cornford, ibid. p. 14
4. Flew 1968, p. 59
5. Sprigge, in Wallace & Walker, eds. 1970, p. 145
6. Huxley, T.H. in Huxley & Huxley eds. 1947, p. 82
7. Simpson 1950, p. 307
8. Monod, 1970, p. 220
9. Huxley Julian in Huxley & Huxley 1947, p. 133
10. Needham 1969, pp. 144-5
11. Monod 1970, p. 220
12. Simpson 1950, p. 314
13. Waddington 1960, p. 177
14. Simpson 1950, pp. 306 and 347
15. Monod 1970, p. 220
16. Huxley Julian in Huxley & Huxley eds. 1947, p. 126
17. Leopold 1953, pp. XVIII-XIX
18. Gerard 1942, pp. 92-120

Chapter 18

1. Ravetz 1971, p. 150
2. Brown 1979, p. 23
3. Carnap 1936, pp. 419-471
4. Popper 1963, pp. 34-35
5. Koestler 1950, p. 68
6. Popper *op. cit.* p. 37
7. Medawar 1982, p. 107
8. Lakatos in Lakatos and Musgrave 1979, p. 119
9. Lakatos ibid. p. 179
10. Kuhn in Lakatos & Musgrave 1979, p. 6
11. Watkins in Lakatos & Musgrave 1979, p. 27
12. Polanyi 1978, p. 289
13. Evans-Pritchard 1937, p. 335 *cit.* Polanyi ibid. p. 289
14. Polanyi, M., *op. cit.* p. 289
15. Polanyi ibid. p. 289
16. Polanyi ibid. p. 291

17. Polanyi ibid. p. 291
18. Evans-Pritchard *op. cit.*, *cit.*
    Polanyi p. 287
19. Lakatos in Lakatos and
    Musgrave 1979, pp. 100-101
20. Polanyi *op. cit.*, p. 294

Chapter 19
1. Hughes 1983, pp. 54-60
2. Plato *cit.* Hughes ibid. pp. 54-60
3. Hughes *op. cit.* pp. 54-60
4. Morgan *cit.* Worster 1977, p. 38
5. Dobzhansky 1962, *cit.* Thorpe
   1965 p. 12
6. de Ricqles in Noel ed. 1979, p. 64
7. Suess 1875, p. 98
8. Lamarck 1964 *cit.* Grinewald in
   Bunyard and Goldsmith eds.
   1988 pp. 1-12
9. Suess *op. cit.*, Grinewald, pp. 1-12
10. Vernadsky 1981, personal com-
    munication from Grinewald
11. Lovelock 1987, p. 87
12. Lovelock ibid., p. 87
13. Lovelock ibid., p. 87
14. Margulis and Sagan 1983,
    pp. 160-167
15. Lovelock 1979, p. 10
16. Lovelock ibid., p. 11

Chapter 20
1. Woodger 1967, p. 300
2. Whorf 1956, p. 20
3. Eliade 1959, pp. 73-74
4. Gesell *cit.* Sinnott 1961, pp. 62-64
5. Bergson 1911, p. 165, *cit.*
   Chaitanya 1975, p. 215
6. Sinnott 1961, p. 60
7. Sinnott ibid., p. 60

Chapter 21
1. Haeckel 1903, pp. 204-229
2. MacLean, *cit.* Koestler 1989,
   pp. 277-278
3. Hearn 1904, p. 38
4. Radcliffe-Brown 1965,
   p. 166
5. see Eliade 1959

Chapter 22
1. Darwin F. ed. 1898, p. 345
2. Simpson 1960, p. 212
3. Dobzhansky in van Dobben and
   Lowe-McConnell eds. 1975, p. 322
4. Thorpe in Koestler & Smythies
   1972, p. 393
5. Weiss in Koestler & Smythies
   1972, p. 46
6. Weiss 1972, ibid., p. 46
7. Dobzhansky 1975, pp. 322-4
8. Monod 1970, p. 159
9. Monod 1970, p. 159
10. Bridges 1971, pp. 19-24
11. Dawkins 1989, p. 19
12. Stanner in Hammond ed. 1971,
    pp. 289-290
13. Odum 1983, p. 47
14. Orians, in van Dobben and Lowe-
    McConnell eds. 1975, pp. 139-150
15. Holling in Jantsch and
    Waddington eds. 1976, p. 81
16. Waddington in Jantsch and
    Waddington eds. 1976, p. 246
17. Holling 1976, *op. cit.*,
    p. 91

Chapter 23
1. Roszak 1972, p. 143
2. Berman 1981, p. 16
3. La Barre 1954, p. 283
4. Calow 1976, pp. 5-6
5. Woodger 1967, p. 264
6. Woodger ibid., p. 270
7. Woodger ibid. pp. 229-
   230
8. Polanyi 1978, p. 142
9. Worster 1977, p. 42
10. Stallnecht 1958, pp. 91-
    92
11. Heller 1957, p. 6
12. Wordsworth *cit.* Worster
    1977, p. 82
13. see Driesch 1908
14. Bergson 1981, p. 12
15. Bergson ibid., p. 98
16. Needham 1936, p. 117
17. Lovelock 1988, p. 35
18. Lovelock 1991, p. 31

Chapter 24

1. Bernard 1878, p. 221
2. Fredericq 1885, p. xxxv
3. Cannon 1932, p. 22
4. Cannon ibid., p. 22
5. Cannon ibid., p. 24
6. Cannon ibid., p. 23
7. Cannon ibid., p. 25
8. Patten and Odum 1981, pp. 886-895
9. Rappaport 1967, p. 4
10. Reichel-Dolmatoff 1977, pp. 4-11
11. Harding 1960, p. 54
12. Patten and Odum *op. cit.*, pp. 866-895
13. Patten and Odum *op. cit.* pp. 866-895
14. Odum 1983, p. 46
15. Odum Howard 1971, p. 331
16. Simberloff and Wilson 1969, pp. 278-290
17. Heatwole and Levins 1972, pp. 531-534
18. Putman and Wratten 1984, pp. 343-344
19. Sagan and Margulis 1983, pp. 160-167
20. Lovelock 1979, p. 10

Chapter 25

1. Waddington 1975, pp. 221-223
2. Orians, in van Dobben and Lowe McConnell 1975, pp. 139-150

Chapter 26

1. Monod 1972, p. 121
2. Huxley 1953, p. 165, *cit.* Chaitanya 1975, p. 83
3. Broadhurst and Ramsey 1968, pp. 300-304
4. Beer 1960, p. 12
5. Riedl 1978, p. 69
6. Waddington 1952 *cit.* Koestler 1978, p. 173
7. Bernal 1969, p. 66

Chapter 27

1. Sherrington 1975, p. 104
2. Barcroft 1938, pp. 73-81
3. Barcroft ibid., pp. 73-81
4. de Beer 1958, p. 16
5. de Haan 1946, p. 59
6. Oatley 1978, p. 166
7. Stent 1978, p. 118
8. Monod *cit.* Stent, p. 118

Chapter 28

1. von Holst 1937, pp. 625-631, 641-647 *cit.* von Bertalanffy, 1973, p. 111
2. Lorenz 1943, p. 235
3. Granit 1974, pp. 1372-1387
4. Linton in Kardiner 1945, pp. 47-100
5. Hardy 1965, p. 176

Chapter 29

1. Merrell 1981, p. 90
2. Merrell ibid., p. 89
3. Merrell ibid., pp. 89-90
4. von Bertalanffy 1972, p. 66
5. Woodger 1967, pp. 149-150
6. Grassé 1973, p. 359

Chapter 30

1. Johnson 1963, pp. 132-138
2. Kalmus 1966, p. 157
3. Hull 1927, p. 224
4. Dixon and Webb 1964, *cit.* Thorpe 1965, p. 45
5. Dixon and Webb ibid., p. 45
6. Waddington in Koestler and Smythies 1972, p. 381
7. Grassé 1973, p. 180

Chapter 31

1. Sherrington 1906, p. 8
2. Herrick 1961, pp. 253-254
3. Skinner 1957, p. 163, *cit.* Koestler 1978, p. 169
4. Skinner *op. cit.* p. 438, *cit.* ibid. p. 169

5. Skinner ibid. p.439 *cit*. ibid. p.169
6. Skinner ibid. p.150, *cit*. ibid. p.169
7. Polanyi 1978, p.150
8. Oatley 1978, p.116
9. Herrick 1961, p.358
10. Krechevsky 1932, p.44 *cit*. Herrick ibid., p.358

Chapter 32

1. Herrick 1954, p.368
2. Nandy, personal communication
3. Binet and Simon 1916, *cit*. Chaitanya 1976, p.230
4. Heim 1970, p.230
5. Harlow *cit*. Roe & Simpson 1964, pp.269-290
6. Harlow ibid., pp.269-290
7. Hingston 1928, p.287
8. Hingston ibid., p.287
9. Hingston ibid., p.285
10. Cuenot 1941, p.222, *cit* Piaget 1979, p.89
11. Piaget 1967, p.66
12. Sherrington 1975, pp.93-94
13. Ramon y Cajal *cit*. Sherrington 1975, p.108
14. Darwin 1971, p.167

Chapter 33

1. Jantsch 1980, p.309
2. Jantsch ibid, p.309
3. Jantsch ibid, p.307
4. Jantsch ibid, p.308
5. Herrick 1954, p.289
6. Thorpe 1965, p.97
7. Huxley *cit*. Thorpe ibid., p.62

Chapter 34

1. Castle *cit*. Sampson 1981, p.82
2. Medawar 1974, pp.244-261
3. Ward 1893, pp.244-261 *cit*. Worster 1977, p.175
4. Ward ibid. pp.244-261 *cit*. Worster ibid. p.175
5. Bakeless 1977, pp.247-249

6. Lee 1969, in Vayda ed. 1969, pp.47-79
7. Park 1984, p.5
8. Crawford 1951, *cit*. Pollard 1981, pp.21-31
9. Bowles in Bethwell & Ogot eds. 1976, pp.195-215
10. Bernier 1984, p.437
11. van der Post 1958, p.276
12 Ch'ien Lung *cit*. Toynbee 1935, p.161
13. Katz and Young 1978, pp.75-85
14. Katz and Young ibid., pp.75-85
15. Lovelock 1991, p.183
16. Wilson 1971, pp.123-6
17. National Academy of Sciences 1991, pp.57-63

Chapter 35

1. Eliade 1971, pp.55-56
2. Pittendrigh 1958, p.394
3. von Bertalanffy 1962A, p.9
4. Weiss 1973, p.25
5. Morin 1977, p.78

Chapter 36

1. Jones 1946, pp.1-10
2. Egerton 1973, p.333
3. Forbes 1880, pp.11-18
4. Allee, Emerson, Park, Park & Schmidt *cit*. Egerton *op. cit*., p.728
5. McKinney 1966, pp.345-346
6. Bernardin de St. Pierre 1797, p.244, *cit*. Egerton, p.338
7. Passmore 1978, p.65
8. Goldsmith 1978, pp.108-109

Chapter 37

1. Patai 1947, p.11
2. Frazer 1935, p.16
3. Campbell 1822, p.34, *cit*. Frazer ibid., p.16
4. Sternberg 1905, p.248, *cit*. Frazer ibid., p.17
5. Cornford 1957, p.78
6. Warren 1888, pp.47-49, *cit*. Frazer *op. cit*. p.18

Chapter 38

1. Hall & Fagen 1956, pp. 18-28
2. Koestler in Koestler & Smythies 1972, p. 197
3. Jantsch in Jantsch and Waddington eds. 1976, p. 38
4. Monod 1976, in Delattre, in Lichnerowicz et alia, p. 34
5. Weiss 1971, p. 99
6. von Bertalanffy 1962A pp. 1-20
7. von Bertalanffy 1962B, pp. 184-186
8. Odum 1983, pp. 3-4
9. Weiss *op. cit.*
10. Koestler 1978, see pp. 23-56
11. see Begon, Harper and Townsend 1990
12. see Whyte 1969
13. see Pattee 1973
14. Mesarovic & Macko in Whyte ed. 1969, p. 29
15. Grene in Whyte, ed. 1969, p. 56

Chapter 39

1. Worster 1977, p. 37
2. White 1902, *cit.* Worster ibid. p. 7
3. Darwin MS, Vol. 30.1, p. 65, cit Ospovat p. 24.
4. Ospovat 1981, pp. 60-85
5. Warming 1909, pp. 82-95
6. Pound *cit.* Boucher 1986
7. Adams 1917, pp. 491-1169
8. Vandermeer and Boucher 1978, pp. 549-558
9. Risch and Boucher 1976, p. 8
10. Boucher in Boucher ed. 1986, p. 6
11. Boucher, James and Keeler 1982, pp. 315-347
12. McNaughton 1979, pp. 695-702
13. Owen and Wiegert 1981, pp. 376-491
14. Mattson and Addy, pp. 515-521, *cit.* Owen and Wiegert, pp. 376-491
15. Boucher in Boucher ed. *op. cit.*, p. 22
16. Janzen in Boucher ed. ibid., p. 20
17. Boucher 1986, ibid., p. 22

Chapter 40

1. Darwin 1971, p. 126
2. Kropotkin 1914, pp. 5-6
3. Boucher, in Boucher ed. 1986
4. Ricklefs 1973
5. Dawkins 1976, p. 140
6. Merrell 1981, p. 425
7. Connell 1980, pp. 131-138
8. Price in Gaud, Price, Slobodchickoff & Williams 1984, p. 354
9. Augros and Stanciu 1987, p. 93
10. Shaw, *cit.* Eibl-Eibesfeldt, p. 116
11. Eibl-Eibersfeldt 1961, p. 119
12. Vayda in Bohannan ed. 1967, p. 367
13. Engels *cit.* Worster 1977, p. 148
14. Zuckerman 1932, see pp. 94-97

Chapter 41

1. Radcliffe Brown 1965, p. 181
2. Von Bertalanffy 1962, p. 123
3. Ungerer 1930, *cit.* von Bertalanffy ibid., p. 12
4. Radcliffe Brown *op. cit.*, p. 181, see in general pp. 178-187
5. Radcliffe Brown ibid., p. 186
6. Putman and Wratten 1984, p. 268
7. Odum 1983, p. 5
8. Monod 1970, pp. 115-116

Chapter 42

1. Boyden 1973, pp. 304-309

Chapter 43

1. McIntosh 1982, in Saarinen ed. 1982, p. 21-22
2. Odum 1983, p. 225
3. Odum ibid., p. 225
4. Washburn and Lancaster in Lee & Devore ed. 1968, p. 293
5. Jackson, personal communication
6. Boyden 1973, pp. 304-309

Chapter 44

1. Weiss 1973, p. 36
2. Shillp, ed. 1959, p. 257
3. Ashmore 1966, p. 70, *cit.*
   Chaitanya 1972, p. 120
4. Weiss 1973, p. 5
5. Waddington 1934, p. 336 *cit.*
   Chaitanya 1975, p. 208
6. Hamberger 1935, p. 67
7. Weiss in Koestler and Smythies
   1969, p. 38
8. Rappaport 1956, p. 307
9. Waddington in Waddington ed.
   1969, p. 336
10. Waddington ibid., p. 337
11. see Singh and Zing 1942

Chapter 45

1. Woodger 1967, p. 295
2. Patten and Odum 1981,
   pp. 886-895
3. Weiss 1973, p. 82
4. Nesbit 1966, p. 108
5. Wing-Tsit Chan *cit.* Perenboom,
   p. 5

Chapter 46

1. see Epstein 1978
2. Damon 1974, pp. 191-216
3. Prior 1987, pp. 457-461

Chapter 47

1. Banfield 1958, see pp. 65-66
2. Lux 1990, p. 195 (quoting
   Seligman 1988)
3. see Population Trends 1990
4. Dalrymple 1991, pp. 9-10
5. Dalrymple ibid., pp. 9-10
6. Dalrymple ibid., pp. 9-10
7. Lewis 1966, pp. 19-25
8. Dickey 1986 *cit.* Lux, *op.
   cit.*, p. 197
9. Pattison and Kim 1991, p. 197, *cit.*
   Tistall, p. 10
10. Taylor, *Daily Telegraph* 1990
11. Cloward & Ohlin 1959,
    pp. 164-176

12. Merton 1951, pp. 142-144
13. see Durkheim 1966

Chapter 48

1. Hall 1974, p. 5
2. Forrester 1971, pp. 4-9
3. Wilson 1976, pp. 342-345

Chapter 49

1. Frankl, in Koestler & Smythies
   eds. 1969, p. 400
2. Frankl ibid. pp. 398-399
3. Roszak 1972, p. 180
4. Monod 1970, pp. 224-225
5. Stent 1978, p. 127

Chapter 50

1. Wynne Edwards 1984, pp. 68-74
2. Wynne Edwards ibid., pp. 68-74
3. Wynne Edwards ibid., pp. 68-74
4. Reichel-Dolmatoff 1977, pp. 4-11
5. Reichel-Dolmatoff ibid., pp. 4-11

Chapter 51

1. Piaget 1967, p. 36
2. Piaget and Inhelder in Koestler and
   Smythies 1972, p. 145
3. Piaget and Inhelder ibid., p. 145
4. see Clements 1916
5. Worster 1977, p. 202
6. Clements *cit.*
   McKintosh 1975, p. 255
7. Tansley 1935, pp. 284-301
8. Malin 1953, *cit.* Worster p. 243
9. Malin 1953, ibid., p. 245
10. Ricklefs 1973, p. 726
11. Putman and Wratten 1984, p. 97
12. Ricklefs *op. cit.*, p. 729
13. Putman & Wratten *op. cit.*, p. 100
14. Putman and Wratten ibid.,
    p. 103
15. Putman and Wratten ibid.,
    pp. 102-103
16. Putman and Wratten ibid.,
    p. 104
17. Putman and Wratten ibid.,
    pp. 103-104

18. Odum 1983, pp. 442-446
19. Odum 1975, p. 151
20. Odum ibid., pp. 150-151

Chapter 52

1. May 1974, p. 39
2. Prigogine and Stengers 1979, p. 178
3. May op. cit., p. 52
4. May ibid., p. 49
5. May ibid., p. 173

Chapter 53

1. Merrell and Underhill 1956, pp. 140-142
2. Waddington 1975, p. 69
3. Jurion and Henry 1969, pp. 444-45, cit. Freeman, p. 36
4. Scott 1978, pp. 75-76

Chapter 54

1. Coleman 1968, p. 103
2. U.S. Dept of Education 1964
3. Raum in Middleton ed. 1978, p. 93
4. Waddington 1975, pp. 285-286
5. Read M. in Middleton ed. 1978, p. 275
6. Coleman op. cit., p. 3

Chapter 55

1. Stanner in Hungerford 1956, pp. 51-56
2. Wheeler 1959, pp. 112-113
3. Armelagos and McArdle 1976, pp. 179-182
4. see McNeill 1976
5. Dubos 1970, pp. 12-15
6. Rappaport 1978, p. 270
7. Krige 1936, pp. 39-53
8. Jaulin 1971, pp. 12-15
9. Geist 1974, pp. 331-350
10. see Levi-Strauss 1975, p. 220-221
11. Hildyard 1977, pp. 46-53
12. Blake 1975, cit. Hildyard, ibid., pp. 46-53
13. Mumford 1967, cit. Dubos, op. cit. pp. 12-15

14. Goldsmith K., personal communication
15. Coomaraswamy 1983, p. 8
16. Plutarch cit. Cornford 1957, p. 53
17. Eiseman 1989, p. 5
18. Reichel-Dolmatoff 1983, pp. 16-21
19. Patai 1947, p. 116
20. Patai ibid., p. 114

Chapter 56

1. Gerard in Whyte, Wilson and Wilson eds. 1969, p. 224
2. Gerard ibid., p. 224
3. Anaximander, cit. Cornford 1957, p. 8
4. Cornford, ibid., p. 10
5. Hildyard A., personal communication
6. von Hildebrand in Bunyard and Goldsmith 1987, pp. 206-236
7. King 1904, p. 48
8. Polanyi K. 1945, p. 53
9. Polanyi K. ibid., p. 53
10. Sahlins in Dalton ed. 1971, pp. 43-61
11. Liedloff, personal communication
12. Park 1970, p. 154
13. Sahlins op. cit., pp. 43-61
14. Thurnwald 1931-35, p. 163
15. Thurnwald ibid., p. 49 and general pp. 46-61
16. Sahlins op. cit., pp. 43-61
17. Akpala 1972, pp. 291-301
18. Huber in Fiske ed. 1978, pp. 158-179
19. Huber ibid., p. 174
20. Kaberry 1939, p. 33
21. Malinowski 1937, p. 232
22. Malinowski ibid., cit. Dalton 1961, pp. 1-25
23. Polanyi K. op. cit., p. 46

Chapter 57

1. Cornford 1957, p. 167
2. Reichel-Dolmatoff 1977, pp. 4-11
3. Reichel-Dolmatoff ibid., pp. 4-11
4. Douglas 1971, pp. 62-87

5. de Garine 1978, *cit.* Fischer 1990, p. 50
6. Liedloff, personal communication
7. Skolimowski 1983, p. 15
8. Fernea 1870, p. 315
9. Voelker 1893, *cit.* Dogra 1983, pp. 84-85
10. Hume 1878, *cit.* Dogra 1983, pp. 85-86
11. Mann 1990, pp. 48-53
12. Payer 1982, p. 33
13. World Bank 1981, p. 35
14. Sharp 1952, in Hammond ed. 1964, pp. 84-91
15. Sachs 1990, *cit.* McCully 1991, p. 249
16. Keyes 1973, *cit.* Mathes and Gray 1975, pp. 119-125
17. Mathes and Gray ibid., pp. 119-125
18. McCully 1991, p. 249
19. Ravetz 1971, p. 63
20. Medawar 1974, p. 125
21. Nelkin in Holton and Morison eds. 1979, pp. 191-209
22. Shapiro, Elon and Beckwith 1969, p. 1337 *cit.* Roszak, pp. 239-240
23. Baltimore 1979, in Holton and Mouson eds. 1979, pp. 37-45
24. Chargaff 1976, *cit.* Culliton in Holton and Mouson eds. 1979, pp. 151-152
25. Cavalieri 1981, p. 64
26. Abian 1991, p. 1 & p. 7

Chapter 58

1. Armstrong 1925, pp. 424-429
2. see Mauss 1954
3. Malinowski 1961, p. 87
4. Dalton 1967, pp. 44-65
5. Douglas in Dalton ed. 1967, pp. 103-122

Chapter 59

1. Odum 1969, pp. 262-270
2. Malinowski 1961, p. 176
3. Polanyi K. 1945, p. 57

4. Gandhi 1949, p. 350
5. Polanyi K. *op. cit.* p. 56
6. Polanyi K. ibid., p. 78
7. Polanyi K. 1957, p. 160
8. Salaman 1949, p. 293
9. Lux 1990, p. 107

Chapter 60

1. see Maine 1854
2. Fustel de Coulanges 1927, p. 194
3. see Morgan 1877
4. Lods 1932, p. 392
5. see Tonnies 1935
6. Pappenheim F. 1968, pp. 66-77, *cit.* Jones 1983, pp. 141-147
7. Rappaport 1979, p. 146
8. see *The Ecologist* 1991, vol. 21, No. 2. March/April
9. Clastres 1974, p. 170
10. Lowie 1921, pp. 344-345
11. Diamond 1974
12. Clastres *op. cit.*, p. 174
13. Banfield 1958, pp. 83-84
14. Banfield ibid., pp. 155-156
15. Diamond, *op. cit.*
16. Popenoe 1991, pp. 65-77
17. McKnight 1978, pp. 112-114

Chapter 61

1. Sheldrake 1988, pp. 150-154 and p. 243
2. Harrison 1927, p. 517
3. Harrison ibid., p. 517
4. Anaximander, *cit.* Cornford 1957, p. 8
5. Cornford ibid., p. 12
6. Herodotus, *cit.* Cornford, ibid. p. 12
7. Iamblichus, *cit.* Cornford 1957, p. 54
8. Homer, *cit.* Harrison, *op. cit.* p. 532
9. de Groot 1910, *cit.* Cornford, *op. cit.*, p. 45
10. de Groot ibid., p. 174
11. Needham 1956
12. Feng Yu-lan 1984, *cit.* Peerenboom 1991, p. 4
13. Feng Yu-lan ibid. p. 5

14. Wing-Tsit Chan 1963, *cit.* Peerenboom ibid., p.9
15. Morenz 1973, p.113
16. Morenz ibid., p.114
17. Bloomfield 1908, p.175
18. Chaitanya 1983, pp.127-128
19. Chaitanya ibid., pp.127-128
20. Hocart 1970, p.112
21. Eiseman 1989, p.12
22. de Groot *op. cit.* 1910, p.166, *cit.* Cornford *op. cit.*, p.176
23. Harrison 1927, p.526
24. Chantepie de la Saussaye 1904, *cit.* Cornford 1957, p.176
25. Murray 1991, p.1
26. Murray 1991, p.1
27. Murray 1991, p.1
28. Chaitanya *op. cit.*, pp.127-135
29. Cornford *op. cit.*, p.33
30. Hughes 1983, pp.54-60
31. Hughes ibid., pp.54-60

Chapter 62

1. Cornford 1957, p.32
2. Durkheim 1964, p.199
3. Durkheim ibid., p.199
4. Lods 1932, p.250
5. Tempels 1948, p.31
6. Tempels ibid., p.69
7. Tempels *op. cit.*, p.33
8. Senghor 1983, in Ndaw, p.32
9. Codrington 1891, p.33
10. Schebesta 1940, p.62
11. Kardiner 1945, p.63
12. Senghor *op. cit.*, p.32
13. Caillois 1950, p.24
14. Douglas 1966, *cit.* Hildyard 1978, pp.166-168
15. Metuh, p.57
16. Metuh, p.57

Chapter 63

1. Kenyatta 1979, p.232
2. Hearn *op. cit.* p.37
3. Robertson Smith 1914, p.30
4. Hearn 1904, p.27
5. Driver 1961, p.428
6. Dubois 1960, *cit.* Kardiner

1965, p.167
7. Kuper 1963, p.58
8. Harrison 1927, p.447
9. Pliny the Elder, *cit.* Hughes 1981, p.13
10. Hughes 1981, pp.196-208
11. Parsons 1964, p.176
12. Harrison, *op. cit.*, p.476
13. Roszak 1972, p.127
14. Berdyaev 1936, p.117

Chapter 64

1. Medawar P. & J. 1977, p.171
2. Margalef 1963, pp.357-374
3. see Jantsch 1980
4. Russell 1982, p.38
5. Russell ibid., p.59
6. Russell ibid., p.60
7. Russell ibid., p.60
8. Russell ibid., p.61
9. Russell ibid., p.62
10. Odum 1983, p.473
11. Medawar 1974, p.127
12. Medawar ibid., p.26

Chapter 65

1. Hughes 1983, pp.54-60
2. Reichel-Dolmatoff 1977, pp.4-11
3. Reichel-Dolmatoff ibid., pp.4-11
4. Turner in Kiev ed. 1967, pp.230-263
5. Bastien 1981, pp.19-37
6. Bastien ibid., pp.19-37
7. Derman in Barker ed. 1984, p.88
8. Schoepf in Barker ed. ibid., p.284
9. FAO 1984, p.94

Chapter 66

1. Stent 1978
2. Polanyi 1978, p.293
3. Polanyi ibid., p.151
4. see Sargant 1957
5. Cumont 1956, see pp.20-72
6. Wallace 1956, pp.264-281
7. Wallace ibid., pp.264-281
8. Taylor 1991, pp.258-266

Appendix 1

1. Brillouin 1968, p. 247
2. Koestler 1967, p. 198
3. Brillouin *op. cit.*, p. 149
4. Waddington in Jantsch and Waddington eds. 1976, p. 244
5. Mason 1956, p. 404
6. Brillouin *op. cit.*, p. 155
7. Brillouin *op. cit.*, p. 147
8. Brillouin ibid., p. 150
9. Brillouin ibid., p. 150
10. Georgescu-Roegen 1971, p. 67
11. Braham 1973, p. 21
12. Braham ibid., p. 21
13. Braham ibid., p. 21

Appendix 2

1. Rogers and Kincaid 1981, pp. 34-35
2. Shannon and Weaver 1949, pp. 15-16
3. Shannon and Weaver ibid., p. 11
4. Shannon and Weaver ibid., p. 27
5. Shannon and Weaver ibid., pp. 13-14
6. Rapoport 1956, p. 306
7. Mackay in Northrop and Livingstone 1964, p. 173
8. Waddington 1975, p. 215

9. Waddington 1975, p. 215
10. Dancoff and Quastler in Quastler ed. 1953, pp. 263-273
11. Dancoff and Quastler in Quastler ed. ibid., p. 270
12. Waddington, *op. cit.*, p. 214
13. Margalef 1958, pp. 36-71
14. Rapoport 1956, p. 307

Appendix 3

1. Hume 1969
2. Worster 1977, p. 336
3. Waddington 1960, p. 54
4. Wilson 1976, p. 345

Appendix 4

1. Koestler 1978, p. 197
2. Haldane *cit.* Koestler 1978, p. 198
3. Grassé 1973, pp. 374-379
4. Baldwin 1896, pp. 354-451
5. Goldschmidt 1935, pp. 38-131
6. Waddington 1975, pp. 59-92
7. Schmalhausen 1949, *cit.* Waddington 1975, p. 75
8. see Piaget 1976

Name Index

Subject Index